100 TURNING POINTS IN MILITARY HISTORY

100 TURNING POINTS IN MILITARY HISTORY

*The Critical Decisions, Key Events,
and Breakthrough Inventions and Discoveries
That Shaped Warfare Around the World*

ALAN AXELROD

Guilford, Connecticut

An imprint of The Rowman & Littlefield Publishing Group, Inc.
4501 Forbes Blvd., Ste. 200
Lanham, MD 20706
www.rowman.com

Distributed by NATIONAL BOOK NETWORK

British Library Cataloguing in Publication Information available

Library of Congress Cataloging-in-Publication Data

Names: Axelrod, Alan, 1952- author.
Title: 100 turning points in military history : the critical decisions, key
    events, and breakthrough inventions and discoveries that shaped warfare
    around the world / Alan Axelrod.
Other titles: One hundred turning points in military history | One hundred
    and one turning points in miitary history
Description: Guilford, Connecticut : Lyons Press, 2019. | Includes index.
Identifiers: LCCN 2019010589 (print) | LCCN 2019011837 (ebook) | ISBN
    9781493037469 (e-book) | ISBN 9781493037452 (hardback : alk. paper)
Subjects: LCSH: Military history—Encyclopedias. | Military history—Chronology.
Classification: LCC D25.A2 (ebook) | LCC D25.A2 A94 2019 (print) | DDC
    355.009—dc23
LC record available at https://lccn.loc.gov/2019010589

♾️ The paper used in this publication meets the minimum requirements of American National Standard for Information Sciences—Permanence of Paper for Printed Library Materials, ANSI/NISO Z39.48–1992.

For Anita and Ian

CONTENTS

Introduction

Traditional military history books present a chronicle of battles and wars and the commanders and troops who fought them. *100 Turning Points in Military History* takes a different approach. It presents battles and wars and people aplenty, but they are not its ultimate subjects. This book is about the *turning points* that not only make military history dynamic but also crucial to the story of humanity and civilization. Here we enumerate and explore the 100 decisions, acts, innovations, errors, ideas, successes, and failures that shaped the evolution of military art and science—strategy, tactics, and technology—and, in doing so, shaped the course of world history.

Please note the absence of the definite article in title of the book. This is not *the* 100 turning points in military history. That is because just as every history book is a story or set of stories, history itself is a fiction. To the degree possible, responsible history is based on records, recollections, and reports analyzed with the intention of objectivity. Nevertheless, the best history can do is achieve the status of plausible fiction. No sequence of human events can be reported with perfect objectivity. Perceptions vary, motives are not objectively measurable, and, while deliberate bias may be avoided, no history should ever be mistaken for an objective presentation of objective reality.

A mere chronological listing of events may seem objective, but in fact it is only tedious and dull and therefore gives the appearance of objectivity. When we read a long, complex novel—Tolstoy's *War and Peace*, say—or see a richly plotted movie—David Lean's classic *Lawrence of Arabia* comes to mind—we can struggle to remember all the names, characters, and scenes, but in truth we do no such thing. Instead, we do what the novelist or the filmmaker wants us to do, which is to focus on what *drives* the story, what we call the "plot," and what propels the plot. These points of propulsion are the *turning points* in the novel or the film. History, I believe, can be very usefully understood not as a chronological recitation of *things, events,* and *people* but as turning points: the decisions, acts, innovations, errors, ideas, success, and failures on which the shape of some key aspect of our collective lives—past, present, and future—depends. In military history, turning points create what we call "destiny" or "direction." They embody strategic, tactical, technological, political, geopolitical, and moral "values" and "ideals" as well as "flaws," "foibles," and "faults" in these areas. They measure the changing pulse of military development through time.

This book does not claim to present "Military History," let alone "What Is Most Important in Military History." Instead, it identifies 100 points at which the course of global military history turned on its way to the state of military power today. Each turning point is a moment at which that course could have gone this way or that. I believe we benefit from knowing something about these points of development and decision so that we can more productively understand and evaluate the history, present state, and future direction of the military enterprise, an enterprise to which nations and civilizations have devoted treasure and lives for better and for worse since the first day human beings organized themselves into communities.

Battle of Megiddo:
The Birth of Warfare (1457 BC)

Near Kibbutz Megiddo, a little less than 19 miles southeast of the Israeli port city of Haifa, is Tel Megiddo. In the fifteenth century BC, it was a fortress city guarding passage into Mesopotamia. Today it is a "tel," an archaeological mound, a historical midden heap, an unnatural hill formed by generation upon generation of human beings living, building, destroying, and rebuilding on one single spot.

Megiddo was the scene of numerous ancient battles, as well as one fought early in the twentieth century between troops of the British Empire on one side and the Ottoman and German Empires on the other toward the end of World War I (September 19–25, 1918). But more famous than any of these was the battle fought between Egyptian forces commanded by Pharaoh Thutmose III (1481–1425 BC) and a rebellious alliance of Canaanite states led by the Mitanni king of Kadesh on or about April 16, 1457 BC.

There are at least three reasons for the battle's renown. Number one, it was the first battle of which there is any appreciable record. It was not the first battle ever fought, but it was the very first to enter history. As far as the study of the past is concerned, it may be regarded as the birth of warfare.

The second reason to pay attention to Megiddo is that it was the first recorded use of the composite bow—a bow made from horn laminated together with wood and sinew. The final reason for the battle's enduring fame is that the site of this engagement, which involved as many as 35,000 combatants, of which some 16,700 were killed, wounded, or captured, gave its name to End Times combat prophesied in the New Testament's Book of Revelation: Armageddon.

Those of a philosophical turn of mind will find this third reason the most important of the three. To be sure, there is a grim poetry in history's *first* recorded battle having bestowed its name on what will be history's very *last* battle. Nevertheless, the first and second reasons are of greater importance for military history—and the second probably even greater than the first. For the status of Megiddo as humankind's first recorded battle has an element of accident about it. It is first, most likely, only because one particular set of records happened to survive while records of other battles, perhaps both earlier and of greater consequence, were lost in time's unforgiving maw. We should note, however, that the numbers involved—10,000 to 20,000 men under the command of Thutmose III versus 10,000 to 15,000 commanded by the king of Kadesh—are considerable (though

Megiddo, Israel, is believed to be the site of the
first battle (1457 BC) of which any account exists.
PHOTOGRAPH (2007) BY JAMES EMERY, WIKIMEDIA COMMONS

many ancient battles involved far more). The butcher's bill this battle produced is terrible as well. Four thousand Egyptians were killed and 1,000 wounded. If we arbitrarily figure the presence of 15,000 men, this represents a casualty rate of 30 percent. For most of the history of warfare, a casualty rate of "just" 10 percent has been considered very heavy, severe, even catastrophic. Let's say that the King of Kadesh led 12,500 men at Megiddo. His losses of 11,700—including 8,300 killed and 3,400 made prisoner—represented total annihilation: Armageddon indeed.

That Megiddo occasioned the first recorded use of the composite bow suggests a genuine turning point in military history. Flighted arrows almost certainly appeared prior to 18,000 BC, more than 3,000 years before Megiddo, but the composite bow used at Megiddo, which featured a wooden core with horn glued to the face of the bow stave and sinew glued to the back, enabled this weapon to be made shorter than the earlier "common," or "self," bow and yet also to store and deliver more potential energy than the longer bow. The compact size made the composite bow much easier to handle on horseback. (Think of the nineteenth-century cavalryman's short carbine versus the infantryman's long musket or rifle.) The increased ratio of the pull to the energy stored and released delivered a deadlier and more accurate flight over a longer range.

The introduction of the common bow had been a game changer in hunting and whatever version of warfare existed before Megiddo. It was history's first true "standoff" weapon—a weapon that extended the killing range of a hunter or soldier far beyond the reach of his arm and hand wielding an edged weapon. The composite bow added to this more accuracy, velocity, and range. It elevated warfare several steps beyond sheer muscle power. In effect, the composite bow democratized combat by empowering more warriors, even those of mediocre strength, to be effective killers.

The Battle of Megiddo followed the decline of Egyptian influence in Palestine and Mittani, a region that encompassed modern northern Syria and southeastern Turkey. Seeking to restore Egyptian power, Thutmose III led a series of campaigns by which he managed first to regain control of Palestine. He then invaded Mittani, only to be checked in his advance by a coalition of perhaps as many as 330 Syrian and Palestinian princes under the military leadership of the king of Kadesh (fl. 1460s BC).

On April 16, 1457—as calculated from an ancient Egyptian account (although scholars have also dated the battle to 1482 BC and 1479 BC)—near what was then the northern Palestinian fortress city of Megiddo, which guarded entry into Mesopotamia, the Mitanni king's coalition troops engaged the Egyptians. The record provides a vivid picture of Thutmose's strategy in this battle. He took the bold and risky step of dividing his forces in the face of the enemy—not just in two, but in *three* contingents, which were arrayed in a concave formation. The two outer wings threatened the coalition's flanks while the center, personally commanded by the pharaoh, led the main offensive against the center of the coalition's line. This enveloping attack was made at dawn and carried out with complete surprise. The will of the somewhat outnumbered coalition army seems to have collapsed quickly and completely, and those troops closest to the town of Megiddo fell back into it, closing the gates behind them. This left the coalition encampment for the Egyptians to loot.

Up to this point in the battle, Megiddo represents a stunning Egyptian strategic and tactical triumph; however, the opportunity to plunder rapidly overcame the discipline of the Egyptian forces. It is recorded that 924 chariots and 200 suits of armor were captured. But, distracted by loot, the Egyptians failed to pursue the scattering coalition forces, and many men, including the king of Kadesh and the prince of Megiddo, found safety within the walls of the city. Those who had already retreated into the fortress town did not dare open the gates. Instead they tied their garments together, improvising ropes that allowed them to pull their brothers-in-arms up and over the walls.

Having succumbed to the temptation of treasure, the Egyptians sacrificed the opportunity to make quick work of the coalition and to capture Megiddo itself. Undaunted, Thutmose laid siege to the city. The operation stretched over weeks and then months. Finally, after a full seven months, the starving occupants of Megiddo surrendered at last.

The victory of Thutmose, delayed though it was, both revived Egyptian power and pushed the Egyptian empire into southwestern Asia. Except for the Mitanni king of Kadesh himself, the other princes of the coalition instantly declared their allegiance to Egypt and its pharaoh. The great kingdoms of Babylonia and Assyria, along with the Hittites, pledged to pay tribute as the pharaoh's vassals. The greatness of Egypt was reborn.

Tiglath-Pileser III: The Birth of Military Civilization (745–727 BC)

King of Assyria from 745 to 727 BC, Tiglath-Pileser returned the kingdom to its former preeminence in the Middle East and transformed it into an empire ruled by an imperial government that lasted a hundred years. His farreaching conquests encompassed Babylonia, Syria, and Palestine. The growth and stability this monarch-commander achieved were products of the military culture he established. It was so thoroughly developed that we may identify Assyria as the birthplace of military civilization.

Son of Adadnirari III, Tiglath-Pileser III came to power in 745 BC by defeating his brother in a fight to succeed to their father's throne. The young Tiglath-Pileser had already served as governor of the province of Calah, where he proved himself a masterful administrator. As king, he made skillful use of his provincial governors, assigning his strongest and most loyal to the larger Assyrian provinces, which, he well knew, had long been agitating for independence. In the outlying regions and in minor provinces, the new king installed governors he judged worthy but who were less well-known to him personally.

When he had assumed the throne, the Assyrian army was a militia composed of peasants called to military service only during times of crisis and released once the immediate need had been satisfied. Tiglathpileser disbanded the militia and created in its place the kingdom's first standing army, a professional force made up primarily of Assyrians but significantly supplemented by foreign mercenaries and troops from vassal states. The army he created was the center of the most efficient and sophisticated administrative and financial system in the ancient world up to this time.

The standing army was the engine of Assyria's economy, which effectively became a state dedicated to the enterprise of making war. Virtually all the growing empire's prosperity was derived from the spoils of military conquest and by the close supervision of trade throughout both the central and outlying, acquired empire. The military command structure was virtually indistinguishable from the bureaucracy that administered the civilian government. Indeed, no state's military and civilian spheres would be as intimately related until the rise of fascism and Nazism in the mid-twentieth century. With the military operating as a seamless extension of the imperial regime, Tiglath-Pileser III was able to establish centralized imperial control over a far-flung empire.

Since the military was both the heart and engine of this empire, no expense was spared to strengthen it. The military focused the energy and efforts of all Assyrian society. In the realm of technology, Assyrians were the first people to recognize and promote the advantages of iron over bronze. The transformation first took place in weapons manufacture, but this was extended to the fashioning of other implements and artifacts. Much as the advancement of military technology in the twentieth and twenty-first centuries spawned innovation in the civilian industrial and consumer sectors, so the technological progress of the Assyrian military advanced Assyrian material civilization as well.

Assyria's transition to iron weaponry began before Tiglath-Pileser, as early as 1100 BC, but the king spurred and accelerated the further development of military technology. Not only did he foster continuous improvement of arms, he also instituted regimens of training that intensively focused on their efficient use. Organization was also key to the Assyrian military. As in other armies of the period, the state's infantry was made up mostly of spearmen. Inherently slow-moving, the Assyrian spearmen during the regime of Tiglath-Pileser were nevertheless swifter and more agile than those of any other comparable force. They were essential to Assyrian combat doctrine, as the objective of any battle was to bring it to culmination in an overwhelming and irresistible advance of massed spearmen.

The operational foundation of Tiglath-Pileser's army consisted of spearmen, but he also developed large units of archers, who were not only better organized than the bowmen of opposing armies but also better equipped. Their bows were stronger, and the arrows they fired were iron tipped. The effect of massed and deadly accurate arrow volleys was to create panic and confusion in the enemy ranks, which laid them open to the next phase of battle, a closely coordinated charge of charioteers and cavalry.

A corps of two-wheeled horse-drawn chariots was the principal shock force of the Assyrian army. Its mission was to smash through enemy infantry lines after they had been initially disrupted by archers. While the chief combat virtue of the chariot charge was its brute force, under Tiglath-Pileser, cavalry troops were closely coordinated with the charioteers to run down the individual enemy foot soldiers as they sought to flee the wheeled onslaught.

All the Assyrian combat arms—archers, spearmen, cavalry, and charioteers—were used in greater numbers than those of the forces defending against them. Tiglath-Pileser's military civilization allowed him to wield forces of unprecedented size, equipped with the most advanced weapons, and operating at a very high state of organization and coordination. Sheer numbers and brute force were important, but Tiglath-Pileser also valued individual training and skill. His cavalry, for example, included Assyrian nobility as well as highly paid Scythian mercenaries. Both fought with skill, daring, and discipline.

Tiglath-Pileser recognized that the scale of his imperial ambitions required that his military develop the art of siegecraft to overcome fortifications. For this reason, the siege trains that accompanied his attack columns brought with them a large assortment of ingenious equipment, including heavy battering rams and the materials to quickly build mobile siege towers, which were protected from defenders' flaming arrows by dampened leather hides. Moreover, because his armies routinely ranged far beyond familiar Assyrian landscapes, Tiglath-Pileser ensured that his forces were trained to move and fight on a wide array of terrain. These expeditionary forces often numbered more than 100,000 men, so he also developed elaborate logistical organization and technology to sustain them in the field. As Tiglath-Pileser saw it, the military was the direct projection of imperial power. As such, it had to combine organizational efficiency with overwhelming force and, last but not least, a willingness to inflict on the enemy both terror and cruelty.

Tiglath-Pileser III introduced military civilization through a series of conflicts historians call the Assyrian Wars. He instigated the first of these in 746 BC and prosecuted them until his death in 727. During this span, he relentlessly carried out a three-pronged strategy aimed at quelling the Aramaean revolt south of Babylonia, annexing Syria, and reclaiming the northern borders around Urartu, northeast of the Tigris and Euphrates Valleys. In 746 he led his forces into Babylonia, where he joined his vassal King Nabu-nasir (fl. 747–734 BC) to fight at Radhan along the Tigris and then to cross that river to the banks of the Uknu. After subjugating this region, Tiglath-Pileser did not simply march on. In each critical city he captured, the Assyrian king left trusted administrators. He also built permanent, amply garrisoned forts, which served as imperial administrative and enforcement centers.

By about 744, Tiglath-Pileser had secured his southern borders. Without intermission, he aimed his further conquests toward the northern territories of Urartu. He knew he would be facing large and well-equipped forces, so he began with a campaign intended to divert them. He campaigned first in Media (modern central Iran) before turning north, toward Uratu proper. After pillaging the unprotected territories around Media, the Assyrian army advanced to Syria and defeated leading elements of an army from Urartu in 743. This accomplished, Tiglath-Pileser deemed his own army ready for a showdown battle at Kishtan against Urartu forces under King Sarduri II (760–730 BC). The result was a massive Assyrian victory in which the Urartu forces were routed and Sarduri II was forced to retreat behind his border.

Urartu was laid open to the Assyrian advance. For the next three years, Tiglath-Pileser laid siege to Arpad—a defiant Urartu-backed city in Syria—until it finally broke in 740, yielding to him more than 70,000 prisoners. To send the message that resisting Assyria meant annihilation, Tiglath-Pileser not only seized and held the prisoners, he leveled Arpad. This set the pattern for all ensuing Assyrian military conquest, and until his death in 727, Tiglath-Pileser III waged virtually continuous warfare. He subjugated Hamah in 739. By the following year, his Assyria comprised about eighty provinces. In 732 he went on to take Damascus and Syria, as well as southern Iraq the following year. The Assyrians drove the rebellious Chaldean prince Ukin-zer (r. 732–729 BC) from Babylon in 729 so that at the time of Tiglath-Pileser's death, the Assyrian Empire stretched from the Persian Gulf to the Armenian mountain ranges and south to Egypt.

The Assyrian Wars were continued by Tiglath-Pileser's successors through 609 BC. By that time, however, Assyria's many enemies had learned the bitter lessons of doing combat against a military civilization. The empire Tiglath-Pileser III had so spectacularly expanded finally began to recede.

Sun Tzu: The Birth of Strategy (c. 511 BC)

In all of China's long military history, perhaps only a single early figure is widely familiar in the West. His name is not that of a celebrated warrior but a strategist—and, at least among nonspecialists, it eclipses all others, including the name of the most celebrated and influential strategist in the West itself, nineteenth-century Prussian Carl von Clausewitz.

For all his enduring fame, remarkably little is known about Sun Tzu (544 BC?–496 BC?). He may have been born in the state of Qi or perhaps Wu. Two important historical texts, *The Spring and Autumn Annals* (official record of the state of Lu) and *Records of the Grand Historian* (a history of ancient China completed about 94 BC by a Han official named Sima Qian), do agree that Sun Tzu was born late in what is called China's Spring and Autumn period, roughly between 771 and 476 BC. Both sources also identify him as a general and military advisor in service to King Helü of Wu, a position he acquired about 512 BC. The two histories paint Sun Tzu as a victorious commander, and both conclude that his military success prompted him to write *The Art of War*. Sima Qian makes specific mention of the Battle of Boju, which, fought in 506 BC, was a decisive Wu victory over Chu. The only problem with this information is that the *Zuo zhuan*, a text written earlier than *Records*, provides history's most detailed account of the Battle of Boju yet makes no mention at all of Sun Tzu. As if this historical obscurity were not sufficiently dense, some historians believe that Sun Tzu was a fiction, a nom de plume applied to a combination of writers.

To read world history is to conclude that war is something of a human reflex, an activity nearly as inevitable and automatic as breathing and eating. The simplest definition of what armies do—they kill people and break things—supports this basic view. Whether he was a person or several people, Sun Tzu was the first military thinker to systematically consider the nature and conduct of war and to reduce it to a subject for logical analysis. His reason for doing this was not idle curiosity but a conviction that "war is a matter of vital importance to the state; the province of life and death; the road to survival or ruin." For these reasons, it "is mandatory that it be thoroughly studied." Thus, Sun Tzu may identified as the father of strategy.

Sun Tzu laid down what today would be called principles of war, the basic factors that successful strategy must deal with. The five principles Sun Tzu described are moral influence, weather, terrain, command, and doctrine. The first of these he defined as the trust of people in their leaders. The second and third are self-explanatory. As for the fourth, "command" encompassed all the skills, qualities, and overall competence of the general. The fifth, "doctrine," took in organization, command and control, and logistics.

Beyond the principles Sun Tzu specifically enumerated were those he derived from some of them. The most important of these are speed, knowing your enemy, and what we might call the art of winning without fighting. This last derivative principle Sun Tzu regarded as the very zenith of military genius.

The art of winning without fighting is about intimidation, the ability to demonstrate to a prospective adversary that armed conflict with your forces would be futile. Some modern historians suggest the famous—or infamous—"Star Wars" program (officially the Strategic Defense Initiative, SDI) begun under U.S. President Ronald Reagan in 1984 is an example of winning without fighting. According to this view, the Soviet Union, America's prime superpower adversary at the time, was intimidated by what its intelligence experts believed was a rapidly developing U.S. military technology capable of neutralizing the Soviet nuclear offensive threat. In truth, the U.S. technology was far from complete, and many in both the military and scientific communities thought SDI was a tremendously costly fantasy. No matter, in panic, the Soviet government spent economically crippling sums in a vain effort to build their own SDI-like system. The resulting financial crisis, some argue, brought the Soviet Union and, with it, the Cold War to an end—all without firing a shot.

Related to the principle of winning without fighting is the concept of the "indirect approach" to war, the earliest articulation of which came from Sun Tzu. To approach war indirectly is to think in terms of neutralizing or paralyzing the enemy rather than killing him. In modern warfare, this may be seen in the so-called island-hopping strategy employed by the Americans in the Pacific theater of World War II. Instead of seeking to attack all Japanese garrisons on every one of the outlying islands that formed a great arc intended to defend the Japanese home islands, the U.S. commanders attacked selectively, destroying the enemy on some islands while leaving enemy forces on others to "wither on the vine" (as Admiral Chester Nimitz put it), neutralized and paralyzed because the U.S. victories elsewhere had cut them off from reinforcement, supply, or retreat.

"Indirect" also described an overall policy of attacking weakness while avoiding strength. In this, Sun Tzu elevated strategic pragmatism above such romantic values as glory and gallantry. In this sense, indirect war may be seen as a principle of modern asymmetric warfare, including guerrilla and insurgent strategies.

In ancient Asia, *The Art of War* figured prominently in the battles of ancient China's Warring States period, spanning 403 BC to 221 BC. During this tumultuous era, many wars were fought among seven nations—Zhao, Qi, Qin, Chu, Han, Wei, and Yan—for control over eastern China. Some historians believe that

The Art of War was not merely influential in this period but also served as a strategic manual for all the principal commanders.

Sun Tzu's work did not reach the West until *The Art of War* was translated by an eighteenth-century French Jesuit missionary to China, Père Jean Joseph Marie Amiot, whose edition was published in Paris in 1772. The book was translated into Russian in 1860 and appeared in several German translations during the later nineteenth century. Yet it was never of more than academic and historical interest in the West until Mao Zedong gave much of the credit for the victory he led in the Chinese Civil War to his reading of Sun Tzu. Assuming this praise was genuine, we can conclude that the 2,500-year-old *Art of War* was instrumental in the birth of a *communist* China, arguably the single most disruptive event in postwar military and political history prior to the collapse of the Soviet Union in 1991.

Beyond question, *The Art of War* did help shape Mao's thinking about the role of indirect war in asymmetric, or guerrilla, warfare, which has been the dominant mode of armed conflict since the end of World War II. Ho Chi Minh ordered a Vietnamese translation of the book for distribution to all his military officers, and, ever since its encounters with Japan, North Korea, and North Vietnam, the U.S. military has made *The Art of War* required reading for all officers.

Yet the true genius of *The Art of War* is that, like the indirect approach to warfare it discusses, it approaches military strategy itself almost indirectly. The book is as much a manual of *Taoist* strategy as it is of *military* strategy. Sun Tzu emphasizes naturalness and "effortless action" to assert one's will in the world, whether it is the will of an individual, a military, or a nation. This Taoist approach to matters military may help to explain why *The Art of War* has enjoyed such popularity among Western civilian readers, especially in the realm of business strategy and the art of corporate leadership. It was never a narrowly military text.

When Sun Tzu wrote his most famous maxim—"Every battle is won or lost before it is ever fought"—he set the battlespace not in the field but in the mind and imagination of the commanders. Indeed, as Sun Tzu saw it, the kinetic action of combat was almost superfluous, since the outcome of battle, barring some accident or freak of nature, was virtually inevitable. Wherever it was applied, *The Art of War* brought a heightened intellectualism both to strategy and to its execution, making the former more efficient and the latter at least potentially less costly in lives and economic destruction.

Spartans at Thermopylae: The Perfection of Military Civilization (480 BC)

In 490 BC, under Emperor Darius, Persia tried and failed to add Greece to its empire. A decade later, in 480 BC and under Xerxes I the Great, Persia tried again. This time, the emperor assembled an army whose size reflected the vastness of his realm. The Greek historian Herodotus (c. 484–c. 425 BC) reported that, marching into Greece, the army paused for water and ended up drinking the River Echeidorus dry. He put Persian numbers at 2,124,000 warriors, but modern scholars estimate that it was more probably between 120,000 and 300,000 men—a number still sufficiently large to have prompted several Greek cities to surrender at the army's mere approach.

Athens united with its traditional rival, Sparta, to resist the invasion. A congress of those Greek city-states that had not yet surrendered was convened early in 480 BC. The Athenian politician and general Themistocles recommended Athens's new fleet of triremes block the straits of Artemisium, which would force Xerxes to land at a place obliging him to march overland through Thermopylae, a narrow pass with very steep walls. This natural bottleneck could be efficiently defended by forces far smaller than the those of the invader. The idea was here to delay passage of the Persians long enough for Greek naval forces to attack the Persian fleet supporting the invasion and for the main body of allied Greek land forces to position themselves advantageously. The more intense the battle at Thermopylae, the costlier it would be to the Persians—even though the Greeks knew the invader would eventually break through.

By this period in Greek history, the Spartans were acknowledged as the region's preeminent military power. The city-state's King Leonidas I decided that the holding tactic could be carried out with a minimal force consisting of the very best soldiers Sparta could deploy. Accordingly, he handpicked just 300 men from his own royal bodyguard. His plan was to attach whatever soldiers from other states of the Greek anti-Persian alliance could be found during the march to Thermopylae. But Leonidas and his men understood that they were about to fight to the death.

The Battle of Thermopylae is history entangled in mythology, but both the history and the mythology tell us that Sparta had created a civilization wholly based on military pursuits. War, for Sparta, was a way of life, and a martial imperative was pervasive throughout society. Spartan culture was shaped to serve this imperative, not with mindless violence—though violence there surely was—but with systematic rigor and discipline.

For male Spartiates—as full citizens of Sparta were called—military service was not only obligatory but the only occupation permitted them. A class of slaves, the Helots, attended to farming and other menial labor. A middle class of free men, called Perioeci, were tradespeople and merchants. Spartiate boys commenced military life when they turned seven. At that age, they were removed from home and family and installed in barracks together with other Spartiate children. Here they were subjected to the *agoge*, a program of military education that seems to moderns—and, indeed, seemed to contemporary visitors from outside Sparta—extravagantly sadistic. Perhaps it was, but the brutality was purposeful and wholly organic to the Spartan social system.

At the *agoge*, children and young men learned a kind of dance called the *pyrriche*, which was performed while brandishing weapons. The idea was to make such martial actions natural—to create a kind of muscle memory for the movements of warfare. The dance also strengthened a bond among warriors-in-the-making.

At twelve, a Spartiate child became a "youth," or *meirakion*. His hair was close-cropped, he went barefoot in all weather and on all terrain, and he wore nothing but a thin veil, the *krypteia*. His military training was expanded to include practical exercises in sheer cunning. The *meirakion*'s rations were severely reduced, and he was now required to devise ways to steal his food—or starve. There was no punishment for theft, but if unsuccessful—if he were *caught* stealing—the *meirakion* would be severely whipped. It was believed that the more painful the punishment, the more quickly the young man would learn to steal successfully, with speed, daring, and stealth, all qualities indispensable in a warrior.

In the barracks of the *agoge*, the *meirakion* were divided into units, each of which was supervised by an older warrior, called an *eirena*, who in turn was under the command of a superior officer, or *paidonomos*. Chain of command, so essential in coordinating successful military action, was continually instilled in Spartan youngsters. At eighteen, the *meirakion* was deemed an adult and was enrolled in the army. He would serve actively until the age of 30, at which point he would continue in less-active roles as needed until he retired at 60. In the army, the smallest organizational unit, the *enomoty*, was the equivalent of the modern company. It was composed of 30 soldiers under the command of a captain (*enomotarch*). Total loyalty was forged within this unit, the members of which swore loyalty oaths to one another.

Each individual warrior was trained to become one with his *enomoty*, with the army, and with the Spartan state. He was also relentlessly drilled so that his weapons became an extension of his body. Spartan weapons were the most technologically advanced in the ancient world. They consisted of a variety of specialized offensive weapons—swords and spears—and a unique shield, often called the

Old Bashing Shield, which combined defensive and offensive functions, warding off blows as well as savagely bashing the enemy. Typically the shield was an heirloom, passed down from father (or widow) to son. Thus, it symbolized family and tradition. It was decorated with the letter *lambda*, standing for *Lacedaemon*, the antique name for Sparta. And so it also symbolized the state. Made of wood clad in bronze and leather, it was much larger and heavier than shields carried by other armies. It was also essential to the basic battle formation of the Spartan land forces: the phalanx. The phalanx multiplied the combat effectiveness of the individual soldier exponentially so that the power of the *whole* of an attacking force quite literally became greater than the sum of its parts.

Spartan warriors typically advanced against an enemy in phalanx, shields strapped to each warrior's left arm and overlapping on front and flanks to create a kind of mobile fortress. In the right hand, each soldier carried a spear. In the front rank of the phalanx, the spears were extended fully, but the next few ranks also aimed their spears outward, in between the interlocked shields. In this way, at least three ranks of attackers brought their primary weapon to bear.

Modern view of the Thermopylae Pass in the area of the Phocian Wall, where the Spartan "300" stood against the Persian legions of Xerxes I
PHOTOGRAPH (2011) BY FKERASAR. WIKIMEDIA COMMONS

The Old Bashing Shield is a practical symbol of Spartan military civilization. It expressed the belief that the individual was indispensable to the triumph of the group and that by protecting the group, the individual defended himself. Moreover, the Old Bashing Shield was integral to each soldier, just as each soldier was integral to the phalanx in which he fought. The phalanx, in turn, was integral to the army, the army to the state, and the state to the army. Thus, at Thermopylae it was not merely a dedicated force of skilled warriors who fought but the projection of the Spartan state itself, the Spartan ethos, and the Spartan civilization.

On the march to Thermopylae, Leonidas and his 300 picked up perhaps 7,000 non-Spartan soldiers from allied Greek states. The entire force was deployed to the narrowest portion of the Thermopylae pass, called the "middle gate," which had a defensive wall the Phocians had built years earlier. When locals told Leonidas that a mountain trail existed by which Xerxes might be able to outflank his position, he sent 1,000 of his Phocian auxiliaries to position themselves at a high point overlooking the trail.

As Leonidas knew would happen, many of the non-Spartan troops were terrified by the prospect of doing battle against vastly superior numbers. They were good warriors, but they had not been raised in a true military civilization. Plutarch writes that when one of these soldiers exclaimed in fear that the "arrows of the barbarians" would block out the sun itself, Leonidas calmly replied, "Won't it be nice, then, if we shall have shade in which to fight them?"

Xerxes sent an emissary to Leonidas, offering terms. All Greeks would remain free men under the honorific title "Friends of the Persian People" if they would allow themselves to be resettled on land that the Persian monarch promised would be better than what they now had.

Leonidas calmly refused this offer, and the emissary delivered the refusal to Xerxes. The emperor sent him back with a demand: "Hand over your arms." To this Leonidas replied, "Come and take them."

As Spartiate solders were thoroughly enculturated as warriors, Spartan commanders devoted much of their time and thought to strategy and tactics. Without question, Leonidas understood that his stand at Thermopylae was ultimately a suicide mission. Yet he did not conceive it as a futile mission. While the army of Xerxes vastly outnumbered his forces at Thermopylae, Leonidas had chosen terrain strategically. It was ideal for infantry on the defense. The landscape was far too rugged for cavalry—the favored arm of Persia—and the middle gate was much too narrow for attack by a wide battle formation of cavalry or infantry. Xerxes would be unable to bring a mass of weapons to bear. Instead he would be obliged to hurl one fraction of his army after another against the defenders. Trickled out this way, he would undoubtedly incur heavy losses—at least until he could finally break through.

The Battle of Thermopylae spanned three days. It began with a barrage of Persian arrows from the bows of 5,000 archers. Although massive, the barrage was ineffective. The arrows were fired from perhaps a hundred yards, which meant that most of their energy was spent by the time they reached their targets. The Spartan shields readily deflected the missiles.

After the failure of the arrow attack, Xerxes sent 10,000 Medes and Cissians against the Spartan position at the middle gate. The defenders fought in front of the old Phocian Wall, where the narrow pass was narrowest. Few attacking troops could be brought into contact with the Spartans at any one time, and by fighting in front of the wall instead of from behind it, the defenders were able to maneuver freely and more aggressively cut down the attackers as they squeezed through the pass. When Greek warriors in the front line tired, they slipped back behind the wall and were continuously replaced by fresh troops.

Unable to maneuver in the confined space of the pass, Xerxes continued to send warriors into the battle by frontal assault, 10,000 at a time, of which number he could bring but a small fraction into contact at any one time. Despite their being far superior in numbers, the Persians were being steadily worn down. Near the end of the first day of battle, wave after Persian wave had been shredded. According to the Greek physician and historian Ctesias, only two or three Spartans had been killed.

Xerxes at last unleashed 10,000 of his "Immortals," a cadre of his most elite troops. Apparently recognizing the higher quality of these warriors, Leonidas adopted a new tactic. He ordered his men to feign a retreat, thereby drawing the Immortals deeper into the pass. As the enemy advanced deeper, the Spartans broke into a run, making the retreat look like a rout. This prompted the Immortals to dissolve their orderly formation and run, helter-skelter, in pursuit of what they took to be the fleeing Spartans. At this point, the Spartans suddenly turned about-face and counterattacked. Stunned, many of the Immortals were killed. And in this way, Day 1 ended.

Xerxes, who assumed the Greek casualties had to be nearly as great as his own, renewed the frontal assaults on the second day. He soon recognized that his assumption was mistaken, and by midday he aborted the assault. Withdrawing into his camp, Xerxes huddled with his lieutenants, struggling to formulate a new tactic. A Trachinian traitor named Ephialtes came to him in camp, offering to guide the Persians to the mountain path Ephialtes believed was unknown to Leonidas. From here the Persians could outflank the Spartan position. That evening, Xerxes put 20,000 Immortals under the command of a general named Hydarnes and tasked him with enveloping the Greek position. Under cover of darkness, Hydarnes deployed his men in the flanking position and awaited daylight before making his next move.

At first light of the third day, sentries among the Phocians stationed above the path heard the rustle of leaves. They alerted their comrades to the presence of the Persians. Instead of attacking, however, the Phocians withdrew to a nearby hill. Instantly recognizing that these soldiers were no Spartans—for they had withdrawn even before battle had begun—Hydarnes decided not to lose the element of surprise by attacking them. Instead he skirted the Phocians and extended his encirclement of the principal Greek force.

Fortunately, a Phocian runner had been dispatched to alert Leonidas to the Persian presence. The king assembled his commanders for a council of war. Some urged withdrawal. Instead of arguing with them or ordering them to stay and fight, Leonidas announced only that *he* would continue to defend his 300 Spartans. Shortly after this, Leonidas explicitly released his non-Spartan allies, but some 2,000 chose to remain. These soldiers battled the Persians head-on in an open field—and were quickly wiped out.

Leonidas was likewise determined to fight to the death. In part, this would serve a moral purpose, showing the Persians how determined Greek warriors were. More tactically, the fatal clash would be a rearguard action that would allow the Greek allies to live to fight another day and to buy time for Greek sea forces to attack and scatter the Persian fleet supporting the ground invasion.

The final day of battle at Thermopylae was the ultimate expression of a military civilization, a state founded on a warrior ethos. Ten thousand Persian light infantry and cavalry charged against the Spartan front line. This time, the Spartan 300 did not merely block the attack. They countercharged, engaging the Persian line as it approached in a wider part of the pass. Leonidas had but one purpose: to slaughter as many of the enemy as possible.

The Spartans fought with their spears until every one of them had been shattered. That is when they took up their secondary weapon, the *xiphos,* or short sword. Herodotus records that this combat claimed the lives of two of Xerxes' brothers, Abrocomes and Hyperanthes. Leonidas was also slain early in the combat, the victim of Persian archers. Although the Persians and the Greeks fought over the body of the slain king, the Greeks retained possession. Herodotus writes that the Spartans "defended themselves to the last, those who still had swords using them, and the others resisting with their hands and teeth."

In the immediate aftermath of Thermopylae, the Greeks yielded all of Attica to Xerxes, who razed Athens to the ground. But he dared not attack Sparta, a city-state saved by its demonstration not merely of military prowess but of a civilization so steeped in war that it was perceived as incapable of surrender.

Battles of Gaugamela and Hydaspes: Alexander Proves His Genius for War (331 and 326 BC)

The son of Philip II of Macedon, who reigned from 359 to 336 BC, Alexander III, known to history as Alexander the Great, was born in Pella, Macedon, and was tutored by no less a figure than Aristotle. He succeeded to the Macedonian throne on the death of his father in 336 BC and immediately turned his attention to matters of security at home, liquidating many of his rivals and consolidating his political power. Accomplishing this by the spring of 334 BC, he embarked on the military expeditions that would occupy the rest of his life. By the time of his death in 323 BC at the age of 32, the undefeated Alexander had conquered the greater part of the known world, building a vast empire that stretched from Greece to northwestern India. In the process, he created a paradigm for global military conquest to loom in the consciousness of empire builders and generalissimos for millennia to come.

After securing his homeland of Macedon, Alexander's first objective was the liberation of the Greek cities in Asia. Crossing the Hellespont with an army of about 40,000 men, he defeated the Persian army under Emperor Darius III at the Battle of Issus (in modern Turkey) and went on to defeat enemies throughout western Asia Minor. In July 332 BC, Alexander stormed the city of Tyre (in modern Lebanon) and then met with Darius III, who desperately negotiated with him in a forlorn effort to dissuade him from further attacks on his empire. When Darius finished his plea, Alexander responded that he intended to take all of Persia. This prompted the Persian to offer him his daughter in marriage. Alexander pointed out that she was already his captive and that he could marry her whenever he wished.

The campaign of conquest continued. During 332–331 BC, Alexander occupied Egypt, which offered little resistance. Learning next that Darius was massing his army in Mesopotamia, Alexander dashed back to Tyre, turned east to cross the Euphrates and Tigris Rivers and came upon a spectacular 200,000-man force arrayed for battle on the Plain of Gaugamela, near Nineveh. To oppose this host, Alexander had no more than 47,000 men. He halted about seven miles from the Persian encampment, where, incredibly, he received another abject offer of appeasement from Darius—though the Persian forces outnumbered him better than four to one. He proposed to give the Macedonian 30,000 gold talents (about

$1 billion in modern money) and half his kingdom. He added—yet again—his daughter's hand.

By way of response, Alexander attacked.

The Persians were deployed in two long, deep lines of infantry, with cavalry protecting each flank. Chariots were arrayed in front of the entire force, and a large troop of elephants were positioned in front of the center. Anticipating that Alexander would make a night attack, Darius kept his entire army standing at the ready all night so that when Alexander finally struck—in broad daylight—they were already exhausted.

The Macedonian commander moved in from the right, advancing "in echelon"—that is, with his fighting units arranged diagonally rather than perpendicular to the line of advance. With his customary genius, Alexander deployed his forces masterfully. He used his fabled "Companions," elite cavalry troops, to deliver the initial punishing blows. In the approach, these warriors were screened by Alexander's light infantry. Behind the Companions and the light infantry were the hypaspists, Alexander's equivalent of hoplites, superb infantry warriors, each armed chiefly with a shield, a long "dory" spear, and short swords—the latter used mainly as backup weapons in case the spear was lost or shattered.

The Companions and hypaspists formed the main phalanx of the attack. Alexander ensured that behind each hypaspist unit a column of light cavalry and infantry was available to protect the flank of the main phalanx. His objective was always to ward off envelopment by the enemy. In addition, he held back a single phalanx of Thessalian infantry to serve as a tactical reserve. Typically, ancients either fought with absolutely every man they had or held reserve forces at some distance from the battlefield. Instead, Alexander used a tactical reserve—a maneuvering force deliberately held back to influence the future course of combat. Military historians believe that Gaugamela was the first recorded instance of the use of such a reserve. It is typical of Alexander's exquisite, patient, and efficient tactical sense.

The echelon approach took advantage of an advancing line's natural tendency to drift rightward in their advance. Most commanders dismissed this drift as a kind of annoying tactical bug. Alexander saw it as a feature. He exaggerated it, and the movement forced the Persians to continually shift leftward, a maneuver that opened up gaps in their line. Alexander knew that such vulnerabilities did not last long, and, sighting a promising gap, he immediately pointed his attack into it. His frontline cavalry and hypaspists charged through the opening in wedge formation. They sliced through, penetrating the Persian line and sending Darius himself into full flight. Not surprisingly, this created panic throughout the units closest to the emperor. The Persian left and center imploded.

Alexander also took note, however, that in the meantime his own left flank had been driven back by a massed Persian cavalry charge. With great personal discipline, he left the ongoing attack to subordinate commanders and rode back to his own lines to personally direct the battle for his endangered flank. He used his tactical reserve to hold the line. Only when he was certain that the threat had been neutralized did he return to leading the main assault, driving it all the way to the Persian rear lines, effectively ending the main phase of the Battle of Guagamela.

Alexander being Alexander, he did not bask in the moment of victory. Instead he rallied his entire army in hot pursuit of the routed Persians. For the loss of 500 killed and some 3,000 wounded, Alexander the Great claimed the lives of at least 50,000 Persians at Gaugamela. Having hounded and scattered the survivors of the battle, he advanced into Babylon, which surrendered to him without a fight.

From Babylon, Alexander marched into the very heart of Persia. After sacking the imperial capital of Persepolis, he swung north to Ecbatana (Hamadan), where Darius had taken refuge. Seeing the approach of the Macedonians, Darius continued his flight eastward. Alexander was not about to let him get away. He detached a flying column of no more than 500 of his strongest men, leading them in a grueling forced march that covered 400 miles in 11 days. This spectacular feat revealed yet another dimension of Alexander's military leadership. A tactical master, he was also willing to require maximum *physical* performance in a single-minded effort to accomplish his mission. By the time Alexander caught up with what was doubtless a stunned Darius, only 60 of his original 500 had managed to keep up with him. The rest were staggered by exhaustion. As it turned out, a clique of Persian nobles led by the satrap of Bactria, Bessus, assassinated their emperor before Alexander closed in. The result of this murder was that the great Persian Empire lay wide open to the great Alexander.

Even now, the Macedonian did not stop. This was a third dimension of his approach to combat. Impeccable tactics and a willingness to take the attack to the extremes of human endurance were joined to relentless tenacity. He now gave chase to the slayers of Darius. In the course of the long pursuit, during 329 BC, Alexander also consolidated his gains and pushed ever eastward, through Parthia and Bactria. At last he overtook Bessus, whom he executed, and then turned toward the north to subdue the wild tribes of Scythia in what is today Central Asia and Eastern Europe. Conquest continued as Alexander pressed into India during 328–327 BC. He found an ally in the King of Taxila (a city-state in what is today the Rawalpindi District of Pakistan's Punjab). The king wanted Alexander to help him defeat Porus, most powerful monarch of the Punjab. Alexander, who desired nothing more than a reason to invade central India, embraced the invitation.

In the spring of 326 BC, Alexander the Great and his army were stalled at the Hydaspes River, which was swollen from torrential spring rains. On the river's far bank was Porus and his army of 35,000. Alexander at this point led perhaps 20,000 men. He was faced with a seemingly insoluble tactical problem. The river was too deep to be forded, but to attempt to cross it in boats against opposition from a numerically superior force was suicide. He decided therefore to camp on his side of the Hydaspes and await the subsidence of the river. In the meantime, he engaged Porus in psychological warfare by continually moving up and down the river, as if preparing to cross. At first Porus's army responded by mirroring Alexander's every feint. With repetition, however, the Indians became complacent.

As always a brilliant observer of his adversary's behavior, Alexander recognized that Porus and his forces were losing their edge. By May the roiling Hydaspes had begun to subside. Alexander had found a place to cross in boats some 16 miles upstream from his encampment. Dividing his already outnumbered army in half, Alexander left about 10,000 men to continue feinting in view of Porus along the near bank. With the rest of his force and under cover of a dark, stormy night, Alexander marched upstream. Boats had been readied, and he stealthily crossed his men throughout the predawn hours, completing the operation shortly after sunup.

For his part, Porus did not know what to make of reports that Alexander had crossed the river. He therefore consolidated his army in a defensive position around his encampment, lining up 100 elephants at the head of his assembled soldiers. Alexander's horses would never charge elephants, Porus correctly reasoned. What he did not take into account was that Alexander rarely launched a simple head-on attack. Arraying his army before Porous—6,000 cavalry and 5,000 infantry—Alexander sent his general Coenus with half the cavalry in a wide sweep around the enemy's right flank. Alexander drew up the remainder of his forces beside the river. Then he sent some of his infantry toward the elephants. They provoked a stampede—not against them, but against the Indians' own lines. A chaos of panic ensued.

While Porus now contended with stampeding beasts and terrified men, his right wing was on the march, seeking to envelop Alexander's exposed flank. By the time the commander of the right wing saw that Coenus and some 3,000 cavalrymen were closing in on their rear, it was too late. Coenus rolled up the Indian right wing, adding to the prevailing chaos and thereby neutralizing the Indians' numerical advantage. Alexander now hit Porus on his front, flank, *and* rear. The Indians fought back fiercely, both inflicting and suffering heavy casualties, but they found it impossible to recover from their disarray. The army of Porus ultimately broke and ran, leaving behind the severely wounded king, who became Alexander's prisoner.

The victorious Macedonian resolved to continue his conquest from the Hydaspes to the Ganges in north-central India, but at the Hyphasis River—today known as the Beas River, in Punjab—his army, exhausted and longing for home, mutinied. Undefeated by any external foe, Alexander bowed to his own men. He commenced a long march back to Persia during 326 BC to 324 BC. All the way back, he grew the ranks of his army by recruiting Persians. This nearly touched off a new mutiny because Alexander, intent on fully assimilating the foreign troops, forced his men to marry Persian women. Determined to resume his career of conquest, Alexander continued the process of augmenting his forces with more and more Persians as he made preparations to invade Arabia. While girding for these new battles, however, Alexander the Great succumbed to what most historians believe was pernicious malaria. He died in Babylon on June 10, 323 BC, before reaching his thirty-third birthday.

Alexander brought the military art to new heights in terms of tactics, charismatic leadership, and the sheer will to conquer. He died undefeated and was thus peerless among his many opponents. In him the great expeditionary campaign was perfected, yet his skill, audacity, and unappeasable appetite for conquest far exceeded his abilities as a political administrator. Narrowly obsessed with conquest, he took no interest in ruling what he had gained. His death brought dissension among the so-called Diadochi ("successors"), the rival commanders, families, associates, and friends of Alexander who now fought for control of all the young man had conquered. The Wars of the Diadochi lasted some 50 years and frittered away the vast empire Alexander had won but failed to consolidate. In the end, the great lesson of this greatest of all ancient generals was that military victory, in itself, is limited—no matter how spectacular. Still, Alexander's vast genius for war set aspirational goals for the likes of Caesar and Napoleon in ages to come.

Battle of Cannae: Hannibal's Masterpiece (216 BC)

Modern writers of military theory and history call him the "Father of Strategy." The literal accuracy of this title is open to dispute, yet it is not undeserved, and the Battle of Cannae, which he fought to a devastating victory on August 2, 216 BC, in Apulia, southeastern Italy, which pitted his Carthaginians against a larger force of the vaunted Roman Republic under Lucius Aemilius Paullus Macedonicus and Gaius Terentius Varro, is universally considered the greatest masterpiece of tactics to emerge from the ancient world.

Son of Hamilcar Barca, the Carthaginian general who had fought the Romans ably during the First Punic War, Hannibal traveled to Spain during his father's campaign there in 237 BC but returned to Carthage to finish his education after Hamilcar's death in 228. He then returned to Spain in command of cavalry under his brother-in-law Hasdrubal the Fair in 224. When Hasdrubal the Fair was assassinated in 221, Hannibal became overall commander of the army and immediately set out across northwest Iberia (modern Spain), which he pacified during two lightning campaigns in 221 and 220.

Following his victories in Iberia, Hannibal determined to exact vengeance on Rome for its victory in the First Punic War. His plan was to attack Italy itself, but he needed a strategy that would avoid the Roman-controlled Mediterranean Sea; therefore, he staged a brilliant, epic overland campaign. He first took Saguntum, an Iberian city-state allied with Rome, which fell after an excruciating eight-month siege late in 219. Hannibal left Iberia in 218 and invaded Gaul (July), evading and outmaneuvering the Roman legion led by Publius Cornelius Scipio the Elder at Massilia (modern Marseille). In August he crossed the Rhone River and by the fall was confronted with the Alps. Undaunted, he organized and executed a spectacular Alpine crossing—elephants and all—entering Italy during September-October 218 BC. He engaged the Roman cavalry and *velites* (lightly armed infantry troops) at the Battle of Ticinus in November and then trounced the main Roman force commanded by T. Sempronius Longus at the River Trebbia in December. Next came the army of G. Flaminius, against which Hannibal assumed the defensive, only to make a devastating surprise attack at Lake Trasimene in April 217.

After these losses, Rome embraced a delaying strategy, seeking to disrupt Hannibal's supply lines rather than fight open battles with him. But Rome could not long tolerate such an approach, and in 216 the new co-consuls, Gaius

Terentius Varro and Lucius Aemilius Paullus Macedonicus, assembled the largest army in the Republic's history with the objective of destroying Hannibal and his army.

When Hannibal marched into southern Italy that summer, seizing a Roman supply depot near the town of Cannae, the co-consuls pursued. On August 2 the Romans and Carthaginians faced off along the River Aufidus. Hannibal had about 40,000 infantry and 10,000 cavalry—horses only, his elephants having by this time died. The Romans had 80,000 infantry and 6,000 cavalry.

Varro (in command that day) deployed in the traditional Roman block formation, a mass of infantry flanked by cavalry. Varro's plan was to break the center of the Carthaginian lines with his massed forces. Anticipating precisely this—for he knew his enemy—Hannibal deployed in what we might call a jiu-jitsu formation intended to use the Romans' own momentum against them. He positioned his Gallic Celts and Spaniards, the weakest of his infantry, in the center and put his best Libyan infantry toward the rear on either flank. Hannibal's cavalry were placed on the far left and right wings. A bird's-eye view would have revealed the Carthaginian line as an extended crescent bulging at its center toward the Roman legions. Hannibal personally commanded at the front, alongside the Spaniards and Gauls.

At the commencement of combat, the two enemies charged toward one another. The first blows were landed by light infantry on both sides, using their standoff weapons—projectiles, javelins, and spears. Then Hannibal sent his heavy cavalry, under his younger brother Hasdrubal Barca (not to be confused with Hasdrubal the Fair, assassinated in 221), in headlong stampede against the right-flank Roman cavalry. The Carthaginian horsemen destroyed the Roman cavalry, which was inferior both in number and fighting quality.

While the cavalry battle quickly unfolded, Hannibal's Gaulish and Spanish infantrymen clashed with the main Roman foot soldiers. As expected, the Carthaginian center slowly gave way, the original bulging crescent becoming a concave pocket into which the Romans, believing they were winning, advanced. They now found themselves lodged between the as-yet unengaged veteran Libyans who formed the flanks of Hannibal's formation. Into the lethal pocket the legionnaires poured, their disciplined ranks becoming a disorderly mob. At this, Hannibal ordered the Libyans to turn inward. They crushed in like the jaws of a great vise.

While the Roman infantry was slaughtered, Hasdrubal moved laterally to rout the Roman cavalry on the left. With both of the Roman horse contingents destroyed, Hasdrubal took the Carthaginian cavalry against the rear of the Roman infantry. Varro's army was now crushed left and right, front and rear—all means of maneuver, including retreat, cut off.

And yet the encircled legionaries, valiant as they were, gave no indication of surrender. This being the case, the Carthaginian troops pressed in, dispatching the Roman soldiers one man after another. It was systematic butchery. Estimates are that between 50,000 and 70,000 Roman warriors were killed on the field. Some additional thousands were made prisoner. Hannibal's losses were perhaps 6,000 men.

At word of this defeat, Rome panicked but then rallied. Hannibal did march into the city of Rome during the summer of 211 and defeated two legions the summer after that. But he could not sustain his gains. His support among Rome's colonial possessions in southern Italy eroded, and he and his army felt the grinding attrition employed by Quintus Fabius Maximus Verrucosus, celebrated as Cunctator—"The Delayer." In 207 Hasdrubal Barca was killed in battle, and the reinforcements he was to bring Hannibal went undelivered. At last Carthage itself withdrew its support for Hannibal's endless campaigning, and he withdrew to Africa to defend against the invasion of Scipio Africanus during the fall of 203 BC.

Battle of Zama: Hannibal's Defeat (202 BC)

Following his triumph at Cannae on August 2, 216 BC, Hannibal attacked Marcus Claudius Marcellus, a Roman praetor (army commander) who had encamped his forces near Suessula, in the Campania of southern Italy. While attacking Marcellus, Hannibal also advanced against the city of Nola. Marcellus defended his forces ably, and although he scored no great victory against Hannibal, he did prevent Nola from falling to him. Despite Hannibal's breakthrough at Cannae on August 2, 216, the Second Punic War now settled into a stalemate lasting from November 216 into June 214. The Romans deliberately shifted to a strategy of attrition under Quintus Fabius Maximus Verrucosus,

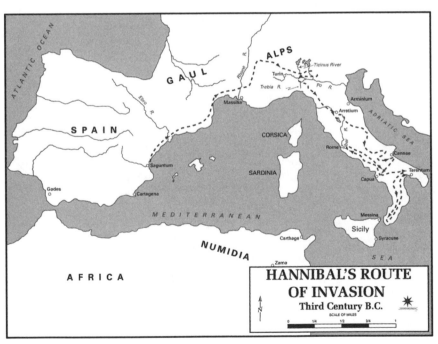

Hannibal's route of the invasion of Gaul
WIKIMEDIA COMMONS

the Republic's dictator. Fabius's delaying tactics earned him the agnomen (nickname) "Fabius Cunctator"—Fabius the Delayer. It was not a compliment, and some complained that his tactics were an ignominious admission that Hannibal was simply superior to any Roman commander. "Admission" it may well have been, but whether or not the admission was "ignominious," the Fabian strategy and tactics worked. Hannibal's poorly supplied forces were wearing down. In March 212 the Carthaginian captured the city of Tarentum in southern Italy, but he failed to pry its citadel from Roman hands. And so the stalemate endured.

Desperate for breakthrough action, Hannibal defeated two Roman armies at Herdonea (modern Ordona, in Foggia, Italy) under Gnaeus Fulvius Centumalus in the summer of 212 BC. In 208 BC his forces killed two consuls in battle, including the celebrated Marcus Claudius Marcellus. But, weakened by the relentless war of attrition, Hannibal proved unable to sustain his gains. Little by little, he lost support among the residents of Rome's southern Italian colonies, even as Fabius Cunctator continued his campaign of delay. From his younger brother Hasdrubal Barca, Hannibal was supposed to receive desperately needed reinforcements, but defeated at the Battle of the Metaurus (the Metauro River) in 207 BC, Hasdrubal charged headlong into the Romans, where he met what he knew would be certain death.

In the end it was Carthage itself that acted on the unrelenting attrition wrought by Fabius. The Carthaginian Senate withdrew support for Hannibal's Roman expeditionary campaign and, in the fall of 203 BC, recalled him to Africa to resist an invasion by Publius Cornelius Scipio, scion of a great Roman military family. In the meantime, the Carthaginians sued for peace to gain an armistice with Rome, which gave Hannibal time to sail from Italy with some 18,000 of his remaining men. As soon as Hannibal was back in Carthage, the Carthaginian Senate broke off peace talks with Rome and backed Hannibal in the rapid recruitment of a new army, which was built around the veterans who had returned with him from Italy.

By the following year, 202 BC, Hannibal had put together a force of 45,000 infantry troops and some 3,000 cavalrymen. With these he marched inland from the city of Carthage southwest to Zama. The objective was to draw Scipio's forces away from Carthage, which the Roman legions were relentlessly destroying. Deciding that completing the destruction of Carthage could wait, Scipio, reinforced by a Numidian army under Massinissa, turned away from the city and marched his 34,000 infantry and 9,000 cavalry to Zama.

Some historians believe that Scipio, about to prove himself Rome's ablest general and earn the agnomen "Scipio Africanus," parleyed with Hannibal briefly before committing to battle. If so, the talks failed, and the two sides prepared to fight a showdown contest.

Scipio deployed his maniples—the basic Roman tactical unit, consisting of 120 soldiers arrayed in three ranks of 40 men—in the usual three ranks, but he added extra space between the ranks and deployed each maniple in column instead of the customary checkerboard formation. Anticipating that Hannibal would begin the battle by unleashing his justly feared war elephants, Scipio was intent on creating lanes through which the beasts could be effectively herded, contained, and thereby neutralized.

For his part, Hannibal also deployed his forces in three ranks. He put his foreign troops—Gauls, Ligudrians, and Moors—in the front rank, his raw Carthaginian recruits in the second, and his trusted veterans of the Italian campaign in phalanx formation at the rear. On the flanks were his cavalry, which was just a third of the size of Scipio's. On his side, Scipio mirrored Hannibal's cavalry disposition so that the opposing cavalry units faces one another.

Hannibal thus went into battle with two serious handicaps. Many of his troops were raw Carthaginian recruits or, worse, conscripts. And his cavalry, always crucial to his tactics, was on this occasion both inferior in number and not nearly as proficient as what he had deployed at Cannae. The Carthaginian was fully aware that he would not be able to execute the brilliantly complex maneuvers that had won the earlier battle.

As Scipio had anticipated, Hannibal led off with his elephants, a weapon that had proved so effective in reducing enemy lines to chaos. But, as Scipio had planned, the modified spacing between Scipio's ranks, along with the variation in formation, made it possible for his men to handle the stampeding beasts. While Scipio's infantry was efficiently managing this aspect of the defense, his superior cavalry—the left wing under the Roman commander Laelius and the right wing under the Numidian Massanissa—were overwhelming Hannibal's cavalry and driving it off the field.

When the main portions of the opposing infantries finally crashed together in battle, Scipio neatly sliced through Hannibal's front and middle ranks, the foreign troops and raw Carthaginian levies and recruits proving no match for them. Undaunted, Scipio nevertheless unleashed his third rank, the Triarii—his older but wealthier and therefore better-equipped legionnaires—against Hannibal's third-rank reserve, the so-called Phalanx of Veterans. Hannibal led these battle-hardened troops personally. They fought valiantly, standing firm against the Roman onslaught and taking a heavy toll on Scipio's Triarii.

But even Hannibal's veterans could not hold out against the whole of the Roman infantry, especially after Scipio's cavalry returned to the main battle. Having dispersed Hannibal's horsemen, Masanissa's right-wing cavalry and Laelius's left wing doubled back to attack Hannibal from the rear. Together they pounded in on both the left and the right. This devastating twin blow brought the Battle of Zama to a rapid and terrible end.

Hannibal and very few survivors fled to Carthage, leaving behind some 20,000 dead Carthaginians. In Roman chains were an additional 15,000 prisoners. Roman losses were 4,000 to 5,000 killed, including more than 2,500 of the Republic's Numidian allies.

The Battle of Zama effectively ended the Second Punic War, a 17-year conflict that ancient historians regarded as the greatest and most destructive military conflict in history. Hundreds of thousands had been killed and many more imprisoned or enslaved. Entire cities were utterly razed. As for Carthage, Rome attempted to wipe it out as an independent country, forcing Carthage to turn over to Rome all of its war elephants and warships. The Romans demanded heavy cash reparations, payable in ruinous installments over a 50-year period. Yet, though defeated, Hannibal showed himself nearly as capable of governing in peace as he had commanded, at his best, in war. Under his leadership, Carthage rose like a phoenix from the ashes, regaining much of its former prosperity. Jealous and suspicious, the Romans accused him of seeking to undermine the peace, and in 196 BC he fled Carthage to offer his military services to Antiochus III the Great of Syria. For this foe of Rome, in 190 BC Hannibal raised and commanded a fleet against Rhodes but was defeated there by the Roman admiral and praetor Lucius Aemilius Regillus at the amphibious Battle of the Eurymedon, fought at the mouth of Eurymedon River in Pamphylia, Asia Minor. Forced to take flight again, Hannibal sought refuge in Crete but was pursued by the Romans to Bithynia (in modern Turkey). Cornered there, he took his own life by swallowing poison. It was a tragic, anticlimactic end to a general whose tactical and strategic genius repeatedly enabled him to successfully pit the inferior military resources of Carthage against Rome, the mightiest military of the ancient world. In Hannibal, military history had its first great paradigm of the insurgent general, the victorious underdog. Rome, it turned out, could not out-general him; but, as Fabius Cunctator proved, it could outspend him and wear him down. Hannibal's final defeat was due primarily to economics. The Republic could afford to endure a war of attrition; Carthage could not. In this, it showed history the limits of military genius.

Reforms of Marius: The Roman Legion as Model for Military Organization (105 BC)

Jugurtha was one of three inheritors of the throne of Numidia, an ancient Berber kingdom (in what is now Algeria) and a key ally of the Roman Republic. The illegitimate nephew of the late king, Jugurtha was not content to share his reign with that king's two sons. Through a combination of assassination and war, with a helping of bribery, Jugurtha assumed sole kingship of Numidia. Because he had acted against Roman allies and, in the course of making war on one of his rival inheritors, killed many Romans who were residing in Numidia, the Republic responded with a military expedition in 111 BC. Jugurtha, however, mounted an extremely effective defense and repulsed the invaders. He then answered a summons to Rome to explain and justify his actions. While there, however, he assassinated his cousin Massiva, who had decided to press his own claim to the throne. The Roman Senate expelled Jugurtha, who returned to Numidia.

In 109 BC and after much delay, the Roman general Quintus Caecilius Metellus led a large African army in a punitive expedition against Numidia. Unable to defeat the invaders in open battle, Jugurtha resorted to guerrilla warfare. In response, the Roman Senate sent an army under Gaius Marius (157–86 BC), a distinguished general and statesman, who would go on to serve as consul for an unprecedented seven terms. Marius continued the campaign of devastation Caecilius had begun, but he failed to extinguish the flame of guerrilla resistance. The war was finally ended not by a brilliant Roman military victory but through the treachery of Jugurtha's father-in-law, who delivered the ruler into Roman hands.

Marius accomplished his mission, returning to Rome with Jugurtha his prisoner, but he also understood that he had not deposed Jugurtha by means of Roman arms. In fact, his legions had proved inadequate to subdue determined insurgents. Marius began contemplating military reforms, but it took another battle to finally move him to action.

The Battle of Arausio was fought on October 6, 105 BC, on the banks of the Rhone River in what is today France. Here a Roman army of 10 to 12 legions—about 80,000 legionnaires in addition to some 40,000 auxiliaries and camp followers—engaged as many as 200,000 Cimbri and Teuton warriors. After an initial skirmish, the legions suffered an apocalyptic rout in which the entire force was simply wiped out. In the worst defeat ancient Rome ever suffered, 80,000 legionnaires were killed, along with all auxiliaries and camp followers. Potentially, Rome had lost a total of 120,000.

In response to the massive shock created by Arausio, Marius, now consul of the Republic, not only took command of Roman Gaul in 105 BC but also set about making massive, highly consequential reforms. In this, he not only redesigned the Roman legions but also created the model for a professional military. Marius's reforms laid the foundation of the legions with which Julius Caesar (100–44 BC) would create the Roman Empire. Indeed, the reforms served as the basis of modern militaries throughout the Western world.

The Arausio cataclysm brought an end to the prevailing Roman militia system in which citizens were levied (drafted) for military service as part of their duty to the state. Marius believed that conscription failed to create a cohesive military force with discipline, motivation, and esprit de corps. He therefore began recruiting soldiers who would volunteer for salaried service for terms of up to 16 years. Under Marius, to be a Roman soldier was to be a professional warrior. He integrated these professionals into a new system of organization. Marius eliminated the traditional aristocratic distinctions that had existed between militia drawn from the lower and upper classes, and he leveled most other distinctions, including those of age and experience. The result was a pool of manpower that could be deployed however circumstances required, giving the legions great operational flexibility and maneuverability as well as efficiency in recruitment and replacement.

A professional army, Marius decided, was the product of intense training. He therefore called on his colleague Publius Rufus to write a new manual of drill regulations to improve and standardize training throughout all Roman forces. Not only would this produce better individual soldiers, but the standardization would make widely dispersed units more interoperable. A soldier trained in the south could be transferred to the north without having to learn new skills. In effect, the armies of Rome were being transformed into a "national" force rather than a collection of local militias.

What military historians call the new "Marian Legion" made the cohort the principal unit of tactical organization. Ten cohorts of 400 to 500 men each composed a legion, with each cohort formed for battle in a line of 10 or 8 ranks along a frontage of approximately 50 men. For maneuvering and the mass launching of javelins, each cohort could be formed in close order, with just three feet between each man. Because this did not leave enough room for swinging even a short Roman sword, the space between men was doubled to six feet in hand-to-hand combat situations. To enable an attacking legion to extend rapidly from a closed to an open formation, the cohorts were separated from one another by a width equivalent to one cohort. This provided sufficient flexibility to maintain a continuous front, without gaps, when transitioning from close order to wide order even while engaged in combat.

When fighting on defense, a legion could form in a line, a square, or a circle. As perfected by Marius, the defensive line, when formed behind fortifications or entrenchments, was usually a single line of 10 cohorts. A defensive square, a formation that armies would use for many centuries, was created from a standard three-line formation by simple facing movements of seven of the cohorts. Three cohorts were left facing front, while three were faced to the rear, and two faced toward each flank. This—or, depending on terrain, the circle—was primarily used to defend infantry against a cavalry assault.

Marius used the square and circle when absolutely necessary, but he favored formations in which infantry flanks were protected by cavalry or light infantry auxiliary troops. He wanted his legion commanders, wherever possible, to maintain a normal line formation so that the pilum (javelin), scutum (shield), and gladius (short sword) could be employed to their maximum advantage. Confronted by such an array of weapons, even a very determined cavalry charge could usually be defeated. In this way, Marius reformed legion doctrine so that a unit could rapidly shift from a defensive to offensive posture. It was a concept of active defense, which would become standard in modern militaries.

Marius added to the new standard legion a contingent of *speculatores*, a detachment of 10 scouts who specialized in reconnaissance. Instead of pressing into service local civilian residents or spies to obtain combat information, legion commanders could rely on the *speculatores* to operate in efficient teams. They were, in effect, light infantry with reconnaissance duties.

Among the most consequential of Marius's reforms was in the Roman cavalry. Under the old order, cavalry troops were drawn exclusively from *equites*, the Roman nobility. Marius removed this limitation and thereby greatly increased both the strength and tactical importance of cavalry. Because these troops were no longer required to be Roman nobles, the legions increasingly drew upon allies and mercenaries to fill out the ranks of the cavalry.

In the old-model militia army, command officers—centurions, tribunes, and staff officers—had to be appointed anew each time a militia levy was made. This cumbersome process was incompatible with creating a truly professional army, since a soldier who served as a centurion one year might be recalled later as a common private. Anything like a military "career" was out of the question. Marius wanted to develop and leverage the continuity and expertise of a professional officer corps. He divided this body of soldiers into two principal classes. The centurions were still promoted from the ranks, but they permanently retained their officer status once they had proven their worth in battle. Field rank officers—tribunes and above—were still drawn from the aristocracy. The centurion in the Marian Legion can be thought of as the equivalent of a modern noncommissioned officer, whereas tribunes and above bear comparison to commissioned officers in modern armies.

In the old legion, command of a legion rotated among its six tribunes. This practice was not officially abolished in the reformed legion, but the far more common procedure was to assign one officer, called a legate, to permanently command a legion. The tribunes acted mainly as staff officers. Continuity of command became increasingly valued in the Roman military. Soldiers began to forge strong bonds with their commanders.

The overall army commander, the *imperator* (general), was assisted by a coterie of *quaestors*, whose roles were mainly logistical and administrative. The *quaestors* may be compared to the modern concept of the staff officer as an intermediate management layer between high command and the officer and troops in the field. *Quaestors* ensured that the commanders' orders were properly executed.

Comites praetorii, aristocratic volunteer aides, served as the imperator's assistants. To this informal arrangement, Marius added an official guard detachment, the *cohors praetoria*. They were the imperator's bodyguard and were invariably assembled from the most trusted veteran soldiers. They became the basis of the Praetorian Guard of Imperial Rome.

The success of the Roman legions after the reforms of Marius is often attributed to improved professionalism, continuity of command, and promotion for merit rather than for social class or aristocratic affiliation. But there was another contributing source of victory that must not be overlooked. The Romans were, of course, renowned as engineers, and the genius that designed the Colosseum and the aqueducts also created engines of war—siege towers, ballistas, bridges, and a host of other structures. To each Roman army, Marius added a dedicated engineering detachment with troops skilled in the design and construction of bridges and siege engines. A special baggage train was attached to every army to carry tools, equipment, and materials required for construction projects.

In his reforms, Marius did not neglect morale. He redesigned the iconic standard of the legion, which was a silver eagle, wings outstretched, mounted atop a staff. This eagle was to be defended from capture at all costs, and those carrying the standard accordingly held positions of special responsibility and honor. In addition to the eagle standard, Marius created a system of legion insignias. Each legion cohort also had its own ensign, a wooden or metal medallion about six inches in diameter, carried on its own staff or, in some cases, at the tip of a lance. Each maniple—the equivalent of a modern company—also had its own distinctive ensign, which served the function of guidon, providing a rallying point in the field. All maniple guidons featured a life-size human fist, fashioned of wood or bronze and mounted on a lance. Below it were emblems uniquely identifying the maniple. Thus the Marian legion combined a standard national and large-unit identity with elements to identify and individuate each smaller unit. In this, too, the Roman army, as reformed by Marius, provided a rich source of models for emulation by many future militaries throughout the world.

Spartacus: History's First Insurgent (73–71 BC)

Most of us know Spartacus through his portrayal by Kirk Douglas in the 1960 movie epic directed by Stanley Kubrick and based on a popular 1951 historical fiction by American novelist Howard Fast. A century earlier, Karl Marx had introduced him to communist and socialist revolutionaries as "the most splendid fellow in the whole of ancient history." Military historians would likely not object to either the Douglas-Kubrick depiction of Spartacus or that of Karl Marx, but for them the more specific significance of Spartacus is as history's first documented insurgent commander—one whose natural skill as a strategist and tactician, along with what must have been charismatic leadership, gave the Roman Republic and its armies, the most formidable state and most powerful military force of the ancient world, a run for their money. Thanks to Spartacus, the Third Servile War (73–71 BC) was the first significant military insurgency, a stunning example of what modern military planners call asymmetric warfare—combat in which a non-state actor assembles and leads a force capable of challenging even a global superpower and its conventional military.

The ancient Greek historical biographer Plutarch described Spartacus as a Thracian of "Nomadic stock." He may well have been a member of the Maedi tribe, which occupied the Thracian borderlands adjoining the Roman province of Macedonia (modern southwestern Bulgaria). Another Greek historical writer, Appian of Alexandria, also identified him as a Thracian by birth and ventured further that he served as a Roman soldier but was subsequently enslaved and sold as a gladiator. Lucius Annaeus Florus, an African-born Roman historian who lived from about AD 74 to 130, elaborated on this, calling him a Thracian mercenary who entered the Roman military service but deserted, was captured, and was enslaved as punishment. His fighting strength was recognized, and he was trained as a gladiator. Plutarch believed that Spartacus was married to a prophetess of the Maedi and that she was enslaved with him.

Spartacus was consigned to a gladiatorial school (*ludus*) near Capua owned and run by Lentulus Batiatus. He was classed as *murmillo*, a "heavyweight" gladiator. These fighters were armed with a heavy, large *scutum* (shield) and an 18-inch-long *gladius* (broad, straight-blade short sword). While it is known that in 73 BC Spartacus was associated with a group of about 70 other gladiators who plotted an escape, it is not known whether he was acknowledged as their leader at the time of the plot's inception.

Neither ancient nor modern historians have reached consensus on the motives of Spartacus beyond his wanting to escape both enslavement and the grim fate of a gladiator. Certainly, no documentary evidence exists that he intended to abolish slavery throughout Rome or in any way reform Roman civilization. Plutarch's opinion is that he wanted nothing more than to escape Italy by fleeing northward into Cisalpine Gaul, where he planned to disband his army and let

This engraving by Nicola Sanesi (1818–1889) depicts the "Final Battle" of the Third Servile War, in which Crassus defeated the slaves and Spartacus was killed.
WIKIMEDIA COMMONS

his men return to their homes. Spartacus's actual movements, however, do not support this interpretation, since he turned south, not north, after defeating the legions commanded by Lucius Publicola and Gnaeus Clodianus, hard-won victories that cleared an escape route over the Alps. Accordingly, both Appian and Florus concluded that he intended to march on Rome, but Appian believed he soon gave up on this idea. Later writers do speculate that Spartacus and the insurgency he led sparked fears throughout the Roman Republic of a general slave insurrection that would culminate in the sacking of Rome. But the rebellion never got that far. It may be that Spartacus and his forces turned south because the fugitive slaves decided it was both better and safer to plunder Italy than to venture over the Alps and into poorer provinces where the pickings were slimmer.

What is known with greater certainty is that the original 70 or so slaves who made their escape fought their way out of the gladiatorial quarters in which they were held by using kitchen knives and other sharp utensils they stole. They were then able to appropriate some wagons that held gladiatorial weapons and armor. With these they defeated the squadrons of troops initially sent to round them up.

Plundering the neighborhood of Capua, the fugitives set about recruiting more and more slaves into their numbers. Then they withdrew to a natural stronghold on the heights of Mount Vesuvius. It may have been there that the band chose Spartacus to lead them. Crixus and Oenomaus, two slaves from Gaul, have also been identified as leadership figures. Early Roman writers believed that this pair were the chief lieutenants of Spartacus, who served as the supreme leader, but some later historians have speculated that the Romans projected their own idea of military order on a slave band that was more democratic (or disorganized) in structure and had no formal hierarchy. At its height, the insurgent army Spartacus likely led was at least 90,000 strong. It engaged against two Roman armies sent to suppress it, the slaves achieving serial victories against the legions of Lucius Publicola and Gnaeus Clodianus.

In 72 BC, while the slave army was raiding south of the Apennines, Spartacus seems to have voluntarily divided his forces. He allowed German and Gallic slaves to follow Crixus and Oenomaus while he retained leadership of the rest. The Gauls and Germans were defeated in battle in Apulia during 72 BC, but Spartacus and his followers pressed northward, presumably with the intention of escaping to Thrace. Once again, however, they decided—perhaps against Spartacus's will—to return to southern Italy and live off the land.

By now, the Roman Senate was swept with panic at the prospect of a massive slave rebellion under way within Italy. The Senate appointed a proven military commander, Marcus Licinius Crassus (c. 115–53 BC), praetor (commanding general) over six new legions in addition to two former consular legions, thereby putting 32,000 to 48,000 trained Roman infantry troops under his command.

When Spartacus and his followers began moving northward again, Crassus led six of his legions in pursuit. He detached two of these under his legate,

Mummius, with orders that they position themselves behind Spartacus but refrain from attacking. Apparently eager for glory, Mummius disobeyed and attacked—only to be overwhelmed and routed. Enraged, Crassus led four legions in an immediate attack, killing at least 6,000 of the insurgents.

Encouraged and emboldened by this victory, the legions of Crassus now attacked at every opportunity, again and again, killing more thousands and driving Spartacus into retreat south through Lucania, all the way to the toe of the Italian boot as far as the straits separating the peninsula from Messina in Sicily. Here (Plutarch writes) Spartacus struck a deal with Cilician pirates to evacuate him and perhaps 2,000 of his men to Sicily. His plan was to stir a slave revolt on the island and reinforce his battered army. The pirates proved treacherous. Taking the payment, they promptly abandoned Spartacus and those with him.

Spartacus retreated toward Rhegium, at the southern tip of the Italian peninsula. Crassus pursued, halted, and built a chain of fortresses to contain and cut off the insurgents. Spartacus and his men continually harassed the legions, but the Roman engineers steadily strengthened the fortifications. Soon Spartacus and his remaining men were totally cut off from supply, reinforcement, or escape. When Spartacus offered to negotiate, Crassus rebuffed him.

In desperation, a portion of the insurgent forces broke through the fortifications and fled north, with Crassus in hot pursuit. The legions engaged them, killing 12,300 insurgents. Although Crassus had also taken heavy losses, his highly disciplined legions remained very much intact, while Spartacus had good reason to believe that his army would soon disintegrate. In desperation, he again turned south and headed straight for Crassus's legions, which were advancing due north. At the Silarius River—the modern Sele River in southern Campania—the two armies clashed. This time the tattered army of Spartacus was routed. Insurgent losses were 36,000 killed in action, including Spartacus (whose body was never recovered). Six thousand insurgents were captured by Crassus and later executed by the prescribed Roman punishment for treason: crucifixion. Another 5,000 were captured by legions under Pompey, which had been dispatched from Rome. These men were also crucified. The final toll on the insurgents was 47,000 killed. Roman republican losses in this final battle of the Third Servile War were 1,000 killed in action.

Despite the lopsided numbers in this battle, some 10,000 Roman legionnaires had been killed in the whole of the Third Servile War—a remarkable toll considering that the vaunted Roman military machine was contending with a ragtag army of untrained slaves equipped only with whatever weapons and supplies they managed to steal. With natural military competence and what must have been a charismatic command presence, Spartacus led an uprising that not only inspired terror throughout Italy but also made him an icon for underdog rebellions down through the ages. He was military history's first great practitioner of asymmetric warfare, the insurgent model destined to topple empires.

The Gallic Wars: Caesar Rising (58–51 BC)

Waged by Roman proconsul Julius Caesar against many of approximately 70 Gallic tribes of Europe, the Gallic Wars not only vastly expanded the Roman Republic over the whole extent of Gaul (chiefly modern France and Belgium) but also laid the foundation for Caesar's rise to sole rule of the Republic. A turning point in Western history and civilization, the Gallic Wars also gave to the history of arms perhaps the very greatest of its "great captains" and, thanks to Caesar's eloquent, detailed, and frank account of his campaigns in *Commentarii de Bello Gallico* (*Caesar's Commentaries on the Gallic War*), provided both a masterpiece of literature and a practical text on the application of military art and science based on the firsthand experience of a superb practitioner. The *Commentaries* emerged as military history's first playbook for waging colonial warfare.

When Caesar was elected consul for 59 BC, the Roman aristocracy, fearing his boundless ambition and great popularity, sought to limit his future power by giving him the backwater assignment of supervising the woods and pastures of Italy rather than bestowing on him the governorship of a province. With aid of political allies, however, Caesar did obtain appointment as governor of Cisalpine Gaul (northern Italy) and Illyricum (southeastern Europe). Later, Transalpine Gaul (southern France) was added to his portfolio. He was given command of four legions and allowed a term of five years instead of the customary single year.

It was one thing for the Roman Republic to claim Gaul as a province and quite another for the Republic to secure control from the Gallic tribes that resisted Rome's dominion. The pacification of Cisalpine Gaul and the conquest of Transalpine Gaul occupied Caesar from 58 to 50 BC. In this span, he expanded the Roman Republic as far as the left bank of the Rhine, subjugating all Gaul so that it remained a secure province throughout the turbulent period of the Roman civil wars, which began in 49 BC and continued through 31 BC.

The Gallic Wars were not just a masterpiece of strategy and tactics; they were no less than the invention of imperial warfare, warfare designed not merely to conquer but to colonize. Alexander the Great was a magnificent conqueror, but he had no interest in governing. Caesar created an enduring empire.

Because his campaigns were expeditionary over a vast area, Caesar had to fight with limited resources. In almost every campaign and battle, he was significantly outnumbered and often underequipped, overmatched in manpower as well as arms by the Gauls, Celts, and Germans he fought. The successes he enjoyed were products of his leadership, his strategic and tactical genius, and his imposition of the systematic military order and discipline that characterized the Roman legions.

When Caesar arrived in Gaul in 58 BC, Rome's northwestern frontier was little changed from what it had been when it was established in 125. It was bounded by the Alps and ran down the left bank of the upper Rhône River as far as the Pyrenees. It then touched the southeastern foot of the Cévennes Mountains and encompassed the upper basin of the Garonne River, but stopped well short of the Atlantic shore. Caesar boldly ventured beyond these borderlands. His first target was the Helvetii, a tribe that had invaded portions of Gaul from their territories in what is today central Switzerland. After achieving victories against the Helvetii, he defeated Ariovistus, a military commander of great skill who led the Suebi (Suevi), chief tribe among a coalition of Germanic warriors who had crossed the Rhine west into Gaul.

In 57 BC Caesar launched a major campaign against the fierce Belgic tribes, who lived in the northern reaches of Gaul. At the same time, Caesar's subordinate commander, Marcus Licinius Crassus, pacified tribes in what are today Normandy and Brittany. This was followed in 56 BC by Caesar's own campaigns against the Veneti, a Celtic tribe associated with the southern portion of modern Brittany. Together with the Morini (who lived near the Strait of Dover) and the Menapii (dwelling along the south bank of the lower Rhine), the Veneti staged a rebellion very broad in geographical scope. Caesar suppressed the Veneti with great aggression but could not complete his campaign against the Morini and Menapii before the onset of winter. Come the spring of 55 BC, he returned to these two tribes, which he annihilated. Of all his Gallic campaigns, those against Veneti, Morini, and Menapi are the only ones that may be characterized as at least bordering on intentional genocide.

In 55 BC as well, Caesar advanced beyond the eastern boundary of Gaul, bridging the Rhine River just below the modern city of Koblenz to make a lightning raid into Germany. He did not linger but instead sought to expand in the opposite direction, crossing the English Channel to raid Britain. He did this once in 55 BC and again in 54 BC but was forced to cut short the British invasion to return to northeastern Gaul to put down a new revolt. He acted against rebellious tribes again in 53 BC and, yet again, threw a bridge across the Rhine to make a second foray into Germany.

The most serious uprising Caesar faced in Gaul came in 52 BC, when Vercingetorix, a chieftain of the Arverni (who lived in what is today the French Auvergne), forged an alliance among tribes in central Gaul to conduct a massive offensive against the Romans with perhaps as many as 330,000 warriors. Vercingetorix proved a highly capable commander of his enormous forces, which he used to execute a strategy intended to cut off Caesar's legions from their sources of supply while also enforcing a scorched-earth policy to deprive them of local forage. In this approach, Vercingetorix showed profound military insight, which he executed ruthlessly. He understood that an invader's weakness is always supply and that an invading force is perpetually vulnerable to being isolated. For him, these vulnerabilities were sources of leverage, whereas engaging the highly disciplined legions in pitched battle put Vercingetorix at a disadvantage.

Fortunately for Caesar, Vercingetorix proved unable to enforce his strict scorched-earth measures on his fellow Gauls, and he was defeated at the siege and Battle of Alesia (September 52 BC). With his surrender, the possibility of a united Gallic insurrection ended, and the winter of 52–51 BC into the spring and summer of 51 BC saw only lesser revolts, most notably among the Bellovaci, who lived between the Seine and Somme Rivers, near what is today Beauvais. Also, at Uxellodunum (believed to be the Puy d'Issolu on the Dordogne River) another force resisted the Romans until their water supply ran dry. With the conclusion of this campaign, the Gallic Wars ended, and Caesar was set up for his next move—the return from Gaul to the heart of the Roman Republic. He would return to a republic racked by civil war, but he would return as the general who had secured all Gaul for Rome.

Crossing the Rubicon: Caesar Triumphant (49 BC)

It is one of the oldest of metaphors and memes—"crossing the Rubicon"—a figure of speech denoting any decision or act that amounts to an irrevocable step committing you to a certain course. The stakes are all or nothing, and it is a path on which there is no turning back, a bell that cannot be unrung.

True Rubicon decisions are relatively few in military history. Most commanders want to keep their options open. Many condemn outright the either/or approach as the very opposite of effective strategy or tactics, which (they say) are all about maintaining the ability to maneuver, withdraw, or side-step. Yet every commander worth his salt envies those generals or admirals who risked it all—and (of course) won. Julius Caesar created the enduring model of either/or, now-or-never decision making in military history when he crossed the Rubicon in 49 BC.

As for the Rubicon, it was a river so shallow and insignificant that no one is quite certain that the stream bearing the name today, near modern Ravenna in northern Italy, is the same one Caesar crossed. To be sure, the Rubicon posed no formidable geographical obstacle to the advance of an individual or an army in 49 BC. There was even a small and convenient bridge over it. But the ancient biographer-historian Plutarch writes that Caesar "became full of thought" as he approached the Rubicon. His "mind wavered," and he "began to go more slowly and then ordered a halt." He walked up alone to the northern bank and stood there "for a long time." Plutarch writes that he "weighed matters up silently in his own mind, irresolute between . . . two alternatives": to cross or not to cross.

What was at issue?

The Rubicon River divided northern Italy—Cisalpine Gaul, one of the provinces the Roman Senate had assigned to Caesar's governorship—from the Roman Republic proper, where the Senate was dominated by Gnaeus Pompeius Magnus, better known as Pompey. Once Caesar's ally and fellow triumvir, Pompey was now his arch rival. What is more, Pompey had the Lex Cornelia Majestatis on his side. This law barred any Roman general from leading an army out of the province to which he was assigned. In other words, if Caesar and the 6,000 men with him crossed the Rubicon, they would commit a violation that would bring down upon them all the legions commanded by Pompey and the Senate of Rome. The crossing would mean civil war, which, on the face of it (unless Caesar could rapidly recruit many more soldiers than a mere 6,000 men), would be impossible to win. And even if he somehow won, the war could be tragic for the nation.

Thus, there were compelling reasons not to cross this otherwise insignificant stream. Yet there was also a powerful reason *to* cross. Caesar believed that failing to act would prolong a peace created by a badly misgoverned Rome. Not to cross surely *seemed* the safer course, but Caesar believed inaction would bring catastrophe sooner or later. For a state misruled cannot long endure.

Caesar's assessment of corruption and misrule arose from a mixture of personal ambition and keen, coldly objective observation. He had been born about 100 BC into a patrician family fallen on hard times. As he entered adulthood, he became determined to revive his family's fortunes by bringing honor and wealth upon himself. At the same time, he saw about him a government and society weighed down by crime and incompetence, beholden to the *equites*—the noble knights—who had enriched themselves on the profits of military and other government contracts. In the meantime, the Roman masses, who supplied the manpower for the armies and the labor for everything else in the Republic, struggled in a political and economic system that only grudgingly allowed them a living. No wonder Rome was in perpetual turmoil, roiled by serial rebellions that necessitated suppression by the Roman legions. With the Roman interior chronically unstable, how long could the Republic endure as "barbarians" menaced the gates at every frontier?

Caesar had made his own climb up the republican ladder, becoming one of three triumvirs ruling Rome and its provinces. In this office, while administering Cisalpine Gaul and Transalpine Gaul, he had put all Gaul—including what is today France, up to the left bank of the Rhine—under complete Roman control. While Caesar was consolidating the two Gallic provinces and therefore absent from Rome, Crassus was knocked out of the triumvirate after losing Syria to the Parthians. This left Caesar and Pompey in contention for sole Roman rule. With the year 49 BC upon them, Caesar was due to resign his provincial governorships and take up a term as consul. Pompey announced his intention to enforce a Roman law obliging Caesar to relinquish his army during the interval between the expiration of his term as governor and the commencement of his consulship. During this span, Caesar would be unarmed and therefore at the mercy of Pompey and other enemies.

Unwilling to risk such exposure, he lobbied the Senate to either eliminate the interval between offices or allow him to retain his army during it. In response, the Senate stalled, and so Caesar now *demanded* of the Senate that Pompey be obliged to lay down his arms simultaneously with him. Offended by Caesar's bold effrontery, the senators replied that Caesar was to be treated as a public enemy if he refused to submit on whatever date the Senate might fix.

And thus matters stood as Caesar stood on the north bank of the Rubicon. Cross, and the full military might of Rome would descend upon him and his men. Cross, and the Roman Republic would be swallowed up in civil war. If he stayed put? Nothing would be gained. But would anything be lost? As Caesar saw it, he might not lose any power, at least not instantly. But it would likely ooze slowly away. Moreover, Rome itself was oozing into premature decay. True, crossing the Rubicon might destroy Caesar. True, it might even destroy Rome. On the other hand, crossing that river was the only hope of elevating Caesar and saving Rome—which Caesar believed only he could do.

Plutarch tells us that Caesar continued to stand on the riverbank, discussing "his perplexities with his friends who were there." He "thought of the sufferings which his crossing the river would bring upon mankind." But then he "imagined the fame of the story of it."

Suetonius, another early Caesar biographer, wrote that the general told his followers: "We may still draw back; but, once across that little bridge, we shall have to fight it out." So, he "stood, in two minds" until, suddenly, he saw a man, "strikingly noble" and of "graceful aspect," who played upon a shepherd's pipe with such beauty that soldiers, including his legions' trumpeters, rushed to the shepherd's side. From one of these martial musicians, the shepherd took a trumpet and ran to the river with it. Putting it to his lips, he sounded a piercing blast. It was the legionnaires' call to advance. Sounding it once more, the shepherd crossed the bridge.

Stirred from his contemplation, Caesar called to his men: "Let us accept this as a sign from the Gods, and follow where they beckon, in vengeance on our double-dealing enemies. *Alea iacta est!*"

And so, another cultural meme—"The die is cast!"—was added to "crossing the Rubicon." For with this exclamation, Julius Caesar crossed the river. As he knew it would, this brought bloodshed. The Great Roman Civil War, which spanned 49 to 45 BC, brought the defeat and death of Pompey and his followers and elevated Caesar to the office of *Dictator perpetuo*—Dictator for Life. Caesar did not become emperor, but, arguably, he ruled like one, and his victory ended most of the political traditions of the Roman Republic, which was formally replaced by the Roman Empire in 27 BC, 17 years after Caesar's assassination.

For general historians, Caesar's decision to cross the Rubicon has led to endless speculation as to the fate of Rome had he chosen otherwise. Most believe that the corrupt and decadent republic was headed for destruction. Most also conclude that by ending the worst of the misrule, Caesar gave to the Roman state—and therefore to Greco-Roman civilization—another four centuries of life in the West and six more in the East. This longevity did much to define the future contours of Western civilization.

For *military* historians, crossing the Rubicon is about the nature and the role of individual command decision in the outcome of battle and warfare. It is a lesson in strategic evaluation and a study of the nexus between military action and political outcome. Surely, it is not the first go/no-go military decision of profound and enduring consequence, but none—save, perhaps, the decision to use atomic weapons in World War II—has proved more important. Moreover, it is the earliest military Rubicon decision into which we have significant historical insight, thanks to the writings of Plutarch, Suetonius, and Caesar himself, whose *Bellum Civile* (*The Civil Wars*) is an account second in historical and literary merit only to Caesar's own *Commentarii de Bello Gallico* (*Commentaries on the Gallic War*).

The Pax Romana Begins: Rome Dominant (29 BC)

One of the most powerful turning points in the military history of the ancient world was more notable for what did not happen than for what did. The Pax Romana ("The Roman Peace") was a long period of peace among the usually contentious nationalities of the Roman Empire, between roughly 29 BC and AD 162. The relative calm within the empire, which encompassed about a third of the known world during this period, contrasted with the conflict that prevailed elsewhere. Moreover, this stability withstood the likes of Caligula, Claudius, and Nero, two of the most infamous emperors in history bookending one of the least competent.

In 29 BC Octavian, successor to Julius Caesar, returned to Rome after defeating Antony and his paramour-ally Cleopatra in the Final War of the Roman Republic (32–30 BC). The victory ushered in the Roman Empire when the Senate conferred on Octavian the title of Augustus in 27 BC, making him Rome's first emperor (*Imperator*). Having defeated Antony and annexed Egypt, Augustus presided over a vast and remarkably stable empire that possessed overwhelming military strength. Augustus's victory showed him to be a superb general, and at least four emperor-generals who followed him—Tiberius, Trajan, Marcus Aurelius, and Septimus Severus—were energetic and competent military figures. None of them, however, with the possible exception of Tiberius, would be classed among history's "great captains" and brilliant strategists. The point is that the military institution and resources established in Rome at this time were so solid that mere competence was quite sufficient to sustain the Roman peace.

The triumph Augustus achieved over Antony and the forces of Egypt exerted great influence over the ancient world and shaped the age. His rational reign continued all that was good about Julius Caesar's governance but without Caesar's overbearing air of boundless personal ambition. Nearly two centuries later, by AD 162, the second year of the reign of Marcus Aurelius, the Roman Eastern War (AD 162–165) began, pitting Rome against Parthia. After an initial defeat, Rome subdued Parthia and regained control of its province Armenia. Although this was a major war, which many historians believe signaled the end of the Pax Romana, Marcus Aurelius not only presided over a final victory but continued to protect the Roman interior from all threats. Some 200 years earlier, Augustus had reduced the Roman imperial army to just 25 legions, perhaps 300,000 men, counting the Praetorian Guard and auxiliary forces. Seeking to fend off threats along the Rhine and Danube frontiers, Marcus Aurelius increased that army to about 400,000. This still meant that barbarian military manpower collectively—and sometimes even singly—outnumbered the legions. But Marcus Aurelius kept the standards of training, discipline, and organization very high, so the Roman army continued consistently to intimidate. Moreover, in AD 6 Augustus capitalized a modest military pension fund, the *aerarium militare*, with 170 million sesterces from his own fortune. To this, a tax was added, creating an endowment from which military veterans were generously paid. In addition, the emperor incentivized the veterans to settle in the frontier provinces, thereby adding a trained military presence to these vulnerable borderlands. The veterans were organized near newly erected small fortresses (*castelli*), which served as advance outposts against barbarian raids and incursions.

Not all the emperors of the Pax Romana were of the caliber of Augustus, Tiberius, Trajan, Marcus Aurelius, and Septimus Severus, the "Five Good Emperors" of Rome. Caligula (AD 37–41), who succeeded Tiberius, was a homicidal psychopath. His brief but violent reign was followed by that of the inept yet treacherous Claudius (41–54) and then that byword for evil, Nero (54–68). The seven emperors who came after Nero were mostly unremarkable, although Trajan (98–117) and Hadrian (117–138) were both able military leaders (Trajan more than Hadrian). After Antoninus Pius (138–161) came Marcus Aurelius (161–180), whose 19-year reign restored much of the rational stability challenged during the reigns of Caligula and Nero.

That the Pax Romana endured even debased emperors and mediocrities demonstrates the enduring influence of a powerful, much-feared military that was nevertheless disciplined, loyal, and subject to Roman law. Although the Pax Romana declined during the reigns of the four emperors between Marcus Aurelius and Septimus Severus (193–211), internal peace remained the rule until the succession of Marcus Aurelius Severus Antoninus Augustus, better known as Caracalla, who ruled jointly with his father, Septimus Severus, from 198 to 211 and then alone until 217. Caracalla was cruel and bloodthirsty, especially in his wars against the German tribes (212–213) and the Parthians (216–217). Appalled by the unpredictability of his gratuitous violence, the commander of his Imperial Guard, Macrinus, successfully plotted his assassination. From this point on, the third century saw the slow but steady decline of the Roman Empire in the West.

That the Pax Romana coincided with what is almost universally considered the "Golden Age" of the Roman Empire has throughout history driven many leaders, both political and military, to associate a strong, dominant military with peace and prosperity. Arguably, this association has some validity, at least in states wealthy enough to raise and support consistently superior military forces. In recent history, we have witnessed what some call the Pax Americana. Despite a 50-year Cold War, the prevalent situation in post–World War II Europe has been mostly peaceful. This stability is often attributed to the strong deterrent force embodied in the very large, well-trained, and well-equipped U.S. military.

Battle of the Teutoburg Forest: The Limits of Imperial Militarism (AD 9)

In the Gallic Wars (58–50 BC), Julius Caesar secured a vast trans-Alpine province for what, under Augustus, was now a full-blown Roman empire. Caesar had probed beyond the western and eastern limits of Gaul, fighting in Britain and crossing the Rhine into the lands of the Germanic barbarians. Seeking stability for the empire, Augustus made the decision to establish imperial frontiers along natural borders that were readily defended. In the northwest and the west, the English Channel and the Atlantic Ocean created the most formidable barriers. In the extreme eastern reaches of the Roman Empire, the Euphrates and the Lycus Rivers as well as the Black Sea provided more than adequate natural frontiers. In the south were the Sahara and Arabian Deserts. This left the European tracts north and east of the Alps, a vast expanse of the empire that was not easily defended. The Teutonic tribes here posed a continual threat, and that meant the prospect of chronic instability in the empire.

Augustus was not content to define the Rhine as the eastern border in Europe. It was simply too close to the prize that was Gaul, which was squarely in the path of Germanic tribal migrations, raids, and outright invasions. The emperor's answer was to establish the northern frontier of the Roman Empire along the Elbe and Danube. The Teutonic tribes in the region revolted during AD 1–5. In AD 4 Augustus dispatched his son Tiberius to suppress the rebellion. In two combined land and sea operations during AD 4–5, the young man crushed the revolts and pushed the tribes above the Elbe. No sooner was this accomplished, however, than Germanic peoples in Pannonia (mostly modern Hungary) rose up. Tiberius turned over patrol of Germany to P. Quintilius Varus and personally commanded legions that stormed into Pannonia. Between AD 6 and 9 he managed to suppress rebellion there. By AD 6 Tiberius secured Moesia as a Roman province comprising the Balkans south of the Danube, what are today Central Serbia, Kosovo, and parts of Macedonia, Bulgaria, and Romania. Within three more years, in AD 9, Pannonia was also a secure province of the Roman Empire.

In the meantime, with five legions and a tribal auxiliary under a German chieftain named Arminius, the Romans kept a lid on German tribal insurgency. As the summer of AD 9 came to a close, Varus prepared to leave his outposts in central Germany on the Visurgis (Weser) River to pass the winter at Aliso on the Lupia (Lippe) River. Unknown to him, Arminius was preparing to rise up against

Rome. At first he staged a minor assault between the Visurgis River and Aliso. At this point, faithful Germans warned Varus, who, convinced that Arminius was loyal, refused to believe that he had anything to do with the current disturbances, let alone that he planned something bigger. He believed he could easily suppress the relatively small ongoing uprising en route to Aliso.

Varus led three legions—about 20,000 men—plus the soldiers' families (some 10,000 civilian noncombatants). In September or October AD 9, they passed over the Visurgis and entered the mountainous woodlands of the Teutoburg Forest. The uphill climbs and the rugged, thickly wooded terrain made for slow going. Finally, torrential rains brought the columns to a halt, making them easy targets for German guerrillas.

At about the location of the modern town of Detmold, Germany, Arminius suddenly peeled away his troops and turned on his former Roman allies. A large Roman detachment was quickly annihilated, an event that sent terror and panic throughout the entire Roman column. Varus responded by attempting to power through. He reasoned that if he could lead his men to fortified Aliso, he would be able to fight from secure cover. The Roman commander brilliantly rallied his troops for the push to Aliso but, to his horror, discovered that this Roman base had already been overrun by local Germans.

Still, Varus kept his head. He decided to turn his columns northward, intending to make his way through the Ems Valley to a Roman outpost on the

Remains of a Roman soldier's sandals found on the site of the Battle of Teutoburg Forest and now in the collection of Museum und Park Kalkriese, Germany Photograph by Carole Raddator, Frankfurt, Germany.
WIKIMEDIA COMMONS

coast of the North Sea. Suddenly the might and majesty of a great imperial Roman column was transformed from asset into liability. Encumbered by a long baggage train and the 10,000 noncombatants who accompanied his legions, the desperate procession became bogged down in a rain-soaked quagmire. Forest roads shrank to muddy trails and muddy trails to brown streams that rushed through the rutted soil. Wagons could move no farther. Arminius's well-armed troops refused to stand and fight but instead continually raided and harassed the exposed columns. As his soldiers frantically hacked new trails through the woods, the Germans redoubled their attacks.

Days passed, each marked by bitter combat. As Varus's columns began to move again, Arminius launched a series of running fights, massing more and more of his men against his former ally. Under unremitting pressure, the legions began to falter and break. Sensing that order was collapsing, Arminius let loose the full strength of his contingent, who cut the Romans to ribbons. In close combat, Varus and his leading officers were all wounded. To avoid capture or a slow death by torture, each took his own life. A few straggling legionnaires survived to carry the tale, but all the noncombatants, mostly women and children, some 10,000 people in all, were massacred somewhere between the modern cities of Detmold and Münster.

In contrast to Varus's three hapless legions, the garrison that manned Aliso managed to fight its way out of winter quarters to make its way to the Rhine and the relative safety of Roman Gaul. As for Augustus, his plan to secure central Germany as a provincial Roman imperial stronghold against the barbarians melted away with Varus's three legions. The catastrophe of the Teutoburg Forest meant the loss of central Germany. It was a loss that would never be made good.

Augustus was stricken. Although he is remembered as the emperor who ushered in the Pax Romana, he would, throughout the rest of his life and reign, repeatedly relive the horror of Teutoburg, groaning through his tears, "Varus, give me back my legions!" He was not, however, paralyzed into inaction. Determined to assert imperial authority, he sent one punitive expedition after another into Germany—yet he never again pursued the idea of adding central Germany to the Roman Empire. He had learned a horrific lesson about the limits of imperial military might. Against sufficiently skilled and determined peoples and in certain environments, the warfare of serried ranks and close-order phalanxes could not prevail. Wildness and wilderness were too much even for the best-armed militarism. Augustus made punitive jabs against the destroyers of Varus's legions, but never again did he try to push the empire beyond the Rhine and the Danube. Those rivers marked the limit of Rome. And it was a limit his successors accepted. The future of the empire, along with the future of Europe in the long, dark Middle Ages yet to come, was determined. Arminius, Roman tribal ally turned enemy of empire, had won a profoundly decisive battle that demonstrated the irresistible power of a determined and ably led insurgency against even the most sophisticated military force the greatest empire of the ancient world could project.

Second Battle of Adrianople: The Western Empire Starts to Fall (378)

By the third century AD, it was becoming apparent to many that the sprawling Roman Empire had become too vast for rule by one emperor. Between 285 and 324 and from 337 to 350, 364 to 392, and 395 to 480, attempts were made to divide the authority and the workload of the Roman emperor. At the heart of most of these attempts was splitting Rome into a Western and an Eastern Empire, with an emperor for each. The empire was intended to remain one indivisible state—a single *imperium*—but the administrative power was to be shared.

The co-emperors often regarded each other as enemies, yet the system, desperate though it was, extended the life of the Roman Empire, at least in the East. The Western Empire was in sharp decline by the third century, but its rate of descent accelerated during the fourth. The turning point came on August 9, 378, near Adrianople, a city built on the site of a Thracian town called Uskudama and founded by the Roman emperor Hadrian, who reigned from 117 to 138. Today called Edirne, it touches Turkey's borders with Bulgaria and Greece. By 377, Valens, emperor of the Eastern Empire, had settled a war with Persia and now turned his attention to Thrace, which was imperiled by invading Goths. Valens dispatched legions under Saturninus, Trajan, and Profuturus to drive the Goths back toward the north and contain them there. The Romans blockaded the invaders in the marshes south of the Danube's mouth until, in a stealthy maneuver, the Gothic chieftain Fritigern led his warriors through the marshland and broke through the blockade. Free of Roman containment, the Goths more than lived up to their fierce reputation, rampaging through Thrace and Moesia, joined in their raids by other "barbarian" tribes, including the Sarmatians, Alans, and Huns, superb horsemen all.

Valens now decided that he had to assume personal command in Thrace. He enlisted the aid of Gratian, his nephew and emperor of the West. At the same time, Fritigern was also making alliances among the Germanic tribes, and in 378 raids exploded along the empire's "border" with the barbarians, from the mouth of the Rhine to the lower Danube. Gratian defeated the Alemanni, a confederation of Germanic tribes, at the Battle of Argentovaria (near modern Colmar, France) in May. It was a devastating blow to the invaders, who reputedly lost 31,000 killed out of a force of some 40,000 men. This victory achieved, Valens's lieutenant, Sebastian, campaigned throughout Thrace during the summer. By the beginning

49

of August, most of the Visigoths and Ostrogoths led by Fritigern, Altheus, and Saphrax were bottled up in a great fortress of wagons on a hill in a valley 8 to 12 miles outside Adrianople. Historians believe they numbered between 100,000 and 200,000 warriors in addition to 200,000 women and children. Desperate for food, the Visigoth infantry held the fort while horsemen foraged and raided throughout Thrace. Jealous of the great successes Sebastian and Gratian had enjoyed and anxious to rack up a decisive victory himself before Gratian—whom he now perceived as a rival—could arrive from the north, Valens decided to attack.

He had an army of about 60,000, two-thirds of this number infantry and the rest a mix of heavy and light cavalry. When his scouts reported Valens's approach, Fritigern ordered Alatheus and Saphrax to recall their cavalry from foraging. In a bid to buy time for the return of the cavalry, Fritigern sent a message to Valens, offering to negotiate. Valens had no intention of talking, but he did recognize the need to rest his troops, so he agreed to parley. On further thought, Valens decided not to let his army rest but to begin deploying into advantageous positions from which to attack the barbarian wagon camp. In his haste, the Roman emperor neglected to provide security patrols on his flank and rear.

It was a grave error made fatal by what happened next. At the approach of Visigoth negotiators, some of Valens's auxiliary troops attacked the negotiating party. At this point, most of Valens's infantry was not yet in position. Valens, however, noted that his cavalry was ready on the flanks, so he ordered an all-out attack.

It might have worked—had it not been for the arrival at this very moment of Alatheus and Saphrax leading their horsemen, who fell upon Roman right-wing cavalry, descending savagely on them from the high ground overlooking the battlefield. The result was a rout, and half of Valens's cavalry was swept from the field just as it was galloping into the wagon camp. Now the Gothic cavalry divided. Some galloped through their own wagon camp while others swung around behind the Roman army, attacking the Roman left-wing cavalry even as Visigoth units counterattacked from within the wagon camp.

In short order, the entire Roman cavalry was annihilated. This left only Valens's infantry, which was as yet incompletely deployed and without space to maneuver for combat. The Gothic horsemen swarmed around the rear and both flanks of the disorganized legions. The Visigoth infantry, in the meantime, charged downhill from their encampment, directly attacking the Roman front lines. Thus the barbarians, with a level of tactical coordination that stunned Valens and his subordinates, enveloped the Romans. The battle rapidly devolved into slaughter. Valens, mortally wounded, died along with Sebastian, Trajan, and some 40,000 Romans. Although the Goths proved unable to take Adrianople or the capital of the Eastern Empire, Constantinople, they ravaged the towns and villages of Thrace mercilessly. It was the worst defeat the Roman legions had ever suffered, and it sent shock waves through the West.

With Valens killed in action, Gratian asked Theodosius to become the new emperor of the East. Establishing himself in Thessalonica, he rebuilt the legions and took a lesson from the insurgent Goths by using small mobile forces to punish them wherever they were found. Through a series of modest victories, he restored the morale of the Roman military, and in 382–383, Theodosius at last led two major campaigns against the Goths. Fritigern was killed during these operations.

Theodosius and his allies saved the Eastern Empire, which endured as the Byzantine Empire until May 29, 1453, when the Ottoman army captured Constantinople. As for the Western Roman Empire, since the publication in 1776–1789 of Edward Gibbon's masterpiece, *The Decline and Fall of the Roman Empire*, the traditional consensus on the precise date of the Western Empire's fall has been the year 476, when Romulus Augustulus abdicated as the last Roman emperor and the Pannonian-born Roman soldier Odoacer was crowned king of Italy. Most historians see the defeat of Valens and the legions at Adrianople as the first definitive military step toward that ending.

Battle of Châlons: The Turning Point That Might Have Been (451)

"Attila the Hun," the popular name for Attila, who ruled the Huns from 434 until his death in 453, has long been a synonym for ruthless invasion and mindless devastation. Attila was, in fact, a sophisticated leader of a tribally based empire that included not only the Huns but also the Ostrogoths and Alans in addition to others. He was also a skilled military strategist and a dynamic commander, one of global history's "great captains."

By the mid-fifth century, his people poised on the territory of Central and Eastern Europe, and Attila meant to lead them in the conquest of both the Eastern and Western Roman Empires.

Attila marched his armies across the Danube on two occasions, plundered the Balkans, and menaced Constantinople, capital of the Eastern Roman (Byzantine) Empire. He also sought to conquer Persia. Failing here, he launched a successful invasion of the Eastern Empire in 441, a triumph that moved him to strike out against the Western Empire as well. This culminated in Attila's invasion of Roman Gaul—essentially the territory of modern France—in a momentous operation that began when he crossed the Rhine in 451, reportedly leading half a million warriors, although modern historians put the number at about 100,000. His soldiers included, in addition to Hunnish cavalry, Ostrogoths, Gepidae, Scrir, Rugi, Thuringi, Bavarians, and Ripuarian Franks. These hordes marched along a front over a hundred miles wide, ravaging most of the towns and villages of northern Gaul. Paris—French legend holds—was spared only through the divine intervention of Saint Geneviève.

To oppose Attila, the Roman general Flavius Aetius, on whom history has bestowed the sobriquet "Last of the Romans," raised a substantial army around a core of Gallo-Roman legionnaires and Roman heavy cavalry. His forces included Franks, Burgundians, German *foederati* (members of client nations pledged to provide military assistance to Rome), and even Alans. Although courted by Attila, Theodoric the Great, king of the Ostrogoths, chose an alliance with Aetius instead.

During May and the first half of June, Attila laid siege against Orléans, bringing the city to the verge of starvation and surrender before Aetius and Theodoric closed in, prompting Attila to retreat. Aetius gave chase, but Attila kept moving until he was able to gather up his entire army, which he deployed at a location between modern Troyes and Châlons, probably near what is now

Méry-sur-Seine. He formed up his large wagon train as a fortress and rapidly dug entrenchments. The field he had chosen, believed to be the Catalaunian Plains, was ground that gave his cavalry plenty of room to maneuver against the enemy. Indeed, the ensuing battle is sometimes called the Battle of the Catalaunian Plains.

By the time he caught up with Attila, it was evident to Aetius that the Hun leader was massively reinforced and had deployed his men formidably for a showdown battle. Aetius therefore slowed his approach, edging forward with caution while also acquiring a substantial number of Frankish deserters from Attila. In the meantime, Attila arrayed his forces in three great divisions. He took personal command of the Huns in the center and placed the Ostrogoths on his left and the other German allies on the right. Aetius deployed Theodoric and the Visigoths—they were mostly heavy cavalry—on his right while he took personal command of the left wing, among which were numbered his legions, his own heavy cavalry, and the Frankish infantry. Aetius took the precaution of placing the Alans, whom he did not trust, in the center, where Roman legionnaires could keep an eye and a heavy hand on them, dissuading them from either deserting or switching sides.

The battle commenced when the son of Theodoric, Thorismund, led an element of his father's force to seize the high ground above the Hun's right flank.

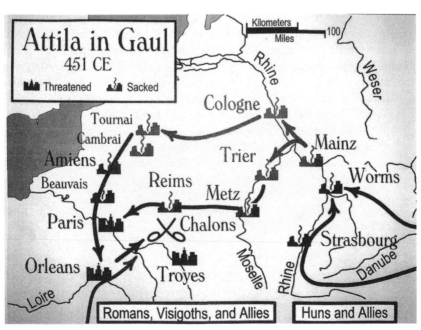

Attila in Gaul at the time of the Battle of Châlons
WIKIMEDIA COMMONS

Attila responded with a massive counterattack, which broke through Aetius's center when the unreliable Alans broke and ran. The Franks and the Romans on the left and the Visigoths on the right stood their ground while Attila sought in vain to dislodge Thorismund's contingent from the high ground.

With the two sides thus engaged, Theodoric counterattacked the Ostrogoths on his front and was killed. The death of their leader served only to galvanize the Visigoths' resolve. They responded by relentlessly pushing back the Ostrogoth attackers. While this action was unfolding, Aetius linked up with Thorismund, who had held out in isolation with his troops on the high ground. This situation threatened Attila with a double envelopment, the realization of which sent panic through some of the Hun's forces, who wavered as darkness fell on the battle.

In the gathering night, confusion reigned. Portions of Attila's vast force were routed, and Thorismund advanced all the way to the Hun camp. Attila managed to repulse his advance, but, recognizing that the battle had turned badly against him, he ordered a general withdrawal. Aetius stubbornly harassed the withdrawing Huns throughout the night, ordering his own wing—the right—to stand at arms through the night in case Attila should turn to attack. In the meantime, Aetius also rallied his center, which had been badly diminished by the flight of the Alans. In this work far forward of his main lines, he narrowly escaped being cut off and captured in the night by the Huns.

Attila girded his men for a fight to the finish come morning. But Aetius chose not to attack and instead allowed Attila to withdraw from the battle. Losses on both sides were very heavy. Modern estimates of the battle casualties are vague, but they certainly numbered in the high tens of thousands. Although Attila was permitted to withdraw—a force defeated but still intact—the Battle of Châlons is counted among history's most decisive because it foiled Attila's bid to overrun the Western Empire. This would have brought about the immediate collapse of Roman civilization and, with it, early Christianity in Western Europe. The continent might well have gone on to develop under Asian cultural and political domination, creating a history doubtless very different from what we know.

Battle of Tours: Muslims v. Franks (732)

Born in 570, the prophet Muhammad began preaching revelations in 610, founding Islam. At an astounding speed, military conquest helped spread the new religion from Mecca (in what is today Saudi Arabia) and then to all Arabia, the Levant, Egypt, Mesopotamia and Persia, the Sindh (in today's Pakistan), the Maghreb (northwest Africa), and, during 711–721, into Hispania (Spain) and Gaul (France). In the meantime, Charles Martel (718–741), a Frankish statesman and military commander, built on the work of his father, Pepin II (c. 635–714) to consolidate Francia—the Kingdom of the Franks—under his rule.

By 814 the empire of the Franks would come to encompass most of Western Europe, and it was Charles Martel who began this process by ensuring that the Franks held sway over the territory that had been the Roman province of Gaul. Once he had consolidated his power against all European rivals, Charles confronted the Islamic advance into Western Europe. As Christians saw it, the conquest was happening at an alarming rate. After conquering Spain in 711, Muslim Arab and Berber forces crossed the Pyrenees (720) and seized Gallia Narbonensis, territory in what is today Languedoc and Provence in southern France. Abdul Rahman Al Ghafiqi, the Arab governor of al-Andalus in Muslim Spain, advanced from Narbonensis into Gaul and then marched toward Tours, which the Franks considered the "holy town" of Gaul.

Abdul Rahman led a large army against the forces of Duke Odo of Aquitaine near Bordeaux at the Battle of the Garonne River (which may have actually taken place at the Dordogne). Abdul Rahman defeated Odo, who immediately turned to his rival, Charles Martel, with an offer of submission and an alliance against the Islamic invasion. Already aware of Abdul Rahman's incursion into Gaul, Martel had begun a hasty return from campaigning against European rivals along the upper Danube. He accepted Odo's submission and planned to link up with the survivors of the Battle of the Garonne River to create a combined force of 15,000 to 20,000 men to direct against the Muslim forces.

Abdul Rahman left a portion of his Berber and Arab army at Poitiers and advanced with between 20,000 and 25,000 men to the Loire, near Tours. Along the way, the Muslim warriors raided and pillaged. No sooner did Abdul Rahman lay siege to Tours itself than he learned of the approach of Odo from the east. Realizing that his lines of communication were now in danger, the Muslim commander sent a supply train laden with his plunder back toward Poitiers and began a slow withdrawal of his combat forces, following behind the baggage train. Charles's Frankish army made contact with the Muslim army south of Tours in October 732. For six days in a row, Abdul Rahman struggled to cover the retreat of his treasure wagons by engaging in repeated skirmishes with elements of the Frankish army. None of the engagements were in themselves decisive, but Charles persisted in pressing the Muslims, pushing them back toward Poitiers. At last, Abdul Rahman decided to turn, take a stand, and force a major showdown battle somewhere between Tours and Poitiers. This became the Battle of Tours (sometimes called the Battle of Poitiers) fought on October 10, 732.

Historians debate the strength of the Muslim versus Frankish forces. Most believe that Abdul Rahman had the edge, but it is possible that the armies were evenly matched or that the combined forces of Charles Martel and Odo were superior. Cavalry played a major role on both sides, but Charles was keenly aware that the Muslim horsemen were quick and agile, though lightly armed and armored, whereas his Frankish cavalry, very heavily armored, was comparatively slow and, worse, not very well disciplined. As an attacking force, Charles reasoned, Abdul Rahman had the advantage, especially if he found a gap to exploit in the Frankish line. Yet he also saw that the Muslim light cavalry would not be able to overcome a massed resistance by heavily armored men. As Charles concluded that Abdul Rahman's cavalry were preparing to make a major attack, he made a bold tactical decision. He ordered the Franks to dismount and form up into a solid *infantry* phalanx. Taking advantage of whatever high ground the rolling hills of west-central France offered, Charles forced the Muslim cavalry to attack uphill into what one contemporary historical account described as a "motionless . . . wall" of armored warriors who were arrayed "like a belt of ice frozen together, and not to be dissolved."

The Arab and Berber warriors hurled themselves against this wall, that "belt of ice," and were cut down by Frankish swords. Time and again, Abdul Rahman ordered his men to attack. The immovable Frankish infantry, time and again, bloodily repulsed them. This went on until night fell. Odo, who led the Franks' right wing, managed to envelop the Muslim left, forcing those troops to withdraw in defense of their camp. Once they reached the camp, the exhausted, dispirited warriors discovered that their leader, Abdul Rahman Al Ghafiqi, had fallen in combat. Apparently, this realization knocked the props out from under them. They panicked, abandoned their treasure train, and fled as a disorganized throng to the south. It is believed that 12,000, at least half the Muslim force, had been killed. Charles and Odo suffered the loss of 1,000 men between them.

For his part, Charles formed up his army at dawn, prepared to resist what he was certain would be a renewed assault. He sent out a reconnaissance force, which revealed that the Arabs and Berbers were on the run. Charles chose not to pursue. Used as infantry, his men had been a deadly defensive wall, but Charles knew they were far from reliable in a fast cavalry pursuit. He had seen in the past how the

Arabs and Berbers drew them into a chase only to turn suddenly and slaughter the Frankish cavalry when, in undisciplined fashion, it had allowed itself to become thinly spread out. Instead of giving chase, he contented himself with their having fled Gaul.

This decision says much about the generalship of Charles Martel. His *tactical* motive for not giving chase was his knowledge of his troops' limitations. But he also had a *strategic* motive. He was intent on recapturing the booty the Muslims had abandoned. Add to this the motive of a statesman. Charles recognized that Odo, highly valuable as an ally, was nevertheless not to be trusted. With the Muslims driven off, Charles reasoned that Odo might well turn on him. The diplomatic solution was to refrain from wiping out the Muslims. Their lingering presence on the margins of the Frankish kingdom would be a strong incentive for Odo to remain submissively loyal to him.

A victory produced by a profound understanding of tactics, the Battle of Tours was a great triumph of strategy. It arrested the advance of Muslim expansion into Europe and afforded Christianity several more centuries in which to install itself firmly across the continent. As for Charles Martel—"Charles the Hammer"—his hegemony over the Franks was ratified by the victory at Tours. It laid the foundation of what would become the Holy Roman Empire, which was founded by his grandson Charlemagne on Christmas Day of the year 800.

Feudalism as a Military Civilization: Epoch of Knight, Armor, Sword, and Longbow (800–1200)

The fall of the Western Roman Empire in the late fifth century ushered in a tumultuous political and cultural period throughout Western Europe in which feudalism arose. Militarily speaking, feudal society was based on the mounted armored knight and the fortified castle. The ideal at the heart of feudalism was that the strong protected the weak—who nevertheless paid a high price for that protection in rendering agricultural service, in the case of the poor, and vassalage, including military service, for those who were better off.

Feudalism may be viewed as a military system with a strong sociopolitical component or as a sociopolitical system with a strong military component. Either way, military civilization is at its heart. As a form of geopolitical organization, feudalism essentially gave direct ownership of the land within a given kingdom to the king. He in turn let portions of his holdings to his principal nobles in exchange for their pledge to maintain and hold in readiness a prescribed number of men at arms to defend the kingdom. Generally, the troops this class supplied were members of the lower order of nobility. By the High Middle Ages (eleventh–thirteenth centuries), they evolved into knights—a military order that soon became associated with an idealized way of life that included adherence to a chivalric code of conduct in which honor, gallantry, defense of the defenseless, absolute loyalty to one's prince, and pious observance of the Christian faith were paramount. Noble knights were mounted, armor-clad fighters who served as the rough equivalent of modern field commanders. They represented in combat the presence and power of both their overlord and the king himself.

Generally speaking, knights fought their social equals, namely other knights. Nevertheless, a knight could be slain by a common archer or a peasant infantryman, but that was not the primary role of the common soldier in a feudal military formation. His principal job was to fight others of his class. From the point of view of the knight, combat between large numbers of infantrymen was something of an obstacle that interfered with the real point of war: the noble armed contest of knight versus knight.

Although the major nobility furnished the monarch with the service of knights, it was the knights themselves who acquired and owned their own very costly heavy weapons, suits of armor, and a stable of war horses. Moreover, each knight was expected to supply and maintain a kind of bodyguard, or retinue, which included one or more squires and other armed servants. In effect, a knight was a field officer, a combatant, and a self-contained fighting unit, with two or more men attached to him.

The knights acquired their real property from the king but were, in turn, allowed to sublet portions of their holdings to lesser nobles and knights, on condition that they supply upon demand some portion of the armed force the principal tenant of the king was required to furnish. As minor nobility. the subtenants did not work their farmlands themselves but leased these to common "copyholders," who in return armed and maintained a sort of militia, composed of men from their leasehold. These men were pledged to march to the banner of their lord when the king called upon him to take part in the defense of the kingdom. Each copyholder supplied a troop contingent called a retinue, which, collectively, was under the command of a knight.

Knights, together with their younger brothers and sons of military age, plus their squires (a squire was a trainee serving under a knight, acting as a servant and shield bearer as well as an auxiliary warrior) invariably fought on horseback. Only knights wore full suits of armor; the other mounted men wore armor abbreviated in varying degrees. The retinues that were under knightly command fought on foot, as infantry. Their "armor" consisted of thick leather jerkins and, sometimes, chain mail or other body armor. Some wore helmets. Whereas knights and squires carried lances, swords, and shields, infantrymen wielded either a spear or a bow—and sometimes other specialized weapons.

There were military variations within feudal society. Some of a king's principal lords, mainly high clergy and the German barons, did not sublet their landholdings to copyholders but instead maintained direct personal control of all their lands. This class of lord was not required to render a retinue for service to the king but *was* required to furnish knights. They did this by hiring so-called household knights in return for monetary payment. These mercenary soldiers formed a small part of most medieval military formations.

Some subtenants of a principal lord held less land than was traditionally the domain of a knight. On the European continent—but not in England— the smaller subtenants were called "sergeants," a title that identified mounted soldiers who were below knightly rank. Sergeants were obliged to supply a certain number of infantrymen, whom they typically commanded in battle. Some sergeants were not obliged to supply the forces, just the leadership for them. In some cases, sergeants served in lieu of the lord himself as field commander of the lord's entire armed contingent.

The major lords in a kingdom not only provided knights but also the services of their own domestic seat, the castle. It was a large fortified building—a fortress, in fact—intended to serve as a strongpoint of area defense and a regional military headquarters. The typical castle occupied commanding high ground, which afforded considerable tactical and strategic advantage.

Armored knights were of a piece with castles, serving, in effect, as mobile fortifications. Their armor evolved from—and improved upon—Byzantine models. The crested helmet of the Eastern Roman Empire became a conical headpiece made of iron. European knights attached to it a nosepiece, which later in the feudal period became a full visor. A shirt of chain mail became a standard item of armor and was steadily lengthened, its flaps (in later versions) reaching below the knees of a mounted knight, providing protection for the torso and all the way down the upper leg. The knight's ancient shield evolved as well. Instead of the curved rectangular Roman scutum or the simple round "target" shield, medieval weapon makers created the kite-shaped shield, which gave greater protection to mounted warriors without the unduly heavy weight of either the scutum or the round shield. In the later feudal period, the word "hauberk" was a synonym for a long mail shirt, but in the earlier period a hauberk was small piece of chain mail worn around the neck to protect the parts of the throat and neck left exposed by the chain mail shirt and the helmet.

Offensive weapons were little advanced from the era of the Roman Empire; however, swords were generally longer and designed more for slashing than thrusting. The battle-ax became popular and was an indication that skill in close combat was now less valued than brute force. Charlemagne (742–814) tried to expand the tactical range of his forces by introducing an important standoff weapon, the bow. But although the Vikings and Turko-Scythian invaders (Bulgars, Magyars, and Pechenegs) were highly skilled archers, it was not until the thirteenth century that archery began to be prized as a military skill. In 1252 an English law called the "Assize of Arms" required that the kingdom's yeomanry constitute a militia of archers. At the Battle of Crecy (1346), some 6,000 English archers launched arrow barrages at the staggering rate of 42,000 arrows per minute, and in 1415 Henry V introduced the magnificent English longbow.

The increasing popularity of the longbow heralded the eventual end of the battlefield supremacy of the mounted knight, and the monarchs of most European kingdoms also began backing up their strictly feudal military systems with the use of the posse comitatus. This was a militia-like force, organized by county or shire and mustered as well as led by the local sheriff. By the late medieval period, laws existed in most European countries requiring men of military age to supply themselves with the best weapons they could afford so that they could serve—armed and ready for combat—whenever called on as a posse comitatus, or militia. The poor equipped themselves as light infantry, carrying into battle a bow or a spear and serving with little or no armor. The more prosperous became medium infantrymen, each armed with a spear and shield and clothed in a padded jacket or an abbreviated chain-mail hauberk called a haubergeon. Many middle infantry troops also wore helmets. Terms of service for members of the posse commitatus were limited by law, usually to 40 days. A king could extend this term by paying the troops; however, peasant soldiers were never obligated to serve abroad and were used only for defensive purposes.

As the feudal system further evolved, there emerged an alternative to a knight's obligation to personally render military service and to supply soldiers. When called upon by the king, the knight could choose to pay scutage, a tax or fine rendered to the king, who could then use the proceeds to hire paid soldiers in place of the knightly retinue. In some kingdoms as many as two-thirds of the knights chose to pay scutage, which meant that many armies consisted mainly of paid soldiers. A king could use scutage funds to pay foreign troops, who fought as mercenaries, or he could pay his own subjects. In this latter practice may be seen the slow emergence of a professional state military, and this military innovation was among the features of later medieval society that brought the feudal period to a close.

Rise of the Raid: Viking Warfare in Ireland, Britain, Western Europe, and Russia (800–1000)

A unique form of warfare and military civilization arose in Europe roughly from the end of the eighth century and into the eleventh. It was the perfection of the amphibious hit-and-run raid by Vikings. These tribal warriors, who came from Scandinavia and were of Norse ancestry, were pagans who raided Christian lands in England and Ireland, expanding their raids into continental Europe and penetrating into Russia.

Their tactics as well as their strategy were rooted in the raid rather than the clash of army against army. As fighters, the Vikings were driven by a warrior culture based on Nordic religion, which elevated a combination of honor and military violence that had been used originally to settle intertribal disputes. Among Vikings, honor was a supreme value, and violence was the sovereign means of defending honor. The Viking warrior accepted death as a highly probable outcome of violence; therefore, fearlessness became the chief virtue of Viking culture.

The Vikings were a seafaring people. In contrast to the peoples of feudal Europe, who were to a large extent landlocked, they developed their style of warfare based on ships and naval tactics, which were adapted to amphibious warfare. Although the Vikings did come to occupy some areas in which they raided, they were generally less interested in long-term objectives of conquest than they were in raids and pillaging. They developed an approach to warfare suited to attacks along coastal regions, which, as they saw it, were vulnerable because a coastline was virtually impossible to effectively block off from attack.

From the end of the eighth century through the early tenth, Vikings waged war mainly through hit-and-run raids aimed at looting treasure, which was brought back to their lands and used in trade—an activity greatly facilitated by their seafaring skills. The traditional Viking longship was an extraordinary achievement in naval architecture. As its development matured, the vessel became capable of high-speed travel on the open sea as well as shallow-draft navigation of inland rivers. This dual capability led, by the eleventh century, to Vikings waging war farther inland in such places as France and Russia.

Based on the so-called Gokstad ship—a ninth-century Viking vessel found in a burial mound at Gokstad, Norway, and today housed in the Viking Ship Museum in Oslo—the classic longship was more than 90 feet long with a beam of more than 16 feet. These vessels carried 50 to 60 sailors, who propelled the ship by galley-style rowing. Construction was of oak, ingeniously split with axes to ensure that the wood grain between planks created a mesh bond with one another. A short mast allowed for hoisting a sail to increase speed, but all steering was done with a single stern rudder. The acutely graceful shallop-style prow gave the longship great speed and remarkable stability, yet the vessel had a draft of little more than three feet.

A Viking longship hull at the Vikingskipmuseet, Oslo, Norway
Photograph (2005) by Karamell.
WIKIMEDIA COMMONS

Longships were crafted in two major types. The drakkar was a battleship, built for strength and speed. Although the basic vessel accommodated 50 to 60 rowers, some were built larger to hold an extra set of rowers, which allowed men to row in shifts so that the ship could travel by day and night. The other known Viking ship type was the knórr, primarily built as a trading vessel. Although smaller than the drakkar, it was built to accommodate cargo and had a deeper draft. Nevertheless, like the drakkar, the knórr was capable of sailing at 12 to 14 knots, which meant it could keep up with the battleships.

The Viking concept of naval warfare was entirely focused on the raid. The drakkar was not intended to fight ship-to-ship battles but to sail swiftly to coastal objectives and be beached rather than docked in harbors. This meant the Vikings could mount an amphibious assault virtually anywhere along a relatively sandy coast.

The ships conveyed warriors who believed themselves to have been endowed with superhuman powers by Odin, god of war. Viking warriors felt themselves connected to the *berserkers*, quasi-mythical fighters whom Odin had rendered impervious to injury on the field of battle. Many historians believe that in combat, Viking warriors did enter into a berserker-like trance, fighting in the intense, wild manner of the berserker—a name, of course, preserved in the modern English word "berserk." Certainly, the Viking style of combat struck terror in the hearts of Frankish and English populations. It was the Vikings who introduced shock tactics into European warfare.

The Viking raids were carried out over a remarkably large amount of territory. The earliest raids were in England during 793–870 and were executed, separately, by Norwegian and Danish Vikings. The latter for a time made alliances with Cornishmen, who rebelled against the Saxons. Although most of the raids were hit-and-run, by 870 Danish Vikings came to occupy more than a third of England. They settled in East Anglia in 865 and expanded into Northumbria the following year. While they continued to raid, they conducted all these operations from land bases to land objectives. Invading York during a period of internal warfare there, the Vikings neutralized Saxon power and influence in the north of England by 870.

During 871–896, Danish Vikings warred against Saxons under King Alfred the Great (849–899) with the objective of extending the territory they had acquired, which was known as the Danelaw. In 878 Alfred attacked the Vikings at the Battle of Ethandun (modern Edington), driving them from the field and forcing them to fall back on Chippenham, to which he laid siege. This prompted Viking agreement to the Peace of Wedmore, by which they pledged to respect the boundary between Saxon Wessex and the Viking-controlled Danelaw.

Contained, the Vikings were not, however, defeated. In 885 they captured London and attempted an invasion of Kent. Alfred repelled the Kentish invasion and recovered London, victories that earned him acknowledgment as king of the

Saxons, making him the first ruler to govern something approaching a united realm. Viking raids continued sporadically until 896.

During 795–1014, Norwegian Vikings raided Ireland and even settled along the Irish coast, where they established several longship ports. They occupied the Shetland and Orkney Islands as early as 795 and, from here, sporadically raided Ireland for the next two centuries. A Viking leader known as Turgeis led the Orkney and Shetland Vikings in notable raids against Armagh, Connacht, Meith, and Ulster, and in 837 sailed up the Liffey River, colonizing some areas, building port towns, and in 841 founding Dublin. By 853 the region around Dublin constituted a miniature Norse kingdom.

Vikings raided France from 799 to 885, when they laid siege to Paris for approximately a year. The Franks suffered mightily under the raids, which were mitigated through a combination of modern urban fortification, the payments of taxes or tribute money known as the Danegeld, and outright bribery. The raiders came separately from Norway and Denmark. From 800 to very nearly the end of the tenth century, Vikings raided the North Sea coasts and islands of Scotland, establishing an enduring presence in the Orkney Islands.

Less well-known than the Viking raids in England and Western Europe are the raids in Russia, from about 825 to 907. The principal raiders were Swedish Vikings, known as the Rus, who clashed with various Russian indigenous peoples and reached as far as Constantinople in the Byzantine Empire. The raids greatly expanded the reach of the Rus, establishing strong trading relations between a realm that became known as Rus and the Byzantine Empire.

Early in the 860s, Rurik, leader of the Rus, was either invited to rule Novgorod or conquered it. He established a trading center on Lake Ladoga, and from this stronghold the Rus navigated rivers to the south, trading as well as raiding throughout southern Russia and the Ukraine. Oleg, successor to Rurik, led the Rus in an attack on Kiev, which fell to them in 882. He then led a fleet down the Dnieper River in 907, exited at the Black Sea, and mounted an invasion of Constantinople, which fell to him with little resistance. Yet he did not seek conquest. Instead he forcibly negotiated an exclusive trade treaty on behalf of Rus.

The later phase of the Viking raids began in France during 896–911, when Danish Viking followers of Rollo (also known as Gonge-Hrolf) colonized Normandy. King Charles the Simple of France made peace with Rollo, who subsequently submitted to baptism to become the 1st Duke of Normandy in 911. In England, the late Viking raids began in 899. Separately, Danish and Norwegian Vikings fought against the Saxons, who sought to reclaim the Danelaw from them. Under Canute the Great, the Danish Vikings not only recovered the Danelaw—which they had briefly lost—but also annexed Mercia to it so that by 1016, Canute had effectively made England a Danish realm. It would continue to be so until 1042. This is the closest the Vikings came to transforming a strategy of raiding into enduring conquest.

Battle of Hastings: Why the Norman Conquest Matters (1066)

Descended from the Viking leader Rollo, first ruler of Normandy, William (c. 1028–1087) became Duke of Normandy in 1035. It was a rebellious realm, and it was not until 1060 that Duke William came to hold Normandy more securely than anyone who had preceded him. In that year King Henry I of France and Geoffrey Martel of Anjou, who had combined unsuccessfully to overthrow him, were dead and had been succeeded by much weaker rulers. Seizing what he saw as opportunity, William led the conquest of Maine, Normandy's southern neighbor, in 1063, and in 1064 or 1065 he received Harold, earl of Wessex, ambassador of his brother-in-law, Edward the Confessor, king of most of England. William persuaded Harold to accompany him on a military campaign into Brittany, which bordered Normandy on the southeast. The pair conquered Brittany.

Content that he had not only secured Normandy but also expanded it, William decided to invade England. His rationale was that in 1051, Edward the Confessor had promised him succession to the English throne. William claimed that Edward had sent Harold to him in 1064 or 1065 to affirm the succession. Yet when Edward died childless on January 5, 1066, Harold assumed the throne, prompting William to make history's second major assault on England across the English Channel after Julius Caesar.

The decision was not impulsive. Long before he crossed the Channel, William had set about putting together a network of the most influential families of Normandy, who became his loyal supporters and whom he richly rewarded for their support. William also built Caen, on the Channel coast, into a formidable fortress that served as both seat and symbol of his power. Early in 1066, William convened a council at Lillebonne, aimed at persuading the most influential leaders of Normandy that the risk was worth taking. He made his case that, for all its power, Normandy was vulnerable to attack from England. Only by conquering England would Normandy be made secure—not to mention immeasurably richer. Not only did William consolidate Norman support, he recruited allies from Flanders, Brittany, and Aquitaine.

He had one more arrow in his quiver. Having made the military and economic case for conquest, William sent an embassy to Rome to secure the blessing of Pope Alexander II. William understood that Harold was supported by many powerful English earls and lords. A papal sanction would be a powerful counter to this support. The pope agreed, and thus the conquest of England was pronounced a holy crusade to remove a usurping king.

Having now established the diplomatic and religious grounds for his enterprise, William set about assembling an invasion fleet. By July, ships carrying a total

This illuminated French manuscript depicts William the Conqueror stabbing the Anglo-Saxon king Harold at the Battle of Hastings in a knightly contest fought, king to king, on horseback. A Norman account reports that Harold was killed by four knights, with William among them, but most other accounts report that he was killed by an arrow that pierced his eye.
BRITISH LIBRARY

of some 7,000 men were ready to sail from the estuary of the River Dives and the harbors of western Normandy. The weather failed to cooperate, and William was forced to wait an agonizing month for favorable winds that would allow him to sail his fleet up the coast to Saint-Valéry-sur-Somme in Ponthieu, a place from which the always treacherous Channel crossing would be relatively short.

William recognized that inaction and delay were great enemies of morale. Accordingly, he took every possible opportunity to display personal leadership. He frequently appeared among his men to exhort and hearten them. At last, on the night of September 27, 1066, the hour for crossing arrived. Landing at last at Pevensey, possibly credible legend holds that he stumbled and fell as he climbed down to the sandy shore. Thinking fast, William transformed what might have been interpreted as an ill omen by quickly gathering up in his hand a clump of sandy earth, rising majestically to his feet, and revealing to all around him the fact that he possessed this clod of English soil.

Landing on "enemy" ground creates the temptation to attack immediately. William resisted. He decided instead to lure Harold to attack him, but to do so where he and his invaders, not Harold, had the greatest advantage. This meant staying as close to the coast as possible so that he could maintain short supply lines while forcing Harold to stretch his long and thin. To draw Harold, William built earthwork castles at Pevensey, Hastings, and throughout the surrounding countryside. From these he launched raids of merciless pillage, burning down villages, killing men, and seizing their women and children. This would give Harold no choice but to march to the defense of his people.

Thus, William demonstrated one of military history's greatest strokes of tactical genius. Invaders rarely have their pick of a battlefield. Typically there is no alternative to conceding the advantage of choice to the defender. By raiding locally instead of directly engaging Harold, William seized an advantage usually denied the aggressor.

At the time of William's landing in the south of England, Harold was fighting a Norwegian Viking invasion at Stamford Bridge in the north. As soon as he repelled these invaders, he led his army on a punishing forced march 200 miles from York to London in the space of a week. In itself, it was the splendid achievement of a skilled military commander. Yet, unquestionably, it left his Saxons depleted and exhausted as they now deployed along the slope of Senlac Hill for battle against William on the evening of October 13. The hill occupied a strategic position eight miles north of Hastings, a village that barred the way to London.

The high ground Harold had chosen was an advantage for him, but William was also aware that the Saxons would be tired. He did not want to give them time to rest. He hastened to launch an attack early on the morning of October 14. While William appreciated that Harold had the natural advantage of high ground, he also observed that the hilltop position limited Harold's ability to maneuver.

Accurately sizing up the field, William devised an attack intended to neutralize Harold's high-ground defensive advantage while simultaneously exploiting Harold's high-ground liability when it came to offense. If Harold had little room to maneuver, William decided to take full advantage of his own mobility. He therefore used his most mobile asset, his cavalry, to attack Harold's infantry, which, perched on a hilltop, was forced into a static defensive posture.

At first contact, it appeared that William had made a terrible blunder. Wielding battle-axes and spears, the Saxons easily repulsed his mounted warriors. Worse, this disrupted William's left flank, which began to retreat in disarray. At this, the Saxon infantry left their strong defensive hilltop to give chase. Seeing this, William rallied the knights in his center. They responded by cutting to ribbons the Saxon counterattack, which was now fully exposed on the open field.

Harold did not panic. Instead he revealed himself as a superb leader. Before William could organize a second attack, Harold succeeded in rallying and re-forming his infantry line. William hurled his knights against what seemed an immovable mass of Saxon foot soldiers. As the hours passed, they held their line.

With daylight fading, William took a new tack. Out of the blue, he feigned a general withdrawal of his cavalry. For his part, Harold was not fooled into taking Williams's bait. But his soldiers fell for it hook, line, and sinker. Despite Harold's desperate attempts to stop them, the Saxon infantry broke the massed formations that had so successfully resisted the Norman cavalry. They charged what they thought was a routed cavalry. It was a willy-nilly pursuit in which the soldiers inevitably spread out. Halfway down the hill, William's knights, in a highly disciplined movement. wheeled 180 degrees to suddenly face the scattered onrush of Saxon men. An army become a mob, they made inviting targets for the Norman swords. Harold's soldiers were cut down like wheat before the reaper.

Seeing that the battle had turned against their king, Harold's personal bodyguards closed round him. But they could not create a human wall high enough or dense enough to stop an arrow from piercing Harold through the eye. He fell, dying instantly, and his bodyguards immediately scattered. Seeing this, the Saxons gave up the fight. Having begun near dawn, the battle was over before sunset. William—now William the Conqueror—had an open road all the way to London, where, on Christmas Day, he was crowned king of England.

The Norman conquest was a spectacular combination of careful strategic and diplomatic preparation, sound logistics, and superb battlefield strategy and tactics. It was a stunning paradigm of amphibious assault as well as one of history's most dramatic examples of the power and the limits of personal command presence on both sides. The Battle of Hastings stands as one of military history's most consequential battles. Its outcome was the transition of Saxon England into a Norman empire, which evolved into a British Empire whose destiny was both independent of yet bound up with that of continental Europe.

War as Pilgrimage: The First Crusade (1096–1099)

Consisting of eight major military expeditions between 1096 and 1291, the Crusades are shrouded in religious lore, popular culture, and depictions in literature and film. It is possible to strip the mythology away by focusing on the pragmatic causes of the Crusades. After the holdings of the Christian Byzantine Empire in Asia Minor fell to the Muslim Seljuk Turks, the Eastern emperor appealed to the West for help. Pope Urban II saw an opportunity to unite fractious Christian elements in feudal Europe. He called for a holy war to recapture Jerusalem, chief city of the "Holy Land," from the Muslims. He believed this would reunite a splintered Church.

Urban II's idea drew on the concept of holy pilgrimage, which is what the series of wars were called. The word "crusade," by which each of these wars is known today, was not applied until the thirteenth century. These so-called pilgrimages

This map from William Shepherd's 1911 *Historical Atlas* shows the extent of territory through which the First Crusaders traveled.

were in fact military expeditions unprecedented in scale and scope. They were the first military operations in which European states united in alliance.

More than any of the religions and political orders of the day, trade benefited from the Crusades. The expeditions were a boon to the commercial trading cities of Italy, foremost among them Venice. Because the ports of Byzantium and the Levant already served as key entrepôts in the trade between Europe and Asia, the arrival of Christian powers in the East ignited worldwide commerce. If anything, as the world became smaller, it also became wealthier, more cosmopolitan, more open-minded, and, paradoxically, less narrowly religious.

On the cusp of the twelfth century, the Muslim world saw the rapid rise of the Seljuk Turks, recent converts to Sunni Islam. In 1071 the Byzantine emperor Michael VII Doulas (r. 1071–1078) led an army against the Seljuks at Manzikert in Armenia, only to suffer a major defeat. All of Anatolia (most of modern Turkey) fell to the Seljuks. Successor state to the Eastern Roman Empire, Byzantium found that as a predominantly Orthodox Christian realm, it could not count on the loyalty of the Catholic West—not, that is, until the ascension of Pope Urban II in 1088. Like a growing number of European Catholics, Urban II had heard horror stories about the persecution of Christians in Syria at the hands of warring Muslims. He also knew that European pilgrims to the Holy Land were exposed to attack. On one level, the pope clearly wanted to reach out even to Orthodox Christians,

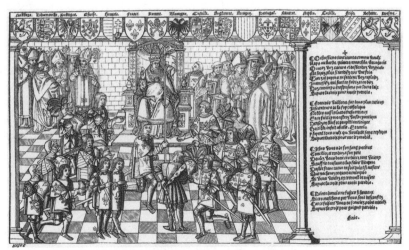

This illustration from a nineteenth-century history reproduces a sixteenth-century woodcut depicting Pope Urban II presiding in 1095 over the Council of Clermont, at which he launched the First Crusade.
FROM P. L. JACOBS'S *MILITARY AND RELIGIOUS LIFE IN THE MIDDLE AGES AND AT THE PERIOD OF THE RENAISSANCE* (LONDON, BICKERS & SON, 1870).

the rivals of Roman Christianity. He seems also to have seized in the Crusades an opportunity to channel the aggression of bellicose knightly armies of Europe away from fighting one another and toward fighting the Muslims. Last but far from least, Urban II reasoned that if the Byzantine Empire became dependent on Western arms for its defense, the global unity of Christendom might be restored.

On November 18, 1095, Urban II convened the Council of Clermont, before which he delivered an impassioned sermon to launch the First Crusade, telling those who went to fight that they would be treated as pilgrims and become temporary churchmen, subject to Church courts rather than the law of any land. To those who might perish in this service, the pope guaranteed a place in heaven. Those who lived to return would earn both salvation and absolution for any sins they might yet commit. The response was overwhelming.

In the West such feudal lords as Raymond IV of Toulouse (c. 1038–1105), Robert II of Normandy (d. 1035), Hugh of Vermandois (1032–1120), Bohemond I (c. 1056–1111) and his nephew, Tancred of Normandy (d. 1148), and brothers Baldwin (1058–1118) and Godfrey of Bouillon (1058–1100) assembled armies and raised money. By August 1096 the main crusading force set off for the Holy Land.

This force, numbering about 40,000, including knights, infantry, and assorted camp followers, began arriving in Constantinople in December 1096, with the last contingent straggling in during April 1097. The Byzantines were not universally jubilant at their arrival, fearing that the true intention of these Europeans was to invade, subjugate, and convert Byzantium to the way of Roman Catholicism. The Byzantine emperor, Alexios I Komeneos (r. 1081–1118), did his best to manage the new arrivals, exacting from them pledges of loyalty in exchange for his support in the form of provisions and other supplies. Most significantly, the European knights swore to render unto Alexios any former Byzantine territory they might recover from the Turks. All was well until Alexios announced that he would not personally participate in the war he himself had initiated. This sowed grave doubt in the minds of the knights, and the antipathy between Byzantine and European Christians poisoned relations throughout most of the twelfth century.

The crusaders nevertheless embarked on the war with gusto. They took the northwestern Anatolian city of Nicaea in 1097, routed the Turks at Doryleum, and seized Antioch, known as the "Cradle of Christianity," in 1098. Meanwhile, the Byzantine force that had joined the European crusaders quickly dwindled to a skeleton crew. Alexios was using most of his forces to follow *behind* the crusaders to ensure the reestablishment of the empire's control over the coast of Asia Minor. In fact, before Antioch fell to the crusaders, Alexios encountered Stephen of Blois (c. 1045–1102), son-in-law of William I (the Conqueror) (1027?–1087), who was en route to Antioch. Alexios persuaded Stephen that the cause of Antioch was hopeless and persuaded him to turn back. This terrible diplomatic blunder gave the crusaders grounds for declining to return Antioch to the Byzantines.

In August 1098 the Fatimid Muslims had taken Jerusalem from the Seljuks. This meant that the Christian army faced a new Arab foe in what was the final drive of the First Crusade. On June 7, 1099, the crusaders, by this time reduced to about 1,500 cavalry and 12,000 infantrymen, camped outside the walls of Jerusalem. In contrast to those within the well-supplied city, the crusaders were short on provisions. The Fatimid governor was confident that he could outlast any siege, at least until reinforcements arrived from Egypt. But men under Godfrey acted quickly. On July 15 they managed to capture and breach a portion of the city wall, opening the gates of Jerusalem to Tancred and Raymond. Overawed by the Christian horde, the Muslim governor surrendered the Tower of David and, under crusader escort, left the city, having secured Tancred's promise that Jerusalem's Muslims would be protected.

The promise may or may not have been sincere. In either case, Tancred was unable to control his Christian infantrymen, who murdered all Muslims—men, women, and children. The city's Jews met the same fate. This was the liberation of the Holy City. This was victory.

After taking Jerusalem, the crusaders attacked a stunned Egyptian relief force, annihilating it and thereby confirming Christian possession of Palestine. This accomplished, most of the crusaders counted their pilgrimage concluded and set off for home. A small contingent remained behind to govern the conquered territory under Godfrey. To his credit, he declined the title of king and instead chose "Defender of the Holy Sepulcher."

Raymond, having also turned down the crown, set off back to Europe, but Bohemond showed up with Daimbert (d. 1109), the archbishop of Pisa, who was proclaimed patriarch of Jerusalem. Presumably, he intended to parlay this ecclesiastical office into secular rule over the city. The death of Godfrey, however, resulted in the recall of his brother, Baldwin, to Jerusalem. Elbowing Daimbert aside, Baldwin assumed the title of king in November 1100. This meant that Jerusalem would not be ruled theocratically as a holy city but as a conventional European-style feudal kingdom.

The coming years would see more crusades and the creation of three additional crusader states to the north of Jerusalem: Edessa, Tripoli, and Antioch. They formed a fragile ribbon stretching 600 miles from the Red Sea to the headwaters of the Euphrates, which, uneasily fusing East and West, came to be known collectively as Outremer (Beyond-the-Sea), the Latin Kingdom, or, simply, the Holy Land. They were in effect Europe's first experiment in colonialism. They did not long endure, and none of the subsequent seven major crusades produced the success (for Europe) of the first. They did, however, create a legacy of mutual resentment between Christian and Muslim, a resentment that has survived into the twentieth and twenty-first centuries to fuel a "Radical Islamist" movement that produced the likes of al-Qaeda and ISIS/ISIL.

Genghis Khan: The "Perfect War Emperor" (1190–1227)

He was born in Mongolia into the Borjigin clan about 1162 and given the name Temujin. His military exploits would ultimately allow him to claim the name Genghis Khan—the latter often translated as "Supreme Ruler" but more rarely and more accurately as "Perfect War Emperor." Genghis Khan became the first great Asian exemplar of the strategic use of warfare to unite disparate peoples—the nomadic tribes of Northeast Asia—into a vast empire. The Mongol Empire he forged grew after his death into the largest contiguous empire in all history.

Although he earned his reputation for merciless brutality, he subordinated its use to brilliant military tactics. Far from being the uncouth barbarian that popular legend depicts, he was a master of tactics, an intelligent strategist, a superb logistician and organizer, and a leader of compelling charisma. Unquestionably, his military triumphs were in large part the products of his skill as a field commander. He was, however, even more effective as a marshal with an uncanny

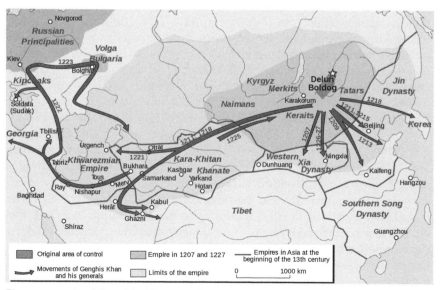

The conquests of Genghis Khan and his generals

ability to get the highest performance from his subordinates, whose absolute loyalty he also enjoyed. He was a builder of alliances and armies, surrounding himself with men in whom he was justified in placing absolute faith and trust, including his own sons. While he was doubtless driven by an insatiable hunger for conquest, he was never prodigal as a plunderer. Those peoples he conquered he generally made better off than they had been when he invaded their lands. His strategy extended beyond military victory to a determination to provide an efficient and just government for those over whom he had triumphed.

When Temujin was just eight or nine years old, his father, Yesukai the Strong, a ranking member of the royal clan, was poisoned by Tatars, members of a rival nomadic band with whom Yesukai had been feuding. With Yesukai dead, the rivals seized control of the clan and cast out Temujin and his mother. The woman responded with a single-minded resolve to raise her son to be a Mongol chief, and the first lesson she inculcated was to surround himself with absolutely loyal men. It was a lesson he heeded lifelong.

Temujin exhibited great prowess in hunting and warfare at an early age and thereby quickly won a large and admiring following. When his new bride was taken and ravished by the Merkit clan, Temujin made a crafty alliance with an acquaintance of his father's, quite literally borrowing from him a fully equipped army to lead against the Merkit in 1180. Not only did he regain his bride, he annihilated the Merkit. This deed won him an even larger following, from which he quickly built his own army of 20,000 men.

While Temujin had been fighting the Merkit, the Jurkin clan took advantage of his absence to plunder his property. Upon his return, Temujin set about exterminating the Jurkin nobility. It was in these two early military operations, against the Merkit and then the Jurkin, that Temujin formulated his most basic doctrine: Leave no enemy at your back. This led to his strategy of serial conquest. He believed in attacking and completely destroying one enemy before engaging another.

With both the Merkit and the Jurkin clans eliminated, Temujin moved against the far more formidable Tatars, who had become allied with the eastern Mongols. In a delayed act of vengeance for the death of his father, Temujin routed the Tartars in battle in 1201 and then systematically slaughtered every person taller than the height of a cart axle. It was an example of his rationalized violence. He reasoned that by killing the adults, he would prevent their hatreds and prejudices from being passed on to the children. This would thereby ensure a second generation he could make loyal to himself.

Conquests of the Naiman and Karait tribes followed in 1203, and by 1204, after establishing his capital at Karakorum, Temujin was master of Mongolia—though not completely without challenge. Jamuka, a Mongol clan leader who had been Temujin's childhood friend, was now at best a tenuous ally who had helped Temujin defeat both the Merkit and the Tatars. After Temujin's brilliant conquests, however, Jamuka's warriors deserted their leader and flocked to

Genghis Khan statue in front of his mausoleum in Ordos, Inner Mongolia, China
PHOTOGRAPH BY FANGHONG. WIKIMEDIA COMMONS

Temujin. He convened them, along with his other followers, at a great assembly on the banks of the River Onon. It was here that Temujin proclaimed himself Genghis Khan.

At this moment, all the major Mongol clans were unified under him. To Genghis, this did not imply the commencement of an age of peace but of warfare beyond the steppe regions. Mastery of the Mongols opened an even vaster stage of conquest. With this, the full scope of Genghis Khan's genius would begin realization, establishing his place in military history.

In prosecuting tribal warfare against highly mobile nomads, Genghis had employed cavalry exclusively. Now that he was going behind Mongol borderlands to conquer other realms, he understood that he had to reinvent his way of making war. To assault great cities, he would have to master the art of siegecraft, including the construction and use of siege engines, catapults, and scaling ladders. He recognized no boundaries and even oversaw such feats of military engineering as diverting great rivers.

Genghis Khan used the entire range of his new tactics when he invaded the Western Hsia Empire in 1205, 1207, and 1209, enlisting Chinese engineers to help him breach city walls. In April 1211 he breached the Great Wall itself to begin his conquest of the Chin Dynasty of northern China. By 1215, Beijing had fallen, and within another two years the last Chin resistance had been neutralized.

This conquest completed, Genghis Khan turned to the south, to Khwarazm, where a local official had made the fatal miscalculation of killing a Mongol trading envoy. Seizing on this as a pretext for war, Genghis Khan hurled 200,000 troops against Khwarazm, devastating not only the enemy army but the people and the very land. Next, in strict succession, Transoxiana (Bukhara and Samarkand), Khorasan, Afghanistan, and northwestern India fell to him. The culminating battle, against Shah Mohammed's son Jellaluddin, was fought on the banks of the Indus River on November 24, 1221.

During 1221–1223, Genghis Khan sent his subordinate generals into southern Russia while he himself led an invasion of northwestern China in 1225, intent on putting down a rebellion against him by the Chin and HsiHsia. After winning a great battle on the Yellow River in December 1226, he prepared to confront yet more rebellious Chins in 1227 but fell ill and died on August 18. He was secretly buried on Mount BurkanKaldan, the place to which he and his mother had been exiled so many years earlier.

Battles of Liegnitz and Sajó River: Mongol Invasions of Europe (1241)

Genghis Khan had laid the foundation for the Mongol Empire, destined to become the biggest contiguous empire in the world. Under Genghis Khan (c.1162–1227) and his successor, Ögedei Khan (c.1185–1241), the Mongols carried out a vast program of conquest that included the subjugation of the Abbasid Caliphate, the Jin (Chin) Empire, and the Song Empire, as well as an invasion of Russia. By 1240, the Mongol army, under the remarkable commander Subutai (1175–1248), who served as the primary military strategist to both Genghis and Ögedei Khan, Mongol forces had overrun Poland. Lublin, Sandomierz, Boleshlav, Chmielnik, and Kraków were either captured or destroyed.

On April 9, 1241, at Liegnitz (present-day Legnica, Poland), Henry I of Silesia (1168–1241) led about 4,000 troops, including a contingent of Teutonic Knights, in a defensive counterattack against a Mongol force numbering between 3,000 and 8,000. Despite the presence of the knights, the European troops were a ragtag lot, poorly disciplined and indifferently led. By contrast, the Mongols were highly trained, intensely motivated, and brilliantly led by Subutai and his subordinates, all of whom were keen students of strategy and tactics.

A shrewd observer of his enemy, Subutai saw that Henry had divided his forces into four units. Accordingly, he chose a tactic known among the Mongols as *mangudai*—"suicide." Subutai sent out a small advance force as a lure to draw Henry out to attack. The mission of this small force was to hold the enemy in place, absorbing its blows long enough for the hidden wings of the Mongol army to descend upon the Europeans, envelop them, and ultimately close upon them as the jaws of a great pincer.

The tactic worked brilliantly. Not only was Henry's mediocre infantry quickly routed, they were killed almost to a man. The Teutonic Knights, the finest warriors of European chivalry, lost just three of their number, having nevertheless miserably failed to prevail against the Mongols. Henry of Silesia fled but could not long evade Mongol patrols, which ran him to ground and beheaded him in a swift and merciless act intended to send a message of thorough intimidation to the citizens of nearby Liegnitz. To Subutai's surprise, however, instead of surrendering at the sight of Henry's severed head, the people were galvanized into resistance. Subutai ordered his army to raze the city, which it did, but at the expense of heavy losses.

From the costly victory at Liegnitz, the Mongols advanced into Hungary via the Carpathian Mountains, Galicia, Moldavia, Transylvania, and Saxony, surrounding the Hungarians on four sides. King Bela IV (1206–1270) of Hungary had foolishly sent most of his army—which was the most formidable in Europe—north, toward Pest (modern Budapest), assuming that the Mongols would make their main attack there. He marched them eastward from Pest, still confident that he would meet and overwhelm the enemy. Reaching the town of Mohi on the Sajó River on April 11, 1241, Bela cautiously divided his 70,000 men, making a probing attack with an advance unit against a small Mongol detachment. Always the master tactician, Subutai concealed his main force and allowed the detachment to take the brunt of Bela's assault. After nightfall, however, the Mongols unleashed their main force, striking the Hungarians, who were asleep in their camp. Surprise was total and resulted in the loss of 40,000 men—more than half of Bela's army.

Totally demoralized following the Battle of the Sajó River, the surviving portion of the Hungarian army fled the field along with their royal commander. This left the great city of Pest at the mercy of the Mongols. They stormed it on December 25, 1241, pillaging it before putting it to the torch. From here, Subutai raided throughout the Austrian countryside during 1242 and doubtless would have continued advancing westward had he not received word that Ögedei Khan was dead. With that, the Mongols withdrew from Europe and returned to Asia—undefeated. In the space of four months of combat in Europe, the Mongol forces had overwhelmed Christian armies, including contingents of knights, totaling five times their own strength. In a clash of civilizations, the West proved militarily inferior to Eastern warriors who, under brilliant leadership, fought with both ferocity and tactical genius.

Swiss Victory at Morgarten Pass: Rise of the Pike and the Mercenaries (1315)

After the fall of the Western Roman Empire in the fifth century, the Swiss, tribes then collectively known as the Helvetii, lived independently, successfully repelling numerous invasions until the late thirteenth century, when they faced their most formidable adversary, the Austrians of the Hapsburg dynasty. In 1291 the so-called Forest Cantons—Uri, Schwyz, and Unterwalden—united as the Swiss Confederation for the sole purpose of hurling the Hapsburg invaders out of their territories.

On November 15, 1315, Leopold I, Duke of Austria, led an army into Switzerland. Historians differ on the strength of this force, with nineteenth-century authorities estimating 8,000 to 9,000 and the most notable early twentieth-century military historian, Hans Delbrück, putting the number at between no more than 2,000 or 3,000. The larger estimate holds that a third of the force was heavy cavalry—armored knights—and Delbrück believes that the *entire* 2,000 or 3,000 were knights. In either case, the mounted knights would have had difficulty negotiating the rugged Swiss topography, and the key moment in the Battle of Morgarten Pass came when a Swiss force of between 3,000 and 4,000 ambushed the Austrians in a rugged defile between a lake and a mountain. Some authorities believe that only about 1,500 of the Swiss were actively engaged in the ambush, which was carried out with two weapons: the mass use of bows and arrows and the individual use of pikes.

Without question, the knights were better trained and disciplined than the Swiss militia. But the "rabble" had taken advantage of the topography and were better equipped. First the Swiss hurled boulders as well as whole trees down upon the column of knights. Then the archers fired into them, producing great confusion. But it was the final Swiss attack, using halberds (a 7-foot-long combination spear and battle-ax) and pikes (18-foot-long spears with a small piercing head) that almost completely wiped out the Austrians.

The news that unarmored peasants had defeated the great knights of Austria spread throughout Europe. It created an instant demand for soldiers—common infantrymen—armed with halberds and pikes, both of which were recognized as powerful hybrid weapons that offered the advantages of standoff in close-contact combat. Both the halberd and the pike could outreach both the sword and the common lance, and either could readily unhorse a knight and pierce his armor.

The Swiss victory was so decisive—and so shocking—that the reputation of Swiss arms became fixed in the late-medieval European mind. The reputation was amplified by the Swiss victory at the Battle of Laupen on June 21, 1339, this time against the combined forces of the Hapsburgs, Burgundy, and Freiburg. The invaders greatly outnumbered the defenders—approximately 17,000 to 6,000—but again, the Swiss victory was overwhelming.

By the fifteenth century, the Swiss had consolidated their early confederation and expanded their territory into the Italian Ticino. What had been derided as a "rabble" at Morgarten was now a highly disciplined and effective militia capable of taking the field on very short notice. The Swiss Confederation, consisting of eight cantons, instituted a regular system of conscription administered by cantonal and local councils as well as trades guilds. Three categories of troops were specified in this arrangement. The *Auszug* were elite troops, young men between 18 and 30, typically bachelors, who constituted the standing army of the Confederation. They also served as the core around which a larger force would be formed when needed. Older men and those who were married were conscripted into the *Landwehr*, a trained militia ready for rapid muster. Last came the *Landsturm*, made up of the oldest group. This was an unorganized militia, available for call-up only in time of grave emergency.

Swiss mercenaries fight German Landsknecht mercenaries in a fierce close combat called "Schlechten Krieg"—literally, "Bad War." Both sides are armed with long pikes, which are ill-suited to hand-to-hand fighting. The engraving is by Hans Holbein the Younger.

ALBERTINA MUSEUM, VIENNA

All of these classes of troops were obliged by law to purchase and maintain their own armor and weapons. If called up, they were also expected to carry sufficient food for four to six days. Self-sufficiency was key, but it also dictated commitment to brief military operations only. When summoned, forces rallied to their cantonal standard—the *Banner*, which referred to the cantonal flag as well as the military unit that carried it. Each banner was commanded by a *Feldhauptmann*, "field captain," the equivalent of a regimental colonel, appointed by the cantonal council. Each banner included a cook, a surgeon, and a scribe, plus a sergeant (*Weibel*), who was responsible for enforcing discipline. An ensign (*Venner*) was physically responsible for bearing the cantonal standard into battle. Each trade guild within the canton contributed a company (*Fähnlein*) consisting of 50 to 150 men, who were armed with crossbows and powder weapons. The general body of conscripts, however, were armed primarily with halberds (prior to the fifteenth century) or pikes (from the fifteenth century on).

After the Battle of Arbedo (June 30, 1422), fought between the Duchy of Milan and the Old Swiss Confederacy (Uri, Unterwalden, Luzern, and Zug) in Ticino, the 18-foot Swiss pike largely replaced the halberd to become the defining weapon of the Swiss infantry. As such, it was the pike that largely dictated combat tactics and formations, especially the phalanx. The phalanx consisted of four ranks of pikemen, who leveled their weapons so as to create a formidable wall against the enemy. Behind these troops, a fifth rank of pikemen stood ready to plug any gaps that might develop in that wall. To bring the maximum number of points to bear against an enemy, the front rank kneeled, holding their pikes low; the second rank stooped, backing up the butt end of each pike under the right foot; the third rank held their weapons at waist level; and the fourth held them head high. The fifth rank was ready to wield their pikes in whatever postures were needed.

Princes and kings all across late medieval Europe were greatly impressed by the performance of the Swiss pikemen, and cantonal governments began negotiating with foreign powers for contracting out their contingents as mercenaries. Most Swiss troops served as mercenaries not individually but as units under the command of their own cantons, which reaped the profit from their service. Soon, former Swiss militiamen hired themselves out individually as soldiers of fortune or banded together in small private companies. Whether fighting under a cantonal banner or as private contractors, Swiss mercenaries earned a reputation for discipline, reliability, and effectiveness. Not only could they be counted on to execute devastating massed pike attacks, they fought ruthlessly, taking no prisoners. To hire them was to hire a machine of war. The Swiss pikemen were not the world's first mercenaries, but they were the most famous, effective, and profitable, bringing mercenary warfare into the mainstream of military history.

Battle of Crécy: Infantry Crushes Chivalry's Flower (1346)

The death of Charles IV of France in 1328 made Edward III of England, his closest male relative, his legal successor. A French court, however, decreed Philip, Count of Valois, Charles's rightful heir, and he was duly crowned Philip VI of France. When the people of Aquitaine continued to favor the English crown, Edward seized the opportunity to proclaim himself king of France in 1340 and invaded France to enforce his claim. Running short of funding, he returned to England to raise money to continue the war, invading again in 1346. On August 22 Edward reached the Somme River, only to find that its bridges had been destroyed. With difficulty he found a fording place near Abbeville and decided to fight at Crécy-en-Ponthieu. He noted that a slope here would put the heavily armored French knights at a disadvantage. Edward deployed his forces with great care. His right flank, near Crécy, was protected by a river, and his left was screened by trees. The English infantry also dug ditches—like the trees, ditches were obstacles to mounted knights.

Estimates of English strength vary from 14,000 to about 20,000. Edward divided these into three divisions, called "battles," with that on the right commanded by his 17-year-old son, Edward, Prince of Wales (later called the Black Prince). The left division was under the Earls of Arundel and Northampton, and slightly to the rear was the division under King Edward's personal command. At the heart of each battle was a phalanx of about 1,000 dismounted men-at-arms, six ranks deep. At the outer flanks of each division were archers, arranged in echelon forward of the rest of the division to create clear and converging fields of fire. Also, in front of the very center of the army, the archers converged in an inverted V pointed toward the enemy. Crécy was almost certainly the first European battle that made significant use of gunpowder weapons. This would prove a notable debut in military history, and yet it would have little tactical effect on the outcome of the battle.

The French army has been estimated at between 30,000 and nearly 60,000 fighting men. All authorities agree that 10,000 to 12,000 of these troops were heavy cavalry, including knights and men-at-arms. Archers, mercenaries from Genoa, were also present, as were other infantrymen. The large French force marched in an exposed column without any advance reconnaissance. When it encountered the well-prepared English line of battle on August 26, it was already late in the day, about six o'clock. At the head of his long column, King Philip VI was totally surprised, and he struggled mightily merely to halt the great train at his back so that he could deploy it for battle.

Wisely, Philip brought his crossbowmen to the front, where they would have a clear field of fire. But his knights, unwilling to yield pride of place to mercenary commoners, lurched forward, creating a chaotic mass just behind the archers. Worse, a sudden downpour turned the field to mud, making it nearly impossible for the knights to control their horses. Despite these impediments, the mercenary archers advanced and then fired—but, at 150 yards from the English front, their bolts fell short. They advanced farther, only to be swept by arrows from English longbows, which proved far more deadly than the Genoese crossbows.

The Italian archers withered, leaving the field clear for the French knights, who charged through the disintegrating ranks of the Genoese. The slope Edward had so carefully chosen turned to slime under the rain, and the heavily armored knights slid out of control along with their horses, trampling the remaining Genoese. The knights and their men-at-arms were no longer a cohesive attacking force but a chaotic, flailing target for English arrows.

Instead of discouraging the ranks behind the French knights, the chaos ahead only drew them forward. Apparently without command, each element of the French column—most of which was still in ranks rather than in anything resembling a line

This depiction of the Battle of Crécy appeared in the illuminated manuscript of Jean Froissart's fifteenth-century *Chronicles*, chapter CXXIX.
BIBLIOTHÈQUE NATIONALE DE FRANCE, PARIS

of battle—hurled itself against the continuing storm of English longbow arrows. Clearly, Edward had amply supplied his archers, who nevertheless rushed into the field to collect arrows for reuse. The barrage continued even into the night until, after some 16 French waves had sacrificed themselves, the army of Philip VI gave up. Tellingly, the English maintained their formations in good order through the dawn.

Among the dead at the bottom of the slope were 1,542 French lords and knights, more than 3,000 men-at-arms, and an unknown number of infantrymen. Thousands of horses lay mangled. King Philip VI was wounded, as were many of his surviving noblemen. English losses, in contrast, were somewhere between 100 and 300 killed.

The English victory sent shock waves through all Europe, especially among the nobility. The English had been developing fierce combat techniques focused on infantry and longbowmen during many wars with the Welsh and the Scots. Of these internal wars, the leaders on the Continent were largely unaware. Thus the disastrous performance of the flower of French chivalry came as a complete surprise. Two armies had met in open combat on an open field, and well-disciplined common soldiery had annihilated the best and noblest European cavalry. Much credit, of course, must be given to King Edward, who understood the value of his military assets and deployed them with tactical genius.

The Battle of Crécy stands as one of military history's most decisive encounters. For perhaps a thousand years leading to August 26, 1346, cavalry, always associated with the nobility, had reigned supreme in warfare. From Crécy forward, infantry—a service arm consisting of "common" men—became the celebrated "queen of battle" and the primary arm of ground forces.

Battle of Agincourt: When the Knights Fell (1415)

King Henry V ascended to the English throne in April 1413 at the end of an uneasy—and often violent—17-year truce in the Hundred Years' War. He was determined to renew the fight against France, with the objective of making good on his claim to the French throne. To this end, he opened negotiations with the French and issued increasingly provocative demands to them in an effort to maneuver England and France into war. At last, during the winter of 1414–1415, Henry began commandeering ships for the transport of an army of invasion across the English Channel. By August he had assembled a fleet at Southampton and landed his army outside Harfleur, to which he laid siege. The people of the

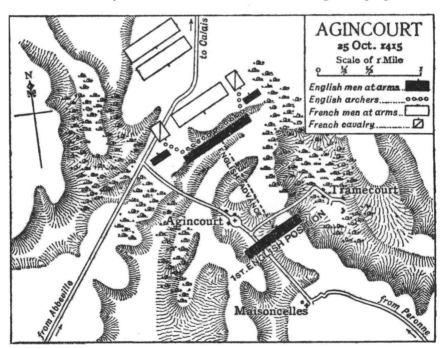

The Battle of Agincourt, October 25, 1415

town held out until September 22, when, realizing that no French army was going to rescue them, they surrendered.

Yet the garrison defending Harfleur had held out far longer than Henry had ever imagined it would. Fifteenth-century armies did not fight in winter, and the campaigning season was fast coming to an end. Moreover, the usually disputatious French barons had united to oppose their common foe, and Henry soon found his forces surrounded. The English king convened a council of war, telling the assembly that he intended to march from Harfleur to Calais. His councilors were appalled. They pointed out that the army could simply reembark on their ships and sail to Calais—at the time a possession of England—without encountering the enemy army or having to make hazardous river crossings over the Seine and the Somme. But Henry insisted, sending a message by sea to the English governor of Calais, ordering him to lead a force to the crossing point in the estuary of the Somme and hold it for Henry's army.

This depiction of the Battle of Agincourt is an illumination painted in the fifteenth century by Thomas Walsingham on the vellum manuscript of *St. Alban's Chronicle*, the author of which is unknown.
LAMBETH PALACE LIBRARY, LONDON

The English invasion force left Harfleur on October 8, 1415, and began the 100-mile march to Calais. When they reached the Somme estuary, they encountered neither the English governor nor an army. Instead, a French force was guarding the crossing. Indeed, the French began assembling all around Henry's army. Soon French troops were guarding the bridges and fords all along the Somme. Henry therefore led his army southeast, up the left bank of the Somme. A French force shadowed him on the opposite bank, ready to check any attempt to cross. At last Henry cut directly across a bend in the river, outrunning the French, crossing the river, and turning back on a northeasterly course toward Calais.

By October 24 the English had marched through the Picardy town of Frévent and were within 30 miles of Calais. Henry's scouts, however, soon came riding back to him to announce that the French were blocking the road into Calais. Clearly, they had—unseen—overtaken the English. When Henry asked one of the scouts, a Welsh man-at-arms named David Gambe, to report on the size of the French army, the man replied: "There are enough to kill, enough to capture, and enough to run away." Nevertheless, the English king kept leading his forces forward. Once they were past the village of Maisoncelles, the French army came into view. It consisted of a large number of knights and attendant men-at-arms. Henry understood that he could not pass them without giving battle. Accordingly, he ordered his army to make camp and prepare for a battle on the next day.

Henry saw that English morale was at low ebb. The weather had turned heavily rainy, and the sight of an enormous French army foretold doom. Nor did it help that the English could clearly hear laughter and music coming from the French camp. Obviously, the enemy was anticipating a great victory.

A skilled leader of men, all through the night, Henry visited his soldiers gathered around their fires. To each group of men, he made encouraging speeches that, judging from their depiction in William Shakespeare's *Henry V*, must have been both eloquent and effective. By the morning of October 25, 1415, the feast day of Saint Crispin, the spirits of his soldiers had been more than revived—they were now eager for a showdown fight. They marched out of Maisoncelles and deployed for battle across the road to Calais, arraying themselves in three divisions of knights and men-at-arms. Those under the command of Lord Camoys were on the right, the Duke of York's men in the center, and soldiers under Sir Thomas Erpingham on the left. Henry's longbowmen assumed the customary inverted-wedge formation along the front. Each archer had a clear field of fire.

The English troops could see the French army ahead, forming for battle. At the front was the constable of France, leading the first French line. The Duc de Bar and the Duc d'Alençon led the second line, while the Counts of Merle and Falconberg led the third. Ahead of the English position, two stands of forest converged close to the road from either side. The battlefield was thus too narrow for the French army to fully deploy in line, and the French knights, all eager to be in front, jostled one another to claim their position. The result was a mass of mounted, armored knights and their men-at-arms, crowded too closely together to maneuver properly or even wield their weapons effectively.

For their part, the English soldiers, led by the example of their king, knelt to kiss the ground in token of their acknowledgment that they might well be committed to the earth before the day had ended. In air thick with anticipation, the English waited for the French to commence the attack. When there was no movement from the enemy, however, Henry assumed the initiative, calling out the command, "Forward banners." With that, the English army began its advance. The French prepared to give battle, but Henry ordered a halt as soon as his forces were just within arrow range of the French front line. Henry's divisions closed up, and his archers set into the ground the pointed staves they carried with them. They fashioned a fence, the sharp ends of the staves raked outward, toward the French. Both armies were now confined by the woods on either side of the road.

Henry ordered groups of his archers and men-at-arms to move through the trees and approach nearer to the French. Then he signaled for the longbowman to open fire on the tightly packed mass of French knights and men-at-arms. The initial shock of the English onslaught was heavy, but the French front line soon recovered sufficiently to begin moving forward to the charge. But by this time, heavy rain had reduced the narrow confines of the battlefield to soupy mud, and the French charge physically bogged down. Into this stumbling chaos, the English let fly their arrows in a barrage that came from the front as well as from the concealment of the woods on either side of the road.

Soon the battle closed in on the stake fence. Across this boundary, the English and French tangled hand to hand. The French knights, astride their horses, had no room to maneuver forward, backward, or to the sides. Much of the cavalry therefore dismounted and began fighting hand to hand with the English. All the while, more of the English joined in from the wooded flanks, and in the space of two hours, they won the Battle of Agincourt.

Casualties among the French nobility were especially high. The Duc d'Alençon was killed by an arrow just as he was about to surrender personally to Henry. The constable of France, Charles D'Albret, was killed in combat, as were the Duc d'Orleans and the Duc de Brabant, among many others. In the meantime, the French soldiery of the third line hung back, uncertain whether it made any sense to risk joining what seemed a hopeless fight. Henry sent a messenger to them with an ultimatum. They must either withdraw from the field or prepare to receive the full fury of the English attackers, who promised to give no quarter. The French third line fled the field.

The main phase of the Battle of Agincourt was over before noon. As French survivors left the field, the English gathered what prisoners they could. But now a rump portion of the French army, led by the knights Isambart d'Agincourt and Robert de Bournonville, making use of their intimate knowledge of the area, descended by surprise on the English baggage train at Maisoncelles. Warned of an impending attack on his rear, Henry ordered his men to kill all their French prisoners. When some balked at the order, the king threatened to hang them as traitors. Thus motivated, the English soldiers efficiently dispatched their prisoners. This done, Henry re-formed his army about-face to confront the threat approaching from the rear. The outnumbered French raiders were quickly repulsed.

Estimates of the numbers of French killed at Agincourt vary widely from a low of 1,500 to a high of 11,000. Between 700 and 2,200 Frenchmen were captured. Among the English, casualties were light, estimated at between 112 and 600 killed. The English, 6,000 to 9,000 strong, had been greatly outnumbered by a French force estimated at a strength of 12,000 minimum and perhaps as large as 36,000, making the English victory all the more spectacular. In view of the withdrawal of attackers and the massacre of the French prisoners of war, however, many of Henry's men considered their triumph severely compromised. They were not bothered by the morality of having killed their prisoners but by the loss of ransom opportunities their deaths, along with the withdrawal of the raiders, had caused.

While Henry completed his march to Calais, from which he sailed to England to celebrate the victory at Agincourt, France's King Charles VI was driven insane at the news of the French defeat and the horrendous losses among the nobility. For military commanders of the era, the takeaway lesson of Agincourt was the terrible destructiveness of the English longbow in the hands of English and Welsh archers. Henry V had created an army in which 8 out of 10 men were archers. They so devastated the French cavalry that commanders began turning increasingly to standoff weapons, longbows and crossbows, over swords and lances. Even more significantly, armies increasingly subordinated the combat role of the noble knight to the yeoman archer.

Joan of Arc in Command: The Power of a "Force Multiplier" (1429–1444)

For much of history, including military history, commanders were kings and kings, commanders. Feudalism in Europe reinforced this formula, affirming that only those of noble birth were fit to command and, indeed, had a duty to command. In the early Renaissance, Joan of Arc emerged as a radically new model of military leadership. In the history of religion, she is portrayed as anointed by the Lord God himself to lead an army. In military history, she is instead a study in the nature of command. With her, the roles of force of personality, conviction, and inspiration came together in what military officers call "command presence." It is the almost mystical power some commanders have to act beyond their strategic or tactical talents. Command presence is a force multiplier: a means of amplifying the basic assets of a military formation—strength of numbers, weaponry, position—without materially adding resources. Whatever effect Joan had on political and ecclesiastical history, her impact on military history was to bring the most intangible aspects of successful military leadership to the fore. She added to warfighting the dimension of dauntless spirit.

Joan of Arc—Jeanne d'Arc or Jehanne Darc—was born about 1412 in the village of Domrémy in the valley of the Meuse. At the time of her birth, Domrémy was in the Duchy of Bar, a part of France loyal to Burgundy, which in turn favored the hegemony of the English and opposed the Armagnacs, who wanted to expel the English to make way for the ascension of the dauphin, Charles VII, to the French throne. In 1420, after years of combat, the Treaty of Troyes instead gave that throne to the heirs of the English king Henry V and disinherited Charles VII. Accordingly, after 1422 the infant king of England, Henry VI, became, at least in name, king of France. A little more than two years after this event, 13-year-old Joan of Arc began to see visions of Saint Michael the Archangel, Saint Catherine, and Saint Margaret.

At first these visions frightened her, but the visual apparitions were soon accompanied by a voice, and it seemed to her "a worthy voice ... sent ... by God." Initially the voice was benign in its commandments, which were simply "to be good, to go regularly to church." Over some four years, however, the single voice became three. They were the voices of Saints Michael, Catherine, and Margaret, and they made far more exacting demands.

Joan was 16 in 1428, a year in which the English laid siege to Orléans and were poised to begin a campaign to conquer the south of France. Joan's voices now told her that she "should come into France"—that is, enter the territory loyal to the dauphin rather than to the Anglo-Burgundian faction. The voices

This exuberant 1854 painting by neoclassical French artist Jean-Auguste Dominique Ingres (1780–1867) depicts Joan of Arc in a full suit of armor at the coronation of Charles VII in the Cathedral of Reims.
LOUVRE MUSEUM, PARIS

persisted, instructing her very specifically to go to Robert de Baudricourt, captain of the town of Vaucouleurs, and obtain from him a military escort to accompany her to Chinon, seat of the dauphin's court. There she was to convince the dauphin, Charles VII, to lead a military campaign to reclaim his throne.

Joan argued with her voices, protesting that she "was a poor girl who knew neither how to ride nor lead in war." The voice of Saint Michael responded that Saints Catherine and Margaret would instruct her, adding that "it was by God's order"—though God never directly commanded her to undertake the mission; the decision was ultimately hers and hers alone.

Presumably it was some combination of religious devotion and patriotism that prompted Joan to leave her village on or about May 13, 1428. She told her father that she was off to visit relatives in Durey-le-Petit, a village near Vaucouleurs. At Durey-le-Petit she talked her uncle, Durand Lassois, into introducing her to Robert de Baudricourt at Vaucouleurs. Reportedly she told Robert that she wanted "to go to France" to have the dauphin crowned. Robert is said to have responded by telling Lassois to take her back home to Durey-le-Petit "and slap her."

In fact, a disheartened Joan returned all the way to Domrémy. Two months later, in July 1428, an Anglo-Burgundian army attacked Vaucouleurs and nearby villages, including Domrémy. On October 12 the English laid siege to Orléans, which controlled a strategic bridge across the Loire, gateway to the south of France.

Now Joan's voices reemerged more urgently. They commanded her to raise the Anglo-Burgundian siege. In January 1429 she left her home village forever and once again traveled to Durey-le-Petit, where she again persuaded her uncle to take her to Vaucouleurs. There, for the next three weeks, she hammered at Robert de Baudricourt, insisting that he must take her to the dauphin. He repeatedly rebuffed her, but stories about Joan were beginning to circulate far and wide. They reached the distant city of Nancy, in Lorraine (at the time part of the Holy Roman Empire). The aging and ailing Duke Charles II of Lorraine summoned Joan in the hope that this visionary of God might have the power to cure him. Joan had no idea whether she could cure the old man, but she knew he was powerful. Perhaps he could help her get before the dauphin. She traveled to Nancy, met the duke, and told him that she knew nothing about how to heal him. She then asked him to "send his son and some men to take me into France," promising that she "would pray to God for his health."

Disappointed, Duke Charles II did nothing more than give Joan safe conduct back to Vauclouleurs, where, on or about February 12, she appeared before Robert de Baudricourt. Before her audience with Robert, she had spoken to Jean de Metz, one of his soldiers. She explained to him that "before mid-Lent," she must "be before the king even if I must wear down my feet to the knees." She was convinced that "no one in the world, neither kings, nor dukes, nor the King of Scotland's daughter, or anyone else can regain the Kingdom of France; there is no aid except myself." In this, students of military leadership may find the secret of command presence. It is the hard-core conviction that no one else can do what must be done.

Once again she pleaded with Robert, who, perhaps impressed that Duke Charles of Lorraine had taken an interest in her, finally gave in. Granting her an escort, he sent her off with the words, "Go, and let come what may."

Joan and her escorts arrived at Chinon on March 4, 1429. The dauphin, Charles VII, whom the French people called *le falot*, "the comical one," was weak and apathetic. He kept Joan waiting two days while he met with his advisors. Finally he granted her an audience, which was witnessed by some hundreds of curious supporters of the feckless dauphin.

Joan told him that God sent "word to you through me, that you will be anointed and crowned in the town of Rheims, and you will be the lieutenant of the King of Heaven, who is King of France." Doubtful, the dauphin sent her to Poitiers, where, for the next three weeks, clerics and theologians examined her. One demanded that she produce a sign of her mission. To this she replied that she had "not come to Poitiers to produce signs; but send me to Orléans; I will show you the signs for which I was sent." Such was the force of Joan's presence that the clerics advised Charles VII to indeed send her to Orléans.

Joan was everything the average feudal military commander was not. She was a girl and a peasant, ignorant of arms. Yet she projected the certainty of rightness to command. In company with the Duke of Alençon, Joan, at the head of an army of 3,000 to 4,000, reached Orléans during April 27–29, 1429. Deployed in boats, the force slipped across the Loire River and past English siege lines. On May 5 Joan led a successful sortie against an English strongpoint. Two days later, on May 7, she led the relief of Orléans itself. In the assault she was badly wounded by an English arrow but nevertheless remained on the field and in the front lines. She broke the English blockade, prompting the Duke of Suffolk, commanding the English forces, to withdraw. He distributed his men into garrisons in an effort to defend the English-held towns in the Loire valley, but over the summer Joan retook most of the towns. On June 19, in the Battle of Patay, she led a surprise attack on the forces of Lord John Talbot and Sir John Fastolf, not only driving the English out of the Loire Valley but capturing Talbot and killing some 2,200 English soldiers for the loss of about 20 Frenchmen and allied Scots. This opened the way for the French forces to march toward Reims for the coronation of the dauphin as Charles VII on the morning of July 17, 1429.

Joan and her subordinate commanders were keen to exploit the momentum of their victories by marching immediately on Paris, but Charles VII called a truce to negotiate peace with the Duke of Burgundy. When talks broke down, which they soon did, Joan led an advance on Paris on September 8. An arrow pierced her leg and, against her protests, the attack was aborted. A terrified Charles VII then ordered a full retreat on September 10. Although she now lacked the king's backing, Joan attempted new attacks elsewhere in November and December. They all failed, and she withdrew until March 14, 1430, when she led a relief force to lift the siege of Compiègne. On May 23, 1430, Burgundian troops captured her and handed her over to the English, who engineered her trial, conviction, and, on May 30, 1431, execution as a heretic. Even after this, Joan remained an inspiration. Both noble and peasant partisans continued to war against the English, even without the support of Charles VII.

Siege of Constantinople: Mehmed II Ascendant (1453)

Founded in the seventh century by Muhammad (c. 570–632), Islam developed and expanded very rapidly, in part driven by its founder's aggressive military genius. Under the Ottoman Empire, Islam spread into Europe, leaving Constantinople, capital of what was now a vestigial Byzantine Empire, an isolated citadel of Christianity at the intersection of Europe and Asia Minor.

Born at Edirne in what is today Turkey on March 30, 1432, Mehmed II was the eldest son of Murad II. Mehmed became sultan for a time when his father retired to Magnesia in 1444, assuming the throne permanently after his father died in 1451. Mehmed II ruled a vast empire that extended to the east and west of Constantinople. Murad had been content to allow the city to exist as an independent quasi city-state in the midst of his empire, but Mehmed began his own reign with a campaign to take Constantinople once and for all.

He started in 1451–1452 by building a fortress, Rumeli Hisari. Located just outside the city, it covered both the European and Asian sides of the Bosporus. When Byzantine emperor Constantine XI protested the erection of Rumeli Hisari as an outrage, Mehmed seized on the complaint as a rationale for declaring war. Constantine XI commanded an army of fewer than 10,000 men against an Ottoman force of 80,000, including the elite corps of Janissaries, the sultan's palace guard. In addition, under the command of a renegade Hungarian artilleryman named Urban, the sultan possessed an unparalleled siege train of 70 heavy cannon.

Constantinople was nevertheless a formidable objective. It was virtually surrounded by water, and its landward defenses were extremely strong. Mehmed began by attempting to push his Turkish fleet into the Golden Horn, the narrow waterway that was the primary Bosporus inlet into Constantinople. The city's defenders, however, had thrown a boom across its entrance. Not to be daunted, Mehmed tasked his engineers with creating an overland passage for his fleet from the Bosporus into the Golden Horn above the boom. His soldiers built a mile-long plank road between the Bosporus and the Golden Horn, greased it with vast quantities of animal fat, and slid 80 warships over it in a spectacular portage. Refloated in the Golden Horn, these ships, combined with land-based artillery, unleashed a withering barrage commencing on April 2, 1453.

Constantinople withstood siege and bombardment until May 29, 1453, when artillery had made a sufficient breach in the city's walls and perimeter defenses to admit a Janissary charge. In the ensuing battle, Constantine XI was killed. The Ottoman Turks pillaged and sacked the city for three days—whereupon Mehmed intervened in an effort to preserve as much of the city as possible. He prevailed upon the learned and the cultured to remain in Constantinople under his protection. Despite the sultan's efforts, however, the city rapidly fell into decay. Having earned his sobriquet Mehmed El Fatih—Mehmed the Conqueror—the sultan presided over a prize much diminished from its former luster. Yet the fall of Constantinople meant the end of the last vestige of the Eastern Empire and permanently installed the Islamic caliphate at the doorstep of Europe.

In 1456 Mehmed II invaded Serbia and laid siege to Belgrade. The Hungarian military and political leader John Hunyadi defeated him in a naval battle there on July 14, 1556, and on land during July 21–22. While the sultan withdrew from Belgrade, he overran Serbia during 1457–1459 and penetrated into southern Greece during 1458–1460, crushing the small empire of Trebizond in 1461 and successfully invading Bosnia during 1463–1464.

Always at odds with Venice, whose great fleet had briefly aided Constantine XI in the defense of Constantinople, Mehmed waged a long war against it beginning in 1463. He raided Dalmatia and Croatia in 1468 and then launched a spectacularly successful amphibious assault on the Venetian fortress of Negroponte in Euboea (Évvoia) from June 14 to July 12, 1470, capturing the city with few losses to himself. Venice persuaded Persia to make an alliance and attack Erzincan (in northeastern Turkey) in 1473, but Mehmed prevailed against this force. Defeating it, he went on to capture the Crimean city of Kaffa (Feodosiya) from the Genoese.

In the meantime, in 1468 Mehmed reconquered Albania, which had been lost in the rebellion of the Janissary Skanderbeg (George Castricata) in 1443. The sultan went on to capture most of the Venetian ports along the Albanian coast and then sent raiders from Croatia across the Alps into Venetia, bringing northeastern Italy to its knees, thus forcing Venice to make peace and recognize the Ottoman conquests.

Early in 1480, Mehmed's army crossed the Adriatic and seized Otranto, in Apulia, at the heel of the Italian boot. He went on to besiege the Knights of St. John on Rhodes during 1480–1481 but suffered a serious defeat. He was planning a second assault on Rhodes when he fell ill at Maltepe (outside present-day Istanbul) and died there on May 3, 1481, having, however, presided over the golden age of the Ottoman Empire that established Islam as a strong competitor to European Christianity.

Cortés Takes the Aztec Empire: Conquest Comes to the New World (1518–1521)

The story of Spain's entry into the New World is so familiar as a turning point in the history of civilization that its role as a turning point in military history is easily lost. We all know that on October 12, 1492, the *Santa Maria*'s lookout sighted land, bringing to an end the first voyage of Christopher Columbus. The natives called their island Guanahani, but that hardly mattered to history as written by Euro-Americans. What counted is that Columbus christened it San Salvador. Most modern historians believe this was present-day Watling Island, although in 1986 a group of scholars suggested that the true landfall was another Bahamian island, Samana Cay, 65 miles south of Watling. Wherever they had landed, precisely, Columbus and his crew were greeted by friendly people of the Arawak tribe. Columbus of course, believing—or wanting to believe—that he had reached Asia, the "Indies," called the native inhabitants Indians. Moreover, because he was supposed to be in the Indies, he sailed on to Cuba in search of the court of the emperor of China, with whom he hoped to negotiate an agreement for trade in spices and gold. Disappointed in this, Columbus sailed next to an island he called Hispaniola (modern-day Santo Domingo). Near Cap-Hatien, a Christmas Day storm wrecked the *Santa Maria*. Columbus ushered his crew to safety ashore and installed a 39-man garrison among the friendly "Indians" of a place he decided to call La Navidad. Columbus and the rest of his crew left for Spain on January 16, 1493, sailing in the *Niña*.

The garrison Columbus left behind among friendly natives set about pillaging goods and ravaging women, apparently as soon as their commander departed. By night the Indians retaliated, killing 10 Spaniards as they slept then hunting down the rest of the garrison. This was a turning point in military history in that Europeans decided to regard the first contact between them and Americans as an occasion for *military* action. War—or warlike behavior—was chosen as the mode of responding to the natives of what, with respect to the Europeans, was a "new world." For their part, the Native Americans responded with warfare as well. When Columbus returned in November 1493, on his second New World voyage, he discovered that not a single Spaniard of the garrison had been left alive. Thus, a cause for war was the very first of the Old World's exports to the New.

The four voyages of Columbus were followed by a military invasion of the New World carried out by *conquistadors*, Spanish for "conquerors." The first contingent was led by Juan Ponce de León (c.1460–1521) in the conquest of Puerto Rico during 1508–1509. Jamaica and Cuba fell next to the Spanish sword in 1510 and 1511.

A more profound military turning point came with the war for Mexico. The first military encounters of the Spanish in the New World were between soldiers experienced in fighting for European empires against other European empires. Hernán Cortés was the first of the conquistadors to lead soldiers of European empire in war against soldiers of American empire. Columbus and the early Spaniards encountered small-scale settlements and civilizations, primitive in their eyes, and responded by waging war against them. Cortés encountered a civilization of great wealth and magnificence, grander even than the imperial courts of Spain. Yet his response was likewise military. He waged war against the empire.

An undated engraving of "Hernando Cortes" from the collection of the Library of Congress.
LIBRARY OF CONGRESS, PRINTS AND PHOTOGRAPHS DIVISION

Hérnan Cortés was a minor nobleman who had thrown over a university education to become an adventurer in the New World. On November 8, 1519, having sailed to America, he led his forces into Tenochtitlan (today's Mexico City), then, as now, a capital city. The Aztec emperor Montezuma II opened his city to the invaders, who, quite understandably impressed, marveled at its wealth and magnificence. We know that Cortés made the decision to conquer the empire he beheld. It is, however, possible that the conquest of Aztec Mexico would have been less apocalyptic than it was—had not another conquistador intervened. Pánfilo de Narváez had been dispatched by Spanish authorities to arrest Cortés for having overstepped his authority in seizing Mexico. Hearing of his approach, Cortés set out to intercept him, leaving affairs in Tenochtitlan in the care of a subordinate, Pedro de Alvarado.

It was another turning point. Under Cortés, the military decision had been made to conquer Aztec Mexico. With Cortés absent dealing with de Narváez, Alvarado devised a new military approach. It was slaughter—a military strategy (if it can be called such) that generations of Europeans and then Euro-Americans would choose when making war on Native Americans. Without warning, Alvarado and his men set upon the celebrants of a feast in honor of the deity Huitzilopochtli and hacked and beat to death men, women, and children.

If the gratuitous brutality was intended to intimidate the Aztecs, it did not. Up to this point, the people of Tenochtitlan had been friendly to the newcomers. Now they rose up against them. When Cortés returned to the city after having defeated Narváez, he arrived in the proverbial nick of time to lead his men in a fighting retreat from the capital during the night of June 30, 1520. It became known in the history of the Spanish conquest of the Americas as the *Noche Triste*—the "Sad Night."

Among the casualties of that "sad night" was the Aztec emperor, Montezuma II. As for Cortés, he withdrew and regrouped. It was a full 10 months before he returned with an augmented force to lay siege to Tenochtitlan. Siegecraft was familiar to soldiers of feudal Europe. Cortés cut off all food and water to the city's inhabitants. They held out for three months until, their numbers reduced by starvation, privation, and an outbreak of smallpox—a disease previously unknown in America and apparently brought to Mexico by an African slave in the service of Narváez—they surrendered to Cortés on August 13, 1521. With that, the conquest of the Aztec empire was essentially complete. Cortés and other conquistadors who came after him used Tenochtitlan as a base from which to mount conquests into the New World hinterlands.

Babur Storms North India: Invasion Becomes Empire (1525–1526)

Except for an interruption between 1540 and 1555, the Mughal Empire spanned 1526 to 1857 and was one of global history's greatest empires, encompassing at its height almost the entire Indian subcontinent and extending into Afghanistan. Mughal rulers claimed more than 150 million subjects, close to a quarter of the planet's population at the time. The empire was founded by one man, Babur (1483–1530), and was brought into being through a single spectacular invasion driven by Babur's dual purpose of overthrowing the sultan of Delhi as master of the region and establishing a new empire.

Born Zahir-ud-din Muhammad on February 14, 1483, near Ferghana in what is today Uzbekistan, Babur embraced a sobriquet derived from the Persian *babr*, "tiger." He claimed descent from both Tamerlane and Genghis Khan and was just 11 years old when he became ruler of Ferghana on the death of his father in 1494. This immediately thrust him into the ancient struggle for Transoxiana—Bukhara and Samarkand—a region hotly contested among all those who claimed descent from Tamerlane. Incredibly, the boy king not only successfully defeated all attempts to wrest Transoxiana from his grip, he also advanced against and captured Samarkand in 1497—when he was 14 years old. He retook it during February–March 1501, but in April–May of that year he was defeated by an Uzbek-Turkoman chief named Shaibani Khan at the Battle of Sar-i-pul.

Forced to withdraw from Ferghana, Babur settled in Kabul, Afghanistan, about 1504. During 1511–1512 he launched another invasion into Transoxiana. When this was repulsed, he turned toward India and there enjoyed far greater success. Starting with Babur's first sortie into northern India in 1515, he waged war almost continuously. From 1515 to 1523 Babur led raids into the Punjab of northern India and then into Afghanistan, where he took and occupied Kandahar in 1522. In 1523 he launched a full-scale invasion of the Punjab, capturing Lahore, which he occupied at first tentatively and then permanently. He used the city as a base of operations for his campaign against the sultan of Delhi, Ibrahim Lodi. In 1525 Babur advanced from Lahore against Panipat, about 30 miles north of Delhi. His army of 10,000 was partially equipped with the first gunpowder firearms in use outside the Ottoman Empire.

Arriving at Panipat on April 13, 1526, Babur settled in for what he thought would be a long, hard defensive war. He moved his cavalry and artillery to the rear and set up a forward defensive line of some 700 baggage carts roped together.

The only gaps he left in this line were to accommodate his artillery. When word spread that Babur's great army was opposing the sultan, several thousand Hindu and Muslim troops flocked to Babur's banner, eager to serve as reinforcements. Nevertheless, Babur still faced long odds. With now perhaps 15,000 troops, he was up against Ibrahim Lodi's army of 40,000 men.

The opposing forces stood idle, facing each other for eight days as if waiting to see who would blink first. Finally, Ibrahim ordered an attack on April 21, 1526. With that, the Battle of Panipat commenced.

Ibrahim's massively superior numbers stalled at the first line of carts. At that decisive moment, Babur opened fire on them. Keeping up a barrage, he ordered his infantry into an aggressively defensive position and then sent out cavalry charges against both flanks of the Delhi army. The enveloping shock tactics proved stunning. Babur routed Ibrahim's army, inflicting some 15,000 fatal casualties upon it. Among those killed in action was the sultan himself.

Babur did not devote a single moment to celebrating his victory. Instead he moved at great speed to occupy Delhi. Within three days, he proclaimed the Mughal Empire in place of the Lodi dynasty. By next striking agreements and alliances with various local chieftains along the Ganges River valley, Babur secured his hold on northern India.

The speed with which Babur turned invasion into empire—and a vast and enduring empire at that—became a landmark in military history. It was an innovative use of new gunpowder weapons, which were used in combination with the sixteenth-century tactical equivalent of mid-twentieth-century blitzkrieg, "lightning war." In wars fought before the Industrial Revolution, speed was difficult to achieve and therefore offered an almost unbeatable edge on those rare occasions when commanders were able to move quickly. By combining high speed and massive violence, Babur prevailed spectacularly, leveraging extreme speed and unremitting violence to conjure up a new empire.

Battle of Mohács: Christian Europe at Bay (1526)

Through much of the Middle Ages, thanks in no small measure to the Crusades, Europe struggled to present a united Christian front against incursions by the Muslim Ottoman Empire. In truth, neither the Christian nor Islamic world was unified. By the Renaissance, however, it was clear that Christian Europe was even more fragmented than the Islamic world. After King Francis I of France was defeated by his rival and sworn enemy, Holy Roman Emperor Charles V, at the Battle of Pavia on February 24, 1525, he joined Pope Clement VII and Venice in the League of Cognac to oppose the Holy Roman Empire. Thus Europe was in political and military disarray when the powerful Ottoman sultan, Suleiman the Magnificent, advanced from Constantinople with 70,000 to 80,000 men on April 23, 1526, to invade Hungary.

Try as he might, Hungary's King Louis was unable to rally the other European states to his kingdom's defense. Louis nevertheless did what he could. He gathered troops and, with about 12,000 cavalry and 13,000 infantry, moved to Mohács by August 15. Some warned Louis that Suleiman had 300,000 men, but Archbishop Tomori, a renowned Hungarian soldier, correctly assessed Ottoman strength and denigrated the capabilities of any Muslim army. Encouraged, Louis decided to take a stand. On August 28 Suleiman reached the southern edge of the Plain of Mohács, where his advance reconnaissance cavalry sighted the Hungarian army arrayed for battle in the center of the plain, southwest of the town of Mohács. Suleiman recognized this flat, open expanse as ideal cavalry ground.

Louis arranged his infantry—a combination of Hungarians and mostly German mercenary troops—in three great phalanxes before the town. The left flank of the infantry was covered by marshes along the Danube, but the right flank was fully exposed. Many of Louis's infantry-men were armed with arquebuses, and he also had about 20 cannon. These he arrayed in front of the central infantry phalanx. He deployed most of his cavalry in the spaces between the three infantry phalanxes, keeping one formation in the rear as a reserve.

Suleiman arrayed his army for battle in three lines. The two front lines consisted of Turkish feudal cavalrymen called timariots. Behind these, Suleiman deployed his Janissaries—elite infantry. The Turkish artillery was in front of the Janissaries, and spahis—North African light cavalry troops—were positioned on the Janissaries' flanks. Suleiman sent a unit of 6,000 timariots on a long sweeping gallop to the west, so that they could position themselves for a surprise attack on the exposed Hungarian right as soon as the armies were fully engaged. The gently rolling hills surrounding the battleground screened their preparatory maneuvers.

On August 29, as the Ottomans advanced, the Hungarians opened up on them with cannon fire. This was followed by a charge of the Hungarian first-line heavy cavalry. The combination of the barrage and the charge drove back Suleiman's first line, prompting the whole of the Hungarian army to advance.

The Hungarian artillery could not keep pace with the advance, and at the precise moment that the Hungarian cavalry charged, Suleiman's second line, those 6,000 timariots, descended on their unprotected right flank, initially wreaking havoc. The second line of Hungarian cavalry, however, rode up to drive off the flank attack, and both Hungarian cavalry lines now smashed through the Turkish second line. At this high point, the Hungarians charged against the third Turkish line, focusing on its center. This is when Suleiman's artillery fired, rapidly piling up heavy casualties. Worse, the charging cavalry could not break through the line of cannons because they were chained together.

The Battle of Mohács is depicted in this sixteenth-century Turkish miniature in the collection of the Castle of Szigetvár, Budapest.
NATIONAL MUSEUM OF HUNGARY, BUDAPEST

While the badly disrupted Hungarians were stalled, the Janissaries and spahis counterattacked, dispersing the depleted and exhausted Hungarian cavalry, which broke and fled in great disorder. Having themselves suffered severe casualties, however, Suleiman's forces did not give chase in any organized way. Independently, some of the timariot units rallied and harassed the fleeing Hungarians. The harassment turned into a rout in which 10,000 Hungarian infantry and 5,000 cavalry were killed. The Ottomans gave no quarter to the handful of prisoners they took, summarily beheading them.

Worst of all, the Hungarian defenders, King Louis and Archbishop Tomori, along with most of the other commanders, were killed in action. Leaderless, the survivors of the routed forces scattered in all directions. Although the Ottoman army was similarly battered, it remained intact and, of course, had been larger to begin with.

Suleiman paused for a full three days to reorganize his ragged but victorious forces before advancing to take and occupy Buda (today, Budapest) on September 10. The demoralized Hungarian military offered no resistance. For his part, Suleiman declined to annex Hungary. Instead he proclaimed it a tributary kingdom under John Zápolya of Transylvania, who had turned traitor against Hungary by absenting himself from the Battle of Mohács. This ignited a civil war in Hungary from 1526 to 1528. In 1527, at the Battle of Tokay, Ferdinand of Hapsburg—brother-in-law of the slain King Louis and brother of Holy Roman Emperor Charles V—having re-formed a new Hungarian army around a German contingent, defeated John Zápolya, who subsequently called on Suleiman to help him.

In 1528 Suleiman made a secret alliance with France against the Hapsburgs, and during 1529 he invaded Hungary yet again with more than 80,000 men in addition to 6,000 Hungarians led by John Zápolya. These combined forces captured Buda during September 3–8, massacring the garrison that held it. Then they marched on Vienna. Suleiman invested the city beginning on September 23, laying full siege from September 27 to October 15. Against very strong resistance, Suleiman finally withdrew—after killing all his adult male prisoners. Austrian forces gave chase but were unable to destroy the Ottoman army, which renewed its invasion of Austria-Hungary in 1532. The following year, Suleiman made peace with Ferdinand of Hapsburg, who, along with John Zápolya, agreed to pay tribute to the Ottomans. At this, Suleiman turned from Europe to pursue conquests in Asia.

The Battle of Mohács awakened Europe to the formidable might of the Ottoman Empire and created a tortured political relationship between the Hapsburg monarchy and the Ottoman Empire as the two presided over a partitioned Hungary. This became the tinderbox interface between Christian Europe and Muslim Asia Minor and would remain so well into the nineteenth century. The Battle of Mohács effectively ended the Middle Ages in Hungary, the last region of Europe that had clung to feudalism.

The Holy League Triumphs at Lepanto: Victory at Sea (1571)

During August and September 1571, Admiral Pasha Ali Monizin-dade waged relentless naval warfare against Venetian possessions in the Aegean and Ionian Seas before sailing into the Adriatic and to within sight of Venice itself. Before he could launch an attack, however, he learned that an allied Christian fleet was being assembled at the coastal city of Messina, Sicily. In response, he immediately made sail to return to the waters of the Ionian Sea, between the Adriatic to the north and the Mediterranean to the south. By September 22, the Christian fleet, comprising about 300 vessels of all kinds, had gathered at Messina under the command of Don Juan of Austria. Having rallied, they sailed the next day, bound for the Gulf of Corinth in search of the Ottoman fleet.

Early on the morning of October 7, 1571, one of Juan's lookouts sighted the Turkish fleet at Lepanto, a port—today known as Nafpaktos—on a bay of the north coast of the Gulf of Corinth. Available for immediate engagement among Juan's fleet were 108 Venetian galleys, 81 Spanish galleys, and 32 other vessels contributed by the pope and small Christian countries. In addition, Don Juan had six Venetian galleasses, very large warships converted for military use from large merchant vessels. Slower and less maneuverable than standard, smaller galleys, they were equipped with 32 oars but nevertheless required the assistance of sails to navigate. Whatever their drawbacks in speed and maneuverability, these large vessels packed superior firepower. Tactically they were the precursors to the ship of the line, which was itself the sail-era precursor of the battleship. Any vessel coming into broadside with such a ship was exposed to massive cannon fire.

On the approach of the Christian fleet, the entire Ottoman fleet sallied out from Lepanto. Ali had more ships, 270 galleys, but most were smaller than the Christian vessels, and it was almost certainly the case that their crews were less experienced than those of seafaring states such as Venice. Naval warfare had changed little since ancient times, and the opposing fleets deployed in a traditional battle formation. Each fleet assembled in a long line of three divisions, with a reserve division held in the rear. There is no documentary evidence that either admiral approached the battle with an elaborate plan. Some military historians, however, conclude that because the Ottoman left wing was larger than its right, Ali intended to envelop the enemy fleet. But the bottom line is that in sixteenth-century naval warfare, the objective was to use each vessel's complement of small cannon to fire as many broadsides as possible. Even more, captains sought to ram and board however many enemy ships they could and to do so as quickly as possible. A sea battle during this period was less about maneuvering than about brawling and boarding. Armed with much larger cannon, the giant galleasses were commanded with the objective of acquiring broadside positions to unleash cannonades capable of sinking the opposing vessel.

Boarding was executed by the soldiers both fleets carried aboard their vessels. The Christian ships held about 20,000 marines, and the Ottoman ships carried some 16,000 for boarding purposes. Some of the Christian marines were armed with arquebuses, long guns, or hand cannons, that appeared in the fifteenth century. Their Ottoman counterparts were armed mostly with bows or crossbows. While the Christians donned light armor, the Turks generally had none.

The fleets, totaling more than 400 warships, were about to fight the largest naval battle in Western history, at least since classical antiquity, and the opposing lines extended over five miles. The fighting began about 10:30 in the morning,

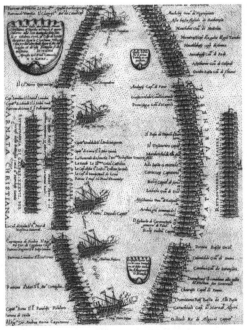

This 1574 map by Camocio Giovanni Francesco shows the disposition of the Venetian and Ottoman fleets at the 1571 Battle of Lepanto.
WIKIMEDIA COMMONS

with clashes erupting all along the lines at an accelerating tempo and with increasingly destructive effect. By noon, both sides were fully engaged in all-out combat, and the great galleasses smashed through the Ottoman line, disrupting it but not decisively so. Instead, chaotic combat raged at full volume for some three hours. Everything depended on the skill of individual captains and their crews, not the upper-echelon commanders. As it stood, the Christian sailors were more experienced and skillful, and they were also better armed. Added to these advantages was a wind that favored the direction of their attack. Gradually, these factors brought the battle to its crisis when the Ottoman right flank, never able to get far from land and the shallows, was driven back against the shore. Run aground, the vessels became sitting ducks and were quickly disposed of. Closer to the center, the battle raged longer, but eventually the Christian fleet prevailed.

It was a different story on the Ottoman left flank, the longest and most numerous of the three lines of battle. Led by Ouloudj Ali, dey of Algiers, a highly skilled naval commander, this flank gave as good as it got—until Ali realized what had happened to the other two lines of the fleet. Isolated and outnumbered, he broke off the battle and managed to escape with only 47 of the 95 vessels under his command. He also possessed one captured Venetian galley.

Ali's 47 ships were the only Ottoman vessels that survived the battle. Sixty others ran aground, 53 were sunk, and a spectacular 117 captured. From the Ottoman fleet, 15,000 Christian rower slaves were rescued and liberated. It is estimated, however, that perhaps 10,000 such slaves drowned in combat. Ottoman losses were between 15,000 and 20,000 Turkish sailors and marines either killed or drowned. Although the Christians captured more than 100 ships, just 300 prisoners were taken. Christian losses were 13 galleys, 7,566 sailors and marines killed, and about 8,000 wounded, including Miguel de Cervantes, who, despite the loss of his left hand, would go on to enduring fame as the author of *Don Quixote*, the first novel by a modern Western author.

It being October and storms likely, Don Juan of Austria decided against pursuing the relatively few vessels that had fled. Nor did he otherwise seek to exploit the massive victory that had been achieved. Further action at sea would have to wait until spring. Nevertheless, Lepanto was among history's most consequential naval battles. It demonstrated the strategic importance of large-scale naval warfare and of major, well-coordinated naval alliances. It brought Christian Europe into rare cooperative harmony, if only rather briefly, and it ended Ottoman domination of the central and western Mediterranean. It was the turning point against Islam's second major assault on Christian Europe. As for the narrower history of naval warfare, Lepanto was the last large-scale battle in the Western world fought between rowed galleys. It therefore marked the spectacular end of a naval tradition that had begun with triremes of the ancient Greek city-states. As warships came to depend increasingly on sails, battle tactics would shift from brute-force engagements to maneuver.

Fate of the Spanish Armada: The "Friction of War" (1586–1588)

Grande y Felicisima Armada, the "Great and Most Fortunate Navy," better known as the Spanish Armada, was a Spanish fleet of 130 ships intended to convoy an army from Flanders to invade England for the purpose of overthrowing Protestant Queen Elizabeth I and restoring Catholicism to her realm. The idea of an armada was recommended to Spain's King Philip II by Admiral Marquis de Santa Cruz, and it was commanded by the Duke of Parma, commander in the Spanish Netherlands.

During April–June, Sir Francis Drake, greatest of England's celebrated "Sea Dogs"—naval raiders—was made aware of Spain's plans. He immediately secured Elizabeth I's permission to lead an English fleet of 23 ships to raid a portion of the Spanish invasion fleet at Cádiz. His raid sank 33 vessels. On his return

An unknown artist painted this spectacular depiction of the Spanish Armada departing from Ferrol, Spain, in August 1588.
WIKIMEDIA COMMONS

from the mission, he led his fleet in attacks on more Spanish shipping, including, in the Azores, a rich treasure galleon, which he captured, greatly enriching the queen's war chest.

Admiral Santa Cruz worked feverishly to repair the damage caused by Drake's raid, but he died—of natural causes—on January 30, 1588, before the expedition was ready to sail for England. At 62, he was not a young man, but many believed he had succumbed not to age but to the continual badgering demands of the Spanish king. Whatever the cause of his death, this unpredictable and uncontrollable event was the first of two destined to doom the Armada. Most historians accept that Santa Cruz was singularly suited to command this difficult mission. He was that rare and important actor in history—the indispensable man. His replacement, Alonso Pérez de Guzmán, Duke of Medina Sidonia, though noble and brave, had no naval experience—or, for that matter, military experience of any kind. He was assisted by Admiral Diego de Valdez, and the fleet carried with it the Duke of Parma, who would assume overall command of the expedition once it reached the Netherlands.

Formerly attributed to George Gower, the Portrait of Elizabeth I of England—also known as "The Armada Portrait"—depicts the queen, left hand resting comfortably on a globe, after the defeat of the Spanish Armada. The ships of the Armada are depicted through the window. On the left-hand side, they are portrayed early in the enterprise; on the right, after meeting catastrophe in storm and battle.
NATIONAL PORTRAIT GALLERY, LONDON

For her part, Elizabeth I selected Lord Howard of Effingham to command the English fleet, with master seaman Drake, a commoner, relegated to the role of vice admiral. Howard, who had only slight naval experience, wisely relied on Drake's expertise. He backed Drake's recommendation to Elizabeth that she authorize a new expedition to raid Spanish ports to prevent the Armada from sailing. She unwisely rejected this advice but did diligently raise a force of 60,000 soldiers to repel the anticipated invasion.

The Armada set sail from Lisbon on May 20, waited out a storm at Corunna, then left that port on July 12, 1588. It consisted of 20 great galleons, multi-decked vessels that were the largest warships in the Spanish navy at the time, 44 armed merchantmen, 23 transports, 35 smaller vessels, 4 galleasses (very large oared warships), and 4 galleys (smaller oared warships). The fleet was manned by 8,500 seamen and galley slaves and carried 19,000 troops. In total, the Spanish warships mounted 2,431 cannon, of which nearly half were heavy pieces, including about 600 culverins, capable of long range. The rest of the artillery were light antipersonnel weapons intended to "clear the decks" of enemy ships to be boarded and to repel enemy boarders.

On July 19 English reconnaissance ships sighted the Armada off The Lizard on the Cornish coast. The next day, Howard departed Plymouth to meet the Armada. He commanded his own fleet of 34 ships; Drake led another 34, also out of Plymouth. A 30-ship squadron was based in London and a 23-ship squadron off the Downs in the eastern English Channel. An additional 50-odd vessels were available mainly as transports and supply ships. In all, the English defensive fleet mounted about 1,800 heavy cannon.

The English first engaged the Armada off Plymouth on July 21, sinking one Spanish ship and seriously damaging others. It was quickly evident that the English were capable of both outsailing and outfighting the Armada—at least in this initial battle. Two days later, on July 23, there was an inconclusive action off the coast of Devon; two days after that, in an intense battle off Dorset, the English made generous use of their ammunition. Fighting in home waters, they had access to abundant supplies. Not so the Spanish. Having been forced to fight much harder than anticipated, Medina Sidonia realized that his vessels were in desperate need of taking on ammunition. Instead of landing on the Isle of Wight, as he had intended, which would have served as a staging platform for invasion, he set sail along the English Channel bound for Calais. Here he planned to replenish his magazines from the Duke of Parma's ample stores.

By July 26–27, the Armada lay at anchor off Calais, awaiting replenishment. By this time, Howard had assembled 136 ships, which he deployed in four squadrons commanded by himself, Drake, Sir John Hawkins, and Sir Martin Frobisher—the last three all celebrated Sea Dogs. Cautious and less experienced than they, Howard fired on the Spanish from long range, fearful of being boarded by the large complement of soldiers carried on the Armada. As for Medina

Sidonia, he called on the Duke of Parma to assist him, but the duke could not leave Bruges, Belgium, because a Dutch fleet was blockading him.

At last, off the coast of Flanders, Howard sent a number of fire ships into the Spanish fleet during the predawn hours of July 28. Medina Sidonia ordered all anchor cables cut, so that his vessels could evade the enemy fire ships drifting toward them. His plan was to return to anchorage once the fire danger was over, but the Spanish captains succumbed to panic amid the flames and the darkness. Their ships caught unfavorable winds and drifted apart from one another, losing the protection of the formation. Seeing their chance, the English pursued and at last closed in on the ships of the Armada. A daylong running fight now unfolded at close quarters. The small guns of the Spaniards were no match for the English heavy cannon.

Sailing to windward, the English captains concentrated their fire against individual ships, firing alternate broadsides. With their heavy ammunition having been exhausted, the exchange of fire was one-sided. Yet no Spanish vessels were sunk. The English were able to close in to board and capture 15 of the most badly damaged vessels, but a sudden squall brought an end to the main battle.

During July 29–30, more unfavorable winds prevented the Armada from breaking the Dutch blockade off the Flanders coast and obtaining the much-needed ammunition. After the fleet was almost driven aground on Zeeland, Medina Sidonia decided to abort the invasion and return to Spain via the North Sea. This required a course that completely circled the British Isles.

En route to the North Sea inlet, the Armada managed to reconcentrate itself. The English fleet pursued but, running short of provisions, returned to their homeports while the Armada passed the Firth of Forth on August 2. The Spanish mariners had failed in their mission of invasion, but at least they had outrun the menace of the English defensive fleet. Yet their ordeal was far from over. During August and September, the Armada contended with acute shortages of rations and water, leading to starvation among the crews. Heavy storms struck after the Armada rounded the Orkney Islands to head southwest along the western coasts of Scotland and Ireland. Of the 130 ships constituting the Spanish Armada, 63 were known to be lost. The English sank or captured 15, and 19 were wrecked in storms. No one knows what became of the other 33. The Spanish death toll overall was about 20,000.

The early nineteenth-century military theorist Carl von Clausewitz (1780–1831) famously wrote of the "friction of war," the numberless imponderables of human frailty, chance, weather, and the sheer physical demands of combat that distinguish war as fought from war as planned. Military history offers no more dramatic example of this "friction" than the ordeal of the Spanish Armada. The death of its original commander and the onset of severe storms combined with the skill of English mariners and the superiority of their weapons defeated the planned amphibious invasion of England.

The defeat of the Armada also profoundly influenced naval tactics. It introduced the art of exploiting "weather gage" (taking advantage of fighting upwind from an enemy vessel) and proved the value of using cannon to sink enemy ships rather than merely to support boarding parties. After the Armada, the English invested in heavier naval artillery and focused on improving naval architecture while intensifying the training of officers and crews. The defeat of the Spanish Armada set a standard for victory at sea that would endure well into the mid-nineteenth century and the twilight of the era of sail.

"Defenestration of Prague" Begins the Thirty Years' War: Old Europe Out the Window (1618)

At 10:19 on the morning of May 23, 1618, a mob of Bohemian Protestants stormed the Hradčany (Prague Castle) and "defenestrated"—pushed out of a window—three representatives of the Catholic king of Bohemia, the Austrian Hapsburg Archduke Ferdinand. The men survived the 60-foot fall, but Europe was thrown into the Thirty Years' War, the bloodiest to that time, with estimates of those killed ranging from 3 million to 11.5 million. Indeed, some historians consider it the deadliest conflict ever fought within the confines of Europe. Rarely in history has a single, contained event—the spontaneous act not of a nation but of a mob—proved the catalyst of so momentous and destructive a war.

The seventeenth century would become known as the Age of Enlightenment, but in that century, the Holy Roman Empire was far more medieval than enlightened. It was a collection of miscellaneous principalities, dukedoms, and city-states loosely governed by an emperor of the Austrian branch of the Hapsburg dynasty. He shared power with an imperial parliament, the Diet, which struggled to keep the constituent states in line. In truth, all that bound them together was allegiance to the Roman Catholic Church, which was now under threat by the Protestant Reformation.

In Bohemia, the Reformation had been started by Jan Hus in the fifteenth century, a full hundred years before a Saxon monk named Martin Luther launched the much larger Protestant revolution with his "95 Theses" of 1517. After another hundred years, in 1618, the Holy Roman Empire had become less and less Roman, Protestantism having made significant inroads throughout it. Within the Protestant movement was a wide spectrum of religious belief, and Bohemia became a cauldron of theological and nationalist ferment. The only way to prevent the jarring religious factions from exploding into war was through religious toleration, which Rudolph II, Holy Roman Emperor from 1576 to 1612, had granted in 1609 via his "Letter of Majesty." This policy was honored by his successor, Matthias, but not by Archduke Ferdinand of Austria, who became king of Bohemia upon Matthias's death in 1617 and would go on to election as Holy Roman Emperor in 1619.

Ferdinand had an uncompromising belief that the dynastic and territorial integrity of his empire depended on complete religious unity. The Holy Roman Empire had to be a Catholic empire. Although Ferdinand publicly declared his intention to honor the "Letter of Majesty," he responded to a Lutheran request to build two new churches by expropriating the land on which these were to be built and turning over the property to the Catholic Church. Local Protestants rose up in protest and were promptly arrested. Protestant leaders then demanded their release. When Ferdinand refused, demonstrators led by Count Jindřich Thurn, a Bohemian Protestant nationalist, gathered outside Prague Castle. Protestant deputies of the Diet soon arrived at the castle, demanding a showdown meeting with Catholic deputies. Many of Thurn's demonstrators followed the Protestant deputies into the castle, and as many as possibly could crowded into the small chamber where four Catholic deputies sat. The Protestant deputies demanded to know if Ferdinand had ordered his Bohemian subjects to bow to his will. They also wanted the Catholic deputies to tell them whether they agreed with such a demand. Two of the Catholics pleaded ignorance and innocence and were allowed to leave the chamber. Two others, Count Vilém Slavata and Count Jaroslav Borsita von Martinitz, made no such plea, and Thurn encouraged the Protestant mob inside the room to show them no mercy. They rushed the two men, pressing them against the tall windows. One among them unlocked the casement, and Martinitz was ejected through the open window to what could only be assumed was certain death. Slavata struggled, clawing at the window frame. Someone knocked him unconscious, however, and he too was flung out. Worked up to a frenzy, the Protestants next seized the deputies' secretary, Philip Fabricius, and hurled him through the open window.

Astoundingly, Martinitz and Fabricius, despite their 60-foot fall, scrambled to their feet on the flagstone pavement below and ran for it. Some in the crowd below, presumably Slavata's servants, carried him away as well, unconscious but alive.

Predictably, Catholics and Protestants offered differing accounts of the survival of the three defenestrated men. The Catholics deemed it a miracle of God— and a clear message as to which side was in the right. The Protestants, in contrast, testified that all three men had had the good fortune to fall on a dung heap, the size of which was commensurate with the size of Prague Castle, reputedly the largest castle in Europe. Some recent scholars suggest that the three men had actually been carried to a lower floor of the castle and tossed out a window— never with the intention of assassination but merely of humiliation.

It matters little. This brutal event with its comic-opera overtones was sufficient to touch off the most catastrophic war Europe would see until the outbreak of World War I in 1914. An issue of Bohemian rebellion against domination by the Austrian Empire combined with the religious conflict of the Reformation to quickly spread far beyond Prague and Bohemia, engulfing the Austrian and

Spanish Hapsburgs and their realms, together with the states of the Holy Roman Empire, as well as France, the Dutch Republic, Denmark, and Sweden. The battlefield was focused on much of Central Europe, which was ravaged by three decades of war. Between deaths caused directly by military action and those resulting from the destruction of farmlands, villages, towns, and cities, the territory most deeply engaged in combat lost between 25 and 40 percent of its population to military action, famine, and disease.

Gustavus Adolphus at Zenith: Creating Military Supremacy (1631)

During the Thirty Years' War, Sweden's King Gustavus Adolphus emerged as one of European history's most efficient dispensers of military devastation. His single greatest tactical innovation was the use of combined-arms tactics. Most notably, he joined squads of musketeers to cavalry units to provide them with fire support. He also attached light field artillery—3-pounder guns—to infantry units, giving their commanders integrated "organic" artillery support. The Swedish monarch came to the aid of German Lutherans against the Catholics, and this meant devastating as much of the Holy Roman Empire in Germany as he could. Here the Swedish army destroyed some 1,500 towns, 18,000 villages, and 2,000 castles between 1630 and 1635.

When Gustavus Adolphus assumed the crown in 1611, Sweden's army was weak, poorly organized, and ineptly led. His initial focus was on recruitment and training, the latter begun the moment a recruit entered the service and continued throughout his service in the army. Gustavus instilled harsh but just discipline, and as the Swedish army racked up a record of victories, morale became a formidable asset.

Gustavus focused on the squadron as the basic unit of maneuver. Each Swedish squadron consisted of 408 soldiers, including 216 pikemen and 192 musketeers, making the combined-arms concept central to the very structure of Swedish forces. In battle, pikemen were characteristically formed into a central block that was six men deep, a formation that allowed four ranks to wield their pikes forward and to the flanks freely. The musketeers were deployed in two wings, six deep, on either side of the pikemen. An additional formation of musketeers was attached to each squadron and was typically deployed on detached duty as outpost sentries and scouts. Three to four squadrons were grouped into a brigade.

The combination of firepower with the pike proved overwhelming. Gustavus's principal tactic of maneuver was the countermarch, in which firepower was maintained almost continuously by rotating the front-rank musketeers to the rear to reload after firing, thereby allowing what had been the second rank to fire. Increasingly intensive training soon taught Gustavus's musketeers to reload considerably faster than what was the norm at the time. This meant that *two* ranks could fire simultaneously and then countermarch together to reload. In this way, the effect of each volley was multiplied by a factor of two. Indeed, the speed and efficiency of the king's musketeers was such that the Swedes perfected a kind of small-arms rolling barrage. They also employed marching fire, advancing while discharging their volleys—protected all the while by the pikemen. At intervals, musketeers were instructed to fire more than a volley. The "salvo" delivered the combined firepower of *three* ranks simultaneously. When this tactic was employed, the pikemen's role became all the more critical, since they had to defend one-half of the musketeer contingent while the men reloaded.

Gustavus did not restrict his pikemen to a defensive role. They were trained not only for force protection but also to deliver the culminating, decisive blow at the climax of an engagement. The musket salvo was generally the signal to bring an encounter to a decision. It was the overture to a massed pike assault, which was the Swedish army's ultimate shock tactic. To render the pike more effective as an assault weapon, Gustavus personally redesigned it. In its traditional version, the pike was some 16 feet long and fashioned mostly of wood. Gustavus shortened it to 11 feet and fully sheathed more of the business end with iron so that the weapon could not be shattered by the blow of a sword. The pike, which was considered obsolescent by the seventeenth century, was now transformed into a versatile modern weapon capable of both defense and offense.

In focusing on his infantry, Gustavus did not neglect the cavalry, whose troopers were armed not only with the traditional saber but also with pistols. The saber charge remained the primary cavalry tactic, however. Only the first rank of horsemen discharged their pistols as they closed with the enemy. They then switched to sabers, and the second two ranks behind them used sabers exclusively—reserving their loaded muskets for dire emergencies. Adhering to the combined-arms approach, Gustavus always positioned detached musketeers between cavalry squadrons to provide suppressing fire before a charge began. Then, while the cavalry charge was under way, the musketeers reloaded in preparation to support a second charge or, if need be, to cover a cavalry retreat. For good measure, cannon attached to the infantry would provide artillery support throughout the engagement.

Combining cavalry with infantry was controversial, since infantry necessarily slowed the initial approach of the cavalry, exacting a price in lost momentum. Yet, time and again, the combined-arms approach proved highly effective and eventually was imitated by most European armies.

Gustavus Adolphus had the services of Lennart Torstensson, who was considered the premier artillerist in Europe. He organized the Swedish artillery into six-company regiments. Four of these companies consisted of gunners, one of sappers (who cleared ground for the placement of artillery), and one of troops who specialized in the use of explosive devices. In addition to artillery deployed independently, each regiment of infantry and cavalry was equipped with one or two 3-pounders, which served as the regimental gun, providing close combined-arms support. The Swedish system greatly increased the flexibility of forces and concentrated much of the tactical leadership of the army in each small-unit commander. This initiated a revolution in military art and science, which shifted much of the conduct of battle from the high-ranking field officers to those of company rank and also elevated the position of the individual soldier. In short, those most closely engaged with the enemy assumed the greatest command responsibility.

The impact of the innovations of Gustavus Adolphus was felt most strongly in the Battle of Breitenfeld, fought four miles north of Leipzig on September 17, 1631. The forces of the Holy Roman Empire were commanded by the Count of Tilly and his chief subordinate, Gottfried zu Pappenheim, who chose Breitenfeld as the place to take a stand against the forces led by Gustavus. Tilly and Pappenheim had some 35,000 men against a combined Swedish and Saxon force of 28,750 available for the battle. Tilly commanded the center and right wing of the imperial forces, Pappenheim the left. Gustavus arrayed his lines facing those of Tilly and Pappenheim, putting the Saxon infantry mostly on the left, the Swedish infantry (with some German units) in the center, and the Swedish cavalry on the right. Pappenheim made the first move, a sweeping attack that targeted the Swedish reserve force. Gustavus's cavalry, however, was flexible and swiftly wheeled toward Pappenheim's attack, pinning his forces between itself and the reserves. This almost instantly dissolved Pappenheim's attack, sending the Catholic troops into disordered flight.

In the meantime, Tilly's right wing attacked the Saxons and drove them from the field. Acting quickly to capitalize on his advantage, Tilly swung around to hit the exposed Swedish left flank but was checked by a swift Swedish shift to the left, which repulsed his attack. Assuming personal command, Gustavus now led his right-wing cavalry, which was closely followed by his infantry, in a sweep around Tilly's left flank. Gustavus recaptured the guns that had been lost in the flight of the Saxons and also took much of the imperial artillery, which Tilly had left behind when he launched his attack on the Swedish left. Gustavus severed the Catholic lines of communication and turned the recaptured Saxon artillery as well as the captured imperial artillery against Tilly and Pappenheim. This shattered the imperial army, which broke and ran while the Swedes pursued until darkness.

Tilly lost 7,000 killed and 6,000 captured. He also suffered grievous wounds. What was left of his forces withdrew from Leipzig the next day, and Gustavus took the city. He had lost 2,000 of his Swedes, and the Saxons lost 4,000. It was a costly but decisive victory that attracted numerous Protestant German states to ally themselves with Sweden against the German Catholic League and the Holy Roman Empire. Gustavus Adolphus was killed the following year, on November 6, 1632, at the Battle of Lützen, a Protestant victory that was badly blunted by his death, which strengthened the Catholic French and greatly reduced the Swedish role in the Thirty Years' War.

Total Warfare Sweeps New England: Race Wars in the Wilderness (1636–1678)

Christopher Columbus set sail on January 15, 1493, for the return leg of his first voyage to America. He left behind a small Spanish garrison at a place he called La Navidad and which is today Cap Haitien, Haiti. No sooner did he leave than the garrison began pillaging native goods and raping native women. The "Indians" (as Columbus called them) retaliated. When Columbus returned to America on his second voyage in November 1493, he found no one from the garrison left alive.

We might consider this the first of many, many wars between Native Americans and Euro-Americans, a series of conflicts that did not end until nearly 400 years later. By the seventeenth century, New England was the scene of racial warfare of a kind that a later generation would term "total war"—war fought not strictly between armies but against entire populations, combatants and noncombatants alike.

In 1634 an English sea captain named John Stone was killed as his ship lay at anchor at the mouth of the Connecticut River. Stone had a nasty reputation as a pirate who had unsuccessfully attempted to hijack a vessel in New Amsterdam, had brandished a knife in the face of the governor of Plymouth Colony, and had been deported from the Massachusetts Bay Colony for drunkenness and adultery. No matter. When Stone turned up dead, New Englanders demanded action against the Pequots, who made their home in the Connecticut River Valley.

As far as we can determine, the Pequots did not want any trouble with their white neighbors. In any case, no one accused any Pequot of having killed Stone. It was generally believed that the murder was the work of a member or members of the Niantic tribe, which was considered a kind of Pequot client tribe. In an effort to avoid a war, Pequot leaders accepted responsibility for the incident and signed a treaty with the Massachusetts Bay Colony in which they promised to surrender those guilty of the killing. They also agreed to pay an indemnity, relinquish rights to a large tract of Connecticut land, and henceforth trade exclusively with the English rather than with rival Dutch colonists.

Although a part of the indemnity was soon paid, the Pequots claimed that all the murderers were dead except for two, who had escaped. The Massachusetts Bay colonists were outraged but made no reprisal for some two years. Then, on June 16, 1636, Mohegan Indians warned the English that the Pequots, fearful that the colonists were preparing to take action against them, were about to

An illustration from Francis S. Drake and Francis Joseph Dowd's *Indian History for Young Folks* depicting the death of King Philip, the Wampanoag sachem. The book was published in New York by Harper & Brothers in 1919.

launch a preemptive strike. Massachusetts Bay leaders summoned Pequot leaders to a conference at Fort Saybrook, Connecticut, and agreements were reached that averted violence.

Unfortunately, word soon arrived of the death of another sea captain, John Oldham, off Block Island. The perpetrators this time were Narragansetts or members of a tribe subject to them. Narragansett sachems wasted no time in sending some 200 warriors to avenge Oldham's death on behalf of the colony, but Massachusetts Bay authorities dispatched Captain John Endecott to Block Island with orders to seize the Indians' stores of wampum, slaughter all the men they encountered, and take captive the women and children for sale as slaves in the West Indies. Learning of these intentions, the Indians fled. Frustrated at the escape of the Narragansetts, Endecott directed his wrath against the Pequots, burning their villages, which lay just beyond Fort Saybrook. This provocation was sufficient to incite Pequot retaliation throughout the Connecticut River Valley. Indians burned one English settlement after another, and the colonists responded against the Pequots in kind.

It was an apparently senseless beginning to a tragically senseless war, but there was a complicating motive. The Native Americans were becoming both players and pawns in a contest among competing European colonial powers. In the case of the Pequot Wars, both competitors were English. The Massachusetts Bay Colony and the settlers along the Connecticut River were locked in a dispute over possession of the fertile Connecticut River Valley. Whichever colony could assert dominion over the Pequots, whose country lay precisely within the disputed territory, would have a legal claim to the region. It is likely that Endecott, a soldier serving Massachusetts Bay, was spoiling for a fight in order to assert Massachusetts Bay's authority over the Pequots, thereby squeezing out the claims of Connecticut settlers.

The problem was that the competitiveness of the New England colonies made effective unified action against the Indians virtually impossible. The war took a terrible toll on the Pequots and colonists alike, and it was not until the spring of 1637 that the disparate colonial forces were able to enlist the aid of the Narragansetts, Eastern Niantics, and Mohegans—all bitter tribal rivals of the Pequots—to mount an effective counteroffensive. Captain John Mason, in command of the colonial-Indian coalition, attacked a village at Mystic, Connecticut, where he killed 600 to 700 Pequots—almost all women, children, and old men—in a "battle" that lasted perhaps an hour.

The Mystic massacre seems to have demoralized the Pequots, who were repeatedly defeated thereafter. On September 21, 1638, the Treaty of Hartford divided the Pequot prisoners of war as slaves among the allied tribes—the Mohegans, Narragansetts, and Niantics. The treaty stipulated that no Pequot could inhabit his former country again and that the very name "Pequot" would henceforth be forbidden to utter.

Destructive though the Pequot War was, it paled in comparison to King Philip's War, also in New England, which broke out less than 40 years after the conflict with the Pequots. Like that earlier war, it started with a murder. On June 11, 1675, a farmer, seeing an Indian stealing his cattle, pursued and killed him. The local Wampanoag chief, called Metacomet by the Indians and (with contempt) King Philip by the English, sought justice from the local garrison. The colonists rebuffed him, whereupon the Wampanoags exacted their own justice. They killed the farmer as well as the farmer's father and five neighboring settlers.

The war was on—though it had been brewing for some time before these violent incidents. Metacomet, King Philip, was the son of Massasoit, a Wampanoag sachem whose benevolence to the early New England settlers is the stuff of both history and legend. Massasoit's son, who experienced both the colonists' insatiable hunger for land and their contemptuous treatment of himself, felt anything but friendly. Beginning about 1662, he forged an anti-English alliance with the Narragansetts and the Nipmucks and began to raid colonial frontier settlements.

Initially, colonial efforts at defense were hobbled by the same lack of unity that had prevailed during the Pequot War. The New Englanders suffered very heavy losses during the first months of the war, and it was only after they finally managed to join forces as the United Colonies—as they dubbed themselves—that Massachusetts, Plymouth, Rhode Island, Connecticut, and the more remote "Eastern Colonies" in what are today Maine and New Hampshire began to gain the upper hand. By the time the war ended in 1676, half of New England's towns were badly damaged and at least a dozen wiped out. The colonial economy was shattered because of the disruption of the fur trade, coastal fishing, and the West Indian trade. Indeed, among the colonists, 1 in 16 men of military age was killed in King Philip's War. The Indians fared worse. Some 3,000 are known to have been killed, and many more were captured and sold into slavery in the West Indies. The Wampanoag, Narragansett, and Nipmuck tribes were decimated. Historians believe that, proportional to the population at the time, King Philip's War was—and remains to this day—the deadliest conflict in American history.

In the many wars between Euro-Americans and Native Americans that followed, the practice of total warfare prevailed, with combat operations not restricted to battle between soldiers and warriors but directed against whole populations. Throughout most of late eighteenth-century and nineteenth-century American military history, the U.S. Army served primarily as a police force intended to control and suppress indigenous people wherever they were perceived to interfere with the transcontinental expansion of Euro-American settlement.

Condé v. Turrenne at the Battle of the Dunes: Clash of the Great Captains (1658)

Louis II de Bourbon, Prince of Condé, known as le Grand Condé, and Henri de La Tour d'Auvergne, Viscount of Turenne, were the military titans of the Enlightenment. In them, strategy and tactics reached new heights and became benchmarks for European military performance through the seventeenth and eighteenth centuries. Napoleon deemed Turenne France's greatest general—excluding himself, of course—and rated Condé just behind him. During the Battle of Wagram (July 5–6, 1809), Napoleon had but one regret—that the great Turenne and Condé could not have fought beside him.

Condé and Turenne began their lives and their careers on the same side, fighting for France, but were fated to oppose each other in the 1658 Battle of the Dunes, which decided the Anglo-French victory in the Franco-Spanish War of 1648–1659. Military historians view that battle as an iconic contest between two "great captains," legendary masters of the art of war.

Born in Paris in 1621, Condé was educated by Jesuits and then attended the Royal Academy in the capital. His abilities were recognized early, and he was appointed governor of Burgundy in 1638, when he was just 17. Two years later he volunteered his services to the Army of Picardy and participated in the siege of Arras (1640) as well as the sieges of Aire (1641) and Perpignan, Collioure, and Salces (all in 1642). Condé made an advantageous union in marrying the niece of Cardinal Richelieu, the powerful chief minister to Louis XIII. This helped him win command of the Army of Flanders, with which he routed the Spanish Netherlands Army commanded by Francisco de Melo at the Battle of Rocroi on May 19, 1643. The battle was not just a crucial French triumph late in the Thirty Years' War but also an object of much admiration and study among Condé's fellow commanders.

Following the victory at Rocroi, Condé captured Thionville (August 16–23) and in 1624 raised a force in Champagne, which he united with that of the Viscount of Turenne on the upper Rhine. Turenne had been born in 1611 at Sedan. Fascinated from childhood by military history, he entered the army of his uncle, Maurice of Nassau, as a private after his father died in 1625. He saw his first action the very next year at the siege of Bois-le-Duc and performed with such dash and brilliance that he was promoted to captain in 1627.

In 1630 Turenne was made a regimental commander of French infantry and fought against Spain during 1630–1634, leading the 1634 assault on La Mothe in Lorraine during the Eighty Years' War. For this he was promoted to *maréchal de camp*, roughly the equivalent of major general. He continued from success to success, prompting Cardinal Mazarin, successor to Cardinal Richelieu, to elevate him to marshal of France. Mazarin tasked him with rehabilitating France's Army of Germany after it was crushed at the Battle of Tuttlingen on November 24, 1643. Turenne led that army in an invasion of the Black Forest in 1643, but finding Baron Franz von Mercy's Bavarian forces numerically superior, he fell back on the village of Breisach, where he joined forces with Condé's Army of Champagne. Together the two generals mounted a brilliant counteroffensive against Mercy, achieving a splendid victory at the Battle of Freiburg during August 3–9, 1644, a major engagement in the Thirty Years' War.

Turenne next led the French Army of Germany into Franconia in 1645, only to be defeated by Mercy in a surprise attack at Mergentheim on May 2, 1645. He withdrew quickly into Hesse and there regrouped. Condé soon joined him in Hesse, and the two invaded Bavaria, engaging Mercy at Allerheim on August 3, 1645. There the Bavarian commander was not only defeated but killed in action. Nevertheless, forces of the Archduke Leopold forced Condé and Turenne into retreat. Condé then returned to France while Turenne bided his time for a year before joining forces with

Painted by Charles-Philippe Larivière in 1837, *Battle of the Dunes (June 14th 1658)* shows the Viscount of Turenne, marshal general of France, directing his greatest victory.
PALACE OF VERSAILLES

Karl Gustav von Wrangel's Swedish army on August 10, 1646, near Giessen. With Wrangel, he enjoyed much success in campaigning throughout Bavaria.

During the French civil war known as the First Fronde (1648–1649), Turenne threw in his lot with the rebel Parlement de Paris during January–February 1649. That same year, Condé took command of loyal French Royalist forces and succeeded in pushing the rebels, including his former comrade in arms Turenne, from their entrenched positions at Charenton, near Paris, by February 8, 1649. Turenne fled to the Netherlands, but Condé did not long bask in his victory. He fell into a dispute with Cardinal Mazarin, who imprisoned him from January 18, 1650, to February 13, 1651. Embittered by this experience, Condé now offered his services to Spain and soon found himself at the head of the Spanish-allied French rebel army in the Second Fronde (1650–1653) rebellion. Turenne, in the meantime, decided to support Louis XIV during Condé's revolt in the Second Fronde.

Once again, Turenne warred against his former ally, defeating him at Given, in the Loire Valley, on April 7, 1652, and then at Porte de St. Antoine/St. Denis, outside Paris, on July 5. Turenne defeated the Spanish at Arras on August 25, 1654, and captured three more towns before the end of the year and another three during 1655, but he was defeated by Condé on July 16, 1656, at the Battle of Valenciennes in the Franco-Spanish War. Condé also bested Turenne at Cambrai in 1657, but at the Battle of the Dunes (June 14, 1658), near Spanish-held Dunkirk—at the time just north of the French frontier in the Spanish Netherlands—it was Turenne who defeated Condé, who had put himself in the service of Spain under Juan José de Austria.

While forces under Britain's Lord Protector Oliver Cromwell, to whom the French had promised Dunkirk in return for allying with France against Spain, blockaded the port at sea and provided some 6,000 infantrymen, Turenne confronted Spanish forces under Juan José, Spanish-allied French rebels under Condé, and several regiments of English, Scottish, and Irish royalists commanded by the Duke of York (later James II), who was seeking to defeat Cromwell and restore the British monarchy. Juan José fielded some 8,000 cavalrymen against just 6,000 under Turenne; but, Turenne noted, Juan José had left his artillery behind to avoid slowing his advance. He also unwisely deployed his forces on the dunes, his right flank on the sea and his left on the Bruges canal. Squeezed by the local geography, he had little room to maneuver, and Turenne was quick to exploit that vulnerability.

The opposing British contingents took the initial brunt of the battle as Turenne's French cavalry swung around the Spanish right wing, finding firm footing on the hard shingle beach that had been laid bare at ebb tide. While Cromwell's navy bombarded the Spanish reserve troops from the sea, Turenne confronted the cavalry charge Condé launched from the Spanish left flank. Condé took heavy losses but was nevertheless gaining the advantage when Juan José's Spanish troops in the center and right were suddenly overrun by an Anglo-French attack. The result was a defeat for both Juan José and Condé. Spain's loss of Dunkirk brought about the end of the Franco-Spanish War.

Condé sought and obtained a pardon from Louis XIV and was repatriated to France in January 1660. Louis XIV named Turenne marshal general on April 4, 1660, which made him supreme commander of the Army of France; eight years later, Condé was given command of a French army. Turenne died in battle on July 27, 1675, during the Dutch War (1672–1678). Condé had fought his own last great battle, at Seneffe, Belgium, the year before, on August 11, 1674, defeating the forces of William of Orange. Although le Grand Condé lived until 1686, severe gout sent him into a quiet retirement after Seneffe.

Battle of Blenheim: The Perfection of Alliance Warfare (1704)

England, Holland, and Austria, fearful of an alliance between France and Spain, formed a new anti-French Grand Alliance in 1701 after the Hapsburg King Charles II of Spain died in 1700, having chosen a Bourbon as his successor. The French supported Charles II's nominee, Philip of Anjou, grandson of Louis XIV, as his successor, but England, Holland, and Austria gave their support to the second son of Hapsburg emperor Leopold I, the obscure Bavarian Archduke Charles. This dispute ignited the War of the Spanish Succession on May 4, 1702, a conflict that not only engulfed much of Europe but also spread to European colonies in America in September 1702, when the South Carolina legislature authorized an expedition to seize the Spanish-held fort and town of St. Augustine, Florida. In America, the conflict was called Queen Anne's War.

The most important campaign of the European phase of the conflict, which did not end until 1713, was Blenheim, an Anglicization of Blindheim, a Bavarian village on the left bank of the Danube. In May 1704 Austria feared an invasion by Franco-Bavarian forces, an event that threatened the fall of Vienna as well as the collapse of the Grand Alliance, which included the Holy Roman Empire, Great Britain, the Dutch Republic, Hapsburg Spain, Prussia, Portugal, and Savoy. Seeking to save both Vienna and the alliance, John Churchill, First Duke of Marlborough and an illustrious ancestor of Winston Spencer Churchill, prime minister of Britain during 1940–1945 and 1951–1955, led his army in a daring surprise advance from the Netherlands down the Rhine Valley with the strategic objective of decisively defeating Maximilian II Emanuel, prince-elector of Bavaria, in his own principality along with his French allies. Only a third of Marlborough's force was British. Two out of every three of his soldiers were either German or Danish, and the duke had to exhibit singularly brilliant military leadership to earn their full confidence.

Marlborough chose his route of march specifically to dupe the French into pursuing him instead of advancing directly to Bavaria to reinforce Maximilian. Such a deception required elaborate planning and execution. Eighteenth-century warfare was not conducive to long marches, which required extensive logistical preparation to avoid shortages of supplies and provisions, to discourage desertions, and to ensure that the army did not melt away through privation and disease. In June, at Mundelsheim, Marlborough held a brief council of war with Margrave

Louis of Baden and Prince Eugene of Savoy to devise their plans. It was decided that Eugene would distract the principal French army, under François de Neufville, Duc de Villeroi, so that this substantial force would not intervene in Bavaria. Baden would accompany Marlborough in the advance against Maximilian.

Marlborough and Baden engaged Bavarian forces under the Comte d'Arco and the Marquis de Maffei at the Battle of Schellenberg on July 2, 1704. The battle was quickly won, at substantial cost to Marlborough and Baden (1,342 killed and 3,699 wounded out of a force of 22,000) who nevertheless inflicted devastating losses upon the Bavarians (some 5,000 killed, including many drowned in the Danube, and another 3,000 captured out of a force of 13,000 men).

Having achieved this victory, which secured Donauwörth, a key crossing over the Danube, Marlborough and Baden laid waste to the surrounding villages and countryside, seeking to draw Maximillian and his French allies into a quick showdown battle. In the meantime, Prince Eugene of Savoy, having discovered that the French force under the Duc de Tallard had eluded him, marched to join forces with Marlborough, who had sent Baden off to lay siege to Ingolstadt. On August 12, Eugene and Marlborough linked up at Blenheim, 10 miles west of Donauwörth. Together, their forces made up an army of 52,000. The

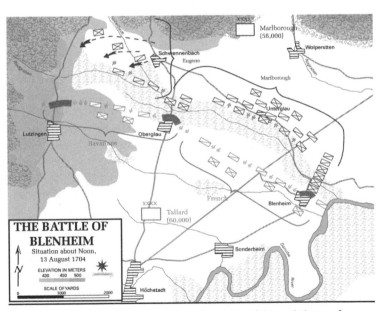

Marlborough's forces are arrayed at the upper right and those of Tallard to the lower left, both poised for a decisive battle at Blenheim on August 13, 1704.

THE DEPARTMENT OF HISTORY, UNITED STATES MILITARY ACADEMY

two commanders faced a Franco-Bavarian force of at least 56,000. Moreover, Marlborough and Eugene were outgunned, possessing some 66 artillery pieces to about 90 on the Franco-Bavarian side. The Duc de Tallard was in overall command of Franco-Bavarian forces, with Maximilian II Emanuel in charge of the Bavarian units and Ferdinand de Marsin commanding the French.

Marlborough and Eugene marched in nine columns and, reaching the battleground on August 13, deployed into position while covering their movements with suppressing fire from their artillery. Tallard was stunned—taken wholly by surprise. He scrambled to deploy and soon found himself in a vulnerable position between Blenheim and the Danube on his right and Lutzingen on his left. Oberglau, a fortified village, stood in the very center of his position. Eugene faced Marsin and Maximilian between Lutzingen and Oberglau. Marlborough faced Tallard from Oberglau to Blenheim.

When the battle began at 12:30 in the afternoon, the Franco-Bavarian forces deployed with infantry in the center and cavalry on the wings, the two wings meeting in Oberglau. Lord John Cutts, on Marlborough's extreme left, attacked the town of Blenheim twice, thereby drawing in the French reserves. This gave Marlborough an opportunity to attempt a breakthrough at Oberglau, the central hinge of Tallard's two armies. Simultaneously, Eugene attacked Maximilian and Marsin in an operation intended to pin them down, thereby preventing them from supporting or reinforcing Tallard elsewhere.

Eugene's attack served to distract Tallard while Marlborough advanced his infantry between his own two lines of cavalry, which he employed to repulse French cavalry charges. Neutralizing the French cavalry allowed Marlborough's infantry to deeply penetrate the Franco-Bavarian line. It was Marlborough who took personal command of the general cavalry countercharge that pushed the French horsemen back and by 5:30 in the afternoon breached Tallard's center at Oberglau. This opened the way for Marlborough's infantry to pour through the gap in Tallard's line, and Tallard became a prisoner of war. Now forces under Marlborough's brother, General Charles Churchill, who had been to the duke's right, shifted left and advanced directly against Blenheim. Fighting was fierce here, but with Tallard out of the battle, the outcome was not in doubt. The town fell at 11:00 that night.

Blenheim emerged as an ideal example of winning coalition warfare. Marlborough and Eugene were perfect complements to each other, coordinating a very complex attack and follow-on operation with flawless cooperation, synchronization, and harmony. Although outnumbered and outgunned, they exploited the element of surprise to inflict a devastating defeat on the Franco-Bavarian force. For losses of 12,484 (4,542 killed and 7,942 wounded), they exacted 27,190 casualties against Tallard, Marsin, and Maximilian II Emanuel—6,000 killed (many drowned in the Danube), 7,000 wounded, and 14,190 captured.

Marlborough and Eugene had not only created a military masterpiece but also saved both Vienna and the Grand Alliance. Yet the costly battle did not decide the war, which ground on until 1713, when King Louis XIV, at last war-weary and heavily burdened by debt, had become eager to end the conflict. Besides, the original source of the struggle—the issue of who would succeed to the Spanish throne—had been by this time rendered moot with the death of Archduke Charles, the Bavarian candidate for succession. Louis's grandson Philip became Spain's king by default, and the French monarch signed the Treaty of Utrecht on July 13, 1713, ending the main phase of the War of the Spanish Succession.

Frederick the Great of Prussia: The Making of a Military Superpower (1740–1763)

Frederick the Great, king of Prussia from 1740 until 1786, forged the beginnings of the modern nation of Germany, began its transformation into a formidable military power, and forever changed the face of European politics and history. Born in Berlin to the Prussian King Frederick William I and Sophia Dorothea of Hanover (daughter of England's King George I), the young Frederick loved art and music and was a passionate Francophile in matters of culture and aesthetics. His stern father, however, relentlessly imposed on the boy the Prussian military discipline he himself had invented. The essence of the Prussian army Frederick the Great would inherit was first distilled by his father.

Born in Berlin like his son, Frederick William I (1688–1740) was the son of Frederick I, who ruled as king of Prussia from 1688 to 1713. Frederick William I was educated in Prussian military schools already known for their discipline and rigid structure. Yet the throne he inherited in 1713 was faltering; Prussia's military was in decay. The new monarch set to work immediately to reconsolidate power in the crown and to rebuild the military. He instituted a regime of Spartan authoritarianism, demanding from civilians and soldiers alike nothing less than "unconditional obedience" to the state. Suspicious of the nobility, he imposed mandatory military service on the children of nobles and required state service from the parents themselves. In 1733 Frederick William I introduced universal conscription and created an elite officer corps, which was soon unmatched in Europe. At the same time, he strove to create efficiency in government, dissolving the hereditary court and, by a 1719 decree, freeing all serfs. In 1723 he established highly efficient ministries of war, finance, and domains, which did away with the traditionally corrupt methods of obtaining and distributing government funds. He then tripled the size of his military, creating a standing army of 80,000, so that by the time his son ascended to the throne in 1740, the military strength of Prussia ranked third in Europe, behind only Russia and France.

Young Frederick chafed under his father's autocratic discipline and, at age 18, fled to England. Frederick William responded by ordering his son's arrest and imprisonment and then threatened to put him to death. The young man returned to the palace at Rheinsberg, but he nevertheless managed to pursue some of his literary and artistic interests, becoming an accomplished flutist and a composer of considerable merit. When he was crowned on May 21, 1740, few in Europe had faith in Frederick's ability to lead. The Austrian ambassador famously observed that the new king was "a poet and can write a hundred lines in two hours. He could also be a musician, a philosopher, a physicist, or a mechanician. What he never will be is a general or warrior."

Within just seven months of his accession to the throne, Frederick marched on Silesia, firing the opening volley in the War of the Austrian Succession (1740–1748). Although his army was badly defeated in Silesia, he acquired that territory

Frederick the Great is depicted as a young commander in this painting from the 1740s, attributed to David Matthieu (1697–1756).

PHOTOGRAPH FROM VAN HAM KUNSTAUKTIONEN, WIKIMEDIA COMMONS

by treaty in 1742, and the kingdom of Prussia thus grew in size. His later military actions in the war were far more directly successful, and Frederick emerged as a superb military commander. Indeed, he took the best aspects of the army his father had created and improved them markedly. Unlike Sweden's Gustavus Adolphus or France's Napoleon, he was not a military revolutionary. Instead, he saw that for all its strengths, Prussian military command was characterized by a lack of tactical imagination and boldness and a tendency to excessively methodical ponderousness. The soldiers themselves, Frederick saw, needed training to improve their slow rate of fire. He resolved to improve these defects, becoming what might be best described as a conservative military innovator. He stressed mobility and speed in everything. He insisted that his soldiers drill relentlessly in the art of rapid fire. By some estimates, he doubled the effectiveness of the Prussian infantry.

Nor did Frederick the Great neglect the cavalry and the artillery. He learned from the examples of the Duke of Marlborough and Eugene of Savoy at the Battle of Blenheim (1704) to use cavalry with boldness and vigor. He even improved upon their example by emphasizing speed, especially in the early stages of an engagement. Always inferior to his enemies in numbers, Frederick the Great nevertheless insisted on seizing the initiative by attacking first.

To the cavalry he added artillery, inventing a new service arm, the horse artillery, which gave cannon fire unprecedented mobility. He accelerated the development of the howitzer, a light cannon capable of being transported rapidly in a cavalry context and designed to fire at high trajectories, which enabled commanders to direct artillery fire against an enemy's rear and reserves, even if these forces were concealed behind high ground.

Frederick's overriding tactic was to create chaos deep in the enemy's lines while concentrating the attack against what later military theorists called the *Schwerpunkt*, the critical point of an enemy's position. In the twentieth century this would become the essence of "Bliktzkrieg"—lightning war—a key aspect of highly mobile, rapidly moving, and massively destructive modern warfare. His idea of combining disruption with a quick and devastating breakthrough multiplied the effectiveness of his characteristically smaller forces. It became the most enduringly influential military doctrine of the next two centuries.

Frederick the Great quickly revealed himself as the very model of the benevolent despot in the Age of Enlightenment. He lifted censorship of the press and abolished penal torture. He decreed general religious toleration. He modernized the entire Prussian government and economy as well as the army, which he perfected as a fighting force second to none. A skilled, wily, and ultimately ruthless continental strategist, he responded to the alliance of Russia, France, and Austria in 1756 by invading Saxony and triggering the Seven Years' War, the European phase of the French and Indian War in North America, and the closest thing to a *world* war before the twentieth century. This long and costly war ended in 1763 with a general reversion to the status quo ante bellum throughout Europe—and yet it demonstrated to the world that Frederick the Great was a military genius and that Prussia was a military power to be reckoned with. In the next century, King Wilhelm I of Prussia, guided by his "Minister President" Otto von Bismarck, would build upon the magnificent military foundation Frederick the Great had laid to win total victory in the Franco-Prussian War (1870–1871). This triumph made Prussia the center of a new German Empire, a development that radically redrew the map of Europe and shaped the destiny of the continent and the world well into the twentieth century.

France and Britain in India: Imperialism by Proxy War (1751–1760)

The post–World War II military landscape was often marked by so-called proxy wars, conflicts instigated by major powers that do not want to be fully involved by directly attacking one another. In these cases, opposing nations generally support smaller opposing countries that serve their interests. During the second half of the twentieth century, possessing nuclear and thermonuclear weapons capable of ending civilization itself, the Soviet Union and the United States frequently became involved in proxy wars ranging from "brushfire" confrontations to such major conflicts as those in Korea (1950–1953) and Vietnam (1955–1975).

The contest between Britain and France for control over the Indian subcontinent in the first half of the eighteenth century may be seen as both a struggle for global empire and one of history's first proxy wars. The conflicts of this period were a turning point from wars fought with geographically limited strategy to achieve local or regional objectives to wars conceived in terms of geopolitical or global strategies and outcomes.

At the opening of the second half of the eighteenth century, four European nations were exploiting India. By the end of the 1750s, however, the role of two of those nations was greatly diminished. Portugal withdrew to the limited confines of Goa, Diu, and Daman, and the Dutch departed the subcontinent entirely. This left Britain and France as the sole contenders for imperial hegemony on a large scale. At this point in Indian history, the once-powerful Mogul Empire was disintegrating amid the rise of the Marathas. The two European powers operated through ostensibly private trading companies—the British East India Company and the Compagnie des Indes—to exploit rivalries between native Indian interests in an effort to claim greater territorial control. The British government went so far as to delegate to the East India Company quasi-sovereign powers. In effect, this commercial enterprise became the Crown's proxy in India, with full authority to make both war and peace with "any non-Christian nation." The Company had its own army, a mixture of European mercenaries and native troops commanded by officers of the regular British army who had been seconded to the Company service. During the early 1750s, a regular British regiment (the 39th Foot, later called the Dorchester Regiment) served as the exemplary core of the East India Company forces. Eventually, many of the regiment's troops and officers permanently transferred to service with the Company.

During September–October 1751, Chanda Sahib, nawab of the Carnatic, a puppet of the French, laid siege to the British garrison at Trichinopoly. Robert Clive, who had come to India as a clerk for the East India Company and had become a soldier in its service, led 500 men with three artillery pieces in a surprise move out of Madras and captured Arcot, Chanda Sahib's capital. This move was made mainly to force Chanda to lift the siege against Trichinopoly. This was done, but Chanda's son Raja Sahib returned with 10,000 men and laid siege to Clive's 500 men at Arcot. Miraculously, Raja Sahib repeatedly failed to breach Clive's position and withdrew in October 1751, having suffered some 400 casualties, while Clive lost four or five men. The failure of Raja Sahib dealt the French a crippling blow, both to their military position and, even more importantly, to their prestige among the Indians. For his part, Clive became the central leader of Britain's remarkably successful efforts to gain dominion over India.

In 1754 the French government recalled Joseph François Dupleix from service as the principal administrator of the Compagnie des Indes. As Dupleix was an able leader, his recall was a self-inflicted wound that put France at an even further disadvantage on the subcontinent. On June 20, 1756, Suraja Dowla, nawab of Bengal, captured Calcutta, a trading town founded by the East India Company, and confined those Europeans who were unable to escape to an underground dungeon that became infamous as the "Black Hole of Calcutta." Allegedly 123 of the 146 prisoners initially held there died overnight, mainly of suffocation and heatstroke. The action prompted a strong British response, and on January 2, 1757, Clive and Admiral Charles Watson recaptured Calcutta. Riding the momentum of this triumph, Clive went on to overrun and capture the French outpost of Chandernagore on March 23. This gave him and British forces a line of communication between British headquarters in Calcutta and the interior, into which he was determined to pursue Suraja Dowla.

On June 23 Clive fought Suraja at the Battle of Plassey on the Bhagirathi River. The Indian commanded some 50,000 troops against Clive's combined force of 1,100 European soldiers (British regulars and mercenaries) and 2,100 native troops. The force was armed with 10 cannon. Clive deployed in a mango grove, which Suraja began to surround while French-manned cannon were arrayed on Suraja's right flank. When a sudden downpour soaked the French powder, rendering the cannon useless, Suraja impulsively sent his cavalry against Clive. Having carefully covered their powder, Clive's gunners blasted Suraja's cavalry with relentless volleys, repulsing the charge with heavy losses. Clive gambled that the costly failure of Suraja's assault would dispirit his infantry. He moved his artillery forward and assaulted Suraja's trenches, also repelling an infantry sortie. The French troops attached to Suraja's army continued to fight but were outnumbered as his native soldiers withdrew in disorder. Suraja himself fell victim to assassination a few days after his defeat, and Clive replaced him with a British ally, Mir Jafar.

By early 1758, French reinforcements under the Irish-born Baron Thomas Lally arrived in Pondicherry, the French trading capital. Lally captured Britain's Fort St. David just south of Pondicherry on June 2, 1758, after a long siege, but his siege of Madras, which stretched to early 1759, began to falter. The British were able to keep the city supplied by sea while preventing the French navy from reinforcing Lally. On January 25, 1759, at the Battle of Masulipatam, a British relief force landed by Royal Navy vessels defeated Lally, who was also forced to lift the Madras siege. The following year, 1760, Pondicherry fell to the British East India Company: and with that, British dominion over the subcontinent was well on its way to assuming an unstoppable momentum. By the mid-nineteenth century, Britain commenced the period of "the Raj," British rule of India, which endured until Indian independence in 1947.

The Battle of Fort Necessity: Young George Washington Starts a World War (1754)

The expansion of European empire into the wilderness of North America brought a new reality into military strategy and military decision that placed it firmly in the context of global geopolitics. Monarchs and parliaments might now make continental and even global plans, but in the end it was the actions of individual commanders operating independently and remote from centers of political power that often determined the course of history. George Washington, a 21-year-old militia colonel in 1754, took an impulsive action in the wilderness of Pennsylvania that began the planet's first world war. As the British author Horace Walpole wrote years later in his 1822 *Memoirs of the Reign of King George II*, "The volley fired by a young Virginian in the backwoods of America set the world on fire."

The treaty of Aix-la-Chapelle (October 18, 1748), which ended King George's War (1744–1748), the North American theater of the War of the Austrian Succession, brought a brief peace to the American frontier but little stability. On March 16, 1749, King George II granted vast western tracts to the Ohio Company, a powerful syndicate of British traders and speculators, with the stipulation that within seven years, the company must plant a settlement of 100 families and build a fort for their protection. The grant and its stipulation immediately renewed enmity with the French and Native Americans, who believed that the new charter meant an English invasion of their lands.

This proved to be the case, as British traders rapidly poured into territories that had been the exclusive trading province of the French. They recruited Indian support against the French in the region, prompting Jacques-Pierre de Taffanel de la Jonquière, Marquis de la Jonquière and governor of New France, to build Fort Rouillé (at the location of present-day Toronto) in an effort to cut off trade between the northern Great Lakes and Oswego, the British stronghold on the south shore of Lake Ontario in New York. La Jonquière also strengthened the fortifications at Detroit and launched a raid against the Shawnees, most powerful among the tribes who traded with the English in the Ohio country. This action served only to drive the Shawnees more deeply into the English fold. For their part, British colonial authorities encouraged aggression among British traders. Colonial negotiators acquired more western land from the Indians, and in 1752 British colonial officials negotiated a treaty at Logstown (Ambridge,

The great Charles Willson Peale painted this portrait of a youthful-looking George Washington in 1772, between the French and Indian War and the American Revolution.

Pennsylvania) between the Iroquois Six Nations on the one side and the colony of Virginia and the Ohio Company on the other, securing from the Iroquois a quitclaim to the entire Ohio country.

The Miami Indian tribe now appealed to the British at Logstown to build a fort to defend them against the French, who had just attacked their "capital" at present-day Piqua, Ohio. When Virginia authorities declined to build the fort, the Miamis joined forces with the French, undermining the Logstown Treaty and ultimately driving English trade out of the Ohio Valley. Seizing on this vulnerability, Michel-Ange Duquesne de Menneville, Marquis Duquesne, who had replaced La Jonquière as governor of New France on July 1, 1752, ordered the construction of a chain of French forts to secure the Ohio country. This thoroughly intimidated the Iroquois, effectively neutralizing a key English ally.

In August 1753, even as British America's few precious Indian alliances were falling apart, Lord Halifax, across the ocean in London, prodded the British cabinet to declare war against France. Using as his basis the 1713 Treaty of Utrecht, which ended the War of the Spanish Succession (Queen Anne's War in America) and stipulated that the Iroquois were to be regarded as British subjects, Halifax asserted English rights to possession of Iroquois lands, including those the Iroquois themselves claimed by conquest, namely the whole of the Ohio country. Halifax argued before the cabinet that the French, in trading throughout the Ohio Valley, had committed an act of war by invading Virginia. Cabinet and Crown authorized Virginia lieutenant governor Robert Dinwiddie to take necessary measures to evict the French from territory under his jurisdiction. Dinwiddie commissioned young George Washington to deliver an ultimatum to Captain Jacques Legardeur de Saint-Pierre, commandant of Fort LeBoeuf (present-day Waterford, Pennsylvania), ordering the removal of the French to prevent the commencement of a war.

Washington set out from Williamsburg, Virginia, on October 31, 1753, with a small delegation. At Fort LeBoeuf, on December 12, 1753, Captain Legardeur politely rebuffed Washington and rejected Virginia's order to vacate. On being told this, Governor Dinwiddie ordered Captain William Trent to build and garrison a fort at the forks of Ohio—the location of present-day Pittsburgh. In April 1754 Captain Claude-Pierre Pécaudy de Contrecoeur, who had replaced Legardeur de Saint-Pierre as commandant of Fort LeBoeuf, sent 600 men against the new British fort's 41-man garrison. The garrison prudently surrendered, and Contrecoeur renamed the stronghold Fort Duquesne. In the meantime, on April 17, the very day the Ohio fort fell to Contrecoeur, Dinwiddie sent Washington with 150 militiamen to reinforce the fort, which, unknown to both Dinwiddie and Washington, the British no longer held.

On May 28 Washington led 40 of his provincials and a dozen Indian warriors in a surprise assault on a 33-man French reconnaissance party in western Pennsylvania. In the ensuing combat, 10 of the Frenchmen were killed and the remaining 23 surrendered. Washington thus claimed the first victory of his military career in an encounter that may be considered the first real battle of the French and Indian War. Mindful that the French would certainly retaliate in strength, Washington scrambled to recruit more Delaware Indian warriors, but he could muster no more than 40. Realizing that he could not withstand an attack by the main body of the French, Washington withdrew. With the French in hot pursuit, however, he decided to take a stand at a place called Great Meadows, in north-western Pennsylvania, not far from Fort Duquesne. Washington ordered the hasty erection of a makeshift stockade, which he dubbed Fort Necessity.

On July 3 Major Louis Coulon de Villiers led a mixed force of 900—including French regulars as well as Delawares, Ottawas, Wyandots, Algonquins, Nipissings, Abenakis, and so-called "mission" (French-allied) Iroquois—to Great Meadows. Vastly outnumbered, inadequately fortified, and fighting in driving rains that dissolved his earthen entrenchments and rendered his small "swivel gun" artillery useless, Washington surrendered Fort Necessity on July 4, 1754, after half his command had been killed. Coulon de Villiers permitted the survivors of the battle to leave, except for two who were taken back to Fort Duquesne as hostages. There the easygoing French, delighted with their victory, treated the prisoners as guests rather than captives. One of the hostages, Captain Robert Stobo, covertly made careful observations of the fort's defenses. Using friendly Delaware visitors, he managed to smuggle detailed plans of Fort Duquesne to Philadelphia, along with an urgent recommendation that Indian allies be used to attack the fort immediately. Stobo's urgings went unheeded, however. This was an example of the contemptuous attitude of British administrators and military commanders to Indians and colonial militia officers alike.

With the fall of the Ohio fort and the defeat of Washington, it was the English, not the French, who suffered expulsion from the Ohio country. In the aftershock of this defeat, the Iroquois, the only Indian allies remaining to the English, wavered. To bring colonial factions into line and to bolster the Iroquois alliance, a panicky congress was convened at Albany from June 19 to July 10, 1754. The Albany Congress not only failed to produce an acceptable plan for unified colonial action but also concluded a poorly thought-out treaty with the Iroquois, which succeeded only in sending the Delaware and other tribes into the arms of the French. The French and Indian War quickly expanded, and during the first three and a half of its nine years, the British footprint in North America contracted under one French victory after another. In 1758 Anglo-colonial military doctrine and policy would become more effective, and it was France's turn to suffer defeat and disaster. In the meantime, the European theater of the war, known as the Seven Years' War (1756–1763) was, as Walpole wrote, setting "the world on fire."

Frederick's Victory at Leuthen:
"Masterpiece of Maneuver and Resolution"
(1757)

The Seven Years' War was a world war, but if there was a single focus of local intensity it was Silesia, on the eastern border of Prussia, territory contested between Prussia and Austria. Frederick the Great attacked and ultimately annexed Silesia from Austria shortly after he ascended the throne in 1740. The 1748 Treaty of Aix-la-Chapelle, ending the War of the Austrian Succession (1740–1748) between Prussia and the allies of Austria's Empress Maria Theresa, gave Silesia to Prussia. Although Maria Theresa agreed to this condition, it was only to buy time for increasing her alliances. She fully intended to retake Silesia someday.

That day came, the empress believed, during the Seven Years' War at the Battle of Leuthen, fought near that Silesian town, six miles northwest of Breslau, on December 5, 1757.

The Austrian army was led by Prince Charles, Maria Theresa's brother-in-law. His was a large force of about 65,000 men, whom he deployed in a magnificent five-mile-long line of battle, facing to the west. Infantry made up the center, with cavalry deployed on either flank. The ground on which he deployed was gently rolling, and Charles predicted that Frederick the Great would see the terrain as favorable for an envelopment. For this reason, the prince retained a considerable reserve of troops behind his left flank, ready to counter any enveloping force. The right flank abutted a marsh, which Charles assumed Frederick would avoid.

In fact, the Prussian leader, who commanded 33,000 men, slightly more than half the strength of his opponent, moved directly *toward* Charles's right, advancing in four columns, the inner two consisting of infantry, the outer two of cavalry. As he reached the cover of a low ridge of hills, Frederick altered the direction of march so that his right-hand columns were positioned obliquely behind the hills, continuing to move rightward while his left-flank cavalry column remained in the rear. He would use this column to make a feint against Charles's right. While Charles could clearly see the cavalry's approach, the two columns of infantry remained hidden behind the hills. The Austrian prince moved his reserves to his right flank to reinforce what he deemed an imminent threat to his right wing.

When Frederick's still-concealed infantry was in a position that over-lapped Charles's left wing, the Prussian ordered his men to face the enemy, and he launched an attack in two echelons from his right. While he increased the pressure on the Austrian left, he opened up an artillery bombardment, focused on the apex of the Austrian left, where Charles's line bent to accommodate the hill separating him from Frederick. The Prussian cavalry on Frederick's right flank charged into the apex of the Austrian line. Disrupted by the artillery bombardment, it had also been stripped of the reserves Charles had sent to cover what he mistakenly believed would be the strongpoint of the attack against him.

Realizing what he had done, Charles scrambled to form a new line but failed, and his left fell back against his center, a catastrophic development. In the meantime, Charles sent the cavalry on his right wing against Frederick's left flank, but the Prussian cavalry attacked the rear of that cavalry attack, scattering it. Riding the momentum of this counterattack, the Prussian cavalry continued forward, charging directly into Charles's right flank. By this point in the battle, the Austrian left had completely collapsed into its own center; the right, under heavy pressure, was likewise disintegrating.

With just half the strength of Charles, Frederick had wreaked havoc on the Austrians. He captured 12,000 men and killed or wounded 6,750. Many other Austrian troops cut, ran, and deserted. A total of 116 magnificent guns also fell to Frederick. All that saved the Austrians from total annihilation was nightfall, which allowed the shattered force to limp back to Bohemia and winter quarters with perhaps half its original strength.

Frederick also paid a high price in the Battle of Leuthen, suffering 6,150 killed or wounded, but when the city of Breslau surrendered to him five days after the victory at Leuthen, he took 17,000 more prisoners of war and had the satisfaction of having created what was universally regarded as a marvel, what Napoleon later called a "masterpiece of maneuver and resolution." It was the greatest battle of the man several generations of military historians came to regard as a tactician without peer. As for Prince Charles, Leuthen was the last battle he ever commanded. The Battle of Leuthen took Austria out of contention for control of Silesia, and it elevated Frederick the Great to the highest possible esteem as a military commander. A new name had entered the pantheon of the world's "great captains."

Lexington, Concord, and Bunker Hill: An American Military Is Born (1775)

Before dawn on April 19, 1775, between 600 and 800 British regulars, army "redcoats" along with Royal Marines, disembarked from the whaleboats that had carried them from Boston to Lechmere Point on the north side of Boston Harbor, in modern-day Charlestown. From here they began a march northwest to the village of Lexington, which lay between Boston and their objective, Concord, where they intended to raid and confiscate or destroy a cache of "rebel" arms and ammunition.

On Lexington's village green, the British encountered 70 or so colonial militiamen. Major John Pitcairn, in command of a detachment of Royal Marines, ordered the "rebels" to surrender their weapons. Although they were greatly outnumbered by the British, militia captain Jonas Parker ordered his men to neither surrender nor attack but simply to disband, taking their weapons with them. At this, Pitcairn repeated his demand that the rebels lay down their weapons. As if in response, shots rang out, and a British soldier was hit in the leg by a ricochet. It is uncertain whether the shots came from the Patriots or the British, but they were sufficient to set off an exchange of gunfire, followed by a British bayonet charge.

Against the onslaught of bayonets, the militiamen scattered. When the "battle" was over, eight of them, including Captain Parker, lay dead on Lexington Green. Ten more were wounded. On the British side, only the marine who had been hit by the ricochet was even slightly hurt. And thus the first battle of the American Revolution ended. The American militia had not fared well.

Doubtless taking heart from the weak showing of the militia at Lexington, the British marched on to Concord. Patriot militia companies marched into this town from the surrounding communities. At the moment of the British army's entry into Concord under Lieutenant Colonel Smith, it is believed there were about 400 militiamen assembled under the command of Colonel James Barrett. From a ridge overlooking the town, these men fell upon Smith's regulars, killing three and wounding nine with their very first musket volley. This sent the entire British contingent running for cover in the center of town.

In the meantime, at Boston, some 1,400 British troops, including 460 Royal Marines, drawing two 6-pound cannon and led by 33-year-old Lord Hugh Percy, were just beginning their march to Concord. All along the way, this column was sniped at by Patriot militiamen crouched behind stone walls and trees, even firing from houses. As Percy's column approached, Smith withdrew from Concord back toward Lexington, his light infantry mounting several successful counterattacks against poorly organized groups of colonial militia. Nevertheless, more militiamen continued to pour into the Concord area, taking up sniper positions on either side of the road, peppering Smith's retreating column with continual fire. After almost 20 hours of a fighting retreat, Smith's force entered Lexington and there joined Percy's column of reinforcements from Boston. Percy trained his 6-pounders against the Americans, which kept them at bay for a time.

More militiamen continually arrived. Fortunately for the British, despite the American numbers, the militia units were ill-disciplined and their action uncoordinated. Yet they were relentless in harassing the now-combined columns of Percy and Smith, harrying them all the way back to Charlestown, where the regulars took refuge within range of the cannon of British men-o'-war riding at anchor in the harbor. Seventy-three British soldiers were confirmed killed; another 26 were missing and presumed dead. One hundred seventy-four regulars were wounded. Among the American militia, 49 had died, 5 were reported missing, and 41 lay wounded.

On June 14, 1775, the Second Continental Congress, meeting in Philadelphia and having already summoned more than 13,000 militiamen to Boston, voted up a proposal by John Adams that the Congress adopt the Boston militia as the "Continental Army," the first army of the United States. Adams understood that merely renaming a collection of militiamen an army would not provide the training, discipline, and arms they needed. But it would, he believed, redefine a collection of local forces as a *national* force. Congress agreed and called for the creation of a Continental Army to be drawn from *all* the colonies, not just the communities around Boston. It was important, they felt, to create a force truly representing all the colonies. Around this army, other forces would rally, including militias from all the colonies. Ultimately, the Congress understood that while militia forces could harass the British army, only a regular army under single command could begin to engage the British on anything like equal terms. They intended to fashion the Continental Army as a European-style regular army capable of fighting formal battles with European discipline.

On June 14 John Adams proposed "George Washington of Virginia" as commander in chief of the new Continental Army. His principal lieutenants, commissioned by Congress, were Artemas Ward (already commanding the Boston militia); Israel Putnam of Connecticut; Philip Schuyler, a wealthy New Yorker; and two recently retired British Army officers, Charles Lee and Horatio Gates, who had both served with British general James Braddock and colonial militia colonel George Washington in the French and Indian War. By the end of 1775, Congress had 27,500 Continental Army soldiers on its payroll, drawn from all thirteen colonies.

While the Continental Army was forming, the Boston army, a conglomeration of local militias numbering some 10,000 men were deployed around the city and held the British regulars at bay. In the meantime, the Royal Navy warship HMS *Cerberus* sailed into Boston Harbor, carrying three major generals from England to assist General Thomas Gage in crushing the rebellion. They were William Howe, the senior officer, John Burgoyne, and Henry Clinton. Gage greeted the arrivals and immediately ordered Howe to destroy the American army in a single blow.

Howe did not flinch. He decided to make an amphibious landing at Dorchester Point, to the right of Cambridge, in coordination with a landing by Clinton at Willis Creek, to his left. This would secure the high ground at Charlestown: Bunker Hill. The twin operations would be well covered by fire from the warships in Boston Harbor. With the high ground secured, the forces of Howe and Clinton could indeed crush the American flanks in a pincer movement converging on Cambridge.

Unknown to the British commanders, the local Patriot "Committee of Safety" operated a highly effective spy ring and had discovered the British war plans. Artemas Ward, in command of the Boston army, sent Major General Israel Putnam, 57-year-old veteran of the French and Indian War, to lead 1,200 men to the heights beyond Charlestown. In company with him was Colonel William Prescott, another French and Indian War veteran. Putnam argued that it was better to occupy Breed's Hill, which was closer to Boston, than Bunker Hill. The two debated, but Putnam ultimately agreed to concentrate on Breed's Hill, leaving some men to fortify Bunker Hill to cover any retreat.

It was a tactical error. Higher, steeper, and farther from the ships of the Royal Navy, Bunker Hill could have been made virtually impregnable. Breed's Hill was lower, not as steep, more exposed, and far more vulnerable. Nevertheless 1,200 Americans furiously dug entrenchments into Breed's Hill. Gage and Howe had 2,500 troops ready to attack. They were supported by land-based artillery and by the cannon of the 68-gun ship of the line *Somerset*, two floating artillery batteries, the frigate *Glasgow*, the armed transport *Symmetry*, a pair of gunboats, and two sloops of war, *Falcon* and *Lively*.

At dawn on June 17, 1775, a Royal Marine sentry sighted the Americans at work on Breed's Hill. *Lively* opened fire, and soon the entire fleet began bombarding the American position. The British generals were upset that the naval bombardment had come prematurely, before they were in position to launch their amphibious landing. Under naval artillery fire, the Americans continued to dig in for six more hours until, at 1:00 p.m., 2,300 British regulars disembarked at Moulton's Point, at the tip of Charlestown Peninsula.

The British regulars quickly found themselves under heavy fire from the well-entrenched Americans. They called on the Royal Navy to help. Instead of intensifying the bombardment of Breed's Hill and Bunker Hill, however, the ships bombarded Charlestown, setting it ablaze. Against a backdrop of flame, the battle continued to rage. Howe positioned 350 of his best troops, the light infantry, along the Mystic River beach and ordered them to make a bayonet charge into the Patriot position fronting the Mystic. As this point, Israel Putnam issued one of the most famous battle commands in American military history: "Don't fire until you see the whites of their eyes! Then, fire low." It was a good, practical command that greatly increased the effectiveness of the militia fire.

The British assault was courageous, but the steady, close-range fire from the ranks of the militia was deadly. After three major American volleys, 96 British regulars lay dead on the sands of the Mystic River embankment. Every member of Howe's personal staff was either killed or wounded. The courageous Howe, always in the forefront of the action, was unscathed—but in shock. He experienced, he later wrote, "a moment that I never felt before."

Seeing that they had repulsed the British onslaught, the American militiamen celebrated—prematurely. Some, without authorization, began to depart the field and go home. For his part, British general Howe rapidly recovered from his initial shock and launched a fresh assault. When this cohort was cut down, he waited and watched. British troops were falling, but the American militiamen were clearly wearing out. They too were shocked by the violence of combat; they also were running low on powder.

Just as the American troops were suffering a crisis of nerve, 400 Royal Marines and British army regulars heeded Howe's call for a third assault. The Americans responded by pouring on the fire, but this time the British managed to breach militia positions on Breed's Hill. Combat became hand to hand there. Because most of the Americans lacked bayonets, Prescott ordered his men to use their muskets as clubs to "twitch their guns away"—to knock the weapons out of the redcoats' hands. As more scarlet-uniformed troops poured over the parapet, Prescott finally shouted to his men: "Give way, men! Save yourselves!"

The militia retreated, suffering in the withdrawal some 450 casualties, including 140 killed. The British took both Breed's and Bunker Hills and thus emerged the victors of the battle. Yet of 2,400 regulars engaged in combat, 1,054 had been shot, of whom 226 died. Against any enemy, such losses would have been appalling. But these were inflicted on European fighting men by a ragtag army of provincials who were outnumbered and vastly outgunned. To his diary, General Henry Clinton confided: "A dear-bought victory; another such would have ruined us." As for Washington, who had not taken part in this battle, he had reason to hope that the militia, organized now under national colors and his command, would make a very creditable army.

Battle of Trenton: Washington's Genius for War (1776)

Before the Revolutionary War battles of Long Island (August 27, 1776), Harlem Heights (September 16, 1776), and White Plains (October 28, 1776), George Washington and his chief subordinates commanded some 19,000 soldiers. After these encounters they were left with just 16,400. Defeat was whittling down the Continental Army and the various Patriot militias. Defeat after defeat pushed Washington out of New York, through New Jersey, and across the Delaware into Pennsylvania. Major colonial cities were being given up to the British.

Thomas Paine, whose pamphlet *Common Sense* had earlier galvanized the cause of independence, was encamped with Washington's army in retreat. He began writing a series of essays that would, after the Revolution, be collected into a volume called *The American Crisis*. The first of these essays was published on December 19, 1776. It began: "These are the times that try men's souls. The summer soldier and sunshine patriot will, in this crisis, shrink from the service of his country; but he that stands it now, deserves the love and thanks of man and woman. Tyranny, like hell, is not easily conquered."

As *Common Sense* had worked its persuasive magic earlier, so this first essay succeeded in drumming up recruits for the Continental Army and the militias. Yet by the Christmas season of 1776, Washington personally commanded no more than 6,000 troops fit for duty. He did not have time to wait for more men to answer Paine's call. The current enlistments were set to expire on New Year's Eve. These would reduce his army, now on the Pennsylvania side of the Delaware, to just 1,400 men. The British were currently encamped in New Jersey, with a contingent of Hessian mercenaries at Trenton and British regulars at Princeton. Washington had rounded up all available boats with the objective of keeping the British bottled up on the New Jersey side of the river, but if the Delaware froze hard, those troops could just march across and attack Washington in Pennsylvania at will.

The time to act was now, Washington reasoned—not just because he would soon lose men and the river could freeze, but precisely because the Hessians and the British thought he was defeated, his army in rags and with dwindling ammunition and spirit. He *needed* to attack. Would he fail? Quite possibly. But the failure to act was worse than defeat. Besides, local Pennsylvania militiamen, acting independently of his command, had lately conducted highly damaging hit-and-run raids against British installations along the Delaware. A good many of the Hessians who had garrisoned Trenton now moved down to Mount Holly, New Jersey, chasing after the militia. The Hessian garrison was as vulnerable as it was ever going to be.

On December 22 Washington received a dispatch from his adjutant, Colonel Joseph Reed. Speaking for his fellow officers, he replied:

> *We are all of the opinion my dear general that something must be attempted to revive our expiring credit, give our Cause some degree of reputation & prevent total depreciation of the Continental money which is coming very fast. . . . Even a Failure cannot be more fatal than to remain in our present situation. In short some Enterprize must be undertaken in our present Circumstances or we must give up the cause.*

He advised attacking Trenton, warning his commander: "Delay is now equal to a total defeat."

Reed was preaching to the choir. Washington immediately summoned his subordinates to a council of war, at which he presented Reed's proposal for crossing the icy Delaware to attack one of the enemy's New Jersey outposts. Not a single officer offered debate. All assented immediately. With that, Washington turned to Colonel John Glover, commander of a regiment of tough Marblehead (Massachusetts) fishermen. He asked him if crossing his army in small boats was feasible. "My boys," Glover assured him, would "manage it." Washington issued operational orders the very next morning.

The objective was Trenton, garrisoned by Hessians, some of the best soldiers in all Europe—and with a reputation for ruthless cruelty in combat. The colonists especially hated and feared them, and that made them all the more attractive as a target. But the first obstacle to overcome was nature itself, in the form of the Delaware River. It had frozen but, under warm rains, melted. Then it refroze—only partially—so that on Christmas night, the wide river roiled in a swift current that sent great sheets of broken ice and miniature icebergs crashing and whirling, posing a grave threat to men in small wooden boats.

No matter. *This* was the night. Washington loaded 2,400 soldiers and 18 cannon into the Durham boats he had hoarded in his effort to keep them out of British hands. He began crossing his men at McConkey's Ferry (the modern Pennsylvania town of Washington's Crossing), nine miles above Trenton. At the same time, roughly a thousand militiamen under General James Ewing prepared to cross at Trenton Ferry with the objective of blocking the possible retreat of Hessians from Trenton. Washington had also ordered Colonel John Cadwalader to lead a diversionary crossing at Bordentown.

Washington is often lauded as a leader of men, but he is just as often crit-icized as a mediocre tactician. His plan for the Delaware crossing was excel-lent, however. In fact, it was more competent—even inspired—than anything he had done so far in this revolution. But plans are not execution, and there were problems from the get-go. Ewing could not manage to get across the treacherous river, and Cadwalader suffered so many delays that he was simply of no use. As for Washington, his intention to disembark on the New Jersey bank by midnight, so that he could advance to Trenton under total cover of darkness, fell victim to the terrible weather. It was three o'clock in the morning of December 26 before the last contingent landed in New Jersey. It was four o'clock by the time the men began to march. There was no way to reach Trenton before broad daylight.

Washington pondered abandoning the mission, but (he later wrote), "As I was certain there was no making a Retreat without being discovered, and harassed on repassing the River, I determined to push on at all Events." And so, he marched his men nine miles from the New Jersey bank of the Delaware River through the stormy predawn gloom. He ordered his men to maintain absolute silence and to refrain from striking any lights. The men were therefore deprived of the comfort of both conversation and a pipe. Snow, sleet, and freezing rain put the reliability of their muskets in question. Unable to count on their guns firing when needed, Washington ordered his men to fix bayonets. If there was no flash when the trigger was pulled, they would have to thrust.

When they at last reached the Hessian camp at Trenton, Washington instantly knew they had been detected. "*Der Feind! Heraus! Heraus!*" ("The enemy! Get up! Get up!") sentries cried out.

Colonel Johann Gottlieb Rall rallied his men, only to be quickly cut down by musket fire. He was mortally wounded in the chest. Now the fight was on. Despite the daylight, surprise was nearly total. No one present had a defini-tive sense of how long the battle lasted. Estimates range from half an hour to two hours. But when it was over, 106 of the 1,200 Hessians engaged lay dead or wounded. The rest were prisoners of war. Washington's forces suffered four wounded. Some authorities believe that no Americans were killed at Trenton, but others report that two men were killed in action and another two froze to death. Either way, Patriot casualties were light. It was a remarkable victory.

Washington wanted desperately to follow up his triumph with imme-diate attacks on Princeton and New Brunswick. But because his subordinate commanders had failed to cross the river or to cross it in a timely fashion, he decided to withdraw back across the Delaware to his Pennsylvania camp. The Battle of Princeton would be fought—to victory—days later, on January 3, 1777. All that mattered now, however, was that his starving, repeatedly defeated army had bested the best soldiers in Europe. The Revolution was alive. The Revolution would continue.

USS *Bonhomme Richard* v. HMS *Serapis*:
The One-Man Navy
of John Paul Jones (1779)

"The Americans," declared Britain's secretary at war, Viscount Barrington, "may be reduced by the fleet, but never can be by the army." The assessment made sense. In 1775 the Royal Navy was the world's biggest and most powerful. The fleet consisted of some 270 vessels in that year, including 131 ships of the line, the heavy battleships of the era. Each mounted a minimum of 64 guns, with the largest of these ships having 90 to 100 or more cannon—and in late eighteenth-century naval warfare, firepower was everything. One ship destroyed another by pounding it with cannonballs. The vessel capable of delivering the most fire most quickly was the vessel that won the battle. (By the end of the American Revolution, in 1783, the total number of Royal Navy ships stood at 468.)

When it went to war against the Royal Navy, the United States had no navy at all. On October 13, 1775, the Continental Congress passed a resolution creating a "Continental Navy" and authorized the purchase of two armed vessels for use in attacking British merchant ships. Six days later, on October 19, 1775, John Adams, a member of the Congress, wrote of creating an "American Fleet," adding wryly that he did not "mean 100 ships of the Line," but some small force. On November 28, Adams drafted the first governing regulations for the Continental Navy, and on December 13 the Continental Congress voted to build 13 frigates within the next three months. By the end of the American Revolution, the U.S. Navy had had 53 ships on the books, not all of which survived to the end of the war. This was still far fewer than the Royal Navy had, of course, but John Adams became a tireless champion of American sea power and spoke of defending the new nation by means of "wooden walls"—a fleet of stout frigates.

Various private vessels and ships operated by several "state navies" were successful in capturing British merchant vessels and commandeering their valuable cargoes. But it was not until March 3–4, 1776, that the *national* navy, the Continental Navy, carried out its first—and last—major planned naval operation in the war. A Rhode Island farm boy turned sailor, Esek Hopkins, was put in command of the navy's first squadron. He used it to surprise British forces on Nassau—at the time called Providence or New Providence—by landing a force of U.S. Marines (in *their* first action of the war) to assault Fort Montagu. They not only captured the fort but took away from it 100 cannon and mortar.

Hopkins had eight vessels under his command, the largest of which were two merchant ships converted into small frigates of 24 and 20 guns, respectively. His officers included four men of the rank of captain—Dudley Saltonstall, Abraham Whipple, Nicholas Biddle, and John B. Hopkins—and a roster of young lieutenants. Among these was John Paul Jones.

A naval hero in revolutionary America, John Paul Jones was depicted as a common pirate in this British caricature.
NATIONAL ARCHIVES AND RECORDS ADMINISTRATION

John Adams and John Paul Jones would meet for the first time in 1779, when both were in Europe. At that time (May 13, 1779), Adams wrote in his diary that Jones was "the most ambitious and intriguing Officer in the American Navy. Jones has Art, and Secrecy, and aspires very high. . . . Eccentricities, and Irregularities are to be expected from him—they are in his Character, they are visible in his Eyes. His Voice is soft and still and small, his Eye has keenness, and Wildness and Softness in it." Before that year was out, Jones would achieve victories so remarkable that he deserved to be called a one-man navy—precisely what the young United States desperately needed.

Born John Paul in Scotland in 1747, the son of a gardener to a Scottish squire, the youth was apprenticed to a shipowner. His early voyages were aboard English ships plying the slave trade, but he later graduated to commanding general merchant vessels. On one of these he flogged the ship's carpenter for neglect of duty. It was a common punishment of the day, but this time the victim died; his father charged Paul with murder, for which Paul was imprisoned briefly, tried, and acquitted. Later, as captain of the *Betsy*, out of London, Paul killed the ringleader of a mutiny. Fearing that his already sinister reputation would result in conviction, he fled to America and assumed the name Jones—John Paul Jones. When the American Revolution broke out, he went to Philadelphia to help fit out the *Alfred*, the first vessel commissioned by the Continental Navy. This position introduced him to influential navy leaders, and on December 7, 1775, he was commissioned a first lieutenant aboard the *Alfred*.

On April 6, 1776, just a little over a month after his triumph at Nassau, Esek Hopkins was leading five Continental Navy ships back from the West Indies when the 20-gun British frigate *Glasgow* attacked the flotilla around midnight off Block Island, east of Montauk Point, Long Island, and 13 miles off the coast of Rhode Island. *Glasgow* inflicted 24 casualties among the American sailors and severely disabled the *Alfred*. The engagement destroyed the morale of the fledgling American fleet, sending officers and crew fleeing the service. Congress relieved Hopkins of command, and Jones received a promotion to captain of the ship *Providence* along with a small supporting flotilla. In this assignment, he quickly captured or sank 21 British warships, transports, and commercial vessels, as well as one Loyalist privateer by the end of 1776.

On June 14, 1777, Jones was assigned command of the sloop *Ranger* and ordered to sail it to France, where he was to take command of the frigate *Indien*, which was being built in Amsterdam for the Continental Navy. When he arrived in December, he found that the American delegation in France had given *Indien* to the French navy, so he continued to sail in *Ranger*, leaving Brest on April 10, 1778, with a crew of 140. During April 27–28, 1778, Jones raided Whitehaven on the Solway Firth in Scotland, spiking the guns of two forts there and burning three British ships. This was the only American military operation carried out on British soil during the Revolution. From here Jones crossed the Irish Sea to

Carrickfergus, where he captured the British sloop *Drake* in a short, sharp action. By the time he returned to Brest, on May 8, he had accumulated seven "prizes" (captured ships) and a host of POWs.

In the summer of 1779, the French, having formally entered the American Revolution on the side of the United States, outfitted for Jones five naval vessels and two privateers (ships sailed by civilians as state-sanctioned pirates, authorized to raid enemy commercial vessels). His flagship was a refitted East Indiaman—a large merchant vessel—called the *Duras*. At this time, Benjamin Franklin was among the American commissioners working with France. His celebrated *Poor Richard's Almanac* was avidly read in the court of Louis XVI, and Jones secured royal approval to call his new vessel *Bonhomme Richard*—the "Good Man Richard." He used it to lead a sweeping voyage clockwise around the British Isles, in which he captured 17 British commercial ships.

On September 23, 1779, off Flamborough Head, along the York coast of the North Sea, Jones sighted two British men-o'-war convoying 40 British merchant vessels. The warships were the 44-gun *Serapis* and the 20-gun *Countess of Scarborough*. As a converted cargo vessel, the *Bonhomme Richard* was not a great combat vessel. It was lumbering and it mounted just 42 guns. But its skipper was the extraordinarily skilled John Paul Jones, and he decided to pursue *Serapis* while the three other vessels with him, *Vengeance, Pallas,* and *Alliance,* chased the *Countess*.

The battle was fought at night, in the moonlight, and did not begin well for Jones. Two of his biggest cannons exploded, which amplified the odds against him. Nevertheless, he managed to outmaneuver *Serapis* and deliberately rammed her stern. This, however, put *Bonhomme Richard* in a position from which none of her guns could be brought to bear on *Serapis*. Noting this, the British commander called out: "Has your ship struck?" meaning, have you "struck" (lowered) your "colors" (flag) in surrender.

"I have not yet begun to fight," Jones replied defiantly. It remains one of the U.S. Navy's proudest utterances.

Bonhomme Richard and *Serapis* broke free of each other, but *Serapis* now collided with *Bonhomme Richard*. Jones instantly commanded his crew to lash onto the British vessel, which was now positioned point-blank to his guns. Using those of his cannon that were still functioning, Jones pounded the captive vessel. After a full two hours of this treatment, it was *Serapis* that "struck" colors.

It was a humiliating Royal Navy defeat. A converted merchant ship had defeated a major British warship. Jones sailed *Serapis* and his other prizes to Texel, Holland, the Netherlands having become an American ally. *Bonhomme Richard* was so badly crippled that Jones had to abandon it at sea, where it sunk on September 25. Jones was obliged by treaty to turn over all his prizes as well as the ships of his own flotilla to the French—save only the *Alliance*. He continued to command this vessel in a campaign of harassment against British commercial shipping until

December 1780, when, as skipper of the *Ariel*, a French military transport, he set sail for America—capturing the British ship *Triumph* along the way.

On his arrival back in the United States, jealous brother officers blocked Jones's promotion to rear admiral. He was, however, given command of the largest ship in the Continental Navy, the *America*. After waiting a year for the vessel to be completed, he was told that it was being given to the French. He therefore sailed with the French fleet until the end of the war, when he offered his services to Russia's Catherine the Great. Jones sailed for Russia as a well-paid mercenary against the Turks. Russian military commanders were as jealous of him as American naval officers had been, and he left Russia for Paris in 1789, discouraged and broken in health. He died in the French capital in 1793, having created for the U.S. Navy not a vast fleet of ships but something even more valuable: a tradition of can-do, must-do leadership and victory. It was not until 1905, however, that his remains were returned to the United States, where they were at last given a resting place of honor, in 1913, at the U.S. Naval Academy in Annapolis, Maryland.

Battles of Hondschoote, Menin, and Wattignies: Kingless Victories (1793)

The French Revolution, which began in 1789, quickly escalated from a domestic civil war to a European war when Austria and Prussia united in alliance against the French revolutionary government on February 7, 1792. By April 20, 1792, a coalition consisting of the Holy Roman Empire (primarily Austria and Prussia), Great Britain, Spain, the Dutch Republic, Portugal, Sardinia, Naples, and other Italian states squared off against France in what historians term the War of the First Coalition (1792–1797).

Fortunately for the fledgling French Republic, the coalition allies had little trust for one another and failed to coordinate their efforts. Nevertheless, the early months of the French Revolution were extremely chaotic, and French forces suffered numerous reversals. By the spring and early summer of 1793, cumulative defeats had demoralized the French, and by later that summer, Maximilien de Robespierre and his Committee of Public Safety had installed the Reign of Terror. Now France was assailed from both within and without. As August drew to a close, the forces of the coalition recaptured Mainz, and the Vendée region of France was roiled by a counterrevolution. Both Lyon and Marseilles declared themselves for the monarchy. The Duke of York laid siege to Dunkirk, and a combined Anglo-Spanish fleet moved in on Toulon, which also declared for the monarchy.

Republican France appeared to be on the verge of collapse when the Committee of Public Safety issued a "Levée en Masse," decreeing universal male military conscription. Within weeks, no fewer than 14 new armies were fielded. On the very day of the Levée, August 23, Marseilles was recovered by Republican forces.

Among the coalition, no one expected a forcibly conscripted army to prevail. But three battles fought in quick succession—Hondschoote (September 8), Menin (September 13), and Wattignies (October 15–16)—proved the coalition's assessment wrong.

Lazare Nicolas Carnot, war minister of the Committee of Public Safety, a no-nonsense military veteran of the ancien régime, actively joined the army and used a combination of terror and patriotism, along with strict military discipline, to rapidly transform raw recruits into fiercely efficient soldiers. His secret was combining veterans from the pre-Revolution army with the brand-new conscripts. This tactic proved sufficient to season the force as a whole.

At Hondschoote on September 8, 24,000 French troops attacked 16,000 men under the Duke of York just east of Dunkirk. The French were raw but enthusiastic. The English were highly disciplined but outnumbered. They could not resist even the clumsy and desperate French charges, which came one after the other. Although losses were about equal on each side, the Duke was forced to yield Dunkirk.

Five days later, on September 13, at Menin, Jean Nicolas Houchard led the French in a rout of the Prince of Orange, but he was subsequently relieved of command and later executed when he failed to eject the Austrians from eastern France. Jean-Baptiste Jourdan, who had risen through the French ranks from private to general, took Houchard's place and during October 15–16 fought the Battle of Wattignies. Coalition forces initially repulsed Jourdan's attack, but on day two of the battle, he led an envelopment of the coalition's left wing, forcing the Austrians to abandon their siege of Maubeuge and retreat to the east, across the French border. Jourdan took heavy losses—5,000 killed and wounded to roughly 3,000 among the coalition armies—but he achieved a great strategic victory in the northeast, accomplishing what Houchard could not do. He pushed the coalition invaders out of France.

Jourdan is remembered as one of the most successful early generals of the wars of the French Revolution, but it was Carnot who earned the title "Organizer of Victory." His skillful transformation of a conscripted army, carefully combined with veteran professional soldiers, created the first truly successful national army without kings and nobles to lead it. Carnot laid the foundation of the kind of forces that Napoleon Bonaparte would use first to win out over the European forces arrayed against the French Revolution and then to expand the French Empire, both under the Republic and then during his own imperial reign.

From Toulon to Campo Formio: The Rise of Napoleon Bonaparte (1793–1797)

Born on August 15, 1769, in Ajaccio, Corsica, Napoleone di Buonaparte attended a French military school at Brienne-le-Château from April 1779 to October 1784. Eager though he was for a military career, his classmates largely spurned him as a provincial bumpkin. Yet he persevered and was admitted to the Military Academy in Paris, from which he graduated with a commission as second lieutenant of artillery on September 1, 1785, assigned to the artillery regiment "La Fère." He was relegated to relentlessly dull garrison duty in Valence, Drôme, and Auxonne. Then, when the French Revolution erupted in 1789, he took a leave of absence that lasted nearly two years, keeping him out of the worst of the Reign of Terror. He returned to Corsica, presenting himself as an anti-French Corsican nationalist yet ultimately supporting the radical French Jacobins. Napoleone managed to get a transfer from the regular French army to the post of adjutant in a volunteer Corsican militia battalion. This soon gained him promotion from second lieutenant to lieutenant colonel. After leading his Corsican volunteers in a riot against a French army detachment in Ajaccio and then ignoring an order to rejoin regular army forces, he was struck from the lists of the French army. To this, he responded boldly by returning to Paris, where he potentially faced court-martial as a deserter—and self-righteously demanded readmission into the army *and* promotion to captain of artillery. Fortunately for him, the French army was in desperate need of officers, and both of his outrageous demands were met in July 1792.

Captain Buonaparte persuaded his superiors to allow him to return to Corsica yet again, this time to assist the great Corsican nationalist leader Pasquale Paoli, who had ostensibly allied himself with the French revolutionary government. Napoleone soon discovered, however, that Paoli had turned coat against France, and, along with the entire Buonaparte family, he fled to the French mainland in June 1793.

Shortly after his return to Paris, in July 1793, Napoleone published *Le Souper de Beaucaire* ("*Supper at Beaucaire*"), a Republican political dialogue that attracted the notice of the younger brother of the Jacobin leader Maximilien Robespierre. This secured Napoleone appointment as commander of Republican artillery at the Siege of Toulon (September 18–December 18, 1793) with the rank of major.

Toulon, on the southeastern French Mediterranean coast, was a royalist counterrevolutionary stronghold that was occupied by British troops who were supported by a Royal Navy fleet riding at anchor in the harbor. The town rose against the Republican government. It was clear to Napoleone that if unchecked, the uprising could rapidly undo the French Revolution. The newly minted major exhibited a combination of tactical mastery, charismatic command presence,

Napoleon Bonaparte—in an unfinished 1797 painting by Jacques-Louis David
WIKIMEDIA COMMONS

and great personal courage in executing a daring plan to take a hill overlooking Toulon's harbor, place his artillery there, and thereby force the British ships to evacuate, taking the occupation force with them. When this stratagem succeeded, the 24-year-old was catapulted to the rank of brigadier general and, on orders of the revolutionary Committee of Public Safety, was awarded command of the artillery arm of the French Army of Italy.

Soon after his victory at the Siege of Toulon, Napoleone di Buonaparte adopted the French spelling of his name, Napoleon Bonaparte, taking particular care to drop the particle "di" as savoring too strongly of the nobility. The subsequent overthrow of Robespierre, however, knocked Napoleon out of favor, and in April 1795 he was transferred to the Army of the West, which was fighting a royalist counterrevolution in the Vendée region of west-central France. The new assignment was a demotion because he had been moved from the elite artillery to the common infantry. Napoleon feigned illness to escape having to accept the new assignment and instead joined the Bureau of Topography of the Committee of Public Safety, an obscure position that cast him even further outside the inner circles of power. To add insult to injury, he was subsequently stricken from the list of regular army generals because of his original refusal to serve in the Vendée.

The relentless course of history came to his rescue.

On October 3, 1795, Parisian royalists rose up against the National Convention. Napoleon was called on to command the defense of the Tuileries Palace, in which the National Convention had assembled and which the royalists were threatening to attack and seize. Napoleon responded by taking the unorthodox step of employing artillery against a popular insurrection intent on overrunning the palace. On October 5 he opened fire on the Royalist insurrectionists, offering them (in the memorable understatement Thomas Carlyle used in his 1837 historical masterpiece, *The French Revolution*) a "whiff of grapeshot." In fact, he ruthlessly mowed down some 1,400 royalists using this antipersonnel ammunition. The feat publicly rehabilitated Napoleon Bonaparte, bringing down on him a sudden shower of fame, wealth, and power.

Promoted to commander of the interior, Napoleon was assigned full field command of the Army of Italy. It was, however, the smallest and most meagerly supplied of the 13 field armies of the French Republic. Perhaps some members of the French governing assembly, the Directory, hoped he would fail and thus fade away. Instead, Napoleon once again proved himself a brilliant logistician and an able tactician. He made up for his army's small numbers by forcing his soldiers to march faster. He worked out maneuvers that allowed him to concentrate more of his army precisely in the places where the Austrians, always superior in strength, were at their weakest and most vulnerable. His early success culminated in the Battle of Lodi on May 10, 1796, in which he defeated the Austrians and drove them out of Lombardy.

An Austrian counterattack at Caldiero on November 12, 1796, inflicted a defeat on Napoleon. He, however, counter-counterattacked at the Battle of Arcola (Battle of the Bridge of Arcole) during November 15–17, by which he regained momentum and forced the Papal States into submission. At this point, radical atheists in the Directory urged Napoleon to invade Rome and dethrone the pope. He refused, not on religious grounds but for strategic reasons, explaining that the pope's removal would only be exploited by the Kingdom of Naples and at the expense of the French position. Austria, he reminded the Directory, was the enemy, not the pope. In March 1797 Napoleon invaded Austria and forcibly negotiated the Treaty of Leoben (April 17, 1797), by which Austria ceded control of most of northern Italy and the Low Countries to France.

Napoleon next invaded Venice, ending its 1,100 years of independence and looting some of its extraordinary treasures. From Venice, as from everywhere else he went in Italy, Napoleon sent wagonloads of riches back to the perpetually cash-strapped Directory.

Napoleon Bonaparte was not a radical strategist. He always claimed to have learned everything he knew from those he called history's "great captains"— Alexander the Great, Hannibal, and Julius Caesar among the ancients; Prussia's Frederick the Great, Marshal Turenne of seventeenth-century France, and Sweden's Gustavus Adolphus among the moderns. He almost always sought to envelop his enemy by making a small frontal attack designed to hold the main enemy force by the nose so that he could swing around with the bulk of his army to attack one or both flanks or a flank and the rear. There was nothing tactically extraordinary in this, but the skill, speed, ferocity, and tenacity with which he executed these time-tested tactics were unparalleled by any contemporary commander. Mobility was the key. Enemy generals were left dazed, bewildered, and intimidated.

Napoleon Bonaparte's sweep through Italy netted 150,000 prisoners of war, 540 artillery pieces, and 170 regimental standards in the course of 67 combat actions, which included 18 important battles. After the French elections of 1797 restored to power many Royalists, who condemned Napoleon's achievements in Italy and his bold diplomacy with Austria, Napoleon responded by sending one of his generals, Pierre Augereau, to instigate a coup d'état in Paris. This culminated in the purge of Royalists on September 4, 1797, and propelled Napoleon to the top of the Republican power pyramid. He was granted full authority to negotiate the Treaty of Campo Formio on October 17, 1797, which brought an end to the First Coalition of nations allied against the French revolutionary republic. The treaty salvaged the French Revolution, stabilized the French Republic, and positioned Napoleon to embark on a career of military conquest and empire building without peer in the nineteenth century. Modern Europe was about be made.

Tactics Triumphant: The Age of Napoleon, Clausewitz, and Mahan (1800–1850)

Napoleon never claimed to be a radical innovator in making war. He was instead an advocate of what today's business leaders might call tactical "best practices"— not as defined by some classic book or modern mentor, but as he gathered them from his study of the military campaigns of what he called history's "great captains," generals from the ancient and modern worlds who consistently achieved victory. He distilled the example of these great captains into an eclectic but coherent system of warfighting that enabled him to rapidly build a record of victory that made his mere presence on a battlefield worth 40,000 men, as Wellington's co-victor at Waterloo, Gebhard Leberecht von Blücher, calculated. Today, Napoleon's battles and campaigns remain the episodes of military history both scholars and commanders most thoroughly study.

Part of Napoleon's success came from the sheer number of battles he fought—probably more than Alexander, Hannibal, and Caesar combined. He learned much from each new engagement. He applied to his own growing experience what he absorbed from the great captains to create his own tactics. They constituted a tactical toolbox, and yet he was careful never to repeat himself, never to become predictable in his actions. His enemies were intimidated by him. Doubtless, Napoleon regarded intimidation as a valuable asset, but he had even higher regard for the enduring ability to surprise. In that respect he was like a great composer, one who creates symphonies that never repeat themselves yet bear the unmistakable signature of their author. While Napoleon's battles held innovations and surprises, they were all conceived according to the same coherent principles. Each bore his signature.

There is no evidence—and, really, no reason to believe—that Napoleon was familiar with the ancient Chinese general and military theorist Sun Tzu. Nevertheless, like him, Napoleon believed that a campaign was won or lost before the first engagement was fought. Napoleon approached combat with dash and daring, but he always had a plan that was generally part of an even larger plan. In addition, he never wanted to engage the enemy on the enemy's terms. Whereas most of his contemporaries deployed for battle and then focused on the fight, Napoleon focused most intensely on the maneuvering *prior* to the engagement. He drilled his armies in rapid marching and agile maneuver, both of which enabled him to employ deception (another foundational element in Sun Tzu's *The Art of War*) intended to put the enemy at the greatest possible disadvantage. Instead of rushing to grapple with the foe, Napoleon often outran him, swinging around his enemy's flanks to sever communications before turning to force the opponent into an engagement that put the hostile ground at the enemy's back. The great set-piece battles of Marengo (June 14, 1800), Ulm (October 16–19, 1805), and Jena (October 14, 1806) were all won before the fighting began.

Almost always, Napoleon faced an enemy whose numbers exceeded his own. He compensated for this disadvantage by deception and by greater speed and agility of movement. He also set his troops to foraging, to living off the land. In part, this ensured a light wagon train of supply—minimal logistical hardware to slow him down. This prebattle tactic also served the purpose of keeping his forces spread out until almost the last possible moment before the attack. In this, Napoleon truly did approach combat in a manner radically different from his contemporaries. The standard approach was to carefully deploy and set up lines of battle. Napoleon avoided such stasis. His armies were accustomed to fan out and then concentrate with tremendous speed when and where needed. Napoleon, it is often said, possessed *coup d'oeil*, the ability to take in and assess a battlespace in the blink of an eye. He would look for the critical point to strike the enemy's line—and then he concentrated his forces against that point, as he famously did at Rivoli (January 14, 1797), Friedland (June 14, 1807), and Dresden (August 26–27, 1813). When the proper circumstances presented themselves, Napoleon sought to concentrate his outnumbered army *between* two enemies and then defeat them in serial fashion. This tactic resembled jiu-jitsu in that it used the opponent's apparent strength *against* that opponent. He did this with great success at Montenotte (Aril 12, 1796) but also, and with ultimately catastrophic results, at Waterloo (June 18, 1815)—which was, however, a battle that the victorious Wellington himself characterized as very nearly a loss or, as he put it, "the nearest run thing you ever saw in your life." Napoleon's apologists are quick to point out that the loss at Waterloo was not due to a deficiency in Napoleonic strategy or tactics but was the fault of subordinates who failed to execute them adequately.

One drawback to being a victorious general is that your enemies are often quick to learn and quick to imitate, using your own tactics against you. Even as he defeated one opponent after another, Napoleon, through his example, raised the tactical level of European warfighting and of warfare itself. Thanks to Napoleon, the division and the army corps became units of tactical maneuver on a large scale. Linear tactics—lines of battle—were increasingly replaced by defense as well as offense in depth. Mobility and maneuver replaced static positioning. Flexibility was elevated above all else so that commanders could concentrate their forces in real time, as needed, to accommodate the dynamic nature of combat on a large scale. Reserve forces were elevated in importance. Instead of being regarded as mere insurance against contingencies, they were used as "closers," the combat units most responsible for bringing the battle to a victorious conclusion and, even more, for exploiting any advantages gained by the battle.

Doubtless, many commanders were made better by either suffering defeat at the hands of Napoleon, serving with him, or simply observing or reading about him. Three major early nineteenth-century military theorists analyzed, distilled, and championed the example of Napoleon into writings that were highly influential on the training of military commanders and on the fighting of wars even into our own day. Jomini, Clausewitz, and Mahon strove to rationalize mass violence into geopolitically useful victory.

Antoine-Henri Jomini (1779–1869) served as a junior officer under Napoleon and was a protégé of one of Napoleon's most celebrated marshals, Michel Ney. Jomini turned coat in the Russian campaign in 1813 and remained in the military service of the czars for the next 56 years. Yet he used his spare time to write analytical works on Napoleon's campaigns, and while *Summary of the Art of War* is his most famous work, his very first book, *Treatise on Great Military Operations*, so shocked Napoleon that he exclaimed, "It teaches my whole system of war to my enemies!"

Jomini's writings were indeed highly influential, forming the foundation of systematic military education and still relevant today. His name, however, is not as familiar outside of military academies as that of Karl von Clausewitz (1780–1831). Born in Magdeburg, Prussia, he served in the Prussian Army during all of its campaigns against Napoleon, from Jena to Waterloo. After the Napoleonic Wars, from 1818 to 1830, Clausewitz was administrative director of the Prussian Kriegsakademie (War College) in Berlin. He wrote voluminous studies on military campaigns, with special focus on those of Napoleon. Yet the single work on which his greatest fame rests is not an analysis of specific campaigns but a treatise on the very nature of war itself. Never finished, *On War* was published posthumously and has had the greatest impact on how both generals and political leaders think about war and use war to achieve various geopolitical aims. Clausewitz's chief source of inspiration for *On War* was surely Napoleon, the most prolific nineteenth-century practitioner of war on a geopolitical scale and the one who achieved the most ambitious geopolitical ends.

The Napoleonic strategic and tactical tradition came to the United States through the teachings and writings of Dennis Hart Mahan (1802–1871), father of the even more famous Alfred Thayer Mahan (1840–1914). The senior Mahan graduated first in the West Point class of 1824. Instead of being commissioned with a field unit, however, he was immediately made an assistant professor. After teaching at the academy for two years, he went to Paris for four years of advanced study, returning to West Point in 1830 as professor of engineering—the most prestigious academic appointment the academy could offer.

Mahan was a pioneer who wrote his own textbook on military engineering for the simple reason that none existed at the time. It became an important text on engineering in the civilian world as well, and he followed it with books on military theory and tactics, all based on the lessons of the Napoleonic Wars. Mahan in effect created the curriculum and texts for West Point, which amounted to the war college of the United States. The officers on both sides of the Civil War (1861–1865) went into battle having been educated by the same teacher, from the same textbooks, and according to the same curriculum. Mahan brought to the United States what Napoleon had brought to Europe: a new tradition of military professionalism.

Barbary Wars: Fighting Terrorism (1801–1815)

The American Revolution (1775–1783) created a new nation, but it alone did not win sovereignty for the United States. In the years following the war, the new republic faced a number of threats to its nationhood, many of them with a military component. Domestically, there was the unremitting guerrilla warfare between the Indians and settlers of the frontier regions, especially in the Ohio country, a region encompassing present-day Ohio, northwestern West Virginia, western Pennsylvania, and a portion of southeastern Indiana. Internationally, friction between France and the United States, close allies during the Revolution, had developed during the peace negotiations that ended the American Revolution, as it became clear that France was more interested in opposing Britain and furthering the territorial ambitions of Spain, a French ally, than in upholding the cause of the United States' independence. Next, the fall of the monarchy in the French Revolution brought renewed warfare between France and Britain in 1793 that further damaged Franco-American relations, as the revolutionary French government accused the United States of deliberately favoring British interests over those of France.

For its part, Britain was also making trouble. The Treaty of Paris that had ended the American Revolution called for the British evacuation of outposts on America's western frontier. Not only did Parliament fail to enforce this provision, American settlers in the region believed that British interests were inducing the Indians to raid. At sea, British warships began routinely intercepting American merchant ships and "impressing"—abducting—certain American sailors (those arbitrarily deemed to be British navy deserters or simply British subjects) for service in the Royal Navy. The so-called Jay Treaty (Treaty of Amity, Commerce, and Navigation, 1795) provided temporary relief but exacerbated Franco-American relations, touching off an undeclared naval conflict historians call the Franco-American Quasi-War (1798–1800). By the time this was resolved favorably to the United States, the French Revolutionary Wars (1792–1802) were segueing into the Napoleonic Wars (1803–1815), and when neither the French nor their English enemies could score a decisive victory, both turned to attacks on the commerce of noncombatant nations, including the United States, in the hope of crippling one another's economies. Most notably, the English resumed the practice of impressing American sailors and also seized American vessels attempting to enter French ports, thereby beginning the long run-up to the War of 1812 (1812–1815).

Against the backdrop of these several threats to American sovereignty came a menace from a much more remote place. The "Barbary pirates" were Muslim seafarers who had been operating off the coast of North Africa since the seventeenth century from what "Christian nations" called the Barbary states (present-day Morocco, Algeria, Tunisia, and Libya). These pirates were not simply freelancing criminals. Their activities were state-sanctioned, and the pirates enjoyed the financial and political backing of wealthy merchants as well as the rulers of the North African Islamic states. Profitable to the Barbary states, the piracy also included a strong element of religious warfare.

From the perspective of the twenty-first century, the activities of the Barbary pirates looks a lot like terrorism. Most "Christian nations" dealt with it by paying extortionary tribute money to the rulers of the states involved. It was cheaper than war, and it kept North African waters open to commerce. At first the United States also paid the tributes demanded, but political leaders and the American public increasingly saw this as both an insult and a threat to American sovereignty. For this reason, the United States embarked on a series of limited naval wars to win the right of free navigation of North African waters.

Historians often call them the "Barbary Wars," and they spanned 1801 to 1815, with the most concentrated action occurring in the Tripolitan War of 1801–1805 and the Algerine War of 1815. While these wars represented a new kind of war, a religiously tinged war against criminality or even terrorism rather than a "traditional" war to gain or defend territory, the conflicts did have a broader, more conventional geopolitical context. In 1785 Great Britain, eager to restrict American trade with North Africa, encouraged the bey of Algiers to capture two U.S. commercial vessels. Thomas Jefferson, at the time American minister plenipotentiary to France, attempted to recruit the aid of Portugal, Naples, Sardinia, and Russia, as well as France, in an anti-Algerian alliance. When France declined to cooperate, the alliance collapsed, and Britain encouraged further Algerian action in which a dozen U.S. ships were captured and more than 100 American sailors imprisoned. This prompted the United States to negotiate a treaty with the bey of Algiers in 1795, pledging tribute to secure release of the captives and to ensure freedom of navigation. Additional treaties were concluded with Tunis and Tripoli.

Despite the treaties, the idea of tribute rankled American sensibilities, and there was a long delay in sending the agreed-to tribute money. Shortly after the inauguration of President Jefferson in 1801, Pasha Yusuf Qaramanli, Tripoli's ruler, unofficially declared war against the United States. Jefferson concluded a coalition with Sweden, Sicily, Malta, Portugal, and Morocco against Tripoli, which forced Qaramanli to back down. For the next two years, one U.S. frigate and several smaller U.S. Navy vessels warded off piracy by patrolling the Tripolitan coast. This mission proceeded successfully until the frigate U.S.S. *Philadelphia* ran aground in October 1803 and was boarded by Tripolitan sailors, who captured 300 U.S. Navy sailors, took the ship as a prize, and prepared to use it against the Americans. In February 1804, however, U.S. Navy lieutenant Stephen Decatur, with great daring and stealth, entered Tripoli Harbor and burned *Philadelphia*. After this, Commodore Edward Preble stepped up the ongoing bombardment of Tripoli, and William Eaton, U.S. consul at Tunis, proposed an alliance with Ahmed Qaramanli, the brother Yusuf had deposed in 1795. Eaton also recruited an army of Arabs and Greeks and joined these to a contingent of U.S. Marines to support the restoration of Ahmed as ruler of Tripoli.

Consul Eaton's force captured the city of Derne in 1805, just as the Jefferson government, which had neither opposed nor supported the Eaton plan, concluded a treaty of peace with Yusuf on June 4, 1805. The treaty ransomed the prisoners for $60,000 and, although it made no explicit mention of the subject of tribute, it put a de facto end to the practice of tribute payment by establishing free and unhindered commerce between the United States and Tripoli.

Americans celebrated the treaty as a triumph, and it suppressed North African piracy for a time. The outbreak of the War of 1812 between Britain and the United States, however, prompted the withdrawal of the U.S. warships that had been keeping the Barbary pirates in check. This encouraged the dey of Algiers to resume preying on American commerce in the region. He also expelled the U.S. consul, imprisoned or enslaved U.S. nationals, and then declared war on the United States for having violated a 1795 treaty by which the United States had pledged payment of tribute in return for safe passage of commercial vessels. In response to the declaration of war and with the manpower demands of the War of 1812 having ended, Decatur led a 10-ship squadron into the Mediterranean. Between March 3 and June 30, 1815, he captured two Algerian warships and then sailed into the harbor of Algiers. Training his artillery on the city, Decatur demanded cancellation of tribute and the release of all U.S. prisoners without ransom. The June 30 Treaty of Peace with Algiers incorporated the dey's pledge to end state-sanctioned piracy.

From Algiers, Decatur proceeded to Tunis and Tripoli, where, again at cannon's mouth, he compelled similar treaties and also secured compensation for American vessels seized at the behest of the British during the War of 1812. The brief "Algerine War" ended American participation in the Barbary Wars and was a triumph of sovereignty for the young American republic. The wars also defined what would prove enduring missions for the both the U.S. Navy and the U.S. Marines—fighting "small wars" and "police actions" to suppress criminal and terrorist activities. To this day, the Tripolitan War is commemorated in the "Marine Corps Hymn," which refers to the "shores of Tripoli."

Annus Mirabilis: Napoleon's Brilliant Year (1805)

From 1805 to 1807, Great Britain and its allies Austria, Russia, and Sweden fought the third of seven "Coalition Wars" against Napoleon. At the outbreak of the war, most of the French army was massed near Boulogne-sur-Mer, on the northeastern tip of France at the English Channel, preparing to invade England. The rest of the army, about 50,000 men, was assembled under Marshal André Masséna in northern Italy. The coalition forces intended to destroy the French in Italy and then advance westward, toward the Rhine and France.

Napoleon discerned the coalition's intentions and, on August 31, 1805, discarded his original plan for a cross-Channel invasion and instead began a secret march with his entire Grand Army—some 200,000 men—eastward. On September 2, unaware of Napoleon's momentous move, Austrian general Karl Mack von Leiberich advanced toward Ulm, Bavaria, with 50,000 troops. Archduke Charles of Austria marched independently with 100,000 men to attack Masséna's force in Italy. Yet another coalition army, consisting of 120,000 Russians, began marching westward. Sweden also pledged a force. The plan was for the Russians and the Swedes to join Mack in an attack on the Grand Army.

On September 26, Mack—still ignorant of Napoleon's whereabouts—was between Ulm and Munich. A force of 33,000 Austrians under Archduke John was massed at Innsbruck, and Archduke Charles was in the Adige Valley, between Trent and Venice. The Russian army was still far to the east., and the Swedes had not gotten under way. On October 6, elements of Napoleon's Grand Army reached the Danube. Marshal Joachim Murat led his cavalry through the Black Forest, engaging Mack at Ulm. While the Austrian was distracted by this frontal attack, the bulk of the Grand Army encircled him in the Battle of Ulm. On October 17, Mack surrendered with nearly 30,000 men.

This spectacular campaign, culminating in a surprise attack by six columns of the French Grand Army, was just the opening of not only the most spectacular year in Napoleon's military career but one of the most spectacular years in all military history. It was a triumph of superior training, grand strategy, and flawless tactics. Rarely had a victory been so overwhelming.

Having defeated Mack, Napoleon detached some of his corps to march southward so as to block any Austrian attempt to advance against him via the Alps. In the meantime, on October 30, Masséna seized the initiative and attacked

Archduke Charles in Italy. He pursued both Charles and Archduke John, dashing the coalition's hope of destroying the French Army in Italy. During November 1 to 14, Napoleon invaded Austria, driving Russian forces under Mikhail Kutuzov before his advance, despite the Russians' gallant delaying actions at Dürrenstein and Hollabrünn.

Having taken Vienna, Napoleon left 20,000 men to occupy and hold the Austrian capital while he marched the major available portion of the Grand Army, about 65,000 men, some 70 miles to Brünn, where he waited for the coalition to make its next move. As November drew to a close, the strategic situation was this: Napoleon was in the very midst of his enemies. Austrian Archduke Ferdinand had 18,000 men in Prague, northwest of him. Emperor Alexander I of Russia and Emperor Frances II of Austria nominally commanded a total of 90,000 men at Olmütz (Kutuzov was in actual field command), northeast of Napoleon. Austrian Archdukes Charles and John had another 80,000 men, which French forces (under Marshal Michel Ney and General Auguste F. L. Marmont) bottled up by blocking their crossing of the Alps. Masséna, with just 35,000 men, continually harassed these superior forces until both archdukes withdrew via Hungary to Austria.

Napoleon nevertheless appeared vulnerable. If the coalition forces could effect a linkup against him, cutting off his line of communication to France through Vienna, he was surely doomed. But the very appearance of vulnerability was key to Napoleon's plan. He offered himself as bait, and when Kutuzov took that bait, moving south to cut the French lines of communications, Napoleon was ready for him.

On November 28, Napoleon, facing east, was positioned two miles west of a village called Austerlitz (today Slavkov u Brna, Czech Republic) in the Moravian province of the Austrian Empire. He deployed his army on low ground, purposely overextending his right wing in a manner he knew Kutuzov's scouts would see and report. In the meantime, Napoleon covertly concentrated most of his forces just east of Brünn, adjacent to the Olmütz road.

The coalition forces reached Austerlitz on December 1, eager to annihilate Napoleon's right flank and then insert themselves between the rest of Napoleon's army and Vienna. They attacked at dawn on December 2, forcing Napoleon's right to fall back. By nine in the morning, a third of Kutuzov's forces were in action, with more coming. It was at this point that Napoleon sent his center, a corps under Nicolas J. Soult, storming the heights of Pratzen, where they split the Russian-Austrian front. Soult and some 8,000 French reinforcements under Louis N. Davout now encircled the coalition's left flank and rapidly rolled it up, forcing it into a rout. The Russians sought to retreat across frozen ponds, only to come under French artillery fire, which broke up the ice. Many of Kutuzov's troops were thus drowned in flight.

Napoleon now unleashed another corps, this one commanded by Marshal Jean-Baptiste Bernadotte, who exploited the gap Soult's envelopment had created. Simultaneously, a corps under General Jean Lanne charged into the coalition right flank on the road to Olmütz. After a fierce fight led by the valiant Russian general Prince Pyotr Bagration, Bernadotte's corps joined Lanne's corps in extending the envelopment of Bagration. By the end of the day, Kutuzov's command—the armies nominally led by Alexander I and Frances II—suffered catastrophic causalities: 36,000 men killed, wounded, or taken prisoner, while the rest were scattered. Napoleon's losses were about 10,000 killed and wounded.

If anything, the Battle of Austerlitz was an even greater victory than the Ulm Campaign, warranting comparison with Alexander the Great's victory at the Battle of Gaugamela (Arbela) in 331 BC, Hannibal's triumph at Cannae in 216 BC, and, far more recently, Frederick the Great's brilliant achievement at Leuthen in 1757. Austria surrendered to Napoleon on December 4, signing the Treaty of Pressburg on the 26th, by which the Austrian Empire not only withdrew from the War of the Third Coalition but also ceded to France vast tracts of territory in Germany and Italy, making Napoleon dominant in western and southern Germany. The year 1805—for Napoleon, an Annus Mirabilis, a year of wonders—ended with the geopolitical map of Europe radically redrawn around France.

Battle of Trafalgar: Nelson's Fatal Masterpiece (1805)

In the course of 1805, Napoleon made France beyond question the dominant military power—on land. He failed miserably, however, when it came to competing with the British Royal Navy for control of the seas. The Royal Navy effectively blockaded France, which not only kept Napoleon from fully mobilizing his own naval resources but also did much damage to the French economy by disrupting trade.

The threat became most acute during the War of the Third Coalition. Napoleon's original strategy for winning the war was to invade Britain. What stood in his way was the Royal Navy. Napoleon therefore ordered the Mediterranean fleets of France and its ally Spain to break through the British blockade there and rendezvous in the Caribbean, from which they were to attack the blockade of the French fleet at Brest. Once that blockade had been broken, the combined fleets would clear the English Channel of Royal Navy ships, thus making way for the barges that would carry Napoleon's armies to an invasion of England.

In April 1805, Admiral Pierre-Charles Villeneuve was able to break through the British blockade of the French Mediterranean port city of Toulon and sail into the Atlantic, where he rendezvoused with a small Spanish fleet. Together, the two fleets, comprising about 20 vessels, made for the West Indies. From April to July, Lord Horatio Nelson, far and away the Royal Navy's most celebrated admiral, pursued Villeneuve to and throughout the West Indies. Villaneuve repeatedly avoided battle with Nelson and, once more, broke into the open Atlantic. On July 22, a Royal Navy squadron of 18 vessels under Sir Robert Calder intercepted the combined Franco-Spanish fleet at Cape Finisterre, a rocky peninsula off the west coast of Galicia, Spain. Although Calder managed to capture two Spanish ships, Villeneuve fled with the rest of the fleet to Cádiz, Spain, where he was reinforced.

By this time, in August, Napoleon had shelved his original plan for a cross-Channel invasion of England. He now had new instructions for his navy. He ordered Villeneuve to sail the combined fleet out of Cádiz and back into the Mediterranean, where he was to join other French ships at the Spanish Mediterranean port of Cartagena. From here, Villeneuve was to sail to Italy to support Marshal André Masséna's army, which was under continued threat by forces of the Third Coalition.

Titled *One Hundred Years Ago 1805–1905*, this engraving was made from an oil painting by Albert W. Holden. The modern (1905) Royal Navy sailor gazes intently at the portrait of Lord Nelson on the centenary of the admiral's victory and death at Trafalgar.

ROYAL MUSEUMS GREENWICH

Villeneuve was a mediocre naval officer, but Napoleon had no better alternative. During the French Revolution, the best officers in the upper echelons of the navy had either been guillotined or had left—"fled" is the more accurate word—the service. Among those remaining, few found favor with Napoleon. To make matters worse, Villeneuve was under no illusions as to his own limited abilities. Napoleon had sent Villeneuve on his mission without knowing that Nelson was still looking to do battle against him. Nor did Napoleon know that the British admiral now had a large fleet of 29 ships of the line. When Villeneuve learned of Nelson's presence, he was inclined to abort his mission—but he resigned himself to fate because he was already under threat from Napoleon, who had menaced him with removal from command for cowardice. He therefore set sail from Cartagena on September 27 with 33 ships, the Spanish contingent of his fleet under the command of Flag Officer Federico Gravina.

While he was off Cape Spartel, at the entrance to the Strait of Gibraltar, Nelson received word that Villeneuve's fleet was in motion. He immediately set a course to intercept, and the two fleets met off Cape Trafalgar, near the Spanish town of Los Caños de Meca.

Villeneuve turned tail, heading back toward Cádiz in an irregular line stretching some five miles. Nelson had, in advance, laid out to his subordinates his unconventional plan of attack. Normal practice was for opposing fleets to engage each other in single parallel lines. This simplified maneuver and ensured maximum broadside fields of fire. Nelson, however, put his fleet in *two* roughly parallel columns approaching perpendicular to the long Franco-Spanish line. His two divisions drove hard and straight into the very center of the enemy fleet, cutting the line in two. For the next five hours, Nelson went about systematically destroying the Franco-Spanish fleet. Of its 33 vessels, 21 were captured—10 French, 11 Spanish—and 1 French ship was sunk. Not a single British ship was lost. Among the French, 3,373 sailors were killed, 1,155 wounded, and more than 4,000 captured. Among the Spanish, 1,022 were killed, 1,386 wounded, and between 3,000 and 4,000 became prisoners of war. Four hundred fifty-eight Royal Navy officers and sailors were killed and 1,208 wounded.

Among those slain was Admiral Nelson, who received a fatal wound and lived just long enough to know that victory was assured. Spanish Flag Officer Gravina was also mortally wounded but did not die until five months after the battle. Villeneuve, who was among the prisoners of war, was paroled but confined to Britain. He was given permission to attend Lord Nelson's funeral.

Horatio Nelson, First Viscount Nelson, was an extraordinary officer. Before he met his end at Trafalgar, he had been repeatedly wounded in battle, losing an eye in Corsica and an arm at Santa Cruz de Tenerife. A peerless strategist and tactician, he was not only personally courageous but also possessed compelling command presence and was universally admired by those who served under him. He always insisted on being in the thick of battle and on leading the fight in full dress uniform. He believed that making himself conspicuous inspired his officers and crew. Doubtless, it was this high-profile display while on the quarterdeck of HMS *Victory* that made him an easy target for the French musketeer-marksman who fired from the ship *Redoutable* at a range of about 50 feet. Reportedly, Nelson's last words were "Thank God I have done my duty" and "God and my country."

Horatio Nelson set an example of audacious, skillful, and committed command, not just for the Royal Navy but for every navy in the world. What he specifically achieved at Trafalgar was the utter destruction of French naval power, which was never restored during the Napoleonic Wars, the course of which ran for nearly another decade. In terms of tactics as well as strategy, Trafalgar stands as the single most decisive naval victory in history—with the possible exception of the World War II Pacific Battle of Midway (June 4–7, 1942).

Friedrich Krupp Starts a Steel Works: Artillery Becomes an Industry and War Is Transformed (1811)

Arndt Krupp made a fortune buying up the property of families who died in and around Essen, Germany, during an epidemic of the Black Death late in the sixteenth century. After Arndt's own death in 1624, his son, Anton, used some of his family's wealth to establish a gunsmithing shop. The Thirty Years' War was in progress and contributed to a great demand for shoulder arms. It was not until the early nineteenth century, however, that the Krupps became involved in modern steelmaking, which led to the Krupp firm's development into the world's premier maker of artillery.

This evolution took time and involved much trial and even more error.

Friedrich Krupp took over management of the family forge in 1807 when he was just 19 years old. He was not a talented businessman and almost immediately turned a profitable family enterprise into a losing proposition, which his widowed mother was forced to sell. Not long after this, however, she followed her husband to the grave, having left virtually the entire Krupp estate to the hapless Friedrich. Seeking to redeem himself and the family business, Friedrich set about discovering the very well-kept trade secret of producing crucible, or cast, steel—a steel of unparalleled strength. At this point in industrial history, cast steel came from just one place, Sheffield, England, where clockmaker Benjamin Huntsman had created the process of making the product in 1740. Those who worked in the industry cooperated with the British government in preserving the secrets of manufacture, forcing the world to import virtually all of their cast steel from Sheffield.

When, as part of the so-called Continental System, Napoleon instituted a blockade against Britain in 1806, the importation of Sheffield cast steel largely ended throughout Europe. Napoleon offered a prize of 4,000 francs to anyone who could devise a way to copy the Sheffield process. This prompted Friedrich Krupp in 1811 to found Krupp Gusstahlfabrik (Krupp Cast Steel Works). It was a good name, but he had yet to figure out how to make cast steel. Nevertheless, Friedrich jumped in with both feet, investing heavily in building a large foundry and a water mill on the Ruhr River. Only after the facility was completed did he discover that the Ruhr was an unreliable source of hydropower, so he built a smaller facility.

While he finally devised a way of smelting steel in 1816, he could not make enough of it to turn a profit; in any case, his product fell short of true cast steel in strength.

Friedrich Krupp died in 1826 at 39. The steelworks he created suddenly became the responsibility of his 14-year-old son, Alfried (he later adopted the English spelling, Alfred), who left school to manage the business. While laboring to produce and sell miscellaneous steel merchandise to keep the family afloat, Alfred continued to pursue the quest for a viable cast steel process. In the meantime, in 1841, his brother Hermann invented a spoon-roller, for which Alfred secured a patent and which he manufactured for companies specializing in making spoons and other utensils out of metal. This financed the enlargement of the Krupp factory and, at long last, the perfection of a cast steel process that allowed the factory to cast very large flawless steel blocks.

In 1847, largely in an effort to promote the great virtue of cast steel—strength—Alfred Krupp cast his first cannon. Four years later, in 1851, he exhibited at London's Great Exhibition a 6-pounder cannon made entirely from cast steel. He also displayed a perfect 4,300-pound cast steel ingot. He topped that considerable achievement at the Paris Exposition in 1855 when he exhibited a spectacular 100,000-pound ingot. In the meantime, Alfred Krupp began producing railway wheels out of cast steel. Because these involved no welded seams, they were extremely durable, and the new product made the Krupp enterprise extraordinarily profitable.

The Krupp Gun Works during World War I
PHOTO BY BROWN BROS., 1915

With his newfound success, Alfred continued to improve the casting of steel cannon. Even after he had created a great product, however, it took much time, effort, and lobbying to persuade inherently conservative military men that cast steel was superior both to bronze and iron for the manufacture of artillery. Eventually, he did win customers in the Russian, Turkish, and Prussian armies.

The Franco-Prussian War (1870–1871), in which Prussia defeated France and Wilhelm I and Otto von Bismarck were therefore positioned to create the German Empire, was widely regarded as a contest between Prussian artillery made of Krupp steel and French cannon made of the traditional bronze. The strength of cast steel allowed for cannon of larger caliber and more firepower, since the heavier shells could be propelled by massive loads of powder that would blow apart any bronze barrel.

In the aftermath of the Franco-Prussian War, Krupp's innovations created a revolution in artillery. The Krupp works became an industrial empire and was soon intimately tied to the German government. Even before that war, Krupp's growing success inspired inventors and industrialists in other countries. The demand for artillery created by the American Civil War (1861–1865) afforded great opportunities to Robert P. Parrott, John A. Dahlgren, and Thomas J. Rodman, who all produced breech-loading cannon of innovative design intended to accommodate very large projectiles and very heavy powder loads. In nineteenth-century England, William G. A. Strong and Joseph Whitworth produced new varieties of ordnance. In France, Henri-Joseph Paixhans invented the first shell guns, naval artillery combining explosive shells and a flat trajectory, which made the demise of wooden ships and the rise of ironclad and steel vessels inevitable. Paixhans also produced massive siege mortars.

Krupp and his international industrial progeny transformed war from contests between men armed with muskets and rifles into armies equipped with massive artillery. World War I (1914–1918) would become known as the "artillery war," and only the development of airpower both on land and sea during World War II (1939–1945) would begin to displace artillery as the delivery system for massive high-explosive devastation.

From Moscow to Waterloo: Napoleonic Retreat (1812–1815)

The year 1805 Brought Napoleon to his first geopolitical and military height. A Fourth Coalition formed to oppose him, yet again, in 1806. Napoleon scored new victories against Prussia at Jena (Auerstedt; October 14, 1806) and then triumphed over the Russians at the Battle of Friedland, Prussia (June 14, 1807). The Fourth Coalition collapsed, and the Treaties of Tilsit (with Russia and Prussia, July 7 and 9, 1807) brought two years of relative peace, broken in 1809 by the War of the Fifth Coalition. The Battle of Wagram, northeast of Vienna (July 5–6, 1809), ended that short-lived coalition, whereupon Napoleon invaded Spain in an effort to further extend the Continental System, designed to bar continental Europe from all trade with Britain. After Napoleon placed his brother Joseph on the Spanish throne in 1808, Spain and Portugal, backed by the British, rebelled, igniting the long and bitter Peninsular War (1808–1814), in which an alliance among Bourbon Spain, Portugal, and the British Empire decisively defeated Napoleon, resulting in his unconditional abdication as emperor of France on April 11, 1814.

Three years earlier, the cordial relations between Napoleon and Czar Alexander I of Russia brought about by the 1807 Franco-Russian Treaty of Tilsit had broken down. In 1811, Alexander defied Napoleon by substantially easing the anti-British trade restrictions of the Continental System in Russia. Learning that Alexander was preparing an offensive against him, Napoleon rapidly expanded his Grande Armée to an unprecedented half-million men and embarked on an invasion of Russia. In this, he committed two uncharacteristic errors, which military historians have explored and debated ever since. The new version of the Grande Armée was the first military formation in which Napoleon sacrificed the quality of his troops for sheer quantity. He turned his back on his own experience, which had proved the effectiveness of relatively small armies made up of superbly trained officers and men. He would soon discover that numbers could be more liability than asset, especially in the vast wastelands of Russia. And that, of course, was Napoleon's second error. He ignored the many who warned him that Russia was the grave of empires. Its measureless distances, harsh climate, and lack of developed infrastructure ate armies alive.

He began the Russian invasion on June 23, 1812. A hoped-for alliance with Poland immediately collapsed when Napoleon refused to give the Polish nationalists what they wanted: his blessing to create an independent Poland. Next he discovered that the Russians meant to avoid a showdown battle with him. As they failed to resist, Napoleon advanced deeper into the belly of the Russian beast. With each Russian military defeat, the czar's forces retreated farther, burning crops and anything else of sustaining value as they withdrew. Napoleon had always depended on living off the land. Now he found himself burdened by a giant army he could not feed. Soon, losses from privation, starvation, disease, and desertion proved far greater than anything combat could produce. By the time Napoleon reached the outskirts of Moscow on September 7, 1812, he had only about 130,000 "effectives" under his command, slightly more than 20 percent of the number with which he had begun the campaign.

On September 7, the Russian army took a stand at the Battle of Borodino. The result was a terrible Russian defeat. Of 120,000 Russian troops engaged, 45,000 were killed, wounded, or captured. French losses were some 35,000 killed, wounded, or captured out of 130,000 engaged. Napoleon and his battered army were too spent to pursue the routed Russians, whom he could have finished off. Napoleon later remarked of Borodino: "The French showed themselves to be worthy of victory, but the Russians showed themselves worthy of being invincible."

Napoleon marched into Moscow, assuming that Czar Alexander I would now seek terms. Instead, the czar ordered the city burned, and the emperor won the ashes of a deserted city.

By the time Napoleon began his return march, the Russian winter had arrived. Through mile upon mile, men starved and men froze. By the time the Grande Armée crossed the frozen Berezina River (in modern Belarus), it had been reduced to roughly 40,000 men, less than 10 percent of its original strength.

Yet, returned to Paris, Napoleon managed to retain his hold over the French. He rapidly rebuilt his army to a field strength of 350,000 by 1813, and much of the rest of Europe—Prussia, Austria, Sweden, Great Britain, Spain, and Portugal—joined Russia in creating the Sixth Coalition. Napoleon engaged the new alliance, winning a series of remarkable victories in Germany. The most important of these was the Battle of Dresden (August 26–27, 1813), in which he defeated a 214,000-man Austrian, Prussian, and Russian army with a force of 135,000 men. The Napoleon of old seemed to be back, but at the Battle of Kulm, in Bohemia (August 29–30, 1813), a French army of 32,000 under Laurent Gouvion Saint-Cyr and Auguste Marmont was defeated by a coalition force. Then, at the Battle of Leipzig (October 16–19), Napoleon's army of 195,000 was overwhelmed and crushed by some 430,000 coalition troops. This was the biggest battle of the Napoleonic wars and, in fact, the biggest European battle before World War I. Napoleon lost 58,000 killed, wounded, or captured. The coalition lost 54,000 killed or wounded.

After Leipzig, the emperor fell back on France with just 70,000 effectives. A coalition army of at least 300,000 dogged his retreat, and he was powerless to prevent the fall of Paris to coalition troops in March 1814. When Napoleon vowed to retake the capital, Marshal Ney led several of his fellow marshals in a mutiny on April 4, 1814. Napoleon abdicated in favor of his son; the Sixth Coalition rejected this conditional abdication. Under the Treaty of Paris, he abdicated unconditionally on April 11, 1814, whereupon the coalition members ordered his exile to the Mediterranean island of Elba, about 12.5 miles off the coast of Tuscany.

Napoleon remained in exile until he somehow managed to elude his guards and, on February 26, 1815, escaped from the island. Two days later, he landed at Golfe-Juan, France. The Bourbon royalists, who now had tenuous control of the government, ordered the 5th Regiment to arrest the fugitive. The troops found him near Grenoble on March 7. Walking up to the column of soldiers, Napoleon announced: "Here I am. Kill your Emperor, if you wish."

With one voice, the men of the 5th Regiment responded, "Vive L'Empereur!"

They escorted Napoleon to Paris, a terrified Louis XVIII fleeing before his approach. On March 13, European leaders met, proclaimed Napoleon an outlaw, and, four days later, announced a seventh coalition, consisting of Great Britain, the Netherlands, Russia, Austria, and Prussia.

Arriving in Paris on March 20, 1815, Napoleon resumed the vacant throne. Within two months he had assembled a loyal army of 200,000. At this point, the Seventh Coalition had not attempted to move against him. Napoleon seized the initiative by moving to block the union of approaching British and Prussian armies. In a favorite tactic, he planned to attack *between* them on a battlefield in and around Waterloo in what is today Belgium but was at the time within the United Kingdom of the Netherlands.

The Waterloo Campaign commenced on June 16, 1815. Napoleon had 72,000 men available against 118,000 of the Seventh Coalition (Britain, Prussia, United Netherlands, Hanover, Nassau, and Brunswick), led by the Duke of Wellington and the Prussian field marshal Gebhard Leberecht von Blücher. They were two of Europe's best commanders not named Napoleon. Wellington was hailed as the "Iron Duke" and Blücher as "Marschall Vorwärts"—Marshal Forward—a sobriquet born of his aggressive fighting style. Wellington had direct command of the Anglo-Dutch forces, Blücher of the Prussian and associated German forces.

Napoleon advanced from the south as Wellington closed in from the northwest and Blücher from the east. Napoleon was relentless in his attacks against Wellington's army, which arrived on the field before Blücher could get into full engagement. His objective was to drive Wellington from the field, which is precisely what he did at a crossroads called Quatre Bras, just south of Waterloo, on June 16.

Yet even in withdrawing, Wellington kept his forces intact, and while Napoleon had been concentrated against Wellington, Blücher arrived at

Wavre. Napoleon defeated him here, but at Waterloo he at last faced the combined forces of Wellington and Blücher. His strategy of attacking between two armies, defeating each, serially, in detail, before they could unite had been quite successful at Quatre Bras and Wavre. Now, however, in this final round, Napoleon's subordinates could no longer successfully execute the master's strategy and tactics. Napoleon's right, left, and finally his center all crumbled. The last day of battle, June 18, 1815, turned into a French rout. By the end of that day, Napoleon commanded no more than 24,000 men, who melted from the field, leaving the forces of the Seventh Coalition to advance into France, where they restored Louis XVIII to the throne.

Napoleon found himself exiled for a second time—not to a pleasant island off the European coast but to Saint Helena, a British-owned speck of earth in the Atlantic Ocean, about 1,200 miles from any substantial body of land. His health slipping into a steady decline, he settled down to dictate his memoirs. On May 5, 1821, Napoleon I died, emperor no more but an enduring object of study, contemplation, and debate for statesmen and soldiers alike.

Choosing War in 1812: America v. Britain (1812–1814)

Up through the post–World War II era, before the Vietnam War became divisively unpopular, many American historians sought to portray the War of 1812 as a "second War of Independence," a fight for sovereignty against British interference with American commerce on the high seas, where the Royal Navy was intercepting American merchant vessels and "impressing" (abducting) sailors arbitrarily deemed to be British subjects liable to conscription for service on British warships.

Such was the long-running narrative of the origin of the War of 1812. In fact, the United States declared war on Britain on June 19, 1812, three days *after* British negotiators had agreed to halt impressment. In truth, the conflict was America's first war of choice rather than necessity. Its true origin is not to be found on the Atlantic Ocean, but in the trans-Appalachian West. In Congress that region was represented by a group of land-hungry "War Hawks," spearheaded by Representative Henry Clay of Kentucky. They saw a fight with Britain as an opportunity to clear "hostile" Indians from the frontier, opening it to white trade and settlement. Moreover, because Spain was allied with Britain against Napoleon—the Napoleonic Wars were still in full swing—so-called Spanish Florida, which extended from modern Florida west to the Mississippi River, was also regarded as up for grabs. Win a war against Britain, and its ally's territory would fall to the United States. That would forge an unbroken link from the eastern seaboard through the recently purchased Louisiana Territory all the way to the Pacific.

Elected to his first term in 1808, President James Madison wanted no war, but, facing a tough reelection battle in 1812, he finally yielded to the War Hawks and asked Congress for a declaration, which they gave him on June 18, 1812. The U.S. Army then consisted of just 12,000 regular troops scattered over a vast territory. The U.S. Navy was in better shape—and had recently prevailed against the French navy in the "Quasi War" of 1798–1800—but it was still puny compared to a Royal Navy that had triumphed over the combined French and Spanish fleets at Trafalgar in 1805. Of course the War Hawks pointed out that most of the British military was engaged against Napoleon, which gave the Americans an opportunity for a successful preemptive war.

Andrew Jackson defends New Orleans against the British in a battle fought *after* the Treaty of Ghent had ended the War of 1812.

FROM DAVID H. MONTGOMERY, *THE BEGINNER'S AMERICAN HISTORY* (BOSTON: GINN & CO., 1904)

U.S. strategists laid out an aggressive approach, beginning with a three-pronged invasion of Canada: a penetration from Lake Champlain to Montreal; another across the Niagara frontier; and a third into Upper Canada from Detroit. These operations all failed miserably in the execution, and on August 16, 1812, Detroit was surrendered to the British. The U.S. northern frontier in what is today the upper Midwest was laid open to raids by British-allied Indians. They quickly gained a strong measure of control over most of the Old Northwest (modern-day Ohio, Indiana, Illinois, Michigan, Wisconsin, and some of Minnesota), but the British, unwilling to commit large numbers of troops to this new war with America, did not exploit the opening.

The performance of the U.S. Navy stood in nearly miraculous contrast to that of the American land forces, which were a loosely organized combination of the diminutive regular army and a patchwork of militias. The British brought to bear 1,048 vessels to blockade U.S. naval and commercial shipping in an effort to strangle the American economy. Opposed to this force were the dozen frigates and 14 lesser vessels of the U.S. Navy plus a ragtag collection of somewhat more than 500 privateers, civilian vessels authorized by the U.S. government to prey on British commercial vessels. The frigates, their commanders, and their crews proved to be extraordinary and bested the Royal Navy in a series of ship-to-ship engagements, the most famous of which were the battles between the USS *Constitution* ("Old Ironsides") and the British frigates *Guerriere*, off the coast of Massachusetts on August 19, 1812, and *Java*, off the Brazilian coast on December 29, 1812. Yet they had negligible impact on the Royal Navy blockade, which continued to drag the U.S. economy to the verge of collapse.

The U.S. Navy responded by innovating an inland fleet. Ill-considered attempts at a second invasion of Canada collapsed in 1813, but in the Old Northwest, General William Henry Harrison, governor of the Indiana Territory and an experienced U.S. military officer, rebuilt his much-diminished militia forces and, by late summer 1813, fielded 8,000 men. In the meantime, a young U.S. Navy officer named Oliver Hazard Perry began building—literally *building*—an inland freshwater flotilla at Presque Isle (present-day Erie), Pennsylvania. While the shallow-draft vessels were under construction, Perry personally trained his sailors in artillery technique. By August he moved the flotilla onto Lake Erie, and on September 10, Perry engaged a British inland squadron in a battle so brutal that he was forced to transfer his flag from the severely damaged brig *Lawrence* to the *Niagara*. From this vessel he directed nothing less than the annihilation of the entire British squadron. To General Harrison, who was fighting the land battle, Perry sent a famous message: "We have met the enemy, and they are ours."

Perry's victory was the first example in U.S. military history of closely coordinated amphibious combined-arms tactics. The inland flotilla cut off British supply lines and forced the British to abandon Fort Malden (at Detroit) and retreat eastward out of the Detroit region. On October 5, 1813, Harrison overran the withdrawing British and their Indian allies, forcing them to a showdown battle at the Thames River. The British suffered about 600 casualties, mostly prisoners of war, and the Native American "confederacy" that had formed around the great Shawnee leader Tecumseh collapsed as soon as he fell in battle.

Perhaps the American victories in the Old Northwest during 1813 might have turned the tide of what had so far been a catastrophic war for the United States. But Napoleon's defeat in Europe and his first exile, to Elba, freed up more British resources for the war in North America. The new British plan was to conduct offensives against New York, along Lake Champlain and the Hudson River, to sever New England from the rest of the Union; against New Orleans, to seize the vital Mississippi River artery; and against the settlements along the Chesapeake Bay, which would force the U.S. Army to transfer manpower from New York and New England to the Chesapeake.

The new British strategy made damaging inroads. By late summer 1814, American resistance to the attack in Chesapeake Bay fell apart. Under Major General Robert Ross, a force of British veterans of the Napoleonic Wars stormed Washington, DC, burning all the major public buildings, including the Capitol and the White House, and forcing President Madison and most of the government into ignominious flight. By early autumn, the United States was essentially broke, and New Englanders, who had always opposed the war, met in a convention to discuss secession from the Union.

Ross did not occupy Washington but instead marched against Baltimore, which he assaulted during the night of September 13/14, 1814, beginning with the bombardment of Fort McHenry in Baltimore Harbor. A young Washington lawyer, Francis Scott Key, detained aboard a British warship in the harbor, anxiously watched the bombardment through the long night and beheld at dawn that the nation's "Star-Spangled Banner" yet waved. As for Ross, he was killed during the overland advance against Baltimore, cut down by American sharpshooters about 12 miles southeast of the city on the morning of September 12.

While Washington burned and Baltimore fell under attack, 10,000 British troops invaded the United States from Montreal. The small American land force between them and New York City was easily brushed aside. But on September 11, 1814, U.S. Navy captain Thomas MacDonough attacked the British squadron—one frigate, one brig, two sloops, and a dozen gunboats—on Lake Champlain with a flotilla consisting of a corvette, a brig, a schooner, a sloop, and 10 gunboats. MacDonough prevailed, capturing the British frigate, brig, and both sloops. With their waterborne means of supply destroyed, the invaders retreated.

The triumph on Lake Champlain added some very high cards to the hand of American peace negotiators then meeting with their British counterparts in the distant Flemish city of Ghent. War-weary after years of fighting Napoleon, the British abandoned their demands for territory. The American negotiators, eager to get out of a bad war, softened their demand for British recognition of U.S.

neutrality rights. The Treaty of Ghent (December 24, 1814) restored the status quo ante bellum.

Word of the treaty did not reach across the Atlantic before General Andrew Jackson fought British Major General Edward Pakenham at the Battle of New Orleans during January 8–18, 1815. Jackson had 3,100 Tennessee and Kentucky volunteers, in addition to New Orleans militiamen and a mob of locals—total force, about 5,700 men. Pakenham launched a fierce artillery bombardment before attacking with his 8,000 veterans of the Napoleonic Wars. Jackson nevertheless won the day, inflicting 2,034 casualties (killed, wounded, missing, and captured) on Pakenham, who also fell in combat. Jackson's losses were no more than 13 killed, 30 wounded, and 19 missing or captured. By January 18, the entire available British force in the South, about 14,000 men, evacuated.

On balance, the United States had barely survived a harsh lesson in the cost of choosing to fight an unnecessary war. Nevertheless, although fought *after* that war had officially ended, the Battle of New Orleans made many Americans *feel* completely victorious. Any cautionary lesson had been lost as the nation gained in Andrew Jackson a brand-new military and political hero—a "Westerner" born and bred far from the traditional seaboard seats of power.

Bolívar: The Art of Liberation Warfare (1812–1825)

Simón Bolívar was born on July 24, 1783, into a privileged Creole family in Caracas when Venezuela was still a Spanish colony. He was educated by private tutors, who, after the death of his father in 1789, essentially raised him. The most influential of these tutor-father surrogates was Simón Rodriguez, a progressive thinker who instilled in young Bolívar a passionate interest in late Enlightenment thought, especially the writings of Jean-Jacques Rousseau. During 1799–1802 Bolívar sojourned in Europe when it was roiled by the French Revolutionary Wars and the rise of Napoleon Bonaparte. He met and married a Spanish noble-woman, with whom he returned to Venezuela, where she soon contracted yellow fever and died. The grief-stricken Bolívar made a second trip to Europe in 1804. This time he experienced a different romance, gravitating toward republican rev-olutionary activism after bearing witness to the self-coronation of Napoleon in May 1804. His emotions were mixed. He was disappointed that Napoleon had made himself emperor, yet he was profoundly impressed by the power of heroism and the cult of personality.

Bolívar returned to Venezuela later in 1804 and discovered that Napoleon's career in Europe was creating political turmoil in South America, making the region ripe for rebellion. This disruptive situation intensified in 1808 when Napoleon deposed the Spanish Bourbons, placing his brother Joseph on the Spanish throne. On April 19, 1810, a coup d'etat established the Supreme Junta of Caracas to replace the colonial administrators. Venezuela was in a state of de facto independence, and in July the junta sent Bolívar as head of a three-person delegation to Great Britain with the objective of securing aid to further the cause of independence. The idea was that the British were now opposed to Spain under Joseph Bonaparte and would be eager to do anything to weaken his reign. In fact, the delegation's efforts proved in vain, but Bolívar did meet the exiled Francisco de Miranda, who had long worked toward Venezuelan independence and had even attempted a revolution in 1806. The delegation persuaded Miranda to return to Venezuela, and Bolívar returned to Venezuela in time to receive Miranda and to participate in drafting a Declaration of Independence, which was proclaimed on July 5, 1811. Although he had no experience in the military, his connection with Miranda, overall commander of the new republic's army, gained him high rank in the force; he was assigned to command the strategically critical fortress of Puerto Cabello on the country's north coast. One of Bolívar's most trusted subordinates, however, betrayed him to the royalists. Worse, Miranda surrendered the Venezuelan army to Spanish general Juan Domingo de Monteverde in July 1812. Bolívar fled to New Granada—present-day Colombia—where he set about personally recruiting a force of volunteers to liberate Venezuela.

What happened next was extraordinary. The army Bolívar raised invaded Venezuela during May 1813, defeating Spanish forces in a series of six bloody battles culminating in his capture of the capital city of Caracas on August 6. With this, he was hailed as *El Libertador,* The Liberator. It was a title he would carry for the rest of his career and life.

Regaining independence was one thing, Bolívar quickly discovered; maintaining it was quite another. His new government faced opposition from the powerful royalist factions that still existed throughout Venezuela, and a bitter civil war ensued. Once again, Bolívar assumed the mantle of military command and proved himself a naturally gifted leader and tactician. He defeated counter-revolutionaries at the Battle of Araure in December 1813, at La Victoria in February 1814, at San Mateo in March, and at Carabobo in May, only to be outmatched and decisively defeated at La Puerta in July.

Once again, Bolívar took refuge in neighboring New Granada. Once again, he raised an army. He had learned three valuable lessons in liberation warfare. The first was to stay alive. The second was never to quit. The third was to create a climate—an environment—of liberation. Instead of simply returning to Venezuela, he focused on the "liberation" of Bogotá, capital of New Granada. He recaptured the city in 1814 and set out to march into Cartagena, where he intended to recruit local forces for the capture of the Royalist stronghold of Santa Marta. Violent political and military disputes with the local government of Cartagena sent Bolívar into exile once again. He fled first to Jamaica, whose leaders rebuffed him; after an attempt on his life there, he fled to Haiti, where he found both refuge and a friend in Alexandre Pétion, president of the new southern republic of Haiti.

While he had been in Jamaica, Bolívar wrote and circulated *La carta de Jamaica (Letter from Jamaica)*, demonstrating to the world that he was still committed to the cause of independence. In December 1816 he returned to Venezuela and defeated Spanish forces near Barcelona on February 16, 1817. At La Puerta the following year, on March 15, 1818, he himself was in turn defeated. Instead of flying into exile, this time he regrouped in the remote Orinoco region, where, during 1818–1819, he built a new army, which he augmented by several thousand British and Irish veterans of the Napoleonic Wars. Instead of immediately returning to battle, Bolívar set about consolidating his army with the forces of other revolutionaries, including those of José Antonio Páez and Francisco de Paula Santander. Once again, he decided not to return directly to Venezuela but to first liberate New Granada.

Bolívar left his headquarters at Ciudad Bolívar on June 11, 1819, leading 2,500 men in an epic and swift march across the wilderness of Venezuela, fording rivers at flood stage and traversing the Andes via the Pisba Pass—widely considered impassable. Descending into the valley of the Sagamosa River (near Bucaramanga, New Grenada) on July 6, 1819, his forces achieved total surprise and defeated the Spanish at the Battle of Boyaca on August 7, 1819. Bogotá fell to Bolívar three days later, and El Libertador proclaimed a republic.

From his new position, President Bolívar convened the Angostura Congress, which proclaimed the creation of Gran Colombia, a federation encompassing presentday Venezuela, Colombia, Panama, and Ecuador. The union was formalized at Cucuta in July 1821, and Bolívar became its president. The following year, 1822, he met with Argentine patriot José de San Martín at Guayaquil, Ecuador, but was unable to negotiate a union with Argentina. Nevertheless, at this time the revolutionary leader Antonio José de Sucre liberated Ecuador (after victory at the Battle of Pichincha in May 1822), and subsequent triumphs in Peru— at Junin (August 1824) and Ayacucho (December 1824)—sent the remaining Spanish forces out of what historians often call the "Bolívarian states": Venezuela, Colombia, Ecuador, Peru, and Bolivia.

Victory over the Spanish did not bring peace to those states, as rivals for power stirred sporadic rebellion. Although Bolívar personally wrote a republican constitution for Bolivia—as the liberated population of northern Peru decided to call their new nation in his honor—defiance of his authority was such that in 1828, El Libertador assumed dictatorial powers over Gran Colombia. Even so, instability persisted, and in spring 1830—discouraged, weary, and gravely ill with tuberculosis—Bolívar resigned the presidency. He died that winter.

He died believing himself a failure. But in fact he had proved himself a remarkable military leader, whose pattern of recruitment, relentless attack, and fighting from the periphery to the center to create a climate of liberation became paradigms for future anti-colonial independence fighters. His *Letter from Jamaica* is still studied as an acute analysis of the Spanish American character; and his *Angostura Discourse* of 1819, basis for the creation of Gran Colombia, and his draft of the Bolivian constitution of 1826 remain models of sound progressive political thought. More than any other figure, Simón Bolívar set the ideal and the practical pattern for the military dimension of the anti-colonial liberation movements of the nineteenth century.

The Wars of Shaka Zulu: A Native Empire in Africa (1816–1828)

For centuries, from the point of view of Euro-American historians, military history was focused almost exclusively on wars and warfare in the nations of the West. It was certainly known that Asian, African, and Pacific civilizations fought wars, but for the most part the military history of these peoples was studied only insofar as it came into contact with the militaries of Europe and America. The first sub-Saharan political-military figure to be examined closely by Western military historians was Shaka kaSenzangakhona, popularly known in the West as Shaka Zulu. He was not only one of the most influential monarchs in the Zulu kingdom but also was a great military figure, the premier warrior and warfighter of the Mthethwa people of South Africa.

Even in a period of European imperial expansion in Asia and Africa, Shaka Zulu earned a reputation as the builder of an empire comparable to those with which Europeans were familiar. Mthethwa tradition portrays Shaka Zulu, born about 1787, as the illegitimate child of Senzangakhona. Because of his illegitimacy, he grew up with his mother in a village apart from his father. Here he became a warrior and the protégé of Dingiswayo, a Mthethwa chief. When Senzangakhona died in 1816, Shaka Zulu returned to the place of his birth and found that his half-brother Sigujana had assumed his father's place as Zulu chief. Eager to confirm his own authority, Dingiswayo placed the equivalent of a regiment under young Shaka Zulu's command. The young warrior used it to stage a coup against Sigujana, killing him and taking his place as chief of the Zulu clan—albeit in vassalage to Dingiswayo, who ruled as monarch of the Mthethwa empire.

As Dingiswayo's vassal, Shaka Zulu fought against the rival Ndwandwe nation, which was led by Zwide. In 1817, Zwide killed Dingiswayo in battle. In the wake of this decapitating blow, the Mthethwa were temporarily dispersed; but in the absence of Dingiswayo, they soon rallied to Shaka Zulu, many no longer calling themselves Mthethwa but Zulus—in tribute to the young man's charisma.

Now elevated to the status of monarch, Shaka Zulu was no longer willing to be vulnerable to overthrow by whatever powerful warrior next emerged. He set about organizing the Mthethwa—or Zulu—people politically, as a nation. He saw an enlarged and well-organized military as an essential aspect of this project, and he began the transformation of Zula warriors from a poorly armed and inadequately trained mob into a highly disciplined force. He equipped them with the assegai, an innovative light javelin he recognized as far superior to the traditional long throwing spear. The assegai was versatile. It could be hurled as a standoff weapon or used in close combat. Shaka Zulu also discarded the small shield that Mthethwa warriors carried and adopted instead a shield large enough to cover the entire front of the body.

Shaka Zulu analyzed and reevaluated traditional warrior strategy and tactics. He made extensive changes. By tradition, Mthethwa warriors fought each other from a distance. They hurled their spears and jeered at one another. After a time, the fight ended, almost always inconclusively. Rarely did a clear-cut victor emerge. Shaka Zulu wanted war to be a serious geopolitical instrument instead of a ritualistic show. He therefore trained his warriors to be fierce combatants. He encouraged them to fight close, hand to hand. He trained them to move in on an enemy, protecting themselves with their large shields while slashing at close range with their short assegais. Under Shaka Zulu, what had been largely ritualized combat escalated into what Euro-Americans thought of as "real" war, bloody war, no mere contest but a contest of life and death.

In 1819, at the Battle of Gqokli Hill, Shaka Zulu led his troops to victory against the far superior numbers fielded by the Ndwandwe. In the rout that followed the Ndwandwe defeat, Zwide was killed and most of the Ndwandwe summarily fled their lands, leaving vast tracts to be gathered up by the Zulus. This victory seems to have inspired Shaka Zulu to embark upon a far more ambitious imperial enterprise, which he called the *Mfecane*—"The Crushing"—a sequence of wars that ravaged the region surrounding Zululand throughout the early 1820s. By the end of The Crushing, Shaka Zulu emerged as "emperor" of an immense Zulu empire, which extended over the region now occupied by Natal and South Africa.

As leader of what was in 1819 the largest and most formidable native army in Africa, numbering some 30,000 men, Shaka Zulu embarked on the systematic conquest of neighboring clans. He compelled all those he conquered to assimilate themselves within the Zulu empire until all the region today encompassed by Zululand and a portion of what is now Natal came under his direct rule.

Shaka Zulu was clearly a brilliant military strategist and tactician. His genius for war was almost certainly in part a matter of natural ability, but it is likely that the mentoring of Dingiswayo played a key role in his early development. To his acumen as a military leader, he joined what seems to have been an exuberant and even gratuitous cruelty. The death of his half brother Nandi in 1827 may have removed the only curb on his tyranny. After Nandi's death, Shaka Zulu became an irrational tyrant, a kind of African Caligula, yet without losing his tactical acumen. Although he had raised the Zulu to dominance over a vast region, he fell victim to assassination on September 22, 1828, at the hands of his remaining half brothers.

He left to the peoples of Zululand a strong warrior culture as well as a sophisticated military system. The effects of these would be felt later in the nineteenth century in clashes with British colonial forces in the so-called Zulu Wars of 1879 and 1887.

Scott Takes Veracruz:
The U.S. Army Conducts Its First
Amphibious Operation (1847)

The War of 1812 was ostensibly fought to defend U.S. sovereignty but was really far more about territorial expansion. In the end it accomplished little to expand the country, but before the middle of the nineteenth century, the opportunity came for a new war that realized the expansion the War of 1812 had failed to achieve.

After Texas won independence from Mexico in 1836, the U.S. Congress resisted approving the newborn republic's bid for annexation. To accept Texas into the Union would not only upset the delicate balance between slave and free states, thereby propelling America into a civil war, but would surely ignite war with Mexico. But when France and England made overtures of alliance to the Republic of Texas, outgoing President John Tyler urged annexation. Under Tyler's successor, James K. Polk, Congress voted to admit Texas into the Union on December 29, 1845. England and France now clearly began to covet California, held so feebly by Mexico that it looked ready to fall into whatever hands were there to catch it. President Polk offered Mexico $40 million for the California territory. When he was rebuffed, he authorized the U.S. consul at Monterey (California) to provoke what became the Bear Flag Rebellion, by which California's independence from Mexico was proclaimed.

The loss of California was doubtless a blow to Mexico, but its government focused narrowly on Texas, disputing its Rio Grande border. Polk dispatched troops under Brigadier General Zachary Taylor to defend the boundary, and on May 13, 1846, after Mexican soldiers advanced across the river, the president asked Congress for a declaration of war. His objective was to obtain all Mexican territory north of the Rio Grande and the Gila River, all the way west to the Pacific Ocean. He directed the army's senior commander, Major General Winfield Scott, to draw up a plan.

It had three parts: Taylor would march west from Matamoros to Monterrey, Mexico; once Monterrey was taken, all of northern Mexico would be vulnerable. At the same time, Brigadier General John E. Wool would march from San Antonio, Texas, to Chihuahua, Mexico. He could then advance farther south, to Saltillo, where he could coordinate further action with Taylor's force at Monterrey. Finally,

Colonel Stephen Watts Kearney would advance out of Fort Leavenworth, Kansas, to take Santa Fe, New Mexico, and from there continue all the way to San Diego, California.

This war plan did not include a deeper invasion to capture the Mexican capital, Mexico City. Both Polk and Scott believed that achieving the objectives of the three-pronged strategy would be sufficient to force Mexico to yield the territory the United States wanted. But Polk rethought the plan in July 1846 and now called for an assault on Mexico City with a force landed amphibiously at Veracruz on the Gulf of Mexico. This new plan would put Scott, as the army's senior officer, in command of the entire war. Polk, however, suspected that

Lieutenant General Winfield Scott, photographed at West Point on June 10, 1862
WIKIMEDIA COMMONS

Scott was too conservative a commander, and Taylor was making progress. He promoted Taylor to brevet major general and put him in charge of all Mexican operations.

During February 21–23, 1847, Taylor prevailed against a Mexican army three times the size of his force and won the Battle of Buena Vista, which neutralized the Mexican army as a threat to the lower Rio Grande. While Taylor won his victories in Mexico, Colonel Kearny took Santa Fe, New Mexico, without firing a shot. He pressed on to California, reaching San Diego in December 1846, and found that a U.S. naval squadron had already secured the California ports.

Despite these remarkable gains, General Taylor proved unable to bring the war to a close. President Polk began to believe that Taylor, not Scott, was the excessively conservative commander. Moreover, he began to fear that Taylor's record of accumulated victories would make him a formidable opponent in the next presidential election. Polk knew that Scott had no political ambitions. What is more, he had been a hero of the War of 1812 and was the most thoroughly experienced officer in the U.S. Army. If anyone could successfully lead the first-ever amphibious operation—the landing of 10,000 men—Scott, Polk correctly believed, was the man to do it, even if this created a conflict of command with Taylor.

On March 2, 1847, Scott commenced operations leading to the landing at Veracruz. Up to this point in its history, the U.S. Army had successfully fought mostly small engagements. Indeed, the regular army functioned principally as a police force tasked with suppressing Indian "uprisings," as violence between Native Americans and white settlers was called. Scott had to manage tactical and logistical issues on a scale that was institutionally unprecedented. In his favor was the fact that, thanks to Taylor's and Kearny's victories, American forces were now in control of northern Mexico. But the task was nevertheless formidable.

Scott and an advance party arrived at Anton Lizardo, Veracruz, in early March and determined that the force should be landed at Collado Beach, three miles south of the city of Veracruz. Scott wanted a regular army unit to make the first landing and chose the 1st Regular Division. It would be followed by a unit of volunteers and then another division of regulars. When Scott commanded forces in the Second Seminole War (1835–1842), he worked with naval officers to create a joint army-navy force known as the Mosquito Fleet, consisting of schooners and barges capable of navigating shallow waters for amphibious operations. Scott now positioned such a Mosquito Fleet within 90 yards of the beach as platforms to supply covering fire for the landing—if necessary. The troops were transported in larger vessels.

Shortly after noon on March 9, the Mosquito Fleet was off Collado Beach, with the main landing force about three hours behind them. At 5:30 the large craft arrived, and Brigadier General William J. Worth, 1st Division commander, shot ahead in a gig that carried him and his staff. They hurriedly waded ashore and gave the signal for the landing to commence. It was accomplished without firing or receiving a single shot. By 11:00 that night, all 10,000 men of Scott's army of invasion had landed. Not a single soldier had been shot at, drowned, or suffered any other mishap. This was the first strategic amphibious landing conducted by the U.S. military. It was an unqualified success.

From the beach, Scott's army marched the three miles to the city of Veracruz, laying siege to its fortress for 18 days, forcing Mexican general Santa Anna to withdraw to the steep Cerro Gordo Canyon with 8,000 of his best troops. Against this position, Scott, a superb tactician, did not make the frontal attack the Mexicans expected. Instead he enveloped the Mexican forces by cutting paths up either side of Cerro Gordo. Santa Anna's troops retreated all the way to Mexico City, with Scott in pursuit.

On September 13, Chapultepec Palace, the seemingly impregnable fortress guarding Mexico City, fell to Scott; four days later, Santa Anna surrendered. The war ended with the hastily concluded Treaty of Guadalupe Hidalgo, which was ratified by the U.S. Senate on March 10, 1848. Mexico ceded to the United States New Mexico (which also included parts of the present-day states of Utah, Nevada, Arizona, and Colorado) and California. Mexico renounced claims to Texas above the Rio Grande. In return, the United States paid the Mexican government $15 million and pledged to assume the financial claims of all Texans against Mexico. As for the spectacular sea-land operation that had made it all possible, amphibious warfare had now been added to the American military toolbox.

The Great Mutiny in India: Birth of the British Raj (1857–1858)

Also called the Sepoy Rebellion and the First Indian War of Independence, the Great Mutiny was an uprising against the British colonial regime in India. It was begun by the *sipahi*, Indian soldiers in service to the British East India Company. The British anglicized the name to "Sepoys." The mutiny began as a rebellion and ended up catalyzing the creation of the British Raj, British colonial rule in India. As such, it is a momentous instance of a counterrevolution that created an empire instead of tearing one down.

The British East India Company was a private enterprise intimately woven into the fabric of the British government at every level. In India it acted with considerable autonomy, serving as a proxy for both Parliament and Crown, a kind of half-step toward global empire. By the middle of the nineteenth century, the company held sway over the region of modern India, Pakistan, Bangladesh, Burma (Myanmar), and Ceylon (Sri Lanka). The Great Mughal emperor of India, once all-powerful, now served largely at the pleasure of the East India Company as a figurehead. Yet the real government was not Parliament or Queen Victoria but a unique class of British civil and military colonial administration. Keeping order on the ground was an army of 160,000 men. The core of this force consisted of 24,000 British officers and enlisted troops. The remainder were native enlistees—Sepoys—in service primarily to the East India Company.

By the mid-nineteenth century, considerable enmity had grown up between the Sepoys and the company that employed them. British officers and managers persistently refused to respect Indian religious and cultural traditions. The situation became a powder keg. Any match, once struck, could set it off.

Late in 1856 a rumor began circulating among the Sepoys that the paper cartridges supplied for the newly issued Pattern 1853 Enfield rifled muskets were waterproofed with a grease made of the fat of cows and pigs. Cows are sacred to Hindus and for that reason must not be eaten. Pigs are regarded by Muslims as unclean and for *that* reason must not be eaten. The problem was that prior to loading a cartridge rifle of this period, the shooter had to bite off the end of the paper cartridge that contained both the gunpowder and ball. In doing so, a soldier's lips, teeth, and tongue inevitably came into contact with the grease. For the Hindu this was blasphemy; for the Muslim it was a pollution.

In the Bengal army, some individual soldiers simply refused to use the new cartridges. In Meerut, northeast of Delhi, the protest was officially deemed a mutiny when 85 men of the 3rd Light Cavalry joined together on April 23, 1857, in refusing to use the cartridges. Tried for and convicted of mutiny, all 85 were sentenced to imprisonment after being fettered, put on public display, and ceremonially "degraded"—stripped of their military insignia. Far from discouraging further acts of disobedience in the Sepoy army, the punishment only incited further rebellion and enlarged the mutiny.

On May 10, 1857, soldiers of the 11th and 20th Infantry Regiments mutinied, storming the stockade and freeing their 85 imprisoned comrades—as well as many Indian civilian prisoners kept there. After this, they engaged in a general riot, killing 40 British officers and civilians in Meerut. From here they marched to Delhi, where additional Sepoy regiments joined what was now a frank uprising. In the city, Sepoys slaughtered many more British soldiers and civilians. Then they made a dramatic show of restoring to power the aged Mughal emperor, Muhammad Bahadur Shah.

This was the inflection point at which a military mutiny became a popular rebellion. News of this development swept the entire subcontinent. Regiments throughout Bengal mutinied. Throughout north and central India, Indian civilians rose up against British rule.

The initial response from the British government and from the East India Company was panic. Clearly, officials were at a loss. As they saw it, the rebellion had come out of nowhere. Unable to think of anything better, British commanders in the Punjab disarmed the Sepoys and assembled a small all-British army to march on Delhi. The force took up a position outside the city. In Kolkata, British officials quickly contained the rebellion and managed to maintain control of the Ganges River and communications lines as far upriver as Allahabad. In central India several thousand British troops fought numerous pitched battles against the forces of local princes and Rani (Queen) Lakshmibai of Jhansi. Seeing the opportunity, all joined the uprising.

Oudh, which the East India Company had only recently annexed in the central Ganges River Valley, became the focus of especially violent rebellion. On May 30, 1857, rebels laid siege to Europeans and Indians loyal to East India Company and British authority, who had taken refuge together within the confines of the British Residency in Oudh's capital city, Lucknow. Very shortly after this, the British garrison at Cawnpore (Kanpur) was held under siege through June 27, when survivors of the onslaught negotiated with the rebel leader Nana Sahib their safe passage out. Although they had obtained permission to leave, they were nevertheless attacked while evacuating to boats on the Ganges. Most of the British soldiers were killed. Some 200 British women and children were captured and subsequently executed in prison.

Outrage swept British colonial society at all levels. The military authorized a general and ruthless reprisal, meting out slaughter that (they believed) mirrored what had been perpetrated against the British. The troops targeted all Indians, combatants and noncombatants alike.

While this was going on, numerous violent but inconclusive battles were under way just outside the walls of Delhi. By September 15 the British army was sufficiently reinforced to storm Delhi; after five days of intense fighting, the army retook the city on September 25. That day a relief column reached the Lucknow residency, center of East Indian Company administration, but it was pinned down there and endured a siege that lasted into late November. That was when a second relief force arrived, breaking the siege and evacuating the survivors.

In February 1858, the British returned to Oudh in company with an army of more than 30,000 men, including Nepalese troops. Lucknow was finally retaken by the British on March 23, and with that, rebel forces in north India dispersed. The rebel fort at Jhansi capitulated in April, and the rani, the Princess of Bengal, was subsequently killed in battle. With this, the mutiny died out but for sporadic outbreaks of violence, which continued into 1859. Early that year, Tantia Topi, the chief general to rebel leader Nana Sahib, was captured. His execution in April 1859 ended what was left of the revolt.

The failure of the Indians to organize and sustain a full-scale uprising had terrible consequences. The British government intervened with its full might, officially and definitively abolishing the Mughal Empire. Old Muhammad Bahadur Shah, the figurehead emperor, was banished to Burma. As for the East India Company, its authority was not elevated but diminished. The pretense of proxy rule was ended as the British Crown and Parliament assumed direct rule of India. The "Raj"—an Indian word meaning "rule" or "royal rule"—replaced the administration of the East India Company.

The British military did not give up on the recruitment of native troops. Indeed, these were regarded as absolutely necessary to maintaining control over the subcontinent. However, recruiters now sought out natives of the Punjab and Nepal. Soldiers from these areas had remained steadfastly loyal throughout the Great Mutiny. The human cost of the rebellion included 2,034 British soldiers and civilian nationals killed in combat and 8,987 dead from disease and other causes during 1857–1859. Nobody thought to count the Indian dead, but in any case the cost amounted to even more than lives lost. As the British regime took over colonial administration, what had been a paternal attitude toward the Indians now became one of mutual distrust. Paternalism gave way to naked exploitation. The Raj grew to magnificent proportions, but, like all one-sided repressive governments, it was from the beginning inherently unsustainable and therefore doomed.

Battle of Antietam: Lincoln Wins a Platform for Emancipation (1862)

In response to an August 19, 1862, editorial by the abolitionist editor of the *New York Tribune*, Horace Greeley, Abraham Lincoln replied that his "paramount object in this struggle [the Civil War] is to save the Union, and is not either to save or destroy Slavery." Without question, the president was personally opposed to slavery, but he believed that the Constitution protected slavery where it existed. He also feared that issuing an executive order emancipating the nation's slaves and transforming the Civil War into a fight to end American slavery once and for all would send the "border states" (slave states that had not seceded from the Union) running into the arms of the Confederacy. He also worried that the Supreme Court would declare an executive proclamation of universal emancipation unconstitutional, a decision that might ensure that slavery in the United States would last forever.

But by the summer of 1862, Lincoln nevertheless wanted to issue an emancipation proclamation. Its content was one problem, its timing another. So far in the war, the Union army had suffered a string of defeats. To issue a proclamation now would look like a toothless act of desperation. A year earlier, Congress had passed the Confiscation Act, which classified as "contraband" those slaves who had been employed directly in the war effort. The act authorized Union officers to "confiscate" such individuals—in effect, emancipate them. Lincoln now called for a broader Confiscation Act. Passed on July 17, 1862, the new law declared free any slaves owned by supporters of what the act called "the rebellion."

Five days later, Lincoln read to his Cabinet the first draft of the emancipation proclamation he had composed. It did not actually set a single slave free. It proclaimed free those slaves living in the parts of the Confederacy not yet occupied by the Union army. Precisely because the United States did not control these areas, these slaves might be declared free but could not be freed in fact. In the border states as well as parts of the Confederacy currently under Union control, slavery would continue. Limited though it was, an emancipation proclamation, Lincoln believed, would give the Civil War the force of a moral crusade.

Now he needed a credible military victory as a platform from which to make the proclamation. Military strategy is generally laid out for military purposes. Lincoln intended to bend military strategy to a moral, spiritual purpose. On

The important Civil War photographer Alexander Gardner took this glass-plate photograph of Abraham Lincoln conferring with Major General George B. McClellan at Antietam, Maryland.

September 5, 1862, Confederate general Robert E. Lee made a decision that handed Lincoln what he needed: an event that made a Union victory both a military and a moral imperative.

Lee decided to radically shift from a defensive to an offensive strategy. He invaded the Union via Maryland, hoping to stir this border state into joining the Confederacy while throwing the North into panic and despair. The commander of the Union's Army of the Potomac, George B. McClellan, a West Point standout who was nevertheless almost pathologically cautious, sent patrols to search out Lee's invading force. For his part, Lee thoroughly intimidated those patrols and established a strong position west of Antietam Creek, near the Maryland hamlet of Sharpsburg.

McClellan proposed a three-pronged assault against Lee, targeting both of his flanks and then attacking his center. It would be a double envelopment—something taught to all West Point men, McClellan as well as Lee. The key to a successful envelopment is meticulous coordination of execution. This was totally absent from the attack McClellan launched on September 17. Still, his subordinate, Major General Joseph Hooker, managed to push Lee's great Stonewall Jackson back very far. Lee had to reinforce him, and had McClellan acted with speed, he could have wiped out a large portion of Lee's Army of Northern Virginia. But he moved cautiously, as usual, and two other Confederate generals, Daniel Harvey Hill and James Longstreet, were able to get their men into position to break up the assault, disrupting all semblance of Union coordination.

McClellan's men fought hard but could not break through. By noon the fighting became concentrated along a sunken farm road held by D. H. Hill. After a battle of five hours, devastatingly lethal to both sides, Union major general Edwin "Bull" Sumner drove the Confederates out of the shallow trench formed by the road. It was now called "Bloody Lane."

While fighting raged there, Major General Ambrose Burnside, commanding the entire left wing of the Union army, frittered away time and men in an effort to capture the bridge across Antietam Creek instead of simply fording the creek and joining the battle. It was late afternoon before he broke through the Confederate line, only to be swatted back by a counterattack from General Ambrose Powell Hill (no relation to Daniel Harvey Hill).

Despite all the Union's errors, McClellan's soldiers fell upon Lee's lines with relentless ferocity. Moreover, they had the weight of numbers on their side: 75,500 Union troops versus 39,000 Confederates engaged. On both sides, Antietam became what military historians call a "soldier's battle," a battle driven less by the plans of generals than by the sheer grit of the soldiers themselves.

Lee was pushed out of Sharpsburg, but McClellan could not persuade himself that he possessed the field. He should have led the Army of the Potomac in pursuit and hammered the would-be invaders before they could get across the Potomac and back into Virginia. Instead he allowed the Army of Northern

Virginia, depleted but intact, to escape. Invasion had been defeated at the cost of 2,108 Union troops killed, 9,549 wounded, and 753 missing out of a force of nearly 75,500. Lee lost 1,546 killed, 7,700 wounded, and about 1,000 missing out of some 39,000 engaged. Even worse, the Civil War would go on through April 1865, bringing yet more death and devastation.

So much blood had been shed for a battle of mixed result. Tactically, Antietam was a draw. Strategically, it was a slim Union victory. McClellan drove Lee out of Maryland yet failed to destroy his army. Nevertheless, Lincoln leveraged this heartbreaking engagement as a turning point in the Civil War by using it as the platform from which, on September 23, 1862, he issued the Preliminary Emancipation Proclamation. The day before, he told his Cabinet: "I think the time has come now. I wish it was a better time. I wish that we were in a better condition. The action of the army against the rebels has not been quite what I should have best liked. But they have been driven out of Maryland."

The Battle of Gettysburg: The Civil War Finds Purpose: (1863)

The Confederacy's principal general, Robert E. Lee, had departed from his defensive strategy in September 1862 when he led the Army of Northern Virginia in an invasion of Maryland. Driven out of Union territory at the Battle of Antietam, he decided to attempt a second invasion in the summer of 1863. His belief was that the Confederacy could not endure a war of attrition much longer and that if he successfully invaded Pennsylvania—a solid Union state, unlike border state Maryland—the North's will to continue the war might be broken.

He invaded Pennsylvania with between 71,000 and 75,000 men at the end of June. He had not determined where he would fight but had certainly not planned a showdown battle in the vicinity of Gettysburg, a small town distinguished only in that it occupied an important crossroads. Chance and circumstances arranged the collision of forces.

Confederate lieutenant general A. P. Hill's corps was in desperate need of provisions, and the prosperous little college town was ripe for foraging. As he neared Gettysburg on June 30, Hill came under fire from cavalry under Union brigadier general John Buford. Buford was also not looking for a battle, especially since he was distantly separated from the main body of the Union's Army of the Potomac, which was led by Major General George Gordon Meade. But Buford was a seasoned commander who possessed coup d'oeil, the ability to assess a potential battlefield with little more than a glance. He saw the importance of the crossroads, and he saw that this crossroads lay below a ridge partially surrounding the town. Whoever held that high ground would control the crossroads. If Lee and his army were nearby, Buford realized, it was essential to hold the high ground until the rest of the Union forces could get into position.

Buford was outnumbered, but he managed to hold the heights long enough for the arrival of the Army of the Potomac's I Corps on July 1. The opening of the main phase of what would be a three-day battle did not go well for the Union. Within moments of the commencement of combat, Hill's troops killed the dashing and much-loved I Corps commander, Major General John F. Reynolds. Shock and confusion exploded through the Union ranks, which nevertheless held their ground until more reinforcements arrived.

But the Army of Northern Virginia also began arriving in force. Later in the afternoon, Hill and Lieutenant General R. S. Ewell linked up in an attack that nearly routed the Federals, sending them into headlong retreat through the center of Gettysburg. What Hill and Ewell failed to do, however, was block their access to Cemetery Ridge, the key stretch of high ground east of central Gettysburg. Here, the Union forces not only rallied but were soon joined by fresh troops from the south and the east. For their part, the Confederates took up an encircling position encompassing Seminary Ridge, on the west side of town, parallel to Cemetery Ridge. With this, by nightfall, the Confederate and Union armies were positioned for Day 2 of the Battle of Gettysburg.

Although he had not planned to fight it out here, Robert E. Lee decided that *here* he was, and *here* was his opportunity to strike a devastating blow against the flagship army of the Union. Defeat it, and there was a real chance that Lincoln would be forced to negotiate an end to the war favorable to the Confederate cause. Lee therefore determined to seize and hold the initiative on Day 2, July 2, 1863. He did indeed inflict heavy casualties—while also suffering serious losses—but he was unable to gain the position he most desperately wanted: a double envelopment of the Union forces.

He came very close. At one point, the entire left flank of the Army of the Potomac was exposed on Cemetery Ridge. The unit at this end of the Union line, on a portion of Cemetery Ridge called Little Round Top, was the severely depleted 20th Maine Regiment, understrength at just 500 men, including some mutinous soldiers from other units, who had been put under the regiment's guard. The 20th was commanded not by a West Point graduate but a Bowdoin College professor of rhetoric, Colonel Joshua Lawrence Chamberlain, who had taken a sabbatical to serve in the Union army. He saw clearly that if his men gave way, even a moderately successful Confederate attack could roll up the entire Union position on Cemetery Ridge. In one of the great, stunning, and awe-inspiring moments of military history, Chamberlain met a fierce onslaught by superior forces with an even fiercer downhill bayonet attack, which prompted the superior 15th Alabama Regiment to surrender. As if this were not miracle enough, Chamberlain's men had made their victorious attack without ammunition, which had run out earlier in the afternoon. They prevailed by bluff, guts, and edged steel.

The achievement of the 20th Maine did not win the Battle of Gettysburg, but it prevented the Union from losing it. Still, Lee closed Day 2 aware that he had made substantial progress against the enemy. His second-in-command, Lieutenant General James Longstreet, counseled Lee to withdraw and regroup. He cautioned that the Army of Northern Virginia lacked the manpower to break through the Army of the Potomac. Lee angrily disagreed, countering Longstreet's advice by pointing out that the second day of battle had unquestionably been a day of victory and that to withdraw after such a success would fatally corrode the morale of his hard-pressed army. The Confederates still held the initiative, and Lee meant to exploit this. After all, a triumph at Gettysburg, far into the United States of America, would almost certainly turn the war decisively in the Confederacy's favor.

Lee decided that on Day 3 the Army of Northern Virginia would not merely stand and fight. It would mount an all-out attack and win. He ordered nine brigades—12,500 Confederate troops—to make an infantry charge across the open ground below the Union position on Cemetery Ridge, push the Union forces off that ridge, and put them in position to be rolled up against the rest of the Army of the Potomac. It would be a devastating blow from which the Union's most important military formation could not recover.

History would call the Confederate operation "Pickett's Charge," even though Major General George Pickett commanded but three of the nine brigades involved. Everyone knew it would be costly. Attacking uphill is rarely a winning tactic, and advancing across a wide-open swath of exposed ground to get to the hill was arguably suicidal. But Pickett's Charge got under way with a magnificence that impressed—nearly overwhelmed—even the Union troops who were its targets. Still, pounded by Union artillery and massed musket fire, the attacking force quickly lost half its number.

Lee saw it all, and, watching the battered survivors return from the failed assault, he turned to a subordinate. "It is all my fault," he confessed. Desperate to win the war at Gettysburg, Lee had made an uncharacteristically desperate tactical blunder. His defeat was catastrophic, but losses were devastating on both sides. Of 104,256 Union troops "present for duty" at Gettysburg, 3,155 perished on the field, 14,529 were wounded (many of them subsequently died), and 5,365 were listed as captured or missing. Confederate figures are less certain. Of perhaps 75,000 troops engaged, 3,903 were killed outright, 18,735 were wounded (many fatally), and 5,425 were listed as missing. The difference was that the North had a much larger population and could afford to lose more men, hardware, and money than the South. The Army of Northern Virginia had no way to make up its losses. Robert E. Lee had predicted that the Battle of Gettysburg would be the turning point in this civil war. He was right. But the outcome did not turn the war in his favor. Lee would never again bring offensive warfare into Union territory.

Months after the battle, on November 19, 1863, President Lincoln delivered a two-minute speech at the dedication of a military cemetery on the Gettysburg battlefield. In terms of its military value—its function as a force multiplier, an example of inspired leadership leveraging victory—it was perhaps the most effective command speech in military history. For President Lincoln defined the meaning of this battle in this war. He successfully argued that it was "for us the living . . . to be dedicated here to the unfinished work which they who fought here have thus far so nobly advanced." He explained: "It is . . . for us to be here dedicated to the great task remaining before us—that from these honored dead we take increased devotion to that cause for which they gave the last full measure of devotion—that we here highly resolve that these dead shall not have died in vain—that this nation, under God, shall have a new birth of freedom—and that government of the people, by the people, for the people shall not perish from the earth."

Total War: William T. Sherman and the Calculus of Victory (1864–1865)

In his monumental theoretical treatise, *On War*, posthumously published in 1832, the Prussian general Carl von Clausewitz developed the concept of "absolute war," or "total war." It was the idea of one combatant nation committing its entire society—not just its military—against the entire society of another. As both civilians and combatants contributed to the prosecution of total war, so civilians and combatants alike became objectives—targets—in total war. The cataclysmic world wars of the twentieth century made total war a horrifically commonplace concept, but at the time of the American Civil War, "total war" was an alien, virtually unknown, concept. Clausewitz's book had been in print for some three decades but was not taught at West Point, not before the Civil War and not during it.

Yet the sheer scale of combat during 1861–1865 made widening the war beyond the battlefield a logical next step. At several points during the war, both

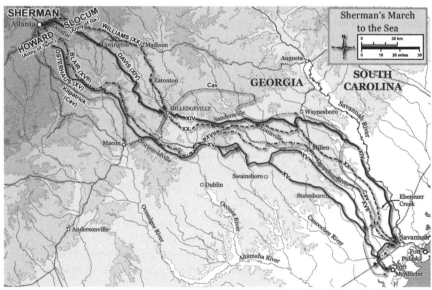

Route of Sherman's March to the Sea

the Union and the Confederacy employed so-called "irregulars"—guerrillas—to wreak terroristic havoc behind enemy lines. In addition, commercial shipping became a target. The Union set up and continually expanded a naval blockade of Confederate ports in an effort to destroy the region's economy and starve its people. The Emancipation Proclamation, issued by Abraham Lincoln in 1862 and put into effect on January 1, 1863—which history regards as a noble effort to transform the war into a crusade to end the obscenity of slavery once and for all—was, in the context of the war, more directly an act of total war, targeting the property, economy, society, and very way of life of the rebellious slave states.

When Ulysses S. Grant, the U.S. Army's general-in-chief, tasked his leading subordinate, William Tecumseh Sherman, to capture the key rail and general transportation hub that was Atlanta, Georgia, in May–September 1864, he also ordered Sherman "to move against [Joseph P.] Johnston's army, to break it up, and to get into the interior of the enemy's country as far as you can, inflicting all the damage you can against their war resources" while he, Grant, continued to battle Robert E. Lee and his Army of Northern Virginia in a fight to the finish.

Sherman took his orders as license for total war on a whole new scale. His campaign against Atlanta was followed by the so-called March to the Sea, the object of which, Sherman himself said, was "to make Georgia howl." War has long brought suffering and devastation to civilian populations—sometimes even deliberately. "*Carthago delenda est,*" Cato the Elder (234–149 BC) repeatedly harangued his fellow Roman senators: "*Carthage must be destroyed.*" And so it was destroyed, utterly, in the Third Punic War (149–146 BC). But in the Atlanta Campaign and the march of destruction that followed it, Sherman made total warfare a deliberate, purposeful, systematic, and strategic element of modern warfighting doctrine. In an era that was just beginning to strive toward international conventions of "civilized warfare"—the first Geneva Convention was promulgated in 1864—Sherman went strongly against the emerging humanitarian grain. The results he produced endured.

The fight for Atlanta was long and deadly, commencing on the far outskirts of the city on May 7, 1864, and culminating in the evacuation of Confederate forces from Atlanta on September 1. Sherman began his occupation the next day, immediately ordering all residents to leave. When the mayor and two city councilmen protested, Sherman responded with a letter refusing to rescind his order, stating, "Our military plans make it necessary for the inhabitants to go away." He acknowledged that his demand was indeed cruel, explaining, "You cannot qualify war in harsher terms than I will. War is cruelty, and you cannot refine it. And those who brought war into our country deserve all the curses and maledictions a people can pour out. I know I had no hand in making this war, and I know I will make more sacrifices to-day than any of you to secure peace. But you cannot have peace and a division of our country. . . . You might as well appeal against the thunderstorm as against the terrible hardships of war. They are inevitable, and the only way the people of Atlanta can hope once more to live in peace and quiet at home, is to stop the war."

Only about half the city's residents obeyed Sherman's order. No matter. The general began transforming Atlanta into a Union military fortress. From it, he launched two armies. One, commanded by Major General George Henry Thomas, advanced west to pursue the army John Bell Hood had withdrawn from Atlanta. The other force, some 60,000 men, Sherman himself led eastward out of Atlanta on a March to the Sea, advancing southeast to Savannah to cut the Confederacy in two, dividing North from South in much the same way as Grant's victories on the Mississippi River in 1863 had divided East from West. The March to the Sea would put Sherman in position to attack Lee's Army of Northern Virginia from the south even as Grant bore down on it from the north, forcing Lee's battered force to fight a two-front campaign he could not possibly win.

But it is what Sherman proposed to do in the course of his long march that would make this an operation of total war. He would burn a swath of ruin, living off the land and putting to the torch whatever his army did not need. As he deprived the Confederacy of Atlanta and Atlantans of their city, so he would tear from the Confederate army *and the Confederate people* all means of sustenance. His objective was to break the enemy army as well as the will of the civilian population to continue to support a government that could not protect it or even provide for its most basic needs.

The March to the Sea began during November 15–16, 1864. Atlanta's function as a Union base of operations had been short-lived, and Sherman set about destroying everything of military value in the city. Union soldiers set many fires, which grew into a great conflagration that consumed most of the city. It is doubtful that the Union commanders intended such a level of destruction, and there is evidence that some of it was the work of Confederates who wanted to deprive Union forces of such valuable commodities as cotton. Whatever the intentions on both sides, the city Sherman left was extensively destroyed.

In the meantime, while Major General Thomas finished off John Bell Hood's Army of Tennessee at the battles of Franklin (November 30, 1864) and Nashville (December 15–16, 1864), Sherman visited relentless destruction on Georgia, exhorting his troops—"bummers," they proudly called themselves—not only to forage aggressively but to destroy at will. When the bummers entered Savannah on December 22, 1864, the terror-stricken city surrendered without a shot. This was the very result Sherman had intended: utter demoralization. "I beg to present you, as a Christmas gift," Sherman telegraphed the recently reelected Abraham Lincoln, "the city of Savannah, with one hundred and fifty heavy guns and plenty of ammunition; also about twenty-five thousand bales of cotton."

Sherman moved next to "punish South Carolina as she deserves. . . . I almost tremble for her fate." His army reached the outskirts of Columbia, the capital, on February 16, 1865. The mayor surrendered the city on the next day. Yet again, the Union occupation was accompanied by horrific fires of obscure origin. On February 17, the Confederate garrison that had occupied Fort Sumter since its fall to the Confederacy at the start of the war, meekly surrendered to Sherman. On February 22, the Stars and Bars were lowered and replaced by the Stars and Stripes over the fort. Weeks later, on April 14, 1865, Robert Anderson, who had been forced to surrender Sumter in 1861, presided over the hoisting of the very flag he had lowered four years and a day before. Hours later, this moment of Union glory was eclipsed by what might be counted the ultimate act of total war. John Wilkes Booth, a civilian operating as a self-proclaimed Confederate agent, assassinated President Abraham Lincoln.

Battle of the Little Bighorn: Shock and Awe on the Northern Plains (1876)

The United States' "Indian Policy" vacillated throughout most of the nineteenth century between attempts at conciliation and aggressive, often violent efforts to enforce confinement to reservations. Authority over Indian affairs shifted back and forth between the civilian government—the Department of the Interior—and the army. Although genocide was never the official policy of the U.S. government, after the Civil War, in 1869, William Tecumseh Sherman became commanding general of the U.S. Army and led it in a program of Native American suppression sufficiently aggressive to verge on genocide. Nevertheless, the size of the regular U.S. Army was far too small to do much more than conduct police actions—many of them brutal.

From April to July 1867, Civil War hero Winfield Scott Hancock fruitlessly pursued the Cheyenne and Sioux through Kansas. The following year, Sherman's most able lieutenant, another former Civil War commander, General Philip Sheridan, conducted a harrowing but futile winter campaign against the Sioux and Cheyenne.

George Armstrong Custer, who had earned fame as the youthful "boy general" of the Civil War through his dashing, reckless, and often nearly suicidal behavior in combat, reverted to his regular army rank after the war. As the flamboyant lieutenant colonel of the 7th Cavalry, he laid claim to the largest body count in "Sheridan's Campaign" at the Battle of Washita River (November 27, 1868) by attacking a peaceful Cheyenne camp, killing 103 Indians, among whom were 93 women, old men, and children. A leading advocate of peace, Chief Black Kettle, was among the slain—along with his wife.

The tragic futility of Hancock's and Sheridan's campaigns were typical of the Indian Wars. The usual pattern was weeks and months of vain pursuit culminating in brief spasms of violence resulting in the deaths of innocent victims alongside militant "hostiles." In July 1874, Custer and his 7th Cavalry rode out from Fort Abraham Lincoln (in what is today Bismarck, North Dakota) on the Black Hills Expedition. Their assignment was to look for suitable sites for a fort, find a viable route to the southwest, and investigate reports of gold in the hills. Custer discovered that those reports were accurate. The government, eager to attract settlers to the Dakota Territory, made offers to the Sioux to buy or lease the Black Hills from them. This land was sacred to the Sioux, who, accordingly, refused all offers. As gold miners began to arrive, federal authorities simply ordered the Indians to vacate. With that, the Great Sioux War of 1876 erupted.

The army, which never had an easy time fighting the Indian Wars, was now confronted by an enemy possessed of formidable riding and warrior skills and driven by religious zeal in defense of a sacred land. In this conflict they were led by the charismatic Tatanka Iyotake, known to the whites as Sitting Bull. On June 17, 1876, he mounted a punishing attack against Major General George Crook's column at Rosebud Creek in what is today Big Horn County, southern Montana. He dealt a hard blow to Crook's force of about 1,000 cavalrymen. That stinging defeat made Custer all the more determined to hunt down and destroy the "hostiles."

On the morning of June 22, 1876, to the strains of its jaunty regimental tune, "Garryowen," the 7th Cavalry passed in review before Generals Alfred Terry and John Gibbon. They were embarking on what the three commanders—Terry, Major General Gibbon, and Custer—planned as a coordinated pincers campaign against the Lakota Sioux and their Cheyenne allies. If they succeeded, they believed this operation would end resistance in the Black Hills.

As Lieutenant Colonel Custer rode off to join his men, Gibbon called after him: "Now, Custer, don't be greedy, but wait for us."

"No, I will not," Custer responded.

An impulsive commander, always hungry for glory, Custer was ill-suited to the frustrating, tedious, and exhausting "police" work that characterized the Indian Wars. He was determined to find a fight to the finish. He was determined to assert the supremacy of the U.S. Army over the Lakota.

On June 25, 1876, Custer's scouts discovered a Lakota Sioux camp and warriors near the Little Bighorn River. His orders were to rendezvous with other elements of the campaign before mounting a major attack. Fearful that the Sioux would slip away, as they usually did, he decided to attack immediately without pausing for reconnaissance to assess the strength of the camp.

He began the attack by sending Captain Frederick Benteen and 125 men south to make certain the Sioux had not moved to the upper valley of the Little Bighorn. Then he sent another 112 men under Major Marcus A. Reno in pursuit of a small body of warriors he had sighted. With his remaining troopers, Custer intended to charge the Sioux camp before him. Before he could begin, however, he saw that Reno and his men were being overwhelmed. Custer therefore dispatched his bugler, Giovanni Martini, to recall Benteen. In the meantime, Custer led his men against the warriors attacking Reno. Almost immediately, all were engulfed by very large numbers of Lakota warriors, who soon enveloped and killed Custer and some 210 cavalrymen.

Reno desperately held off disaster to his detachment and was joined by the returning Benteen. Together, their 368 officers and men endured a relentless two-day siege. In the end, U.S. Army casualties totaled 268 killed and about

55 wounded. Sitting Bull later reported 36 of his warriors killed and some 168 wounded. Another Native American leader present, Red Horse, put the numbers at 136 killed and 160 wounded.

News of the "massacre" of Custer's command spread rapidly, shaking the U.S. Army leadership to its core. Instead of provoking an immediate thirst for vengeance, the Indian triumph, so complete and devastating against so renowned an officer, cowed the Western forces into a state of timid hesitancy. For a time, the white American public and the government grew reflective about Indian policy. Some believed that the Battle of the Little Bighorn might prove a stunning turning point in nearly four centuries of white-Indian warfare on the North American continent.

But the Battle of the Little Bighorn proved to be the last major Indian victory of the Indian Wars. Two army leaders emerged, Colonel Ranald S. Mackenzie and Colonel (later Lieutenant General) Nelson A. Miles, who were willing to use the memory of the Little Bighorn as a battle cry in an accelerated push for a final, punitive victory against the Sioux. They led a series of engagements in which the Lakota warriors were repeatedly defeated. The Indian Wars dragged on through the rest of the 1870s and 1880s, but Native American resistance was rapidly wearing down.

Industrial Firepower: Hiram Maxim's Machine Gun (1884)

Born in Sangerville, Maine, in 1840, Hiram Maxim was a mechanical engineer who earned patents on everything from mousetraps and hair-curling irons to steam pumps. He experimented with aircraft and even laid claim to having invented the incandescent electric lamp—before Edison. But he is remembered for just one iconic invention: the Maxim gun.

In 1862, the multi-barrel Gatling gun, invented by American innovator Richard Jordan Gatling, made its debut in the Civil War. Although it was used very little in that conflict, it became famous as the first "automatic" weapon. In fact, it was a hybrid, since the automation, such as it was, came from a man turning a hand crank. Thanks to its ingenious gearing, the weapon was capable of firing 200 rounds per minute. In contrast to Gatling's human-mechanical hybrid, the weapon Maxim invented was a truly automatic gun, the world's first *machine* gun. Its remarkable design recycled the energy of its own recoil to advance the weapon's firing mechanism from one round to the next. Moreover, it had only a single barrel and was fed by a fabric belt of cartridges, which was drawn through the gun mechanically by the recoil-powered action. Maxim's original model was capable of firing 550 rounds per minute—a rate so high that a large water-circulating jacket had to be built around the barrel to cool it, preventing both structural damage to the metal and the possibility of the intense heat generated by rapid fire cooking off the ammunition on the belt, with catastrophic results to the crew manning it.

By the time he developed the weapon, Maxim had moved from the United States to the United Kingdom. He would be naturalized as a British subject in 1899 and knighted by Queen Victoria herself. By then, he had already entered into partnership with the British Vickers company, which produced the version of his invention that became a staple, iconic weapon of World War I. The Vickers Maxim fired 0.303-inch ammunition fed from a 250-round fabric belt at a rate of 450 to 500 rounds per minute with a devastating muzzle velocity of 2,240 feet per second. The gun itself weighed 33 pounds, and it was mounted on a 50-pound tripod. It was manned by a crew of two, a shooter and a feeder.

The Vickers Maxim and the many other machine gun types that followed it transformed warfare by multiplying the lethal potential of each soldier (or pair of soldiers) armed with the weapon. Advantageously positioned and firing from adequate cover, a two-man Maxim team could mow down 100 to 200 approaching attackers in the space of minutes. In a very real and horrific sense, the machine gun was both product and symbol of the triumph of industrialization in the late nineteenth century. The gun automated killing and killed impersonally, without the need to aim individually, at the rate of a mass-production machine. In World War I the weapon ensured that the advantage in combat would always go to the defender. It was not a weapon carried forward in an attack but one fired from a trench or a "machine-gun nest" against oncoming attackers. The proliferation of the machine gun was instrumental in creating the bloody stalemate of trench warfare on the Western Front of 1914–1918. Attackers could rarely achieve a decisive breakthrough against a line of trenches well defended by machine guns.

Like chemical weapons (so-called poison gas) and heavy artillery, the machine gun was a product of industrialized warfare. Creating any of these three classes of weapon required the combatant nation to possess a massive and advanced industrial capacity, and the weapons themselves embodied the industrial technology used to produce them. Precision machined and mass produced, the machine gun killed with considerable accuracy and on a large scale. Indeed, it was more machine than gun.

Serbian soldiers train on Vickers Maxim MG 11 machine guns during World War I.
MILITARY MUSEUM, BELGRADE

Reliance on the machine gun helped change the focus of military tactics early in the twentieth century from offensive to defensive. Because it was such an effective defensive weapon, however, the machine gun soon stimulated the development of new offensive weapons. In World War I these included improvements on the hand grenade and on mobile weapons platforms, including light artillery and, most important, the tank. Still, the 1914–1918 war ended before the technology of offensive weaponry had significantly closed the gap with defensive weapons. As a result, most military leaders failed to envision that the technology prevailing in the next world war would favor mobility and attack over static fortification and defense. Combatants such as Germany and the United States, both of which had begun earnestly developing highly mechanized, highly mobile warfighting platforms, therefore seized a valuable advantage in the 1939–1945 war.

Battle of Wounded Knee: How the "Indian Wars" Ended (1890)

By the mid-1880s, with the arrest of the Apache leader Geronimo, the conflict between the United States and the Apaches—the last major Indian War in the Southwest—came to an end. This marked a point at which almost a quarter of a million Native Americans were confined to reservations. Among these was Thathanka Iyotake—Sitting Bull—the most prominent leader of the Hunkpapa Lakota Sioux, who were now living at the Standing Rock Reservation on the South Dakota–North Dakota border.

Although Sitting Bull acquiesced to life on the reservation, he continued a kind of passive resistance, refusing to cooperate with the federal agent in charge. He did all he could to avoid contact with the white world. In the meantime, out of the general misery of reservation life in the late 1880s, there arose a prophet, a Paiute shaman's son named Wovoka. He was also known as Jack Wilson, having worked since the age of eight for a rancher named David Wilson and his wife, Abigail. To the Paiute religious traditions he had absorbed from his father, Wovoka added elements of Christian theology learned from the Wilsons. And so he preached to the others on the reservations a Native American version of the Second Coming, which would open a world in which only Indians dwelled and in which buffalo were again plentiful. It was nothing less than a general resurrection of Native American civilization.

While Wovoka spoke prophecy, he also exhorted his followers to hasten the coming of deliverance not through war with the white man but through the peaceful invocation of the Ghost Dance. Soon, numerous western reservations were alive with Ghost Dancing, which many nervous white people viewed as a kind of frenzy. They feared it was the prelude to violence. Among the Sioux of Standing Rock, the Ghost Dance was practiced with great intensity. Wovoka's message of peace, which should have accompanied it, was suppressed, and Short Bull and Kicking Bear, Teton Sioux apostles of the Ghost Dance religion, began openly urging a militant campaign to destroy the white man.

The pervasiveness of the Ghost Dance alarmed white authorities. On November 20, 1890, cavalry and infantry reinforcements arrived at the Pine Ridge and Rosebud Reservations, prompting some 3,000 Indian residents to gather on a plateau, dubbed the Stronghold, at the northwest corner of the Pine

Ridge Reservation. Officials feared that these men were plotting a total uprising on the reservations.

General Nelson A. Miles, who had military command over the area, ignored the protestations of Standing Rock Indian Agent James McLaughlin and summoned the great showman of the Wild West Buffalo Bill Cody to travel to Standing Rock and persuade Sitting Bull to give himself up. Miles knew that Sitting Bull had been featured in Cody's famed Wild West Show, and the general had been told that Cody was the only white man Sitting Bull trusted. There was likely truth in this; however, Agent McLaughlin was afraid that Buffalo Bill would simply draw too much curious attention to the unstable reservation. This in itself was likely to set off a general uprising. McLaughlin arranged for Buffalo Bill's train to be met. The showman was kept occupied in a saloon until orders could be secured canceling his mission and sending him home.

On December 15, 1890, with a great sense of relief at having rid himself of Buffalo Bill, McLaughlin dispatched 43 reservation policemen—Native Americans all—to arrest Sitting Bull before he could leave Standing Rock and stir the Indians to violence. McLaughlin believed the chief's removal would leave

An unknown photographer took this photograph of the grim aftermath of the Wounded Knee Massacre. It was published by Trager & Kuhn, Chadron, Nebraska.
WIKIMEDIA COMMONS

the impending Ghost Dance uprising leaderless, and it would simply peter out. Instead the arrest went bad. There was a scuffle during which Sitting Bull was shot in the chest. Seeing that the chief had been severely wounded, reservation police sergeant Red Tomahawk administered the coup de grâce, shooting Sitting Bull in the back of the head. No one knows if the scuffle was a setup and the shootings a deliberate assassination or was a case of spontaneously escalating violence—something all too common at the time. Either way, the Ghost Dancers now had a martyr.

Critical as the situation now was, there was worse to come. Nelson Miles was aware of another Ghost Dance leader to contend with. Big Foot was the chief of the Miniconjou Sioux, who lived on the Cheyenne River. Miles did not know that Big Foot had concluded that the Ghost Dance was futile and had renounced the Ghost Dance religion. Miles was also unaware that Chief Red Cloud, a Pine Ridge leader friendly to the whites, had pleaded with Big Foot to come to Standing Rock and use his influence to persuade those occupying the Stronghold to surrender. All Miles knew was that Big Foot was en route to the Stronghold. He assumed that he meant to join the other "hostiles."

Seeking to contain the coming explosion, Miles deployed troopers across the prairies and badlands to intercept all Miniconjous, including, in particular, Big Foot. A squadron of the 7th Cavalry located the chief and about 350 followers on December 28, 1890, camped near a stream called Wounded Knee on the Lakota Pine Ridge Reservation in what is today South Dakota. At the same place were some 120 warriors under Spotted Elk. The cavalrymen set about disarming these warriors, moving among them under the cover of 1.65-inch Lewis guns—rapid-action Gatling-style weapons—that were arrayed on the high ground overlooking the camp. Predictably, an argument broke out between some of the troopers and warriors who resisted giving up their weapons. As the dispute became physical, the Lewis gunners opened fire against the warriors and their camp. Between 150 and 300 Native Americans were slain, including both Big Foot and Spotted Elk, as well as women, children, and old men. While the U.S. Army classed the encounter as the "Battle" of Wounded Knee, most Americans called it the Wounded Knee Massacre, and it generated considerable sympathy for the Native cause. Too late, however. Two weeks later, on January 15, 1891, the entire Sioux nation formally surrendered to U.S. Army officials. With this, the Indian Wars, which had been fought sporadically since the first voyage of Columbus in 1492, ended.

The USS *Maine* Explodes: Finding an Excuse for War (1898)

The "Indian Wars" ended with the surrender of the Sioux Nation in 1891. A year earlier, the U.S. census of 1890 revealed that all unclaimed public lands had now been settled. The American frontier was, in effect, "closed," and some predicted that America's restless appetite for the republican equivalent of empire would now begin to reach beyond the confines of the North American continent.

In February 1896, the government of Spain sent General Valeriano Weyler to restore order in its rebellious colony of Cuba, just 90 miles off the coast of the state

Chicago lithographers Kurtz & Allison published *Destruction of the U.S. Battleship Maine in Havana Harbor Feby 15th, 1898*, shortly after the event.
LIBRARY OF CONGRESS, DEPARTMENT OF PRINTS AND PHOTOGRAPHS

of Florida. Among Weyler's first acts was to build "reconcentration camps" for the incarceration of rebels as well as other citizens accused of supporting them. From American politicians as well as the public, calls rose up for intervention against the Spanish atrocities being perpetrated on America's very doorstep. Locked in their own war, a war over circulation, New York rival newspaper publishers Joseph Pulitzer and William Randolph Hearst vied with each other in running lurid stories of Spanish cruelty in Cuba. The American public began to heat up with war fever. President Grover Cleveland and then his successor, William McKinley, resisted increasingly strident demands for intervention until, at last, a reluctant McKinley ordered the armored cruiser USS *Maine* into Havana Harbor as a show of force intended to protect American citizens and property there.

It was not public empathy for Cuban suffering alone that fueled America's enthusiasm for war against Spain. By the late nineteenth century, many American businesses had made major investments on the island, especially in sugar plantations. Revolutionary unrest threatened profits, but a successful revolution, properly supported by the United States, could install a nominally independent Cuban government that was, in fact, a compliant American client. An alternative was territorial annexation.

On February 9, 1898, the Hearst papers created a sensation by publishing an intercepted private letter in which the Spanish minister to the United States insulted President McKinley by calling him weak and interested only in gaining favor with the crowd. This turned up the fever, and when news broke on February 15 that the *Maine*, moored in Havana Harbor, had exploded and sunk with the loss of 266 sailors and officers, that fever rose beyond remedy. Most current historians are convinced by evidence that the ship's powder magazine spontaneously ignited through no hostile action. To give President McKinley due credit, he did not jump into war but convened a naval court of inquiry to investigate and determine the source of the explosion. Their conclusion was that the ship "was destroyed by the explosion of a submarine mine"; however, the court declined to assign responsibility for the detonation. Was it a Spanish mine set by Spanish agents? Or was it the work of rebels, eager to provoke U.S. entry into their struggle against Spain? The Hearst and Pulitzer papers had no doubt. They both implicated Spain, and the United States soon rang loudly with the battle cry of "Remember the *Maine* . . . to hell with Spain!"

President McKinley secured a congressional resolution demanding Spain's withdrawal from Cuba and authorizing the use of military force to aid in the cause of Cuban independence. Spain responded by severing diplomatic relations with the United States, which on that very day, April 21, 1898, established a naval blockade of the island. Spain warned that an American invasion of Cuba would mean war. Congress declared that a de facto state of war already existed and issued an ultimatum demanding that Spain surrender control of Cuba. When Spain failed to respond in what was deemed a timely manner, the war was on.

As was the case with the War of 1812, the United States was quite unprepared to wage a major war, let alone one outside its continental limits. The leaders of the small U.S. Army endorsed the Navy's proposal to continue the war mainly through a naval blockade. Congress and the public, however, demanded more positive action in the form of an invasion. The regular army numbered about 26,000 officers and men; the National Guard enrolled about 100,000 more, almost all of them poorly trained and ill equipped. Beyond this, no ready plan existed for conducting a foreign invasion. In belated preparation for war, Congress had passed a Mobilization Act on April 22, 1898, which provided legal authority for deploying National Guard units outside U.S. borders and authorized the recruitment of 125,000 volunteers, to which an additional 75,000 were soon added. There was even a special 10,000-man force, called "the Immunes," which consisted of men "possessing immunity from diseases incident to tropical climates." Finally, the Mobilization Act also increased the size of the regular army to about 65,000. (By the end of the brief 10-week war, the regular army numbered 59,000 and the volunteer forces 216,000.)

Logistics were inadequate to transport the army quickly and efficiently to Cuba, but the U.S. Navy was sufficiently manned and equipped to strike the first aggressive blows. On May 1, 1898, the American fleet attacked and destroyed the Spanish fleet in Manila Harbor, Philippines, at the time a Spanish colony. The United States decided to force Spain to attend to two fronts simultaneously.

It was not until May 1898 that General Nelson A. Miles was ready to send army units to Cuba from Tampa, Florida. U.S. Marines coordinated with the Navy to neutralize Spanish batteries guarding Havana Harbor, and on June 14, V Corps, consisting of three divisions—17,000 men, mostly regular army—under Major General William R. Shafter, left Tampa. It was June 20 before the convoy, made up of leased commercial vessels, arrived near Santiago, the troops having suffered under brutal tropical heat and in overcrowded, unsanitary conditions. Admiral William T. Sampson implored Shafter to land at Santiago Bay and immediately storm the fort on the east side of the entrance to the bay to drive the Spanish from their guns, but Shafter had failed to transport heavy artillery and doubted his troops could take the fort without those weapons. He decided instead on a less direct approach, landing at Daiquiri, east of Santiago Bay.

Disembarkation began on June 22 and was not concluded until June 25, amid great confusion. Equipment was stranded, and cavalry mounts were tossed overboard, left to swim ashore on their own. Many swam out to sea and were lost. Had the Spanish commanders responded at all competently, they could almost certainly have devastated the landing force. Spain had at least 200,000 troops in Cuba, of which 36,000 were stationed in Santiago. Against this was an initial U.S. Army force of no more than 22,000 men supplemented by some 5,000 local insurgents under General Calixto Garcia. But the Spanish did nothing at all to repel the landings, and elements of V Corps soon advanced west toward the high ground of San Juan, a series of ridges east of Santiago.

On June 23, Brigadier General Henry W. Lawton led an American army advance force along the coast from Daquiri to take and hold Siboney, which became the principal base of U.S. operations. The next day, Brigadier General Joseph Wheeler marched his dismounted cavalry units inland along the road to Santiago and captured Las Guasimas.

V Corps units, now just five miles outside San Juan Heights, halted, awaiting the arrival of the rest of Shafter's divisions. That commander, however, feared the debilitating effect the tropical conditions had on his troops. He decided that speed was of the essence and ordered an immediate frontal attack against San Juan Heights, which stepped off at dawn on July 1.

The attack began badly. Troops fell victim to the heat and to Spanish artillery. Nevertheless, by midday, American forces made a vigorous assault on San Juan Heights. Among the army units participating were the 9th and 10th Cavalry—both segregated African-American regiments—and the 1st U.S. volunteers, a regiment known as the Rough Riders and commanded in the field by its dashing lieutenant colonel, Theodore Roosevelt. These three cavalry regiments all fought on foot because their mounts had failed to arrive in Cuba. They seized and occupied Kettle Hill as U.S. regular infantry charged up San Juan Hill and overwhelmed the defenders. Short of food, water, and ammunition, the Spaniards abandoned San Juan. Simultaneously, U.S. ships engaged and destroyed the Spanish fleet; on July 16, Spanish commanders in Cuba surrendered.

During July 21–25, General Nelson A. Miles led more than 3,000 troops out of Guantánamo, Cuba, and landed at Guanica on the southeastern coast of Puerto Rico. Meeting virtually no resistance, they advanced to the port town of Ponce. From there, Miles led four columns toward San Juan but suspended the campaign on August 13 when news arrived that Spain had signed a peace protocol.

Shortly after the American army and navy triumphed in Cuba and Puerto Rico, VIII Corps, consisting of about 13,000 volunteers and 2,000 regulars under Major General Wesley Merritt, began landing near Manila, the Philippines. By the start of August, 11,000 U.S. troops were arrayed to the rear of the Filipino insurgents just outside the capital, which some 15,000 Spanish troops stood ready to defend. Admiral George Dewey and General Merritt appealed to the Spanish government in Madrid to surrender. When the government refused, VIII Corps attacked on August 13, supported by Dewey's naval bombardment. The Spanish garrison soon gave up. On August 14 the Manila surrender was formalized—two days after Madrid had signed a general peace protocol. On December 10 the Treaty of Paris was signed, securing Cuban independence, and President McKinley successfully pressed his negotiators to obtain cession of Puerto Rico, Guam, and the Philippine Islands. The United States had taken its first step toward becoming a global power.

Boers Hold Off an Empire: The High Cost of Insurgent Warfare (1899–1902)

Britain colonized South Africa during the Napoleonic Wars but failed to resolve the tension between the new colonial rulers and the original Dutch and Huguenot colonizers. During the 1830s, to evade Britain's empire-wide ban on slavery, the Boers (Afrikaans for "farmers") left the coast and trekked into the interior, where they established two colonies of their own—one beyond the Vaal River (the Transvaal Republic), the other beyond the Orange River (the Orange Free State).

The Boers twice handed the mighty British Empire embarrassing defeats, the first in the Transvaal Revolt of 1880–1881 and the second in the Jameson Raid of 1895–1896. After the British installed the much-hated Cecil Rhodes as prime minister of South Africa, the Boers demanded the withdrawal of troops protecting British mining interests in the Transvaal. When the demand was ignored, the Boers declared war on Great Britain in October 1899 and came out swinging.

From all appearances, the South African Republic (Transvaal) and the Orange Free State made for a puny enemy. They lacked a navy, a regular army, and an industrial base of any kind. They were nothing more or less than insurgents daring to take on an empire. Nevertheless, every Boer was a sharpshooter, for all practical purposes a born hunter, and each knew the land intimately. Like the Indians of the American Plains, they were superb horsemen. They armed themselves with modern repeating rifles and even had a few pieces of French and German field artillery.

They scored initial easy wins. Led by General Piet Joubert, veteran of the Transvaal Revolt, the 15,000-man main force prevailed against General Sir George White's Natal Defense Force and bottled up his troops in Ladysmith on November 2, 1899. Transvaal general Piet Cronjé took Mafeking on October 13, and Free State forces besieged Kimberly two days later. British attempts to relieve this major mining center failed at great cost, and the siege stretched on and on.

General Sir Redvers Buller attempted to defeat the forces of Free State general Louis Botha at Colenso on December 15, only to be cut to ribbons by Boers hiding in the bush, who relentlessly drove back his troops. Buller was so demoralized that he advocated the outright surrender of Ladysmith. The London government responded by relieving Buller of principal command and replacing him with Field Marshal Lord Frederick Roberts, who steamed into Cape Town in January 1900 with reinforcements and his chief of staff, General Lord Horatio Kitchener. A brilliant tactician, Roberts quickly understood that the key to the Boers' insurgent success was their incredible mobility. Going against the conventional wisdom of conservative British tacticians, Roberts decided to build up a mounted infantry around existing militia units. By January 10, 1900, he had radically reorganized British forces. The new mobility of his mounted infantry enabled him to bring the Boer siege of Kimberly to an end on February 15. Positioned to next defeat Piet Cronjé's South African Republic forces, Roberts fell ill and had to be replaced by Kitchener, who impulsively launched a piecemeal frontal attack that was easily spoiled by Boer marksmen. Roberts was well enough to resume command on February 19 and laid siege against Cronjé at Paardeberg. The South African forces were starved into surrender.

On February 28, General Buller, now in a subordinate command, reached Ladysmith and, after two failed assaults, broke through with a third attack on February 17–18, forcing the Boers to lift their siege and scatter. This was the turn in the tide of war. Heavily reinforced, the British advanced on all fronts. Roberts marched into the Orange Free State and seized its capital, Bloemfontein, on March 13, 1900. From here he fanned out to occupy the rest of the country. During May 17–18, Major General Bryan T. Mahon relieved the garrison at Mafeking, which had been under siege for seven months. At the same time, the British invaded the Transvaal, capturing Johannesburg on May 31 and Pretoria on June 5, crushing all Boer resistance on the battlefield. Britain annexed the Orange Free State on May 24, 1900, and the Transvaal Republic of South Africa on September 3.

Lord Roberts considered the war over and won. Leaving Kitchener in charge, he sailed for home in December 1900. The mistake both Roberts and the British government made was failing to understand the intense commitment of true insurgents. The Boers quietly shifted to guerrilla commando tactics, trading set battles for relentless raids. Small bands of horsemen struck the slow-moving British infantry and its supply columns, hitting, running, and vanishing. By the time reinforcements arrived to give chase, the guerrillas had invariably evaporated.

Kitchener addressed the insurgency with a logic as brutal as it was bloody. Unable to defeat 20,000 Boer horsemen with the quarter-million British troops he had on hand, he built some 8,000 blockhouses out of corrugated iron and stone, siting them first along the railway lines then across the veldt itself. They were a chain of forts, linked by barbed wire, and located within rifle shot of one another, able to set up crossfires. This system of fortifications seemed impregnable—except that it was not. The raiders broke through at will.

Kitchener then copied the savage tactics Spain had used to subjugate Cuba, sweeping through the now-compartmentalized Boer nations with flying columns of mounted infantry. He encouraged his officers to lead his men as if they were hunting big game. He also ordered them to scorch the earth, burning the Boers' crops and farms to bare ground. Kitchener waged total war. Every Boer was an enemy. There were no civilians. He swept up large numbers of Boers and carted them off to one of his newly constructed "concentration camps"—his term, which he invented—24 of which were built and administered by the army. They were hellholes, breeding typhoid and other diseases. Some 117,000 Boers were confined to the camps during the war. As many as 28,000 died in them.

Despite the terrors mounted against them, the Boer commandos—led by Botha, De La Rey, Christiaan De Wet, and Jan Smuts—continued their raids; but in a war of attrition, it is the underdog that generally loses.

When the Boers first sued for peace in March 1901, Kitchener rebuffed them. By May 1902 they were thoroughly demoralized and simply capitulated. By the Treaty of Vereeniging (May 31, 1902), the Boers accepted British sovereignty. And this is where Kitchener and the other British administrators suddenly changed their tune, extending very lenient terms. No Boer lost his property. No Boer was taxed with war indemnities. Far from it, in fact. The Crown agreed to pay the Boers £3 million in compensation for the destruction of farms and crops. Boers were encouraged to teach both English and Afrikaans in their schools, and the British agreed to delay settling what was antiseptically referred to as "the issue of nonwhite suffrage."

The mighty British Empire consumed three years in subduing the tiny Boer nations. Before the war ended, Britain had committed more than a half-million men to South African service, draining manpower from armies stationed around the world. The Boer population probably offered 83,000 males of military age, but the insurgents never actually fielded more than 40,000. Nearly 6,000 Britons had died fighting the Boer War; another 22,829 were wounded. No one knows much about Boer casualties. Most estimates guess at 4,000 killed. Victorious though it was, the British military had learned a sobering lesson. Experience fighting formal and self-contained European wars was useless against determined insurgents. The most effective tactic was precisely what critics of Kitchener condemned as his "methods of barbarism."

The Boxer Rebellion: Leveraging a Little War on China (1900)

The so-called Boxer Rebellion of 1900 occasioned the formation of the first modern international military coalition, creating a model for transnational military command and cooperation against a third-party nation. For the United States, participation in the coalition signaled a new willingness to play a military role on the global stage.

It began in 1899, when U.S. secretary of state John Hay communicated to the governments of France, Germany, Great Britain, Italy, Russia, and Japan America's endorsement of an "Open Door Policy" (first suggested by British customs official Alfred E. Hippisley) toward China. Hay proposed that the United States, all European nations, and Japan should have equal access to Chinese trade. Initially, Japan objected, but the Western nations unanimously approved. China, the object of the policy, was not even consulted. That ancient empire was on the brink of disintegration, held together only very tenuously by Cixi, the empress dowager, who, in desperation, issued a proclamation (on January 11, 1900) approving an uprising of a militant secret society, Yihe Quang, loosely translated as the "righteous harmony of fists" and called by Westerners "the Boxers."

By spring, the Boxers were on the rampage, menacing foreigners as well as Chinese Christians and sabotaging rail and telegraph lines. As usual in an international crisis, the U.S. Navy was the first American military service called on to respond. Two ships, USS *Monocacy* and USS *Newark*, were dispatched to Taku Forts on the Hai River in northeastern China. Their mission was to protect Americans and American interests, and on May 27 the *Newark* joined a flotilla of European warships off Taku Bar. Just two days later, in response to a request from the U.S. consul in the coastal trading town of Tianjin, 49 U.S. Marines were landed and were soon augmented to a ground force of 150. The marines became the first foreign ground troops in Tianjin, but they were rapidly joined by units from England, France, Russia, Austria, Italy, and Japan.

While the coalition forces assembled in Tianjin, European diplomats in Beijing demanded permission for the coalition forces to travel by train to the capital to reinforce the inadequate contingent of European embassy and legation guards. With permission granted on May 30, Captain John Twiggs Myers took 55 marines and joined more than 300 troops from the other coalition nations on the 90-mile rail journey to the capital. In the meantime, Boxer riots intensified.

Looting and arson were common, as were assaults on Chinese Christians. On June 6 the Boxers severed the railroad between Beijing and Tianjin. The coalition forces agreed to unified command under a British Royal Navy vice admiral, Sir Edward Seymour.

Two days after Seymour assumed command of the coalition fleet, Boxers cut the telegraph lines into Beijing. Seymour authorized what would come to be called the Seymour Expedition, four trains carrying 2,006 coalition troops from Tianjin to Beijing. The first train left on the morning of June 10; others followed during the rest of the day, but progress was slow due to Boxer sabotage of the railroad track.

No sooner did the Seymour Expedition pull out of Tianjin on June 10 than Chinese forces started shelling foreign sections of the city. Just 1,100 foreign troops and the small U.S. Marine cadre remained in Tianjin. Overwhelmed and outgunned, the expedition was supremely vulnerable. In conference, the leaders of the European-American coalition decided that time was running out for the relief of Tianjin. To capture and hold the city, coalition commanders decided that taking the forts at Taku and the rail station at Tongku was the key to defeating the Boxers. Accordingly, Russian, German, British, Japanese, Italian, and Austrian officers issued a joint ultimatum to the commander of the forts on June 16, demanding surrender. In response the forts fired on the warships at Taku Bar. The vessels returned fire for four hours, driving the Boxers out of the forts, which Euro-American forces seized and occupied.

The American ships refrained from contributing to the bombardment or the capture of the forts because the U.S. commanders interpreted their mission as strictly defensive. They felt authorized to act only in the direct defense of American nationals. Cixi, however, responded to the shelling of the Taku Forts by ordering, on June 18, an Imperial Army attack on the Seymour Expedition. Troops hit transport trains near Anting, 25 miles outside Beijing, and cut rail lines behind the train so that it could neither return to Tianjin nor advance to Beijing. Vastly outnumbered, Seymour burned the train and ordered a retreat, on foot, to Tianjin. The column reached Hsi Ku Arsenal, five miles from Tianjin, on June 22.

In the meantime, Imperial troops laid siege to the international quarter at Tianjin and to the European diplomatic legations at Beijing. On June 17, the Chinese intensified bombardment of the international quarter. Under the leadership of future thirty-first president of the United States Herbert Hoover, then a young mining engineer working for a British firm with Chinese interests, the foreign civilians and Chinese Christians valiantly defended Tianjin.

On June 20, U.S. Marines from the Philippines landed at Taku and set off for Tianjin to force an end to the siege. They joined with a Russian battalion along the way, the combined force engaging Chinese troops on June 21. Outnumbered, the Russo-American force fell back until reinforced by British troops. What was now a Russo-Anglo-American force then resumed the advance to Tianjin on June 22, engaging Chinese forces several times before arriving at Tianjin on June 24. They relieved the Seymour Expedition at the Hsi-Ku Arsenal on June 25 and destroyed the arsenal to keep it out of Chinese hands. In the meantime, Tianjin was evacuated of non-Chinese residents. At this point, the American commanders expanded their mission to a more proactive and aggressive role. During July, the coalition, Americans in the forefront, continuously operated against both the Boxers and Imperial troops in and around Tianjin. All the coalition powers sent reinforcements into China. U.S. forces, including elements of the 9th Infantry, the 14th Infantry, the 5th Field Artillery, and the 6th Cavalry, together with additional marine units, were dubbed the China Relief Expedition and put under the command of U.S. Army general Adna Chaffee.

By August 4, the coalition had become a polyglot force of more than 20,000. They now marched from Tianjin to Peking. On August 5, Chinese Imperial troops attacked the Japanese, in the vanguard of the international column, hitting the Japanese left flank. In a six-hour battle, Japanese and British troops routed the Chinese.

Acting on their own initiative, Russian troops advanced into Peking on August 13 only to be immediately overwhelmed. Other coalition units rescued them. On August 14, elements of the 14th U.S. Infantry and a contingent of marines captured a section of the fabled Tartar Wall. From here the Americans covered British troops, who entered the Outer City to relieve the besieged legations. On August 15, marines cleared the barricades from Chien-mien Gate and established artillery positions there. The cannon destroyed the gates of the Forbidden City. With this action—and the relief of the legations—the Boxer Rebellion dissolved. The coalition nations now drew up the Boxer Protocol, a document that imposed an exorbitant $333,000,000 indemnity against China and which also compelled the nation to agree to the permanent stationing of U.S. and other troops in the country.

Back on July 3, Secretary Hay began to suspect that the other members of the coalition intended to exploit the Boxer Rebellion as a pretext to abandon the Open Door policy and carve up China among themselves. Hay issued a "circular letter," in which he stated the policy of the United States "to seek a solution which may bring about permanent safety and peace to China, preserve Chinese territorial and administrative entity, protect all rights guaranteed to friendly powers by treaty and international law, and safeguard for the world the principle of equal and impartial trade with all parts of the Chinese Empire." After victory had been won, the United States, which was entitled to share in the indemnity against China to the tune of $24,500,000, agreed to reduce its share to $12 million. Years later, in 1924, the United States forgave the unpaid balance due on that reduced amount.

The Boxer Protocol proved the final undoing of the Qing, or Manchu, dynasty, which had ruled since 1644. Humiliated and weakened by the protocol, it was overthrown in the Chinese Revolution of 1911. China was plunged into decades of civil war and revolution, emerging in 1949 as the People's Republic of China, by far the largest of all the Communist countries. The United States had earned considerable prestige in the Boxer Rebellion but soon discovered that military action on the global stage risked a cascade of unintended, unforeseen, and unforeseeable consequences. Nevertheless, coalition warfare entered the American military playbook.

The Naval Campaign of Tsushima: Japan Redefines Victory (1905)

First, the battle. Fought between Russia and Japan during the Russo-Japanese War (1904–1905), it is distinctive for three reasons. It was the first naval battle in which radio (wireless telegraphy) played a tactical role. This stands as an enduring turning point in the use of electronic communications technology in combat. The second distinction is that Tsushima was the only engagement in which modern steel battleship fleets met in a decisive sea battle. In retrospect, this fact stands as one of military history's most paradoxical turning points. On the one hand, Tsushima was such a shock to the world's major naval powers that massive steel battleships were instantly regarded as the "ultimate" naval weapon. In 1906 the British Royal Navy commissioned HMS *Dreadnought*, first of a class of battleships intended to revolutionize naval power. It mounted massive

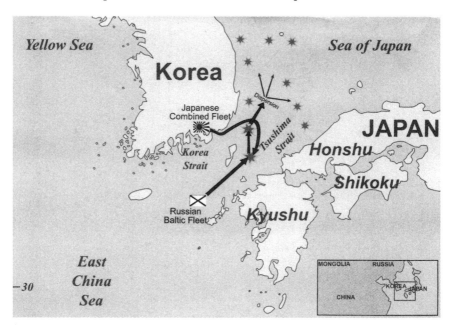

The Battle of Tsushima
WIKIMEDIA COMMONS

12-inch artillery only, was very heavily armored, and was fast, making 21 knots. Yet history would quickly render the battleship obsolete. In World War I the epic 1916 Battle of Jutland, pitting British and German naval fleets, both organized around Dreadnought-class battleships, proved eminently indecisive, and in World War II the aircraft carrier immediately eclipsed the battleship as the queen of battle at sea.

The third distinction was that both the battle and the war marked the first time in modern history that an Asian power defeated the military of a European nation.

Although Tsushima inaugurated the era of electronic battle communications, it was the death knell of the very battleship technology it launched. It was fought during May 27–28, 1905, in the Tsushima Strait between Korea and southern Japan. The Japanese fleet—5 battleships among a total of 89 vessels—commanded by Admiral Tōgō Heihachirō destroyed two-thirds of Admiral Zinovy Rozhestvensky's Russian fleet, consisting of 8 battleships and 30 other vessels. The Japanese sunk 6 of the major battleships and one so-called coastal

This 1905 photograph shows the damage done to the Japanese armored cruiser *Nisshin* after both guns in one of its turrets exploded in intense firing during the Battle of Tsushima. Injured in the blast was Isoroku Yamamoto, future architect of the World War II Japanese attack on Pearl Harbor.
WIKIMEDIA COMMONS

battleship along with 14 other vessels—a total loss of 126,792 tons. Russian personnel casualties were 4,380 killed and 5,917 captured. Japanese losses were minimal: 3 torpedo boats sunk (a 450-ton shipping loss), 117 sailors killed in action, and 583 wounded. The one-sided catastrophe that befell the Russian fleet has been compared in historical importance to Lord Nelson's lopsided triumph over the French navy at Trafalgar a hundred years earlier in the Napoleonic Wars. The defeat created a public clamor in Russia for immediate peace, and a treaty, brokered by U.S. president Theodore Roosevelt, ended the conflict in September 1905 without any further battles.

The background of the battle may be traced to February 8, 1904, when the Japanese fleet laid siege against a Russian naval squadron anchored at Russian-controlled Port Arthur on the Liaodong Peninsula in southern Manchuria. This surprise action triggered the world's first large-scale use of massive sea power and, on land, brutal battles between soldiers equipped with modern rapid-fire weapons. The attack was the product of some 50 years of Japanese anxiety over the expansion of the Russian Empire into eastern Asia, which was a challenge to Japan's own imperial ambitions. After China's decadent Manchu dynasty lost a war with Japan in 1894, it joined Russia in an anti-Japanese alliance, yielding to Russia a railroad right-of-way across Manchuria to Vladivostok and ceding to Russia control over a strategic strip of Chinese territory. Four years later, Russia pressured the Chinese into leasing Port Arthur (modern Lu-shun) for a Russian naval base. In 1903 Czar Nicholas II refused to honor his pledge to withdraw Russian troops from Manchuria. Japan's government saw a dagger pointed at the heart of the nation.

Japan had long been building up its army. By the late nineteenth century, all that kept it from launching a major war against Russia was the British Royal Navy. In 1902, however, Great Britain made an alliance with Japan to curb the expansionist ambitions of Nicholas II. Before commencing war, Japan engaged in talks with Russia late in 1903. Japan proposed that each side recognize the other's special interests and economic rights in both Manchuria and Korea. The Russians refused to come to an agreement, and on February 6, 1904, the Japanese ambassador broke off negotiations. On February 9 Japan sank two Russian warships at Chemulpo (Inchon, Korea) and launched a devastating torpedo attack on the Russian fleet at Port Arthur.

The West regarded Japan as a quaint, backward country and was confident that Russia would easily defeat it. But the Port Arthur attack was devastating, and because the rest of the Russian navy was icebound at Vladivostok, Czar Nicholas II could do little. Even more shocking to the Western powers was the velocity with which the Japanese army overran Korea and crossed the Yalu River into Manchuria. By May 1, 1904, vast areas in Korea and China were under Japanese control. By September, the Russians had been forced west to Mukden (Shenyang). Port Arthur was now surrounded. Russian ground forces responded in two bloody but indecisive battles then retreated farther north. Port Arthur fell to Japan on January 5, 1905.

Although overmatched and outgunned, Nicholas II refused to back down. Before the fall of Port Arthur, he dispatched Russia's Baltic Fleet to the Pacific. At the straits off the Japanese island of Tsushima, that fleet was forced to its doom. At the same time, Japanese land forces defeated the Russians in Mukden.

The cost was high to both nations. Russia, fielding some 1,365,000 men, lost 71,453 killed and 141,800 wounded. Japan, with forces numbering about 1.2 million, suffered 80,378 combat deaths and 153,673 wounded. Yet it was the Russian Empire that was brought to its knees. By the Treaty of Portsmouth (New Hampshire), mediated by President Roosevelt between August 9 and September 5, 1905, Russia recognized Japan's conquest of Korea and ceded to Japan control of the Liaodong Peninsula and Port Arthur. Russia also agreed to evacuate southern Manchuria. Two months after signing the treaty, Czar Nicholas II faced the Russian Revolution of 1905, which he managed to crush. This bought the Romanov dynasty, at the time nearly 300 years old, just 12 more years of life.

Assassination in Sarajevo:
Bringing a World to War (1914)

June 28, 1914, was a day of religious and nationalist celebration in Sarajevo, capital of Bosnia and Herzegovina. Called Vidovan, the holiday marked both St. Vitus's Day—the holy day of Bosnia's patron saint—and a Serbian victory against the Ottoman Empire in 1389. It was on this very day that the heir apparent to the Austrian throne, Archduke Franz Ferdinand (with his wife, the Grand Duchess Sophie), made a state visit to Sarajevo. The choice of day was intended to intimidate the rebellious Balkans, most of which were tenuously under Austro-Hungarian control, by boldly asserting imperial authority in an important Balkan provincial capital.

During this period, much of the Balkans was seeking independence under the "pan-Slavic" ethnic umbrella of Russia, which offered itself as the defender of all who proclaimed themselves Slavs. At the same time, Serbia, then the most powerful independent state in the region, was home to a secret society called "Unity or Death" but better known as the Black Hand. It covertly reached out to would-be revolutionaries throughout the region, sowing anti-Austrian violence. Its leader, a former Serbian colonel who called himself Apis ("The Bull"), specialized in recruiting radically inclined university students. He often sought out desperate young men infected with the universal plague of the turn of the twentieth century: tuberculosis. Among his recruits was Gavrilo Princip, who had become involved in Bosnian nationalism. His handler in Sarajevo was Danilo Ilić, a Bosnian Serb and member of the Black Hand, who connected Princip and five other assassins with Apis. The latter supplied them with Belgian-made Browning FN M1910 9-millimeter pistols, ammunition, six grenade-style bombs, and what he said were cyanide suicide capsules. Their assignment was to assassinate Franz Ferdinand on Vidovan.

Ilić deployed his recruits and himself along 300 yards of the Appel Quay, principal avenue of Sarajevo. The archduke's timetable and route had been published in the local newspapers, so the seven assassins, armed variously with pistols and bombs, were certain they would not miss a close-encounter opportunity. The first assassin, positioned at the Cumuria Bridge, had a bomb; the second, a bomb and a Browning; the third was armed only with a bomb. Ilić and another had Brownings, as did Princip, who was positioned second to last. He believed at least one of the others would score a kill before him.

Franz Ferdinand refused to accept special protection in a city of *his* empire. He ordered his military units to clear out of Sarajevo and stay out, retaining only a small unit of body guards. After arriving by train, he and the grand duchess mounted an open-top limousine, which displayed to greatest advantage his full-dress uniform and his wife's white silk dress, red sash, flamboyant picture hat, and ermine-trimmed cape. They passed Cumuria Bridge without incident—the first assassin, gripped by panic, failing to hurl his bomb. The next did throw his grenade, but it bounced off the back of the archduke's limousine, rolled in front of the car following it, and exploded with sufficient force to damage the second vehicle and injure a number of spectators as well as members of the archducal entourage. Even Sophie felt the sting of a miniscule splinter in her cheek.

For his part, the driver stepped on the gas, moving fast enough to leave Ilić and the next would-be assassin in line too confused to act. Both Princip and the hapless young man positioned after him were similarly confounded. The archduke's car moved too fast for aim or action. Dejected, Princip drifted away to a table at an outdoor cafe. He ordered coffee, the small pistol still heavy in his coat pocket.

In the meantime, Franz Ferdinand and Sophie put the assassination attempt behind them and attended a scheduled reception at the town hall. This finished, the archduke ordered a change in the planned itinerary, insisting on a visit to the local military hospital, where those injured by the bomb blast had been taken. Unfortunately, his driver did not know the way to the hospital and ended up at the corner of the Appel Quay and Franz Josef Street, down which he turned. The archduke's military aide shouted out that they were going the wrong way. Thoroughly rattled, the driver clumsily attempted a U turn. Suddenly hemmed in by a crowd, he was forced to stop. The automobile was now positioned broadside to the cafe-delicatessen of Moritz Schiller—and Gavrilo Princip was just five feet from the archduke and the grand duchess.

Princip later told police that he "recognized the heir apparent, but as I saw that a lady was sitting next to him, I reflected for a moment whether I should shoot or not. At the same moment I was filled with a peculiar feeling and I aimed at the heir apparent from the pavement—which was made easier because the car was proceeding slower at the moment. Where I aimed I do not know. But I know that I aimed at the heir apparent. I believe I fired twice, perhaps more, because I was so excited. Whether I hit the victims or not, I cannot tell, because instantly people started to hit me."

The time was 11:15 a.m.; the date, June 28, 1914. Princip reached into his coat pocket, withdrew the small black pistol, and leveled it at point-blank range. An alert police officer lunged at the young gunman, but an out-of-work actor named Pusara shoved the officer out of the way. Princip squeezed off three rounds before the policeman regained his balance. By that time, Princip had spun around and was about to take flight. Another bystander, Ferdinand Behr, gave him a helping hand by punching the officer in the stomach. Princip could have made a run for it. He should have. Instead he stood stunned, giving another bystander—who was obviously more sympathetic to Austrian rule—the opportunity to knock the pistol out of his hand. Still others in the crowd swarmed Princip and rained blows down upon him.

Gavrilo Princip's first shot had passed through the car door, hitting Sophie in the abdomen. The second shot buried itself in the archduke's neck, clipping the carotid artery and lodging in his spine. There was a great deal of blood, and husband and wife died within seconds of each other.

Austria-Hungary's foreign minister, Count Leopold von Berchtold, demanded more blood. He blamed Serbia for the assassination, even though the Serbian-based Black Hand sought to overthrow the current Serbian government. No matter. Berchtold was determined to punish Serbia so severely that Bosnian nationalism would be crushed along with, he hoped, the entire pan-Slavic movement.

Berchtold did not intend to start a European war, much less a world war, the greatest and most destructive in history to that time. He wanted only to humiliate Serbia by defeating it in a swift and contained war. On July 23 he sent 10 demands to Belgrade, Serbia's capital city. All were humiliating, but one in particular required a renunciation of nationhood. Berchtold demanded that Serbia turn over the assassination investigation exclusively to Austria, whose officers were to be given total authority to operate within Serbia. The Serbs accepted 9 of the 10 demands, balking only at giving Austrian officials absolute authority in Serbia.

Austria-Hungary responded to this refusal by declaring war on Serbia. On July 28, 1914, Russia mobilized to protect Serbia, whereupon Germany declared War on Russia on August 1. France mobilized to help defend Russia, prompting Germany to declare war on France on August 3. German troops began the invasion of France via neutral Belgium. Britain, bound by treaty to protect Belgian neutrality and bound by treaty to help defend France, declared war against Germany on August 4. On August 6 Austria declared war on Russia. Japan—although on the other side of the world—declared war on Germany on August 23, and Austria declared war on Japan on August 25. Italy declared war on Germany on May 23, 1915, but it was April 6, 1917, before the United States joined in.

An assassination, barely pulled off by a tubercular young man in an obscure European capital, became the turning point from peace to total war thanks to the shortsighted machinations of an Austrian diplomat desperate to keep a faltering empire from dying. An act of impulsive desperation magnified by political stupidity in the context of a Europe bound by entangling alliances and counter-alliances set off a world war beyond the ability of any single combatant nation to stop. Perhaps no war had ever been started so mindlessly, only to be fought so far beyond the point of futility.

From Schlieffen Plan to the Miracle on the Marne: How the Fog of War Descends (1914)

From the 1860s until 1890, Otto von Bismarck dominated not only German political affairs but those of all Europe as well. He positioned Prussia at the center of a new German empire, which he and his monarch, Kaiser Wilhelm I, created after victory in the Franco-Prussian War of 1870–1871. Bismarck redrew the map of Europe and wove between its nations a network of treaties and diplomatic agreements that brought some two decades of unprecedented stability and peace to the Continent. Underneath the placid surface, however, the European states were not only arming themselves for a new major war but making plans to fight it.

The assassination of Austria-Hungary's Archduke Franz Ferdinand and his wife, the Grand Duchess Sophie, put into motion Austria-Hungary's Plan B—the plan for a local war against Serbia. This quickly shifted to Plan R, the script for a general war against Serbia and Russia. France had its own Plan XVII for fighting Germany—which possessed what became the most famous war plan of them all.

Its first iteration was drawn up at the start of the twentieth century by Count Alfred von Schlieffen and was repeatedly modified and honed. Worked out to the smallest detail, the so-called Schlieffen Plan was intended to prepare for precisely what Bismarck had always aimed to avoid: a two-front war against France in the west and Russia in the east. What was significant about this was that the Germans assumed that every other major European government had essentially the same conception about the next European war—that it would be, of necessity, an all-encompassing continental war. To a large extent, the assumption proved true, but the Schlieffen Plan also became a self-fulfilling prophecy.

When Germany committed to a general mobilization on August 1, 1914, it also committed its army to unwavering adherence to the Schlieffen Plan. It was a good plan in that it was very thorough and aimed at solving the problem of a two-front war. Was it the best possible plan? The question is irrelevant because it was Germany's only plan.

Designed to fight against France and Russia, the Schlieffen Plan assumed that the French, whose army was more modern and more efficiently led, would get into action much more quickly than the Russians. The czar's forces were more numerous but poorly equipped and very poorly led. As Schlieffen figured it, Russia would take a minimum of six weeks to mobilize effectively. For this reason, his plan called for a rapid offensive strike against France while fighting a lower-grade defensive war against Russia. The objective was to invade France with such overwhelming speed and force that the nation would surrender in little more than a month. That should provide enough time for a smaller German force to hold off a Russian invasion of Germany from the east. Once France was neutralized, German troops could be shifted to the Eastern Front to commence an offensive campaign against Russia. It was war meticulously planned and intended to be fought on a schedule as precise and unalterable as a railroad timetable.

The genius of the Schlieffen Plan is that it did not call for a direct east-to-west frontal assault on France. Instead it charted a "great wheel," a wide turning movement northwestward through Flanders Plain (northeast of French territory), followed by a southwesterly arc that descended into France from the north. The idea was that the full force of the kaiser's armies would hit the French army's left flank while also hooking around from behind. In all, five major German armies would sweep wide from Alsace-Lorraine in a broad arc. All the fighting would be done in France and—as Schlieffen figured it—would be done very quickly. The French forces would be hit all along their left and from the rear. The key was to ensure the widest possible wheel. As Schlieffen admonished, "Let the sleeve of the last man on the right brush the English Channel."

Indeed, it is easy to see why the Schlieffen Plan became a veritable talisman among German commanders. It not only was a blueprint for destroying the French army by hitting it where any army is most vulnerable, flank and rear, but it also ensured that the devastation would be meted out within France, far from German soil. If strategic retreat became necessary, there would be plenty of France in which to maneuver.

The only apparent drawback of the plan was that to succeed, Schlieffen's "great wheel" *had* to advance through Belgium, a neutral country—whose neutrality Great Britain was pledged by treaty to defend. The Schlieffen Plan would inevitably bring Britain into the war so that Germany would face three principal adversaries: France, Russia, and Britain. No wonder British foreign secretary Edward Grey, looking into the twilight of August 3, 1914, remarked to a friend: "The lamps are going out all over Europe. We shall not see them lit again in our lifetime."

But bringing into the war a third enemy was not the only flaw in the Schlieffen Plan. The very clockwork structure of the plan, a war fought by timing and miles and numbers, failed to account for the element of war the great Prussian military theorist Karl von Clausewitz wrote about in his treatise *On*

War, published posthumously in 1832. He wrote of the "friction of war" and the "fog of war," explaining friction as a "concept that more or less corresponds to the factors that distinguish real war from war on paper," that is, war as fought versus war as planned. Friction is the collective effect of the sheer physical demands war makes, which are magnified and complicated by the paucity of clear information and the abundance of ambiguous information in actual warfare, the general state of chaos that Clausewitz called the "fog of war."

Friction and fog diverted Schlieffen's great wheel. Once diverted, there was no way to correct the course. On August 29, 1914, with the First and Second German Armies poised to attack and overrun Paris—which would likely have ended the "Great War" in its first month—the French commander in chief, General Joseph "Papa" Joffre, typically a slow-moving, mediocre tactician, saw that the flank of German general Alexander von Kluck's First Army was vulnerable. He ordered the French Fifth Army to attack it, a move that prompted General Karl von Bülow to deviate from the Schlieffen wheel by bringing part of his German Second Army to Kluck's aid. In this way, the relentless German advance was stalled, and Bülow himself was now exposed to French counterattack. Seeing this, Kluck turned his First Army, the entire right wing of the German invasion. The men whose sleeves were supposed to brush the English Channel were turned away from that landmark. The "great wheel" had become a flat tire. Kluck acted on incomplete information—the fog of war. He mistakenly believed that he was turning toward the exposed left flank of all that remained of the battered French army. It was a fatal mistake.

Joffre saw his second opportunity. He put at the disposal of General Joseph Gallieni, the crusty old military governor of Paris, the entire French Sixth Army, which suddenly marched out of garrison in the French capital and into battle against Kluck. This was the start of the First Battle of the Marne (September 6–10, 1914), a desperate, costly fight destined to be called *Le Miracle de la Marne*. It saved Paris, even as it doomed Europe to four years of war in which death and futility would be produced on an unprecedented scale. What started out as a quick German invasion of France quickly congealed into a Western Front marked by the utter stalemate of trench warfare. This would be Europe's reality until November 11, 1918.

Unrestricted: Submarine Warfare in World War I (1915–1917)

After Germany's initial thrust into France ended at the First Battle of the Marne (September 6–12, 1914), the Western Front in World War I coagulated into a trench warfare stalemate as bloody as it was futile. While the Allies and Central Powers slaughtered one another across no-man's-land, Britain used its Royal Navy to blockade goods going in and out of Germany. The objective was to simultaneously destroy the German economy and starve the German people into submission. For its part, the German *Kriegsmarine* (navy) focused much of its resources on submarine warfare aimed at disrupting Allied trade and breaking up the British blockade.

The submarine—or U-boat (from the German *U-Boot*, for *Unterseeboot*)—became increasingly important to Germany. By 1916, food riots were sweeping Germany and Austria-Hungary. The submarines were seen as Germany's only hope for retaliation on the high seas. German U-boats attacked not only British and French merchant marine but the commercial shipping of other nations as well. The first commercial vessel a German submarine sank was the British merchant steamship *Glitra*, torpedoed on October 20, 1914, and on January 30, 1915, two Japanese liners, *Tokomaru* and *Ikaria*, were sunk. The British and the French took particular notice that in the 1914 encounter, the U-boat surfaced and gave warning before attacking. This provided sufficient time for all hands and passengers to abandon ship in lifeboats. In the 1915 attacks, however, the U-boat launched its torpedoes while submerged and without warning. Referred to as "unrestricted submarine warfare," this practice was widely considered a violation of the basic rules of civilized warfare.

But even by early 1915, the situation in Germany was growing desperate, and Germany responded to international protests by announcing on February 4 that it intended to regard the waters around the British Isles as a war zone in which all Allied merchant ships would be targeted without warning. The safety of no ship would be guaranteed, whatever its flag.

Unrestricted submarine warfare was, of course, a naval policy. But it was demanded by Germany's generals, whose troops were being consumed on the Western Front, despite the tremendous propaganda liability. It was not just that the torpedoing civilian ships—without warning, no less—made Germany look barbaric; it was the very real risk that the policy would finally prompt the United

States to enter the war on the side of the Allies. As German secretary of state Gottlieb von Jagow had warned the admiralty back in 1914, "If we take up unrestricted U-boat warfare, the attitude of all neutral Powers will be changed against us and we shall have to calculate upon establishing new fronts. Germany will in such case be looked upon as a mad dog." For the United States, freedom of navigation of the high seas and freedom of trade were well-recognized rights of

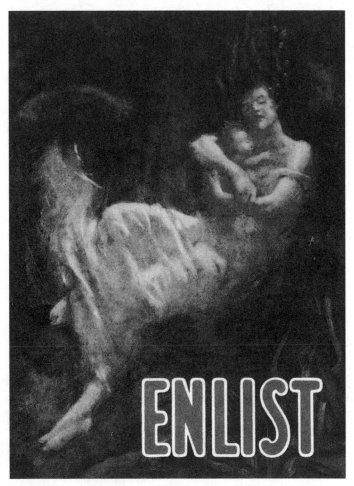

Fred Spear created this remarkable poster in 1915 for the Boston Committee of Public Safety after the sinking of the *Lusitania*. Although the United States was not yet in the war, Spear's message to America's young men was clear: ENLIST.
WIKIMEDIA COMMONS

neutral nations and were essential to national sovereignty. Beyond these political and moral principles, however, the export trade had become economically vital to American business and financial interests during this war. Both the American people and American commercial interests were increasingly outraged by the German menace to trade.

The people of the United States were outraged by Germany's disregard for freedom of the high seas, but few Americans wanted any part of what they called the "European War." Then, in April 1915, RMS *Lusitania* arrived in New York City. Built for £1.2 million and launched in 1906, Cunard's *Lusitania* was the fastest, largest, and most luxurious liner plying the Atlantic. But it was not strictly a civilian vessel. The British Admiralty carried it on the Royal Navy official lists as an "auxiliary cruiser," and it was not only fitted with gun mounts hidden beneath its wooden decks but also took on a cargo of rifle cartridges and other munitions, including a cargo of gun cotton (nitrocellulose), from American manufacturers. It also carried a small detachment of Canadian soldiers bound for European service. Indeed, the German embassy in Washington published a paid warning in 50 American newspapers, including every paper in New York City:

NOTICE!

TRAVELLERS intending to embark on the Atlantic voyage are reminded that a state of war exists between Germany and her allies and Great Britain and her allies; that the zone of war includes the waters adjacent to the British Isles; that, in accordance with formal notice given by the Imperial German Government, vessels flying the flag of Great Britain, or any of her allies, are liable to destruction in those waters and that travellers sailing in the war zone on the ships of Great Britain or her allies do so at their own risk.

Travelers paid little heed. Even worse, by May 1, 1915, when *Lusitania* embarked from New York bound for Liverpool, the British Admiralty had intercepted German radio traffic giving the position of U-boats operating south of Ireland. The captain of *Lusitania* was not informed of this. He also was not told that the British cruiser HMS *Juno*, which was supposed to escort the liner through the perilous waters off the southern Irish coast, had been recalled. Nevertheless, most passengers were aware that German U-boats had recently been operating under "Cruiser Rules," which obliged warning to be given before an attack. These passengers did not know that the newly widespread use of "Q-ships"—fully armed Royal Navy surface vessels disguised as merchant ships—had moved the German admiralty to give U-boat captains full authority in deciding whether or not to surface and issue warning before attacking.

On May 7, when Kapitän-Leutnant Walter Schweiger saw *Lusitania* through the periscope of his submarine, *U-20*, he chose to attack without warning. He fired just one torpedo, which hit *Lusitania* at 2:20 in the afternoon as she passed some 10 miles off Old Head of Kinsale, southwest Ireland. There was a powerful explosion followed by a second, more destructive blast moments later. This has led many historians to conclude that the torpedo touched off the munitions on board. Within just 18 minutes, *Lusitania* sank in the shallow coastal waters. Of 1,962 passengers and crew, 1,198 were lost. Among these were 128 Americans.

News of the sinking stirred fevered outrage in the United States. Although President Woodrow Wilson's closest advisor, Texas politician Edward M. House, urged him to instantly bring the nation into the war, Wilson sensed that the American people were not sufficiently outraged to go to war. He told an audience in Philadelphia that "there is such a thing as a man being too proud to fight—there is such a thing as a nation being so right that it does not need to convince others by force that it is right," but he did send a stern diplomatic note to Berlin, demanding an end to attacks on merchantmen. Although the government of Kaiser Wilhelm II did not respond to Wilson's note, the kaiser did suspend the policy of unrestricted submarine warfare.

Despite the kaiser's order to stop attacking passenger liners without warning, more ships were sunk—*with* warning, including in August the British-registered SS *Arabic*, resulting in more American deaths and a new U.S. protest, and, in September, the SS *Hesperia*. When the German government publicly announced the suspension of U-boat activity in the English Channel and west of the British Isles, however, America's clamor for war quieted.

Throughout the rest of 1915 and through the end of 1916, Germany, fearful of American entry into the desperate war, refrained from unrestricted submarine attack. By the end of 1916, German high command was convinced that the European Allies were losing the war. This was probably an accurate assessment. On the other hand, Germany and the other Central Powers were certainly not winning. The war was more intractably stalemated than ever before, and the tempo of death and destruction had only quickened. It was a war of attrition—in which *both* sides were being worn away. While some on each side debated who would wear away first, others pointed to the very real possibility that the Allies and the Central Powers would simply beat one another to death.

How long could the civilian populations tolerate the war? How long would the soldiers keep fighting? By the end of 1916, the German high command had come to the conclusion that American entry into the war was no longer a matter of *if* but of *when*. The generals calculated that "when" would come in about five months. The German admiralty calculated that if the German U-boat fleet could sink 600,000 tons of Allied shipping during each of these five months, American entry into the war would be rendered moot by British surrender, which would compel France to give up as well. This was something like good news, and the kaiser embraced it. On January 9, 1917, he ordered the navy to resume unrestricted submarine warfare, commencing on February 1.

The submarine in World War I was an incredibly consequential weapon. Given the stalemate on land, unrestricted submarine warfare—in strictly military terms—held the promise of tipping the balance toward German victory. But if the submarine was a turning point in total warfare—war that made no distinction between civilian and military targets—it was also a turning point in political terms. Perceived as too monstrous, too treacherous, too evil—even in a war that produced human casualties at the pace of a great factory producing automobiles or cookware—unrestricted submarine warfare produced tactical victories but brought strategic defeat. For Woodrow Wilson it became a public motive for entering the war on the side of the Allies, on the side of democracy—and, yes, on the side of those powers on whom American financiers and industry had wagered their funds, their investment houses, their factories, their workers, and their personal fortunes.

Exit the Russians, Enter the Americans: The Disruption of World War I (1917–1918)

Following the assassination of Archduke Franz Ferdinand and his wife, the Grand Duchess Sophie, in Sarajevo on June 28, 1914, the major combatant nations fell to fighting with astounding speed. Austria-Hungary's response to the assassination—a declaration of war against a single small nation, Serbia—instantly activated a complex network of both public treaties and secret alliances. In an astoundingly short span, virtually all of Europe (and more) was at war: Austria declared war on Serbia (July 28, 1914), Germany on Russia (August 1), Germany on France (August 3), Britain on Germany (August 4), Japan on Germany (August 13), Turkey allied with Germany (October 29), and Russia declared war on Turkey (November 2), as did France and Britain (November 5). Italy joined the Allies on May 23, 1915.

The rapid genesis and metastasis of the "Great War" was in itself a turning point in military history, which demonstrated the dark side of global geopolitics and grand-scale diplomacy instigated by Germany's Otto von Bismarck late in the nineteenth century. On the one hand, Bismarck's diplomatic initiatives gave Europe an unprecedented degree of stability. On the other, they created the conditions of diplomatic lockstep that escalated a small war into a world war.

The structure of the warring alliances—"Allies" (mainly France, Britain, Russia, and Italy) versus the "Central Powers" (mainly Germany, Austria-Hungary, Bulgaria, and Turkey)—turned out to be surprisingly vulnerable, however. Russia entered the war under Czar Nicholas II, the latest member of the Romanov dynasty, which had ruled Russia since 1613. Nicholas had already survived and suppressed a 1905 revolution, which followed the ruinous and humiliating Russo-Japanese War of 1904–1905. Although the army he took into the war was the largest in Europe, it was also the least competently led, least adequately trained and equipped, and technologically the least advanced. Catastrophic defeats—earliest and most notably at the Battle of Tannenberg (August 26–30, 1914), in which 170,000 out of 230,000 Russian soldiers were killed, wounded, or captured—came quickly and greatly weakened the czar. The so-called February Revolution of March 8–16, 1917, resulted in the czar's abdication, imprisonment, and, on July 17, 1918, execution—along with his wife and five children. In the meantime, the new Bolshevik (Communist) government of Russia signed with Germany the Treaty of Brest-Litovsk (March 3, 1918), by which Russia—and Europe's largest army—withdrew from the Great War.

With the Allies and the Central Powers locked in a bloody trench warfare stalemate on the Western Front, the worst sort of war of attrition, the sudden withdrawal of Russia positioned the Allies for defeat. That defeat would have been virtually certain had it not been for a new entrant into the war.

Ever since the summer of 1914, the government and people of the United States had taken comfort in geographical and political isolation from what they called the "European War." During 1914–1915, President Woodrow Wilson (who had been elected in 1912) scrupulously maintained U.S. neutrality. When a German U-boat torpedoed and sunk the British liner *Lusitania* on May 7, 1915, with the loss of 1,198 lives, including 124 Americans, calls began for U.S. entry into the war. Nevertheless, Wilson won a narrow reelection victory in 1916 largely on the strength of his campaign slogan, "He Kept Us Out of War," and on a pledge from Kaiser Wilhelm II to end the practice of "unrestricted" submarine warfare—attacking merchant vessels without warning.

On January 9, 1917, with Germany starving because of a highly effective British naval blockade, the kaiser ordered resumption of unrestricted submarine warfare effective February 1. President Wilson severed diplomatic relations with Germany on February 3, 1917, after the U.S.-flagged steamship *Housatonic* was torpedoed and sunk. Shortly after this, British intelligence authorities released to President Wilson a telegram they had intercepted between Germany's foreign minister, Arthur Zimmermann, and the German ambassador to Mexico. Transmitted on January 16, 1917, this so-called Zimmermann Telegram instructed the ambassador to propose a German-Mexican alliance to Mexican president Venustiano Carranza. In return for a Mexican declaration of war against the United States, Mexico would receive Germany's support in a military campaign to recover the "territory in Texas, New Mexico, and Arizona" Mexico had lost in the United States–Mexican War of 1846–1848. Zimmermann also wanted the ambassador to ask Carranza to invite Japan to join the anti-American alliance. Wilson made the telegram public, and on April 2, 1917, he addressed a joint session of Congress to ask for a declaration of war.

Wilson's "War Message" made clear that joining the fight was not, strictly speaking, a war of necessity but a war of moral and ideological choice: "Our object . . . is to vindicate the principles of peace and justice in the life of the world as against selfish and autocratic power and to set up amongst the really free and self-governed peoples of the world such a concert of purpose and of action as will henceforth ensure the observance of those principles. . . . We have no quarrel with the German people. . . . It was not upon their impulse that their Government acted in entering this war. It was not with their previous knowledge or approval. It was a war determined upon as wars used to be determined upon in the old, unhappy days when peoples were nowhere consulted by their rulers and wars were provoked and waged in the interest of dynasties or of little groups of ambitious men who were accustomed to use their fellow men as pawns and tools." He concluded: "The world must be made safe for democracy."

For the first time in American history, certainly—and perhaps for the first time in world history—a war was declared on the strength of an ideology or ideal. It was a turning point in American foreign policy, American history, and the military history of both the United States and other world powers.

Hutier Tactics: A German General Changes Modern Warfare at Riga (1917)

Erich Ludendorff, Germany's ruthless generalissimo—possessing absolute authority over the army and nearly absolute authority over war-related civilian affairs—was greatly alarmed over the United States' entry into the "Great War." Congress had declared war on Germany on April 6, 1917, but was slow to build up a sufficient force in Europe to make an effective contribution to the fight on the Western Front. Hoping to break the trench warfare stalemate that had existed since the end of 1914, Ludendorff planned a series of all-out offensives against the British and the French before the Americans could arrive at the front in force. The first of these offensives was launched along the Somme River, beginning on March 21, 1918. From north to south, the German Seventeenth, Second, and Eighteenth Armies attacked the British in northern France on their right flank along a 60-mile front from Arras to La Fère. The British held the northern portion of the Western Front; the French held the southern portion, including the territory nearest Paris.

Some historians of World War I have referred to Ludendorff's offensives as "desperate." They were, in fact, carefully thought out to divide and conquer the Anglo-French forces. Ludendorff noted that the British were always concerned to maintain lines of communication with (and, if necessary, withdrawal to) the English Channel ports, whereas the French always operated with the defense of Paris in mind. In effect, the British and French had conflicting strategic priorities. Ludendorff reasoned that even if he hit the British very hard, the French would not send large numbers of troops to their ally's aid but would focus on defending Paris. He understood that Paris figured so prominently in the French national identity that if it were captured, France would surrender. All the German army had to do, Ludendorff believed, was menace Paris while attacking the British, and the French would withhold reinforcement from the British. That might well knock Britain out of the war, which would give France no alternative but to negotiate a favorable peace with Germany.

To ensure that the Spring Offensive would succeed, Ludendorff began with a massive artillery attack that included poison gas. He then employed what the Allies had learned to call "Hutier tactics" to break through the British lines. The name came from German general Oskar von Hutier, who in September 1917 unleashed what he believed would be a level of attack so intense that it was capable of breaking the trench warfare stalemate. Hutier employed his tactic not on the Western Front but on the Eastern, against the strategically vital Baltic Sea port of Riga (today in Latvia) and its associated fortress.

Hutier trained his Eighth Army in a radically innovative approach. Traditional attacks, such as those that had been repeated over and over on the Western Front, always began with a long and massive "artillery preparation," a prolonged artillery bombardment intended to soften up the enemy's defenses. Such barrages were indeed horrific and devastating, but they also gave defenders plenty of warning of an attack and a good deal of time to prepare for the onslaught of troops that would follow. Another drawback of a prolonged bombardment was that it so thoroughly cratered no-man's-land—the ground between opposing trench lines—that the leading ranks of the attackers, who needed to move with maximum speed, were always slowed down by the pockmarked and therefore difficult terrain.

Hutier's radical approach was to begin with an intense but very brief artillery bombardment. This was immediately followed by an infantry advance against the enemy lines. Moreover, instead of focusing the initial artillery fire against the enemy's front lines, Hutier aimed at the rear. This had two effects. First, it prevented the rear echelons from reinforcing the front. Second, it cut off the major route by which the front lines could fall back and maneuver. It held the front lines in place while they were being attacked, depriving them both of reinforcement and the option to withdraw.

As the advance was ready to step off, Hutier masked the movement of the attackers as well as positions from which they advanced with smoke shells and the very concentrated use of poison gas. These brutal measures sowed confusion and ensured that the element of surprise would be maintained until very nearly the last possible moment.

Hutier's tactics required the use of light, very fast infantry units. They were shock troops Hutier called *Sturmbattaillon* (Storm Battalions). Their assignment was to break through—storm through—enemy lines very quickly at weak points that had been identified by pre-battle reconnaissance. Such penetrations would ensure that the rest of the attacking force, which followed, would have wide latitude for maneuver.

Shock troops fought to achieve local superiority at key points along the front while artillery support *accompanied* the infantry advance. This was key. Hutier did not use an extended artillery preparation, but he did extensively use artillery simultaneously with his infantry. It was a "combined arms" approach to combat. The artillery was used with great agility, shifting from fire directed against enemy artillery positions—so-called counter-battery fire, intended to wipe out enemy artillery—to fire that directly supported the infantry's advance. This highly dynamic use of artillery the Germans dubbed the *Feuerwalz*, or fire waltz. The Allies sometimes referred to it as a rolling barrage, because it was directed just ahead of the advancing attackers.

At Riga, the effect of Hutier tactics was staggering. The Russian Twelfth Army simply melted away before the advance of the German Eighth. Although they were hardened by battle, the Russian troops panicked and ran from the field.

Ludendorff intended to scale up Hutier tactics for the Spring Offensive. With a half-million troops freed for transfer to the Western Front after Russia's withdrawal from the war, Ludendorff had about 1.5 million men to draw on. At Riga, Hutier had just 60,000. At first the Spring Offensive looked to be very successful. As Ludendorff had predicted, France's Marshal Henri Philippe Pétain moved to protect Paris rather than reinforce the British. What Ludendorff failed to predict, however, was the effect of a protest from the British chief of staff, General Sir Henry Wilson, who demanded that Pétain be replaced with "[Ferdinand] Foch or some other French general who will fight."

In response to the protest, the Allied Supreme War Council, the administrative body responsible for managing the operational aspects of the military alliance, declined to remove the conservative Pétain from overall command of the French army, but it did name Foch commander in chief of the Allied forces in France. In his willingness to fight all out, to risk everything over and over, Foch proved a match even for the relentless Ludendorff. More German offensives followed, but increasingly these confronted more and more freshly arrived American troops. The Ludendorff offensives failed to drive the Allies into defeat, but the use of the tactics Oskar von Hutier had developed—based in part on both British and French infiltration tactics—survived World War I to be used in World War II. Between the two wars, Hans von Seeckt, head of Reichswehr (the greatly reduced German army permitted by the Treaty of Versailles), transformed Hutier tactics into the combat doctrine popularly called "Blitzkrieg." It was the ultimate application of combined arms in attack, and it changed the tactical course of warfare profoundly.

Rush to Disarm: The London and Geneva Conferences (1930–1934)

Many of those who lived through World War I and into the 1920s and 1930s were so disgusted by the bloody futility of Western Front trenches that political leaders of many nations met hopefully and repeatedly in an unprecedented global effort to bring an end to warfare. In part, this movement was philosophical and moral. In part, it was a practical effort to preempt war with a massive program of disarmament. The idealists saw the London Naval Conference of January 21–April 22, 1930 and the World Disarmament Conference at Geneva (1932–1934) as turning points in *world* history precisely because, as they saw it, these events held the promise of bringing an end to *military* history, to realizing President Woodrow Wilson's aspiration, that the Great War would be the "war to end all wars."

The two conferences were preceded by the work of the Disarmament Preparatory Commission, which was created by the League of Nations in 1925 to prepare for a World Disarmament Conference. For the next seven years after its establishment, the commission debated and negotiated in an effort to reconcile French demands for security guarantees as an absolute prerequisite for arms reduction with German demands for parity in armaments with British demands for sufficient arms to defend its far-flung empire, its scattered possessions, with American postwar isolationist opposition to anything like collective security, which American leaders saw as involvement in the very "entangling alliances" George Washington had warned against.

Despite the endless wrangling by the commission, Great Britain, the United States, and Japan met independently at Geneva during June 20–August 4, 1927, in the Three-Power Naval Conference. Their aim was to establish a schedule of ratios for strength in cruisers, destroyers, and submarines. The idea was that by maintaining parity in national naval armaments, aggression from any of the three conference signatories would be discouraged. The conference ended in a failure to reach agreement.

Whereas the Three-Power Naval Conference dealt with numerical ratios, United States secretary of state Frank B. Kellogg met with French minister of foreign affairs Aristide Briand in creating a pact that simply renounced "aggressive war." Officially called the General Treaty for Renunciation of War as an Instrument of National Policy, it was familiarly known as the Kellogg-Briand Pact and was signed on August 27, 1928, by the United States, France, Great Britain, Germany, Italy, Japan, and nine smaller nations. An idealistic statement, it provided no practical means of implementation and absolutely no provisions for enforcement or sanction.

From January 21 to April 22, representatives from the United Kingdom, United States, and Japan, plus France, Italy, and several other states met in London to attempt what the earlier Three-Power Naval Conference had failed to do—achieve parity among the naval powers and also impose certain limitations. The most important of these included the formulation of rules to limit, or "civilize," the tactics of submarine warfare and to set specific limits on both the tonnage and artillery caliber of submarines. Limitations were placed on aircraft carriers, extending provisions agreed to in the 1922 Washington Naval Treaty, and the signatories agreed to scrap a number of warships by 1933. While Britain and the United States agreed to a formula that gave them parity in the combat effectiveness of cruisers, the effect of these limitations was to meet Japanese demands to strengthen its own naval position relative to that of the British and American navies. The London agreement was set to expire in 1936. At that, it also included an "escalation clause" that permitted increases in tonnage limits if the "needs" of any signatory required it.

Despite its limited window and its "escalation clause," the London Treaty was a serious attempt at arms limitation. With tragic irony, it had the effect of clearing the way for Japan—which neither the British nor the Americans seriously considered a potential adversary—to become a very formidable naval power.

In 1932, two years after the London Naval Conference, the member nations of the League of Nations plus the United States (which was not a League member) met in Geneva for the World Disarmament Conference. The Preparatory Commission had drafted a disarmament treaty for discussion. Although it included protocols for arms control and inspection, it left out any precise formulas for equitable force ratios. This plagued the conference throughout its two years. Even worse was a generally pessimistic outlook, which was a far cry from the idealism of the 1928 Kellogg-Briand Pact. But the 1932–1934 conference was confronted by the realities of a worldwide depression, Japanese aggression in China, and rise of Hitler and Nazism in Germany.

The French proposed the "Tardieu plan," which called for an international police force, strict security guarantees, and not outright disarmament but the placing of the most powerful weapons of war in an "escrow" account controlled by the League of Nations. The plan proved a nonstarter because it was seen as too deep an incursion on national sovereignty. Germany demanded nothing less than equality with the other major powers. To both the French and German positions, Britain responded with a counterproposal of both "proportionate" and "qualitative" arms reduction. So-called "aggressive weapons" were to be banned outright.

After the British proposal was rejected, the United States offered two sweeping approaches. The first was to ban all offensive weapons, period. When this was spurned, the American delegation suggested an across-the-board arms reduction of one-third.

In the midst of what was proving hopeless discussion and debate, Japan withdrew from the League of Nations in March 1933), and Germany withdrew from the disarmament conference as well as the League in October 1933. In June of the following year, the World Disarmament Conference adjourned without any agreements having been made. No further attempts at abolishing war or even limiting arms would be made until after World War II, a conflict that broke out just two decades after the end of the "war to end all wars." The turning point all of the noble efforts had reached was not an end to war but an expansion in scope, destruction, and amorality.

Rehearsal for a Second Act: The Spanish Civil War Goes Global (1936–1939)

The simplest definition of a "civil war" is *war between citizens of the same country*. By this definition, a civil war is a contained war, confined to a single country. The Spanish Civil War of 1936–1939 was the product of intense political division in Spain, which was greatly exacerbated by the hardships of the worldwide Great Depression, an economic crisis that hit Spanish farmers and workers especially hard. The war also developed against a global background in which the forces of Communism squared off against the forces of fascism and Nazism, with the Western democracies looking on with great anxiety. In 1917, while World War I raged, the Russian czar, Nicholas II, was overthrown, and, after a brief interlude of quasi-democratic government, Russia became a Communist country. As conceived by its father, Karl Marx (1818–1883), Communism was of necessity an international movement, and the Russian Communists were eager to disseminate Marxism globally. At the same time, fascism, concentrated in Benito Mussolini's Italy and, as Nazism, in Hitler's Germany, competed directly against the rise of international Communism.

The victory of the left-wing Popular Front in Spain's 1936 general elections installed a Communist-leaning government, sparking a coup d'etat by the right-wing Falange, a fascist political party led by General Francisco Franco. This, in turn, ignited a civil war that quickly spilled far beyond Spain's borders. Germany, Italy, and Russia saw it not as a civil war but as a contest between fascism and communism and, therefore, a conflict with global consequences. All three nations sent troops, weapons, and funding—Germany and Italy to back Franco and the fascists (and their domestic allies), Russia to back the Popular Front (and its domestic allies). The Western democracies, including Britain, France, and the United States, remained officially neutral in the war, but idealistic citizens of these countries volunteered to serve—the vast majority joining the forces of the leftist government.

The Spanish Civil War began in earnest on July 18, 1936, when Franco took over the Spanish Foreign Legion garrison in Morocco and staged an army officers' revolt at Melilla, bordering Morocco on the north coast of Africa. This touched off similar mutinies in Spanish military garrisons at Cádiz, Seville, Burgos, Saragossa, Huesca, and elsewhere. While these uprisings were under way, Franco airlifted Foreign Legion units to Spain late in July. These troops were joined by other rebel soldiers as well as by insurgent pro-fascist "Nationalists."

Fascist revolutionary and future dictator of Spain Francisco Franco poses in 1930 wearing his winter uniform cloak.

Together they overwhelmed government forces and quickly seized control of southern and western Spain.

During late July and into August, Franco led a motorized advance on Madrid, the Spanish capital, but was repulsed by government forces during fighting in September and October. By this point, the country was bitterly divided into "government" (also called "Loyalist" or "Republican") territories and Nationalist (fascist or pro-fascist) territories. The situation on the ground was rarely clear-cut, as many factions existed on a political spectrum that spanned leftist and rightist extremes. Allies often turned against one another, depending where each stood along the spectrum. Nevertheless, on September 29, 1936, the Nationalists proclaimed their own government, with Franco at its head. In April 1937 he was also named head of the fascist Falange Party. Although well to the political right, the Nationalists were not all at the fascist extreme. But Franco's Falange was.

Unfolding during what turned out to be the eve of World War II, the Spanish Civil War became a kind of dress rehearsal for what was seen as a looming global conflict between fascism and Nazism on the one side versus communism on the other. Many outsiders flocked into what was, after all, a civil conflict. Italy, ruled by Benito Mussolini, the creator of modern fascism, committed some 40,000 to 60,000 Italian troops to the war. Adolf Hitler, a Mussolini ally who led the Nazi Party and Nazi-dominated government of Germany, sent some 20,000 Germans, including, most importantly, members of the Luftwaffe, the German air force. German pilots came to regard the Spanish Civil War as a golden opportunity to hone, practice, and perfect their deadly craft, especially the elements of tactical aerial bombardment, which would become a key feature of "Blitzkrieg" combined-arms warfare in World War II.

The Spanish government—the Loyalists or Republicans—attracted volunteers from Britain, France, and the United States, who defied their governments' official policies of neutrality to join the struggle. Only the Soviet Union gave its official support to the Loyalists, sending between 634 and 806 aircraft, 331 to 362 tanks, and 1,034 to 1,895 artillery pieces to government forces. The Soviets committed somewhere between 2,000 and 3,000 military personnel, who were characterized as military advisors. Indeed, it was the volunteer brigades from the Western democracies that, fighting as insurgents, proved most effective against the Falangists.

Ultimately, aid from the Soviets and the volunteers was no match for the Franco's Falangists and the major support from Italy and Germany. On March 31, 1937, Italy's Aviazione Legionaria and Germany's Legion Condor bombed Durango, a town of 10,000 located at a key crossroads and rail junction in Biscay. Some 250 residents were killed, and Durango, a Republican stronghold, fell to the Nationalists, who now controlled a major route to the front lines. More infamous was the bombing of Guernica, in Spain's Basque region, on April 26, 1937, again by Italian and German aircraft. Casualty estimates vary from about 150 to as many as 1,650 killed, but the attack drew worldwide attention and condemnation. In contrast to Durango—arguably a transportation hub—Guernica had no strategic importance. The bombing was a terrorist attack and in particular served the Legion Condor as a live-munitions training mission. Several prominent poets and artists attempted to portray the obscenity and horror of the Guernica attack, but none so memorably as the painter Pablo Picasso, whose large canvas *Guernica*, completed in June 1937, remains the most powerful antiwar painting since the paintings and prints Francisco Goya produced during Napoleon's Peninsular War (1807–1814). Both the bombing and Picasso's painting foreshadowed what World War II would bring: a commitment to total war—warfare not merely fought out between armies but also directed against civilian populations, warfare that employed large-scale terrorism as a key aspect of strategy and doctrine.

The attacks on Durango and Guernica heralded the impending triumph of the fascists in Spain. The Falangists increasingly dominated the Nationalists and enjoyed a growing degree of unity, whereas the Republicans were torn more and more by dissension, especially on the extreme left. When a bloody anarchist uprising broke out in Barcelona in May 1937, a new Republican government had to be formed. It moved far to the left and, in so doing, alienated many. After an 80-day siege, on June 18, 1937, Bilbao, in Basque country, fell to the Falange. A Loyalist counteroffensive captured Teruel, in Aragon, late in the year, but Falange insurgents retook it in mid-February 1938. At this point, Joseph Stalin, recognizing that the Republicans were doomed and no longer willing to antagonize Mussolini and Hitler (he would soon forge an alliance with the latter), suddenly withdrew Soviet support to Spanish Communists. With this, the left quickly collapsed and the Republican forces were fatally diminished.

On January 26, 1939, Francisco Franco took Barcelona, and Republican resistance throughout Spain folded. Madrid fell on March 28, 1939, ending the war and establishing Franco as dictator of Spain. In this, the first great contest between the forces of fascism and Nazism on the one side and Republicanism (fortified as well as weakened by communism) on the other, the biggest loser was democracy, which came off as weak and uncommitted. Yet both Mussolini and Hitler failed to reap the strategic rewards they hoped their intervention in the Spanish Civil War would deliver. While Franco remained a fascist, he steadfastly refused to abandon neutrality and join the Axis during World War II.

Blitzkrieg: Germany's Combined-Arms Invasion of Poland (1939)

World War II, the biggest and costliest war in history—with some 73 million people, military and civilian, killed as a direct result of the conflict—began with the killing of a single human being, the hapless victim of a Nazi fraud.

On the evening of August 31, 1939, an inmate from one of Adolf Hitler's concentration camps was dressed in the uniform of a Polish soldier, taken to the German town of Gleiwitz on the border with Poland, and shot by the German secret police, the Gestapo. The next day, Hitler broadcast that a "Polish soldier" was shot during a Polish attack on a German radio transmitter at Gleiwitz. Hitler explained that *this* "act of war" was the reason he had ordered a general attack on Poland, which had begun at 4:30 that morning, September 1, 1939.

From the very beginning, the invasion was a combined-arms operation on an unprecedented scale. Aircraft of the German Luftwaffe cratered Polish airfields while German ground forces surged across the border. Even a German battleship, which had been "visiting" the Polish port of Danzig (modern Gdansk), opened fire on the port's fortifications. The Germans—at the time allied with the Soviets—surged into Poland with massively superior forces, some 2.5 million troops opposing about 280,000 Polish soldiers. It was all part of *Fall Weiss*—"Operation White"—Germany's master plan for the invasion of Poland.

Operation White was the essence of what journalists of the day called "Blitzkrieg," literally "lightning war." The tactic, one of the most consequential in modern military history, had been under intensive development in Germany since the 1920s and was an outgrowth and amplification of the so-called Hutier tactics first unveiled in the Battle of Riga (September 1–3, 1917) during World War I. Blitzkrieg was intended to overwhelm, overawe, and paralyze a defending army through the application of great numbers, great speed, and great mobility highly coordinated among multiple arms—armor, mechanized infantry, massed artillery, and airpower—all of which were supplemented by shock-troop special forces that worked to disrupt and degrade the defenders' logistical resources and means of communication and supply. The objective was to create chaos and panic, to advance fast and far, gaining territory while rolling up the opposing army. At the same time, attacks on the defenders' rear echelons were intended to paralyze its capacity to coordinate any effective defense using reserve forces.

Blitzkrieg was a radical departure from traditional invasion tactics. Throughout most of military history, invaders focused on breaking through front lines and border defenses. Blitzkrieg merely called for these frontline defenses to be disabled, mainly by disrupting supply and communication. Such disabling was all that was needed to concentrate force for rapid and deep penetration of the enemy's country. Blitzkrieg was like a knife attack. Stab the enemy quickly and deeply, and he would be rendered defenseless.

Blitzkrieg against Poland was accomplished by charging through a narrow front—called the *Schwerpunkt* (loosely translated as the "critical point")—with the objective of immediate and deep penetration. Tanks, mechanized artillery, and aircraft—especially the Junkers Ju-87, single-engine "Stuka" (dive bomber)— were all used in conjunction with infantry. The Stuka was capable of pinpoint tactical bombing, which punched holes in the enemy's defenses while sowing terror and panic. After a Stuka pilot had dropped his bombs, he circled around to strafe fleeing survivors of the bombing attack with the aircraft's three 7.9mm machine guns. This was the essence of a key Blitzkrieg tactic called close-air support, the use of high-performance tactical aircraft to support forces on the ground.

Their stunned expressions speak volumes. These are Polish prisoners of war, taken during the Nazi Blitzkrieg invasion of Poland that began World War II.
WIKIMEDIA COMMONS

The combined-arms penetration of the *Schwerpunkt* effectively opened a gaping wound in the defensive line. It was crucial to swarm through the wound before it could be "bandaged" by enemy reinforcements. Shock troops advanced rapidly, widening the *Schwerpunkt* gap as they also deepened the penetration through it. The objective now was to create pockets in which the defending units were held, isolated from one another. Cut off, these men had no alternative except to surrender.

Poland's armed forces fought with great bravery, but the German tide was relentless. Poland had gallantry but lacked military leadership, weaponry, and numbers to resist such overwhelming and skillfully applied force. Moreover, Poland's "Plan Z," as its defensive operational program was called, prescribed nothing more than creating a cordon in the west to delay—not defeat but delay—invading forces long enough for the arrival of troops from France and Britain, both of which were bound by treaty to come to Poland's defense. Not only did Plan Z fail to contemplate anything like Blitzkrieg, it did not consider that the Western democracies would prove incapable of providing timely aid. Nor did Plan Z take into account that the Soviet Union, sworn enemy of fascism and Nazism, would collaborate with the German invaders. The result was that the world witnessed a demonstration of Blitzkrieg at its most devastatingly successful. Polish defenders, deployed along the entire length of the Polish frontier with Germany and Slovakia, were rolled over—not so much destroyed as simply rendered irrelevant. The air attacks achieved instant air superiority, which opened the way for German bombers to penetrate far to the rear, where they destroyed supply depots and centers of communication. The destruction of the rear came even before many of the forward units were engaged in battle. This was unprecedented.

By September 3, 1939, the German Third and Fourth Armies linked up in the north, cutting the so-called Polish corridor, which had been created by the Treaty of Versailles, ending World War I, to serve as Poland's lifeline to the west. Of the two Polish armies in the north, one was essentially destroyed, the other forced to withdraw. As the northern action was taking place, German Army Group South broke through defensive lines to attack the great cities of Lodz and Kraków so that by September 5, the fifth day of World War II, Poland was, practically speaking, a defeated nation.

Winston Churchill Becomes Prime Minister: The Role of the Great Man in War (1940)

Born in 1874, the son of Lord Randolph Churchill, who was descended from the 1st Duke of Marlborough, and American Jennie Jerome, Winston Churchill did not appear destined for greatness. He did not take well to schooling—at Harrow— and rejected the university education that befitted his aristocratic station. He enrolled instead at Sandhurst, training academy for British army officers and, after an undistinguished tenure there, graduated in 1894 to a commission in the 4th Hussars—the cavalry being considered the place for the army's dimmer officers. He led a restless, adventurous life, taking a two-month leave from the army in 1895 to cover unrest in Cuba as a war correspondent and then returning to his regiment for duty in India, where he served in the Malakand expedition to the Northwest Frontier during 1897. He also continued to write as a newspaper correspondent and published the first of his many distinguished books, *The Malakand Field Force*, a vivid account of siege of the Malakand garrison.

In 1898 he served with Lord Kitchener in the Sudan and published a two-volume account of his Sudanese experience in *The River War* (1899). Early in 1899, Churchill resigned his commission to enter politics. After losing his first bid to enter Parliament, he sailed to South Africa on assignment from the *Morning Post* to cover the Second (Great) Boer War. Taken captive by the Boers, he pulled off a daring escape that catapulted him to world celebrity and helped him win election to Parliament in 1900 as a Conservative.

Churchill quickly made a mark as a brilliant debater, but he shocked the political world in 1904 by bolting to the Liberal Party. When the Liberals came to power the following year, he was named under-secretary of state for the colonies and in 1911 was appointed first lord of the Admiralty. He set about modernizing the Royal Navy in preparation for what he believed was the coming of a world war. During that conflict, Churchill's boundless confidence in the navy he had been instrumental in creating led him to plan an audacious amphibious assault on the Dardanelles in 1915. The naval campaign failed disastrously, as did the subsequent land campaign at Gallipoli, precipitating Churchill's removal as first lord of the Admiralty and, ultimately, from the government altogether. Churchill served briefly in combat in France before rejoining the government under Prime

Minister David Lloyd George as minister of munitions (July 1917–December 1918). In this post he championed the development of the tank and spectacularly improved the production of guns and ammunition.

After the war, Churchill served in other important cabinet posts but lost his seat in Parliament after Lloyd George's government fell in 1922. He promptly realigned himself with the Conservative Party and was returned to Parliament in 1924, joining the cabinet of Prime Minister Stanley Baldwin as chancellor of the exchequer. His tenure—1924 to 1929—was disastrous, as he was singularly unsuited to lead financial policy. His ill-advised return of Britain to the gold standard in 1925 deepened a depression that had followed the Great War, and when the nation was roiled by a general strike in 1926, Churchill condemned the strikers, alienating British labor forever afterward. As the hyper-liberal Labour Party ascended, Churchill withdrew from the Baldwin government in 1930 and began a decade in which he languished well outside the inner circle of British government.

As Hitler and Nazism began to rise in Germany, Churchill became a tireless Cassandra, warning of the growing danger and advocating rearmament. Like France, Britain was still war-weary, and the majority of politicians and public turned a blind eye on the rearmament program Hitler was leading in defiance of the Treaty of Versailles. Churchill urged Parliament to fund a program to match Germany's growth in airpower, reasoning that Hitler would use his air force to attack Britain from the air in preparation for an invasion. A mere member of Parliament, without any cabinet office, Churchill opposed the ongoing disarmament policies of Stanley Baldwin and the more infamous appeasement policy of his successor as prime minister, Neville Chamberlain.

In fairness to Chamberlain, he did begin to reverse disarmament and rebuild the British military, but he believed that he had to buy time by "appeasing" Adolf Hitler's aggressive expansionism. Through appeasement—which Churchill loathed and condemned—Chamberlain connived in Germany's annexation of the Sudetenland, the German-speaking region of Czechoslovakia, in return for the führer's pledge to refrain from further annexations. Churchill argued that no dictator could be appeased and that sacrificing Czech sovereignty was not only immoral and cowardly, it was strategic folly. Czechoslovakia's central position made it the keystone of middle Europe, and its factories and coal fields were of tremendous economic and military value. When Chamberlain returned from the Munich Conference (September 29–30, 1938), having yielded to Hitler the Sudetenland and claiming to have achieved thereby "peace for our time," Churchill bluntly labeled the act a "total and unmitigated defeat."

When Hitler invaded Poland in September 1939, bringing a new world war to Europe, Chamberlain, acknowledging Churchill's vison, offered him his former post of first lord of the Admiralty. Believing that maximum aggression was called for, Churchill instigated an assault on Norway to dislodge the Germans there. Like the Gallipoli campaign of World War I, the assault proved a fiasco and had to be aborted. But it was Chamberlain, not Churchill, who took the blame. Chamberlain resigned in May 1940, and although he wanted to be replaced by Lord Halifax—whose intention was to negotiate peace with Hitler—Churchill was the only prime minister a coalition government would accept.

Churchill assumed office at the nadir of British fortunes in World War II and set about not only creating a turning point in that conflict but also building a stunning example of how one exceptional leader can not only save a nation and its military but also lead both to victory.

He took upon himself all the responsibilities of a war leader. As continental Europe rapidly fell to the Germans, he engaged the neutral United States, creating an intensely personal relationship with President Franklin D. Roosevelt, whom he gradually persuaded to gravitate toward an alliance. The first step was the development of the Lend-Lease policy, which provided Britain (and soon other Allies, most notably the Soviet Union) with arms, materiel, aircraft, and ships, not on the traditional cash-and-carry basis but in a moneyless exchange for strategic cooperation with the United States.

Still, through 1940 the German juggernaut seemed unstoppable. France, Britain's most important Western European ally, was invaded and crushed during late May through early June. The entire British regular army was sent to France but was forced into retreat and almost pushed into the English Channel at Dunkirk on the Channel coast. A nearly miraculous trans-Channel evacuation (May 27–June 4, 1940) saved 85 percent of the British professional military—some 300,000 men. In early autumn, the Battle of Britain commenced as the German Luftwaffe did precisely what Churchill had predicted years earlier. It conducted the "Blitz," a massive bombing campaign of London and other English cities from September 7, 1940, to May 11, 1941. Churchill prepared his people to resist invasion with everything they had, delivering on June 4, 1940, a speech that galvanized the nation and impressed the world: "Even though large tracts of Europe and many old and famous States have fallen or may fall into the grip of the Gestapo and all the odious apparatus of Nazi rule, we shall not flag or fail. We shall go on to the end, we shall fight in France, we shall fight on the seas and oceans, we shall fight with growing confidence and growing strength in the air, we shall defend our island, whatever the cost may be, we shall fight on the beaches, we shall fight on the landing grounds, we shall fight in the fields and in the streets, we shall fight in the hills; we shall never surrender."

It was such eloquence, honesty, and confidence that created what military commanders call a "force multiplier"—a force or entity other than a new weapon or fresh troops that amplifies the effectiveness of a nation's military effort. To the stunned dismay of Hitler, the British emerged victorious in the Battle of Britain, the Royal Air Force (RAF) defeating the Luftwaffe and foiling invasion.

Churchill was more than a great orator and an icon of gritty determination. He engaged fully in every aspect of the conduct of the war, never tyrannizing over the generals and admirals but forging a working partnership with them. He did insist on fighting offensively whenever and wherever possible. He also set aside his own intense anti-Communist convictions to create an alliance with Joseph Stalin and the Soviet Union, all the while continuing to cultivate a remarkable relationship with President Roosevelt. He greeted FDR as a comrade in arms when the Japanese attack on Pearl Harbor thrust America into the war on December 7, 1941. From that point on, the two leaders collaborated on most of the major strategic decisions. They also forged an ironclad pact that neither would make a separate peace with the enemy and that, in fact, nothing less than the unconditional surrender of the Axis powers would bring the war to an end.

Churchill was not a great strategist, and historians still question the wisdom of his insistence that an Allied invasion of the European mainland be postponed until North Africa and the Mediterranean had been cleared of the enemy. Over the vigorous objections of top U.S. generals George C. Marshall and Dwight D. Eisenhower, President Roosevelt acceded to Churchill's plan, and it was not until the summer of 1943 that the Allies invaded Sicily and Italy, having fought the first part of the "European" war in North Africa. Nevertheless, a year later, Churchill was an unwavering champion of the principal invasion of Europe via Normandy on "D-Day": June 6, 1944.

By this time, Churchill's influence over the day-to-day conduct of the war had diminished, and he quietly turned to planning for the postwar future—one in which he saw the West's Soviet ally as an emerging threat. He advocated a drive by the British and American forces directly into Berlin, specifically to preempt the city's occupation by Soviets. President Roosevelt and his successor, Harry S. Truman, supported General Eisenhower's decision to crush what he mistakenly believed would be major German resistance in southern Germany and Austria, leaving Berlin to the Soviets. Arguably, Eisenhower's course was safest and least costly, but Churchill believed it to be an error. Nevertheless, he maintained absolute public solidarity with Eisenhower and Truman.

When Stalin made expansionist moves in Eastern Europe after the war ended, Churchill turned to warning the world of the dangers of a Communist "iron curtain" descending upon Europe. The Soviet ascendency dampened the Allied victory for him, but even more crushing was his defeat in the general election of July 1945. He would, however, be returned to office in 1951, as Britons looked to his leadership during the economically difficult early postwar years. They felt the need, once again, for a "force multiplier."

Total War: The Blitz, Battle of Britain, and Rationale for Strategic Bombing (1940–1945)

By any measure, the scope of World War II was staggeringly vast. The most dramatic and consequential measure, however, are the fatalities directly caused by the war. Conservative estimates put total military deaths at greater than 24 million. Civilian deaths are conservatively estimated at more than 49 million. Thus, noncombatant fatalities outnumbered combatant fatalities by more than 50 percent.

Why?

The simple answer is that in World War II, there were no noncombatants. There were no civilians. World War II was the most extreme instance of total war in military history. It was a war between states—peoples—not just the militaries of those states. It was a war that pitted economic, industrial, and institutional infrastructures against one another, not just armies, navies, and air forces. It was a war of civilizations, cultures, ideologies, and peoples.

Among the first military expressions of the conflict's approach to total war came from warfare's newest arm, the air force. Aerial bombardment may be divided into two broad categories, tactical and strategic. Tactical bombardment targets discrete military objectives—fortresses, bases, ammunition dumps, military formations, and the like—whereas strategic bombing targets population centers and does so on a large scale.

On July 16, 1940, Adolf Hitler issued Directive No. 16, preparations for the invasion of England. The first preparation was a tactical bombing operation to destroy Britain's Royal Air Force (RAF) by targeting air bases. Hitler did not want to attempt a cross-Channel invasion until the RAF had been neutralized. He had every reason to believe this would not be a difficult task. In the summer of 1940, the German air force, the Luftwaffe, consisted of 2,679 aircraft, including 1,015 medium bombers, 350 Stuka dive bombers, 930 fighters, 375 heavy fighters, and various reconnaissance aircraft. The RAF at this time had about 900 fighters, of which just 600 could be deployed at any given time because of a shortage of pilots.

As it turned out, the Luftwaffe was shocked by the skill and courage with which the outnumbered RAF defended the British homeland. The Germans suffered surprising and serious losses, which so angered Hitler that he diverted many of his bombers from tactical military objectives to a strategic bombing campaign against cities, especially London, intended to demoralize the British population and destroy the nation's will to continue making war. This proved to be a fatal error. Spanning September 7, 1940, to May 11, 1941, the "Blitz," a sustained campaign of air raids lasting eight months and five days, killed about 43,000 civilians and injured between 139,000 and 200,000. Perhaps 20 percent of London's buildings were severely damaged or totally destroyed. In this effort, the Luftwaffe lost 2,265 aircraft and 3,363 aircrew. As devastating as the civilian casualties were, they only strengthened the British resolve to win through to victory. Worse for Hitler, by targeting cities the Luftwaffe missed its chance to destroy RAF bases and RAF planes on the ground. The Blitz and the aerial Battle of Britain that accompanied it demonstrated that a nation could absorb catastrophic *civilian* losses but keep fighting as long as it possessed the *military* resources to do so. (RAF losses were heavy: 915 fighters, 481 pilots killed or missing, and 422 pilots wounded.)

A bus lies in a crater in Balham, South London, after a German air raid during the London Blitz.
IMPERIAL WAR MUSEUMS

The Blitz had another effect on the practice of total war. The Allies, British and American, overcame moral objections to strategic bombing by citing the example of the Blitz. After the Dutch city of Rotterdam was devastated by a massive German raid on May 14, 1940, the RAF launched a major strategic bombing campaign against German-occupied Europe and Germany itself.

The RAF raids were not precision-bombing missions but so-called carpet-bombing runs, in which large formations of heavy bombers dropped massive bombloads not on specific targets but on entire cities and portions of cities. Because precision aiming was not required, the raid could be conducted at night, which provided a measure of cover for the incoming bombers. Carpet-bombing created many civilian casualties even as it failed to guarantee the destruction of targets of high military value, such as armament factories.

When the U.S. Eighth Army Air Force arrived in England at the end of 1942, U.S. air commanders decided to risk the hazards of precision bombing in daylight. While British crews and planes maintained the night shift, American crews flew by day, targeting specific factories, mines, and portions of cities directly associated with military activity. The first American raid against Germany came on January 27, 1943, and from that point on, the Allied strategic bombing campaign was a 24-hour program, with missions flown whenever weather permitted.

The lumbering heavy bombers—the principal U.S. four-engine bomber aircraft used in Europe were the Boeing B-17 Flying Fortress and the Consolidated B-24 Liberator—were vulnerable to ground-based antiaircraft fire and to attack by German fighter aircraft. The Allied fighter aircraft available early in the campaign lacked the fuel capacity to escort bombers all the way to their targets and back, which left them wide open to enemy interceptors. Later, as such long-range fighters as the P-51 Mustang and P-47 Thunderbolt arrived in theater and Allied air bases moved farther east, bombers could be escorted to and from targets even deep inside Germany. Still, casualties among Allied airmen were staggering. Of 3.4 million U.S. Army Air Forces (USAAF) personnel in all theaters, 54,700 were killed in action and 17,900 wounded.

Major Allied strategic raids included a British attack on Cologne, which destroyed most of the center of this historic German city during the night of May 30/31, 1942. On July 24, 1943, a combined Anglo-American raid using incendiary bombs set off a firestorm that devastated Hamburg, killing about 50,000 civilians. On August 1 of the same year, the U.S. Eighth and Ninth Air Forces raided the oil refineries of Ploesti, Romania. The Ploesti raid badly damaged the refineries, but they were quickly repaired. Fifty aircraft and aircrews had been sacrificed for little long-term gain. Less than three weeks later, on August 17, U.S. bombers raided Schweinfurt, Germany, and its ball-bearing plants and aircraft factories at Regensburg. Again, the damaged plants were quickly repaired. The Schweinfurt raid alone had cost 60 bombers downed and 122 badly damaged. On October 14,

1943, a second raid was launched against Schweinfurt, resulting in the loss of another 60 bombers and damage to 138 others.

During November 18, 1943, and March 31, 1944, the RAF raided Berlin 35 times, extensively damaging the German capital but losing 1,047 bombers in the effort. The USAAF conducted its own major offensive, "Big Week," during February 20–26, 1944, targeting aircraft factories and wiping out almost half of Germany's fighter production capacity. U.S. losses were 226 bombers. On March 11, 1944, the RAF hit oil and railroad facilities at Essen, Germany, causing devastating damage without suffering heavy losses.

The results of strategic bombing were mixed and the losses to aircraft and crews severe. The value of the strategy was bitterly debated and has remained controversial. The greatest controversy came as a result of the massive Anglo-American raid against Dresden on the night of February 13/14, 1945. The bombers used a combination of high explosives and incendiaries to destroy the jewellike medieval city. A catastrophic three-day firestorm was created in which temperatures rose to more than 2,730°F and an estimated 135,000 German civilians were killed. Allied losses over this poorly defended target were six bombers. To this day, the "Dresden Fire-Bombing" remains a monument to the prodigal cruelty of total war.

Enigma and Ultra: Information Becomes War's Ultimate Weapon (1939–1945)

Codes and ciphers have likely been used in war since organized militaries first fought one another. The earliest cipher machine—a mechanical device for encrypting and decrypting messages—was probably the one invented in 1470 by Leon Battista Alberti, an Italian polymath who was history's original "Renaissance Man." It was a cipher disk consisting of two concentric circular copper plates mounted on top of each other. The larger plate was stationary, the smaller one movable. Two alphabets were engraved on the plates so that they moved relative to each other, enabling users to match "coded" letters to their "clear" equivalent.

"Enigma" was a twentieth-century electromechanical elaboration of such simple cipher wheels, and it was used during the World War II era by the German army (Wehrmacht), Schutzstaffeinel (SS), Luftwaffe (air force), navy, and Abwehr (secret service) as well as by the German state railway system. The original design was patented in 1919 by a Dutch inventor, H. A. Koch, and was extensively modified and improved in 1923 by a German engineer, Dr. Arthur Scherbius. In 1929, while Germany was in the early stages of covertly rearming in defiance of the Treaty of Versailles, which had ended World War I, the German army and navy purchased all rights to the Enigma from Scherbius. By the beginning of World War II, all the military services and the railroad were using various versions of it.

Enigma was the state of the art in electromechanical cryptography. It was the most complex encryption-decryption device in use by any nation and was widely believed capable of encoding messages impossible to decrypt without the proper key. The basic machine—there were many variants—resembled a typewriter. In addition to a keyboard, however, the military Enigma had an electric plugboard, a light board, and a set of three rotors and half rotors (called "reflectors"). The rotors could be set independently to create a library of 16,900 substitution alphabets so that, provided the message was not longer than 16,900 characters, there would be no repeated use of a letter substitution within any given message. Since repetition of patterns is the key by which codes are traditionally broken, there simply seemed no way to decrypt an Enigma cipher. As if the lack of repetition were not challenging enough, the Enigma machine added additional complications. The sequence of alphabets used was different if the rotors were started in position ABC, as opposed to ACB, CBA, and so on. There was also a rotating ring on each rotor that could be set in a different position. Additionally, the starting position of each rotor itself was variable. The military version of the Enigma added the *stecker*, an electric plugboard, by which some key assignments (depending on the model of the machine) could be changed. In sum, even the most basic three-wheel military Enigma with six plug connections generated 3,283,883,513,796,974,198,700,882,069,882,752,878,379,955,261,0 95,623,685,444,055,315,226,006,433,616,627,409,666,933,182,371,154,802,7 69,920,000,000,000 coding positions. It was a staggering number.

Complex encryption is valueless unless it can be swiftly and correctly decrypted by the intended recipient. The genius of the Enigma machine was that its complex combination key could be communicated to a recipient by supplying just a few values: what rotors to use, the rotor order, the ring positions (within the rotors), the starting positions of each rotor, and the plugboard settings. For good reason, the Germans placed such confidence in the Enigma that it was used not just by high headquarters but by every military echelon and unit.

Yet there were four unrecognized flaws in Enigma. First, regardless of how complex a coding system may be, underlying it is an alphabet of just 26 letters, several of which are used very rarely. Second, although the Enigma gave the impression of producing a confounding randomness, it was governed by one absolute principle: No letter could stand for itself. This in itself provided a basic reference—a key—for code breakers. Third, Enigma ciphers were alphabetical, not alphanumeric. Without numerals, numbers had to be spelled out. This furnished yet another key, since the spelling of numbers was easily inferred from very few clues. Finally came the greatest flaw of all. Neither German engineers nor military leaders appreciated that all machine-generated codes have a cardinal weakness: Created by a machine, their ciphers can be broken by another machine.

As early as 1932, Polish cryptologists had begun to expose the flaws and were beginning to read some intercepted Enigma traffic. With war looming in mid-1939, Polish cryptologists secretly communicated much of their knowledge to the French and the British. On the basis of this work, British mathematician Alan Turing and others at Bletchley Park, the British center of cryptanalysis located just outside of London, set about creating an electromechanical computer capable of reading Enigma intercepts. The product of these decrypts was a body of intelligence dubbed "Ultra." It proved central to the Allied war effort.

The name Ultra was coined by British intelligence and at first applied exclusively to its decrypts of German Enigma communications. Before World War I ended, U.S. cryptographers adopted the term as well, applying it to all intelligence derived from any important cryptanalytic source. The name indicated that the intelligence was ultra-secret, beyond "top secret," and was accessible to only a small number of top-level commanders and political leaders.

Ultra decrypts, whether derived from Enigma or other sources (including the "Purple" ciphers used by Japan's diplomatic services or the "Orange" ciphers

A German naval Enigma machine. This four-rotor model was called the M4.

used primarily by the Japanese Imperial Navy), were of incalculable value to the Allied war effort. The power to decrypt enemy communications without the enemy knowing that their codes had been broken had to be exercised sparingly, lest the enemy guess that its ciphers had been compromised. Were this to happen, the enemy would move quickly to change its codes. Often, Ultra intelligence was purposely withheld from commanders in the field or carefully disguised. For instance, when information relating to the location of U-boats was received, the intelligence was never disseminated without an accompanying cover story. For instance, commanders of vessels hunting U-boats might be told that a search plane had "accidentally" discovered a boat at a certain location. So scrupulous were the keepers of Ultra that neither the Germans nor the Japanese discovered that their major codes had been broken and that their radio communication was being continuously intercepted and read.

Ultra intelligence became available too late to be of help during the air war over England known as the Battle of Britain (July 10–October 31, 1940), but it existed for almost every major operation after 1940. As Prime Minister Winston Churchill noted, "It was thanks to Ultra that we won the war."

The Aircraft Carrier: A New Platform for War (1942)

In the early twentieth century, the Dreadnought-class battleship, with very large-caliber artillery and heavy armor plate but the capability of maintaining a swift cruising speed, emerged as the ultimate weapon at sea. Two generations of senior naval officers came to think of the battleship as the queen of naval combat and planned all significant naval engagements accordingly. The battleship became the iconic geopolitical projection of a nation's military might.

November 1910 saw the unlikely beginnings of new type of ship destined not only to dethrone the battleship but to render it obsolete. In that month and year an American civilian aviator, Eugene Ely, took off from a platform built on the deck of the USS *Birmingham*, a cruiser. On January 18, 1911, Ely also became the first pilot to successfully land an airplane on a seagoing vessel, setting down on a larger platform built over the quarterdeck of the battleship USS *Pennsylvania*. For this feat, he used wires extended across the platform and attached to sandbags to serve as arresting gear to stop his plane before it rolled into the sea. This innovation—with many refinements, of course—became a central feature of aircraft carrier design, making it possible to land aircraft in spaces much shorter than those of a ground-based landing strip.

The British Royal Navy was the first sea power to seriously contemplate introducing an aircraft carrier in combat, converting a civilian ocean liner into HMS *Argus* during World War I. The ship displaced 15,750 tons (full), was 565 feet long with a beam of 68 feet, and had a 21-foot draft. It could accommodate about 20 aircraft and was powered by Parsons turbines driving four screws to a top speed of 20.2 knots. The armistice ending the war was signed before *Argus* could be deployed, but its example inspired both the United States and Japan to experiment with carriers.

The U.S. Navy built a flight deck on a converted collier and launched its first carrier, USS *Langley*, in 1922. Later that same year, the Japanese Imperial Navy launched *Hosyo*, the first vessel designed and purpose-built as an aircraft carrier rather than converted from an existing hull.

The *Langley* displaced 11,500 tons, was 542 feet in length, and had a beam of 65 feet. It drew a little less than 12 feet and was capable of making a modest 15 knots. *Hosyo* displaced just 10,000 tons (full), was 551 feet, 6 inches in length, and had a 59-foot beam and a draft of 20.4 feet. It could carry 11 to 26 aircraft and achieved a brisk top speed of 25 knots.

Early aircraft carriers were met with a great deal of institutional resistance, especially from American flag officers, who stubbornly clung to the ideal of the battleship. Nevertheless, as combat aircraft continued to develop after World War I the demand for aircraft carriers grew. The Washington Naval Treaty of 1922, signed by the great powers as an arms control measure after World War I, allowed each of the major signatories to convert two of their existing capital ships to carriers of no more 33,000 tons' displacement. Carriers purpose-built from scratch could displace no more than 27,000 tons. Moreover, the treaty limited carrier guns to eight inches, about half the caliber of those on a World War II battleship. In fact, the conversions made by the United States (*Lexington* and *Saratoga*) and Japan (*Akagi* and *Kaga*) exceeded the treaty limits on displacement. The new carriers built by these two nations during the 1930s (*Yorktown* and *Enterprise*, *Hiryu* and *Soryu*, respectively) adhered to the 27,000-ton limit, however. Britain converted two World War I–era light battle cruisers, HMS *Courageous* and HMS *Glorious*, to carriers, and then began construction on a new carrier, HMS *Ark Royal*, in 1935.

A new prewar naval treaty, concluded at London in 1936, placed more stringent size limitations on new carriers—23,000 tons, maximum—but also removed all restrictions on the number of carriers a signatory could build. Britain's Royal Navy introduced the Illustrious class of 23,000-ton carriers, but the United States, in the throes of isolationism, did not lay down any more carriers until World War II began, an event that rendered the 1936 treaty restrictions moot. The U.S. Essex class, built after the outbreak of war, displaced 27,500 tons and could carry more than 100 aircraft. Carriers of this class served as the main fleet carriers of the Pacific throughout World War II. Also during the war, the United States began construction of the mammoth 45,000-ton *Midway*, with armored flight decks, already used on Royal Navy carriers but not on existing U.S. vessels. No ships of this class, however, were completed before the war ended.

In addition to the large fleet carriers, the United States, Britain, and Japan also built and deployed light carriers, ranging from about 9,000 to 20,000 tons, which were designed for quick construction. Even the smaller escort carriers, also built by all three of these nations, displaced 7,000 to 17,000 tons. They were intended to protect merchant convoys from submarine attack. Most escort carriers were converted from light cruisers or merchant hulls. Britain's Royal Navy even added flight decks to some tankers and grain transports, allowing these vessels to serve as flight platforms while still carrying out their original cargo roles.

When the Japanese attacked the U.S. Pacific Fleet at Pearl Harbor on December 7, 1941, all the battleships anchored there were either sunk or badly damaged. The three aircraft carriers assigned to Pearl Harbor were out on patrol that morning and therefore survived to fight from the beginning of the war. It was at the Battle of the Coral Sea, fought during May 4–8, 1942, that aircraft carriers received their baptism under fire. The American and Japanese fleets in this battle had two fleet carriers each—and no battleships. The engagement was fought chiefly by aircraft launched from the carriers, so Coral Sea became history's first sea battle fought "over the horizon," the opposing ships never visually sighting one another, with all combat taking place in and from the air. Both sides publicly claimed victory after the battle. In fact, however, Coral Sea was a tactical defeat for the U.S. Navy and a strategic defeat for the Imperial Japanese Navy. The incontrovertible loser in all respects was the battleship—absent from this battle and not missed. It was well on its way to becoming all but irrelevant in naval warfare, which was undergoing a transformation into sea-air warfare.

The Battle of Midway: What a Turning Point Looks Like (1942)

At 6:00 a.m. local time, air forces of the Japanese Imperial Navy launched a pre-emptive surprise attack on the U.S. Navy's Pacific Fleet at Pearl Harbor, Hawaii. The first wave of aircraft used commercial radio broadcasts to home in on Pearl; then, as they neared their target, the pilots followed a bombing grid drawn up by the Japanese consul general stationed in Honolulu. Moored in the harbor on that sleepy Sunday morning were 70 U.S. warships, including 8 battleships. Fortunately, the heavy cruisers and fleet carriers were away at sea—something the Japanese planners had not anticipated.

The first wave of torpedo bombers and dive bombers attacked the battle fleet and bombed and strafed the airfields from 7:55 to 8:25 a.m. Fifteen minutes after this, a second wave of aircraft, high-level bombers, attacked. At 9:15 the dive bombers of that second wave swooped in, withdrawing at 9:45. In all, some 360 Japanese planes were involved in the operation. The toll they took was terrible: The battleship *Arizona* was completely destroyed and the *Oklahoma* capsized; the battleships *California*, *Nevada*, and *West Virginia* were sunk in shallow water. Three light cruisers, three destroyers, and four other vessels were damaged or sunk. One hundred sixty-four aircraft were destroyed on the ground and another 128 were damaged. Casualties included 2,403 U.S. service personnel and civilians killed and 1,178 wounded. Japanese losses amounted to 29 aircraft and 6 submarines—one I-Type and 5 "midget" subs.

Except for the absence of the carriers and heavy cruisers, the attack succeeded beyond Japanese expectations, but Admiral Chūichi Nagumo, in command of the attack fleet, decided against launching a planned third wave of aircraft because he feared a counterattack. Had that final wave been launched and, as planned, had it bombed the base's repair facilities and fuel installations, Pearl Harbor could have been knocked out of the war for a long time, perhaps permanently. Because these installations were undamaged, however, the base returned to service almost immediately. As for the fleet's losses, severe as they were, they were not fatal. The damaged battleships were repaired; even those that had sunk in shallow water were subsequently refloated. Six of the eight battleships hit at Pearl Harbor eventually returned to service, along with all but one of the smaller ships sunk or damaged.

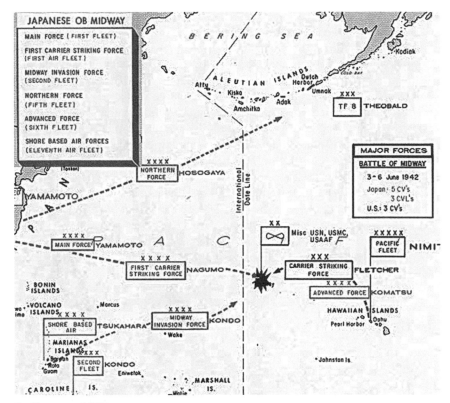

Battle map of Midway
UNITED STATES MILITARY ACADEMY

Japan's Admiral Isoroku Yamamoto, who had planned the Pearl Harbor attack, now conceived another plan to finish the work left incomplete by that operation. He devised a means of luring the U.S. Pacific Fleet into a single decisive battle, one he hoped would severely cripple if not utterly destroy the fleet, forcing the United States to seek a negotiated peace in the Pacific theater.

Midway Island, 1,000 miles west of Hawaii, was a strategically located piece of land from which either side could launch major attacks against the other. Yamamoto knew that the Americans wanted to maintain control of Midway, and he planned to draw the U.S. fleet to it, ambush it, and administer a deadly blow. He sent a diversionary force to the Aleutian Islands, part of the U.S. territory of Alaska in the northern Pacific. Because this was an attack and landing on American soil, Yamamoto knew that the U.S. Pacific commander, Admiral Chester W. Nimitz, would have to send some of his ships there, almost half an ocean from Midway. In charge of the main fleet targeting Midway was none other than Admiral Nagumo, the same overly cautious officer who had led the ultimately incomplete attack on Pearl Harbor. He led to Midway a four-carrier striking force followed by an invasion fleet, a total force of some 88 vessels.

Thanks to "Ultra" decrypted intercepts of Japanese radio transmissions, Admiral Nimitz was able to anticipate Nagumo's every move. Far from avoiding the Japanese trap, Nimitz decided to give Yamamoto the decisive battle he wanted. What he also proposed to deliver, however, was a very different outcome: a decisive American victory. Nimitz rushed to assemble two task forces east of Midway: Number 16, under Admiral Raymond Spruance, and Number 18, commanded by Admiral Frank Fletcher. In addition to the aircraft launched from the large carriers *Enterprise*, *Hornet*, and *Yorktown*, land-based planes would operate from Midway itself.

The battle began when some of those Midway-based planes attacked a portion of the Japanese fleet more than 500 miles west of Midway on June 3, 1942. The attack failed to do significant damage, and American aircraft losses were heavy. On the morning of June 4, the Japanese seized the initiative, sending 108 planes against Midway, causing heavy damage, including the loss on the

The U.S. aircraft carrier *Yorktown*, hit by a Japanese Type 91 aerial torpedo, begins to list. It was photographed from USS Pensacola during the Battle of Midway, June 4, 1942.

NATIONAL ARCHIVES AND RECORDS ADMINISTRATION

ground of 15 of the 25 Marine Corps fighter planes defending the island. At the same time, U.S. torpedo bombers launched a second air attack against the Japanese fleet. They hit not a single ship and lost seven aircraft. In a second strike this day, 8 of 27 Marine Corps dive bombers were lost, again having inflicted no damage. At last, 15 heavy B-17 bombers, flying out of Midway, attacked, but—incredibly—the Japanese carriers once again escaped unscathed.

The battle seemed lost when all three U.S. carriers launched yet another attack on the Japanese fleet, this time with torpedo bombers. Once more, they managed to inflict little damage. Worse, 35 of the 41 bombers engaged were shot down. But—and this was essential—the attack had forced the Japanese carriers to launch all their aircraft in defense. This left the carriers wide open and vulnerable to a follow-on attack. As the Japanese crews were still preparing their aircraft, which had just returned from defending against the American torpedo bombers, 54 dive bombers from the *Enterprise* and *Yorktown* (the *Hornet*'s planes had been launched but failed to find their targets) descended on three of the great Japanese carriers—*Akagi*, *Kaga*, and *Soryu*. All were loaded with just-recovered aircraft not yet ready to take off. In a mere four to five minutes, all three ships were sent to the bottom, along with crews, aircraft, and pilots. A fourth carrier, *Hiryu*, was sunk in a separate attack later in the afternoon—although not before the *Hiryu*'s planes had savaged the *Yorktown*, ultimately sinking it.

The Battle of Midway was costly for American pilots and sailors, but it was fatal to the Japanese. Having lost four aircraft carriers, many aircraft, and—perhaps worst of all—many of its best naval aviators, the Japanese withdrew from the waters around Midway on June 5. The American task forces were too battered and depleted to give chase—although they did manage to sink a heavy cruiser, the *Mikuma*, when they encountered it on June 6.

Decided in mere minutes by a single spectacular attack, the Battle of Midway is one of the great turning-point engagements in military history, an example of how one critical encounter can determine the course of a war. Seven months after suffering a catastrophic defeat at Pearl Harbor, the U.S. Pacific Fleet made a bold gamble and reversed the course of the war in this theater. Until Midway, Japan had been an offensive juggernaut, unstoppable. As a result of Midway, Japan was reduced to fighting an entirely defensive war, which loosened Japan's grip on the vast Pacific one finger at a time. The United States bought this turning point for the price of 150 planes, 307 men, a destroyer, and the carrier *Yorktown*. Japanese losses were 275 planes, 4 carriers, a heavy cruiser, and nearly 5,000 sailors and airmen—the latter an irreplaceable loss. The empire would never regain the initiative.

Holocaust: The Wannsee Conference Plans the "Final Solution" (1942)

Anti-Semitism and the scapegoating of Jews for the political and economic woes of Europe in general and Germany in particular were instrumental in the rise of Adolf Hitler. None of these themes was original with Hitler. Europe had a long anti-Semitic tradition. But Hitler, his Nazi Party, and his government, the Third Reich, transformed anti-Semitism into a political and cultural crusade, one of the major motives for world war. Total war had been fought before. This time, Hitler and the Nazis made total war—war that did not distinguish between combatants and noncombatants—more than a strategy and warfighting doctrine. It became a cause for war. For Adolf Hitler, a principal purpose of World War II was genocide.

As initially developed by the Nazis, Germany's national anti-Semitic program required purging Jews from "German" life. The *Endlosung*, the "Final Solution," was code for what happened when purging was defined as genocide. Hitler rose to power on a pledge to "free" Germany of Jews and "Jewish influence," which he purposely confounded with Marxism and Communism. He claimed that the Jewish "race" would pollute the pure "Aryan" blood of Germany, and he therefore posed to the German people the *Judenfrage* ("Jewish Question"): What was to be done to make Germany "Jew-free" (*Judenrein*)?

The first "answer" was internal exile, the expulsion of Jews from rural Germany, from villages and small towns, and their concentration in ghettoes located in the larger cities. The next "answer" was voluntary emigration abroad, which was encouraged (but not required) by the government. Emigration constituted official Reich policy from 1933 to the outbreak of war in 1939. Although emigration was voluntary, German law prevented Jewish émigrés from retaining real property or taking their belongings and most of their monetary assets with them. Virtually everything was forfeited to the government. Nevertheless, between 1933 and 1938, more than half of Germany's 500,000 Jewish citizens emigrated, driven out by passage of the 1935 Nuremberg Laws, which deprived Jews of German citizenship, and pogroms such as Crystal Night (*Kritallnacht*), a government-sanctioned general riot against Jews during November 9–10, 1938.

On January 20, 1942, with World War II raging—and the Russian Campaign beginning to turn against Germany—a meeting was called at Wannsee, a villa on Lake Wannsee in southwestern Berlin, to hammer out the "Final Solution" to the Jewish question.

Presiding was Reinhard Heydrich, director of the Reich Main Security Office and head of the Gestapo. Present were high officials of the Schutzstaffel (SS) and principal administrators of the German civilian government. By the time of the meeting, the Final Solution—genocide—was already under way, SS Einsatzgruppen ("deployment groups") murder squads were already executing Jews in the occupied territories of Eastern Europe and the Soviet Union. The task of the conference was to lay out official but covert policy for "extermination" on a much larger and systematic scale. With his assistant, Adolf Eichmann, Heydrich digested the minutes of the conference into a document historians call the "Wannsee Protocol." It summarizes the shift in policy from removing Jews by coaxing or forcing emigration to deportation, forced labor, and, ultimately, genocide. "Deportation" was a code word for confinement to concentration camps. Forced labor was both a means of extracting labor essential to the war effort and, because the work was especially grueling, of literally working the Jews to death. Outright execution, genocide, increasingly became the direct and immediate fate of Europe's Jews under the Nazi regime.

Among the tactical and technical issues discussed at Wannsee were the obscene mechanisms of genocide, which would be conducted mainly at concentration camps converted for industrial-scale mass murder and disposal through industrial-scale cremation. Early in this process, death would be by asphyxiation, using carbon monoxide generated by the redirected exhaust of prisoner transport vans. To increase "production," specially designed mass gas chambers, which were typically disguised as shower or delousing facilities, were to be built in the "death camps." As a more efficient alternative to carbon monoxide, Zyklon B, a cyanide preparation originally intended as a pesticide, would be used to produce extremely lethal cyanide gas. Once the method of genocide had been settled on, the biggest problem remained the disposal of corpses, which was to be carried out mainly in large multi-oven crematoria located in the death camps. In this way, the Holocaust, as the genocide of some 6 million European Jews came to be called, was perpetrated as a discrete objective of Hitler's war. Wars had been fought in the past for conquest, for religion, for independence, and even to establish political ideologies. But not since Rome had sought to annihilate Carthage in the Third Punic War of 149–146 BC had a war been fought with the explicit aim of exterminating an entire class of humanity.

Battle of Stalingrad: The Tide Turns on the Eastern Front (1942)

The eruption of World War II was not a surprise to most observers of Europe. What shocked the military experts, however, was how very different World War II was from World War I. Before the new war broke out, the general assumption among military experts was that the new war would closely resemble the old one, at least in Europe. It would be another trench war, in which battle lines would rapidly congeal along extended static fronts. The reality of World War II could not have been further from this vision.

Two things made the difference. First was the German "Blitzkrieg" tactic, the intensive use of combined-arms operations in an overwhelming attack. Second was a major transformation in weapons technology. In World War I, the development of weapons of defense—especially massive artillery and the machine gun—outpaced the development of offensive, highly mobile weapons. For this reason, the available weaponry favored defenders fighting from entrenchments and other covered positions, putting attackers at a great disadvantage. This calculus was reversed 20 years later in World War II. Development of weapons of maneuver and mobility outstripped those of defense. Mechanized artillery, tanks, and aircraft dominated the battlefield.

At the outbreak of the war, German exploitation of these new weapons systems drove extraordinarily rapid invasions of Western Europe, especially France, and Russia in the East. On June 22, 1941, Hitler suddenly betrayed his nonaggression pact with Stalin by invading the Soviet Union with a force of nearly 3.6 million troops, 3,600 tanks, and more than 2,700 aircraft. Stalin's Red Army formations available on the Western Front included 140 divisions and 40 brigades—some 2.9 million men. Although about 15,000 tanks and 8,000 aircraft were available to the Soviets, the vast majority of both were obsolescent and certainly inferior to their German counterparts.

Stalin was initially stunned into a kind of paralysis by the surprise invasion, but in a remarkable show of resilience, he soon recovered and proved to be an effective and inspiring leader, rallying both the civilian population and the military to great sacrifices in resisting and defeating the invaders. Operation Barbarossa, as the German invasion was called, penetrated very deeply into the Soviet heartland, causing massive loss of life; yet despite early triumphs at the battles of

Bialystok-Minsk and Smolensk, German field commanders began to realize that they had seriously underrated the Red Army—not so much for its military skill set as for its sheer fighting will to resist. Even when German commanders outgeneraled their Soviet counterparts—which frequently happened—the defeated Red Army forces withdrew, regrouped, and continued to fight. Worse for the invaders, who had aimed to quickly wipe out Soviet industrial capacity, Stalin ordered the rapid mass evacuation of Soviet industry far to the east. War production continued almost uninterrupted. Obsolescent Soviet equipment, especially aircraft, was destroyed in great quantity, only to be replaced by more modern and formidable equipment, including the revolutionary T-34 medium tank, widely considered the finest tank of World War II.

The German plan called for the rapid occupation of Leningrad and Moscow, as well as the destruction of the industrial Donets basin. After a devastating victory at the Battle of Smolensk (July 16–August 6, 1941), Hitler ordered his forces to divert from direct assaults on Moscow and Leningrad and instead invade Ukraine in the south and capture the industrial and mining areas outside Leningrad in the north. This shifted the main thrust of the invasion from the center to the wings. German Army Group Center, poised to take Moscow, now had to assume a defensive holding posture. It was a fatal strategic blunder that gave the Red Army time to organize effective counterattacks and develop stronger defensive positions. Still, by the end of September, Kiev, capital of Ukraine, was totally encircled. Seizing on this success, Hitler simply ignored the problems at the center of the German invasion. When he finally ordered an advance on Moscow, it was too late, and the operation bogged down. By the beginning of December, the German panzer armies had broken off their attack on the capital. As December ended, the Red Army had definitively repulsed the German attempt to take Moscow, marking the failure of Operation Barbarossa and shattering the powerful myth of German invincibility.

One result of Hitler's incompetent decision to refocus the invasion of the Soviet Union on its northern and southern wings was that Stalingrad (today called Volgograd) became a prime German objective. In part, Hitler was determined to capture a major manufacturing and transportation hub; but, even more, he believed that defeating the Red Army in a fight for the city that bore the name of Stalin would deliver a blow to Russian morale that could not be overcome. He further reasoned that Stalin would sacrifice unlimited resources to defend his namesake city. Hitler thus saw an opportunity to bleed the Red Army white.

The epic battle spanned June 22, 1942 to February 2, 1943. In the initial German attack, Field Marshal Fedor von Bock led Army Group B against Stalingrad while, to the right (south) of Army Group B, Army Group A set as its objective the oil fields of the Caucasus. Bock's attack came on June 22 from the line formed by the upper Donets River. His left wing advanced to the Don River at Voronezh on July 1 but could not hold Voronezh. Outraged, Hitler replaced Bock with Field Marshal Maximilian von Weichs on July 13.

While the Voronezh attack faltered and failed, Hermann Hoth led his Fourth Panzer Army in a 100-mile race to the Don and then turned southeast to drive between the Donets River and the Don. This provided support for Paul von Kleist to advance his First Panzer Army across the lower Don as it moved into the Caucasus and the oil fields there. Simultaneously, Friedrich von Paulus led the Sixth Army east from the bend of the Don toward Stalingrad on the right (west) bank of the Volga.

By August 24, German forces had reached the western margins of Stalingrad. At this time, the Sixty-Second Red Army, amply reinforced by local civilian volunteers, mounted an urban warfare defense, fighting the Germans house by house. At terrible cost, the Germans advanced to central Stalingrad by September 22. It was by this time a city in ruins, leveled by incessant artillery fire. Yet the Red Army was determined to prevent the Germans from capturing even the ruins of a place named for Stalin. The Soviet commander in charge, Georgy Zhukov, cautiously reinforced the Stalingrad garrison to hold the Germans, preventing their reaching the Volga River. At the same time, Zhukov built up his flanks both north and south of the city and, on November 19, unleashed a counterattack under Konstantin Rokossovski. After descending from the north of Stalingrad, Rokossovski crossed the Don at Kalach on November 21, breaching the German lines and opening the way for General Nikolai Vatutin to rout three Axis armies: the Third Rumanian, Eighth Italian, and Second Hungarian. The Germans responded with a counterattack from Panzer Corps H but were repulsed.

While this exchange was fought north of the city, General Andrei Yeremenko advanced from the south on November 20. Over the next five days, he scored total victories against the Fourth Rumanian Army. This accomplished, the two Soviet forces converged from north and south, linking up west of the city. Although the German Sixth Army was now in a hopeless position, Hitler personally denied permission for a withdrawal. Thus, on November 23, the Red Army enveloped the Sixth Army in the Soviet city. With communication and supply cut off, Luftwaffe chief Hermann Göring promised to airlift 300 tons of supplies each day. The promise went unfulfilled, and the Sixth German Army starved and froze in Stalingrad. Hitler at last gave Erich von Manstein permission to lead a relief force, called Army Group Don, to break through the Red Army envelopment. It failed, and General Paulus and his Sixth Army were left to fend for themselves.

On January 8, 1943, the Soviets issued a surrender demand. Once again, Hitler denied permission for surrender, and on January 10 the Soviets launched a massive artillery attack, followed by an assault from three sides. By January 16, the German airfield had been captured, and on January 24 the Soviets again demanded surrender. Hitler responded with an order to fight to the last man. It was ignored. Part of the Sixth Army surrendered on January 31; the rest did so two days later. Of the Sixth Army's roughly 285,000 men, 91,000 survived to be taken prisoner.

The Battle of Stalingrad was, in strictly operational terms, the turning point of the war on the Eastern Front. Beyond this, it shattered the myth of Adolf Hitler's vaunted "military genius" and revealed the German military, formidable as it was, to be vulnerable to ultimate defeat. It was thus a political turning point and a turning point for Allied morale in addition to being a major strategic turning point. For military history, Stalingrad emerged as a symbol of heroic resistance driven in large part by the cult of personality surrounding Stalin. It also stands as a symbol of defeat likewise caused by ceding military decisions to a cult of personality—that surrounding Adolf Hitler.

Operation Overlord and the D-Day Landings: Breakthrough from the West (1944)

World War II gave rise to some of the most ambitious projects in military history. The Allied invasion of Normandy, popularly known as D-Day, on June 6, 1944, was one of these—the biggest and almost surely most consequential invasion in military history. Equally ambitious was the project of military engineering Adolf Hitler ordered with the intention of transforming the entire European continent into a fortress (*Festung Europa*) behind, on its western sea margin, an "Atlantic Wall" (*Atlantikwall*). The encounter on D-Day between that invasion force and that wall and fortress was the greatest and most consequential operation in the long, long history of invasion assault versus fortification. It proved, perhaps once and for all, the futility of fixed fortification in warfare as practiced in the context of highly industrialized nations.

Operation Overlord was the code name for the planned Allied invasion of German-occupied northwest Europe. Overlord's first stage, the landings themselves, was separately code-named Operation Neptune. The Overlord concept was authorized in January 1943 at the Casablanca Conference primarily between President Franklin D. Roosevelt and Winston Churchill. The first task of planning was the determination of a landing area. After much study, the Baie de la Seine, between Le Havre and the Cherbourg (Cotentin) Peninsula, was decided on because Cherbourg offered a major port to sustain the invasion forces, the German defenses were determined to be less than insurmountable here, and the location was close enough to roadways into the interior to facilitate a post-landing breakout.

At the Quebec Conference in August 1943, the initial plan was presented. Churchill, recalling the failure of the earlier Dieppe Raid (August 19, 1942), an assault on the German-occupied port of Dieppe, called for a 25 percent increase in the initial assault force. Indeed, in January 1944 it was decided to make that force even larger, expanding it from three to eight divisions, including three airborne assault divisions. In February, SHAEF (Supreme Headquarters Allied Expeditionary Force) was created under U.S. general Dwight D. Eisenhower as supreme Allied commander, Europe. British general Bernard Law Montgomery would serve as commander of the invasion's ground component, Air Marshal Trafford Leigh-Mallory as commander of air forces, and Sir Bertam Ramsay as commander of all naval components. These men oversaw the planning for Operation Neptune, the landing and initial assault phase of the invasion.

Scheduling, timing, and coordinating Operation Neptune were intricate. There were advantages of operating under cover of darkness, but so many ships and aircraft were to take part that it was decided to land after dawn, yet no more than about one hour after low tide, so that German coastal obstacles and mines would be accessible to assault engineers. In addition, airborne troops, to be dropped in by parachute prior to the landings, required a full moon. Together, these prerequisites allowed for a very narrow window between June 5 and 7.

Overlord was cloaked in the most stringent secrecy of the war, and an elaborate program of deception (Operation Mincemeat) was launched prior to the invasion, including the dissemination of disinformation through a network of

U.S. Army soldiers, under full fighting equipment, wait on the deck of a Coast Guard assault transport, about to begin crossing the English Channel to waters off the Normandy coast.

NATIONAL ARCHIVES AND RECORDS ADMINISTRATION

double agents, the creation of phony radio traffic, and the erection of decoy camps and equipment. Everything was aimed at persuading the Germans that the landing would take place not in Normandy but at the Pas-de-Calais. In addition, between April 1 and June 5, 1944, more than 11,000 Allied aircraft flew more than 200,000 sorties, dropping 195,000 tons of bombs on rail and road networks, airfields and other military facilities, factories, and coastal batteries and radar outposts, all to weaken the so-called Atlantic Wall. They also engaged in many decoy missions in and around the Pas-de-Calais. In France itself, the Free French resistance worked with the British Special Operations Executive (SOE) and the American Office of Strategic Services (OSS) to supply on-the-ground intelligence, undermine German defenses, and commit acts of sabotage, especially against rail lines.

By May 1944, 47 divisions—about 800,000 combat troops—had been assembled in Britain, ready to cross the English Channel for landings along a 50-mile expanse of Normandy coast, from Caen west to the base of the Cotentin Peninsula. Tactically, the landing zone was divided into five beaches, code named, from east to west, Sword (to be assaulted by the British 3rd Division), Juno (Canadian 3rd Division), Gold (British 50th Division), Omaha (U.S. 1st Division and part of the 29th), and Utah (U.S. 4th Division). The first landings would be made by about 156,000 troops.

On and behind the Atlantic Wall were the German Seventh Army under Friedrich Dollmann and a part of Army Group B, commanded by the legendary Field Marshal Erwin Rommel. One of Rommel's armies, the Fifteenth, commanded by Hans von Salmuth, was held north of the Seine River under the assumption that the Allies would invade via Pas-de-Calais. Overall German command in the West was under Field Marshal Karl von Rundstedt, who had 36 infantry and 6 Panzer divisions in the coastal area.

A severe storm forced a one-day delay in the launch of the invasion, which finally took place on June 6, 1944, on the morning after an airborne assault by U.S. and British paratroopers. The U.S. 82nd and 101st Airborne divisions were tasked with capturing exits into the Cotentin Peninsula; the British 6th Airborne parachuted onto the eastern margin of Sword Beach to take bridges over the Orne River and the Caen Canal to protect the invasion's left flank. Four thousand ships constituted the invasion fleet, and the air component of the invasion included 4,900 fighter planes and 5,800 bombers.

The landings began at dawn on June 6, supported by massive naval bombardment and accompanied by close air support. The landings went remarkably well on all beaches except for Omaha Beach, where German resistance was heaviest. Nevertheless, by the evening of the first day, four of the five beachheads had been completely secured. Allied casualties in the first 24 hours were about

11,000 (including 2,500 killed in action)—costly, yet far lighter than had been anticipated.

Over the next six days, the invaders successfully joined their five beachheads together into an 80-mile-broad lodgment with an average depth of 10 miles. During this period, eight additional combat divisions landed. By D-Day +11, it was clear that the Allied invasion would not be pushed back into the sea; however, the breakout into the French interior would be difficult. On the left flank (east end) of the invasion, German panzers (armored forces) kept the British Second Army out of strategically vital Caen for weeks after the landings. On the right, three corps of the First U.S. Army defended the perimeter from Caumont to Carentan. North of Carentan, the U.S. VII Corps attacked to the west across the base of the Cotentin Peninsula. Inland progress was greatly impeded by the *bocage*, or hedgerows, of the Normandy coastal farmlands, but on June 18 the Americans were able to turn north, and on June 20 the U.S. 9th, 79th, and 4th Infantry Divisions reached the outer defenses of Cherbourg. From June 22 to June 27, the Americans battered Cherbourg's defenses and ultimately secured the port as a major artery of supply.

Elsewhere along the widening front, the battle for Normandy increased in violent intensity. The Allies raced to build up forces behind their initial lodgment so that they could make a major breakout to the interior. The Germans scrambled to bring up reinforcements in a desperate bid to contain the invasion. On June 28, Seventh German Army commander Dollmann was killed and replaced by SS General Paul Hausser. Adolf Hitler, never a steady hand, was in a panic. On July 3 he summarily relieved Rundstedt—one of Germany's most capable marshals—and replaced him with Field Marshal Günther von Kluge, a lesser light newly transferred from the Eastern Front. On this very day, the First U.S. Army attacked to the south but made little progress. Still, that army managed to take Lessay, which anchored the invasion's right flank, and, on July 18, also took Saint-Lô, at the approximate center of the American sector. On the left flank of the invasion, the Second British Army captured at least part of Caen on July 8, but it was not until July 20 that the British secured the rest of the town.

By July 20, the invading forces held only a bit more than 20 percent of the area that had been assigned to them, but by July 24 they were poised to begin the general breakthrough (Operation Cobra). Total Allied casualties up to this point were 122,000 killed, wounded, or captured; 117,000 for the German defenders. In the contest between fixed fortifications and well-planned, highly motivated assault forces, the fortifications had lost. The liberation of Europe was under way.

Hiroshima, August 6:
The New Wages of War (1945)

On September 2, 1945, General Douglas MacArthur, supreme Allied commander in the Pacific, made a radio broadcast to America from the battleship USS *Missouri*, riding at anchor in Tokyo Bay, after he had accepted the surrender of the Empire of Japan and brought World War II to an end. It was not a joyous speech of victory. Instead, he spoke of a "new era" that brought "profound concern, both for our future security and the survival of civilization. The destructiveness of the war potential, through progressive advances in scientific discovery, has in fact now reached a point which revises the traditional concepts of war. Men since the beginning of time have sought peace. . . . Military alliances, balances of power, leagues of nations, all in turn failed, leaving the only path to be by way of the crucible of war. We have had our last chance. If we do not now devise some greater and more equitable system, Armageddon will be at our door."

On behalf of the grand alliance that had won the most destructive war in history, the military leader of the Pacific theater did not celebrate the end of that war but warned that the end of humankind itself was now militarily possible.

He had good reason.

Hiroshima was a Japanese city and manufacturing center of some 350,000 people about 500 miles from Tokyo. On the morning of August 6, 1945, a Boeing B-29 Superfortress bomber—which pilot Colonel Paul Tibbets named *Enola Gay*, for his mother—took off from an airfield on the Pacific island of Tinian. The aircraft had been modified to carry a single bomb—a unique, nearly 8,000-ton, 9-foot, 9-inch munition called "Little Boy." It contained 141 pounds of uranium-235.

At 8:15 a.m. (local time), *Enola Gay* dropped Little Boy on Hiroshima. Slowed by parachute, it descended for 44.4 seconds before detonating, as designed, at precisely 1,900 feet above the city. The blast, a result of a very rapid atomic chain reaction, released an energy equivalent to 16 kilotons (16,000 tons) of TNT, an explosion that also instantly released tremendous heat and radioactivity, including lethal contamination in the form of radioactive fallout.

Hiroshima had been selected by a U.S. target committee because it had not yet been bombed by U.S. Army Air Forces. Its pristine condition would allow the Allies to assess the effect of the revolutionary new bomb and, even more important, demonstrate to the Japanese government and people the destructive force of this terrible weapon. All the city's wooden buildings within a 1.2-mile radius of the point of detonation (the "hypocenter") were destroyed. Reinforced concrete structures were destroyed within 1,625 feet of the hypocenter. An area of five square miles was largely incinerated, and 62.9 percent of the city's 76,000 buildings were completely destroyed by blast or fire. A mere 8 percent of Hiroshima's buildings escaped substantial damage.

The immediate human toll was 50 percent killed among those located within three-quarters of a mile of the hypocenter. An estimated 70,000 to 126,000 civilians were killed instantly or nearly so. About 20,000 soldiers garrisoned within the city were also killed. Another 30,524 persons were considered severely injured, and 48,606 were classified as lightly injured. About 4,000 residents of Hiroshima went missing and have never been accounted for. Of the approximately 350,000 persons believed to have been in Hiroshima at the time, only 118,613 were confirmed uninjured through August 10, 1946. The longer-term effects of radiation exposure included elevated rates of genetic and chromosomal damage, as well as birth defects (including stunted growth and mental retardation) of some children born to parents who survived the blast. However, the greatly increased rates of cancer that had been predicted did not materialize.

Little Boy and a second bomb, called Fat Man, which was dropped on Nagasaki on August 9, were products of an effort code named the Manhattan Project, the largest wartime scientific and industrial enterprise ever undertaken

A victim of the Hiroshima bombing on August 6, 1945
NATIONAL ARCHIVES AND RECORDS ADMINISTRATION.

by the United States. Officially begun in August 1942, the origin of the project may be traced to 1939, when a group of American scientists, including recent refugees from European fascist and Nazi regimes, became alarmed by what they knew to be work ongoing in Germany (led primarily by Nobel laureate physicist Werner Heisenberg) on nuclear fission, a process by which the energy of the binding force within the nucleus of the uranium or plutonium atom might be liberated to produce an explosion of unprecedented magnitude. Hungarian expatriate physicist Leo Szilard and other scientists prevailed on the nation's most celebrated refugee scientist, Albert Einstein, to write a letter to Franklin D. Roosevelt on August 2, 1939, advising him of the urgent necessity of beginning work on a military fission project in light of the dangers posed by Germany. Under the military direction of Major General Leslie R. Groves and the scientific direction of physicist J. Robert Oppenheimer, the Manhattan Project transformed cutting-edge theoretical physics into an operational fission weapon in the space of just two years.

It was hoped that the bombing of Hiroshima would elicit an immediate offer of unconditional surrender. When it did not, Nagasaki was bombed on August 9, instantly killing another 39,000 to 80,000 people. On August 12, Emperor Hirohito told his family that he had decided to surrender. On August 14 he recorded a surrender announcement for public broadcast, which came the next day. The formal Japanese surrender, aboard the battleship USS *Missouri*, occurred 19 days after this. As General MacArthur recognized in the speech he made following that ceremony, this great turning point in world history, in science, and in World War II amounted to a turn toward, quite literally, a dead end.

The National Security Act Is Passed: The United States Remodels Its Military (1947)

On September 18, 1947, the National Security Act of 1947 came into effect. It was a momentous restructuring of the American military and the American intelligence community. The act merged the Department of War and the Department of the Navy into the newly created Department of Defense, which encompassed what was now called the Department of the Army and the Department of the Navy in addition to the Department of the Air Force. The latter was created in conjunction with the separation from the U.S. Army of an independent U.S. Air Force, which had functioned up to and during World War II as the U.S. Army Air Forces. In addition, while the U.S. Marine Corps remained under the Department of the Navy, it was recognized as an independent service operationally separate from the Navy. Finally, the 1947 act created the National Security Council (NSC) and the Central Intelligence Agency (CIA). This was the nation's first peacetime nonmilitary intelligence agency; however, the fact that the CIA was created under the same legislative umbrella as the restructuring of the armed forces had the effect of defining the mission of all these organizations as national security.

More than a bureaucratic evolution, the National Security Act was a turning point in the military history of the United States. American independence and the revolution that won it had been motivated in part by a popular objection to the maintenance of a large standing army—the hated British "redcoats"—among the civilian population. Ever since the American Revolution and up to World War II, the majority of Americans looked upon a standing army with suspicion and even disdain. The 1947 legislation effectively integrated a large military and intelligence community into the government. No longer was there a "War" Department. Military matters were now functions of "Defense" and "National Security," permanent, organic fixtures of government. The American military was seen as an extension of the American national identity. Military affairs and politics grew closer together.

Passage of the National Security Act came in the same year that President Harry S. Truman, the chief executive who had made the decision to use nuclear weapons against Japan, announced a new foreign policy in response to a threatened Communist takeover of Greece and Turkey. Called the Truman Doctrine, it was based on the theory of "containment" put forward by the State Department's brilliant George F. Kennan, in the so-called Long Telegram he sent from Moscow to Washington, the contents of which he later digested in an article for the influential journal *Foreign Affairs*. Two grim new realities overshadowed the Allied victory in World War II. The first was the existence of nuclear weapons, which, as General Douglas MacArthur had noted in his broadcast to America following the Japanese surrender on September 2, 1945, were instruments of Armageddon. The second was the Soviet Union's aggressive efforts to spread Communism throughout Europe and elsewhere. The USSR would not test its first nuclear weapon until August 29, 1949, but American military and political leaders knew that the U.S. monopoly on such weapons would not last long. The question was how to confront the Soviet threat without triggering World War III.

Kennan's answer was a policy of containment. Wherever the Soviets attempted to spread their influence, the United States would confront them and contain their efforts using (Kennan advised) economic incentives wherever possible but resorting to the use of limited force if necessary. The result was the Cold War—a contest of economic influence (such as the Marshall Plan) as well as the limited application of military threat and actual force. To maintain this state of continuous low-level hostility, a new approach to "national security" was required. And so the National Security Act was crafted and passed. In effect, the United States was put on a perpetual low-level war footing.

While most Americans were comforted by the creation of a Department of Defense, the CIA was a more divisive matter. The late 1940s and early 1950s brought a "red scare" to America, a tremulous climate in which the new agency was rapidly scaled up as an espionage organization, becoming in some contexts a shadow government. Intended to provide political leaders with the intelligence needed to make effective foreign policy and military decisions, the CIA mounted covert actions that too often proved not merely unsuccessful but also counterproductive. Some threats were exaggerated, others minimized or ignored. The CIA's operation of U-2 spy planes over the Soviet Union—the aircraft belonged to the CIA, but the pilots were Air Force aviators seconded to the agency—led to a major diplomatic embarrassment for President Dwight D. Eisenhower. On May 1, 1960, a U-2 flown by one of these seconded pilots, Francis Gary Powers, was shot down over Soviet territory, leading to the angry cancellation of a key summit conference. When the CIA became deeply involved in a guerrilla action, the insurgent invasion of Cuba at the Bay of Pigs during April 17–20, 1961, political disaster befell the new administration of President John F. Kennedy, who threatened to dismantle the agency.

That the CIA has weathered many controversies since then demonstrates how thoroughly it has become woven into the fabric of national security it shares with the regular military establishment. Arguably, the National Security Act was a major step toward both reaffirming and amplifying civilian control over the military, but Americans have also learned to accept their military as a permanent part of American life and American civilization. Since 1947, the United States has been, in some degree, a military state.

Berlin Blockade and Berlin Airlift: A Model Cold War Victory (1948–1949)

The business of the military, it is often said, is to kill people and break things. From June 24, 1948, to May 12, 1949, the militaries of the United States and United Kingdom saved people, put things back together, and, in so doing, stymied Soviet aggression in Europe while avoiding the path toward a third world war. It was an American-led triumph of military logistics and an unprecedented role for a brand-new American service arm, the U.S. Air Force.

Toward the end of March 1948, Joseph Stalin, leader of the Soviet Union, decided to take steps to break up the alliances being formed by the Western democracies. He was especially wary of the Western allies' commitment to transform their zone of postwar occupied Germany into a permanent and separate capitalist state: West Germany. Accordingly, the Soviets began detaining troop and supply trains bound for the Western-controlled zone of Berlin, a city 100 miles inside the Soviet-controlled eastern sector of the defeated and divided country. In defiance of Soviet action, on June 7, 1948, the United States, Britain, and France officially announced the advent of West Germany. Little more than two weeks later, the Soviets blockaded access to West Berlin, arguing that this city, deep within what would now become East Germany, could not possibly be part of West Germany.

In accordance with his policy of "containing" the spread of Communism and Soviet aggression, President Harry S. Truman was determined to act. He needed, however, to act in a way that would not ignite outright war with the Soviets. Rejecting the idea of an armed overland convoy to West Berlin but convinced that the loss of the city would ultimately mean the loss of all Germany, and urgently aware that the *people* of West Berlin needed food and, as winter approached, both food and fuel, he asked General Hoyt Vandenberg, chief of staff of the newly independent U.S. Air Force, if a massive airlift was feasible. Vandenberg worried that mounting so large an operation would impair the Air Force's ability to respond to some crisis that might break out elsewhere. Having decided that an airlift involved less risk than an armed ground convoy, Truman nevertheless directed Vandenberg to put together the operation. The immediate responsibility fell to Lieutenant General Curtis E. LeMay, at the time commanding U.S. Air Forces in Europe (USAFE). When General Lucius Clay, commander in chief of U.S. Forces in Europe, asked him if he could "transport coal by air," LeMay answered: "Sir, the Air Force can deliver anything."

LeMay immediately summoned to West Germany virtually every USAF transport plane in the world. He put Brigadier General Joseph Smith, commander of the Wiesbaden Military Post, in charge of what was now called Operation Vittles—the Berlin Airlift. The first 32 C-47 Skytrains took off for Berlin on June 26, carrying a total of 80 tons of cargo that included milk, flour, and vital medicines. Two days later, the British Royal Air Force (RAF) made its first flight in the operation. Smith believed that the airlift would last perhaps three weeks. He committed to having 65 percent of available aircraft in the air every day, regardless of the weather, each plane to make three round-trips to Berlin daily from the Rhein-Main Air Base and Wiesbaden. He organized a "block system" to convoy together aircraft capable of maintaining speeds. This was aimed at making air traffic control, ground traffic control, and cargo handling more efficient. Smith set up a special Air Traffic Control Center to handle the airlift exclusively.

After three weeks, there was no sign that the Soviets intended to lift the blockade. Therefore, on July 23, 1948, Operation Vittles was assigned for the long term to the USAF logistics wing, the Military Air Transport Service (MATS), under Major General William H. Tunner. He set about transforming

Berlin kids living near Tempelhof Air Force Base play a game they call *Luftbucks*—"air bridge." West German toy shops sold many models of USAF aircraft used in the Berlin Airlift.

NATIONAL ARCHIVES AND RECORDS ADMINISTRATION

the airlift into a sustained and sustainable enterprise, orchestrating flight and ground operations according to what he described as a "steady rhythm, constant as the jungle drums." Tunner did the math, calculating that each day consisted of 1,440 minutes. He intended to land an aircraft every minute. In the end, he averaged one every three minutes—still an astounding achievement. Aircrews were forbidden to leave the side of their aircraft after landing at West Berlin's Tempelhof or Gatow airports. They had to be ready for immediate return. When a plane landed, an operations officer and a weather officer drove up to brief the pilot while another jeep delivered hot coffee, hot dogs, and doughnuts. Tunner brought in civilian time-motion experts, who worked out a system that allowed a dozen men to load 10 tons of bagged coal into a C-54 Skymaster in six minutes. Crews assigned to unloading were able to cut a normally 17-minute process to 5 minutes. Refueling was slashed from 33 minutes to 8.

Flying round-the-clock serial missions, regardless of weather, was as hazardous as flying combat missions. But accidents were few, and the people of Berlin were fed and warmed. What was projected as a three-week operation stretched out to nearly a year. On May 12, 1949, the Soviets at long last blinked, lifting the blockade. The airlift continued after this, though at a reduced volume, for nearly five more months, to stockpile reserves of food and fuel. The last flight was completed on September 30, 1949, USAF crews having made 189,963 flights over Soviet-held territory and RAF crews 87,606. The Americans had transported 1,783,572.7 tons of food, coal, and other cargo; the RAF, 541,936.9 tons.

A Treaty Signed in Brussels: The Creation of NATO (1949)

World War I may have been triggered by the assassination, in an obscure Balkan capital, of the heir apparent to the Austro-Hungarian throne, but it quickly became a cataclysmic *world* war because the nations of Europe were bound to one another by a dysfunctional network of treaties, alliances, and agreements—some public, some covert—virtually ensuring that any little brushfire would almost instantly be fanned into an all-engulfing conflagration. Yet worse, the war ended with a document even more dysfunctional than the network of treaties that had created it. The Treaty of Versailles transformed what President Woodrow Wilson hoped would be a "war to end all wars" into a war to end all peace. It made the eruption of a *second* world war almost inevitable.

The end of World War II brought an extraordinary turning point in military history. It was a will, shared by most of the combatant nations, to avoid repeating the mistakes of World War I. Among the Western victors there was a desire—perhaps unprecedented in history—to create recovery and healing, to restore the shattered economies and infrastructures of all the devasted nations, friend and former enemy alike. As American political leaders put it, "We won the war. Let's not lose the peace."

The most dramatic and compelling expression of the will to peace that followed World War II was the enactment of the Marshall Plan, an American program for revitalizing a ruined and war-weary Europe. Winston Churchill called it "the most unselfish and most unsordid financial act of any country in all history." And yet the Marshall Plan had the unintended consequence of widening and hardening the gulf that was opening up between the Soviets and its former allies in the West. Joseph Stalin denounced the program as a capitalist plot even as he plotted to overthrow the emerging democratic governments of fragile new republics throughout Eastern Europe and to partition Germany so as to create a buffer of satellite states to insulate the Soviet Union against Western influence, which he correctly saw as a threat to his dictatorship.

Even as the United States promoted peaceful recovery with the Marshall Plan and other aid initiatives, Stalin supported (through Yugoslavia, Albania, and Bulgaria) the Communist Party of Greece in the Greek Civil War (1946–1949) and backed a Communist coup in Czechoslovakia in March 1948. The Western European states, Great Britain, and the United States responded by pressing ahead with the unification of the western zones of German occupation and the establishment of a West German currency and government. This prompted the

Russians to storm out of the Allied Control Council, which had been set up to administer the Allied occupation of Germany. Three months after leaving the council, the Soviet occupation forces in the eastern zone of Germany shut off Allied access by road and rail to the western zones of Berlin, the divided city deep within Soviet-controlled East Germany.

President Harry S. Truman, deeply concerned over the aggressive expansion of Soviet influence, was persuaded by the "Long Telegram" sent from Moscow by American diplomat George Kennan and urging the adoption of a policy of "containment" toward Stalin. The idea was to counter Soviet expansion wherever it was under way—by nonmilitary economic means (such as the Marshall Plan) where feasible and by military means where necessary.

For his part, Truman had already begun to set up a national security apparatus, which was largely authorized by another turning point, the National Security Act of 1947. The United States would have a new Department of Defense, unifying the services, a permanent Joint Chiefs of Staff, an independent U.S. Air Force—including a Strategic Air Command (SAC) to take the lead in managing the nation's growing nuclear arsenal—and a Central Intelligence Agency (CIA) to counter (mostly) Soviet espionage.

Truman had also already concluded the Inter-American Treaty of Reciprocal Assistance, better known as the Pact of Rio, which was signed on September 2, 1947. It became a model for several regional mutual-defense agreements that connected the United States to nations adjacent to the Soviet Union or its satellites. But the president wanted to do more, to "get tough" with the Soviets in fighting what was already being called the Cold War. The first test of the new policy was Truman's response to the Soviet blockade of West Berlin. The U.S. commander in Berlin, General Lucius Clay, and Secretary of State Dean Acheson advised sending an armed supply convoy straight through the Russian zone to Berlin. The newly created Joint Chiefs of Staff objected, as did the British and the French. All were unwilling to risk provoking a major war with the Soviet Union. Truman responded with the Berlin Airlift, brilliantly executed by the newly created U.S. Air Force. It kept West Berlin supplied with food, fuel, and medicine—and was yet another turning point in crafting a military response to aggression without igniting World War III.

Whatever Joseph Stalin hoped to accomplish by his aggression against West Berlin, what his blockade did succeed in doing was move the Western powers to take bolder measures to contain the Soviet threat than they might otherwise have implemented. On April 4, 1949, the foreign policy heads of the United States, Great Britain, France, Italy, the Netherlands, Belgium, Luxemburg, Portugal, Denmark, Iceland, Norway, and Canada met in Washington to create the North Atlantic Treaty Organization (NATO), the most important Cold War multinational mutual alliance and arguably the most successful military alliance in modern history.

The preamble to the North Atlantic Treaty clearly established the purpose of NATO:

The Parties to this Treaty reaffirm their faith in the purposes and principles of the Charter of the United Nations and their desire to live in peace with all peoples and all governments.

They are determined to safeguard the freedom, common heritage and civilization of their peoples, founded on the principles of democracy, individual liberty and the rule of law.

They seek to promote stability and well-being in the North Atlantic area.

They are resolved to unite their efforts for collective defence and for the preservation of peace and security.

If there is a heart to the document, it is Article 5:

The Parties agree that an armed attack against one or more of them in Europe or North America shall be considered an attack against them all, and consequently they agree that, if such an armed attack occurs, each of them, in exercise of the right of individual or collective self-defence recognized by Article 51 of the Charter of the United Nations, will assist the Party or Parties so attacked by taking forthwith, individually, and in concert with the other Parties, such action as it deems necessary, including the use of armed force, to restore and maintain the security of the North Atlantic area.

Any such armed attack and all measures taken as a result thereof shall immediately be reported to the Security Council. Such measures shall be terminated when the Security Council has taken the measures necessary to restore and maintain international peace and security.

With the end of the Cold War and the disbanding of the Soviet-dominated Warsaw Pact alliance formed to counter NATO, some Europeans called for replacing NATO with a less exclusively military organization. Indeed, in the early 1990s, the United States took steps to reduce its NATO presence, substituting for large standing NATO forces contingency plans that relied on smaller "rapid deployment forces," with reinforcements available from the United States and other signatories in time of need. Immediately following the terrorist attacks against the United States on September 11, 2001, the NATO members invoked Article 5 for the first—and so far only—time in its history, pledging themselves to come to the defense of the United States. Despite this and despite the role NATO has played in preserving the post–World War II peace in Europe, calls have sporadically persisted, including from President Donald Trump, to end the alliance.

The Birth of "Limited War": Finding a "Substitute for Victory" in Korea (1950–1951)

On June 25, 1950, the Cold War turned hot in Korea. Like West and East Germany in Europe, this Asian nation was divided at the end of World War II. The territory north of the 38th parallel was designated a Soviet occupation zone; south of the parallel was a U.S. zone. In November 1947, the United Nations voted to create a unified independent Korea, but the Communists barred free elections in the north. Elections were held in the south, and on August 15, 1948, the Republic of Korea was born. The following month, in the north, the Communists created the Democratic People's Republic of Korea in September 1948. As the Soviet Union and the Communist government of the People's Republic of China supported communist North Korea, the United States and other Western powers supported the democratic government of South Korea. On June 25, 1950, forces from the north crossed the 38th parallel into South Korea. The United States secured a United Nations sanction against the invasion and then contributed the majority of the UN coalition troops to repel it. Chosen to lead the UN military effort was General of the Army Douglas MacArthur, the larger-than-life American army officer who, instrumental in the defeat of Japan, accepted the Japanese surrender on September 2, 1945, and went on to head the occupation government of that country.

The U.S. military had rushed to demobilize after World War II and now, much diminished, scrambled to mount a credible defense against the invasion. Very rapidly, the North Korean troops, who had been trained and equipped by the Soviets and the Chinese, drove the South Korean defenders back from the 38th parallel and toward the southern tip of the Korean Peninsula. It was the start of a proxy war between the United States and its allies on the one side and the Soviet Union and "Red" China on the other.

MacArthur faced a desperate situation. Struggling to hold the critical southern port of Pusan (now Busan) to buy time until the arrival of reinforcements, he attempted not only a defense but also a daring counteroffensive by making a high-risk amphibious landing at Inchon, on the west coast of Korea, *behind* North Korean lines. A spectacular success, the perilous landing was MacArthur's tactical masterpiece—an achievement that elevated him to the status of one of

First Lieutenant Baldomero Lopez, USMC, leads the 3rd Platoon, Company A, 1st Battalion, 5th Marines over the seawall on the northern side of Red Beach, as the second assault wave lands, 15 September 1950, during the Inchon invasion.

NATIONAL ARCHIVES AND RECORDS ADMINISTRATION

military history's "great captains." By October 1, 1950, the Communist invaders had been driven all the way back to the northern side of the 38th parallel.

At this moment of triumph, President Harry S. Truman was faced with a grave decision. MacArthur was eager to cross the 38th parallel and invade North Korea. Should he be allowed to? Although such a move was sanctioned by the UN—which had voted for the unification of Korea—it could well convert a proxy war into World War III. Fail to defeat the Communists in their own territory, however, and all Korea might be "lost" to Communist domination. Truman decided on a compromise. He authorized the crossing but took steps to continue fighting a "limited war" intended to avoid provoking the Chinese and the Soviets. He ordered MacArthur to bar troops from entering either Manchuria or the USSR, both of which bordered North Korea. Furthermore, he specified that only South Korean forces would operate near those borders.

Once again, on October 7, the UN called for the unification of Korea and added its authorization of the invasion. It moved quickly. On October 19 the North Korean capital of Pyongyang fell, and North Korean forces were driven far north to the Yalu River, the border with Manchuria.

In the United States and elsewhere in the West, it was widely assumed that the Korean "Conflict" was over. Then, during October 14–November 1, approximately 180,000 so-called volunteers crossed the Yalu from China. That Communist nation was now in the war—with a major force. MacArthur responded with a counteroffensive on November 24 but was driven back. The UN troops retreated across the 38th parallel, and in January 1951 the South Korean capital of Seoul fell to the Communists. Nevertheless, MacArthur was able to arrest the retreat south of Seoul, and American and allied units began probing northward in a relentless but gradual offensive the soldiers themselves called "The Meatgrinder." By March 1951, the UN forces had clawed their way back to the 38th parallel. They dug in, creating a strong defensive position.

General MacArthur was not satisfied with playing defense. He did not request but instead demanded authorization to retaliate by bombing Manchuria. Both President Truman and the UN refused permission, fearing that such an attack on China would provoke a nuclear war with the Soviets. American politicians and the American public became deeply divided. Many sided with the general against the president. In direct violation of the constitutional chain of command assigning the role of military commander in chief to the president, MacArthur publicly blamed the military setbacks on Truman. The president was patient until March 25, 1951. On that day, immediately after Truman had completed preparation of a cease-fire proposal, MacArthur broadcast an unauthorized ultimatum to the enemy commander. This forced Truman to shelve his proposal. That was bad enough, but MacArthur also sent a letter to Republican House Minority Leader Joe Martin excoriating Truman's war policy. Martin read the letter into the *Congressional Record*. Deeming MacArthur's letter an act of gross insubordination, an unconstitutional breach of the chain of command, the president relieved MacArthur of command in Korea on April 11, 1951.

On April 19, having returned to the United States, MacArthur appeared before a joint session of Congress to announce his retirement. In the speech he memorably quoted a traditional barracks ballad—"Old soldiers never die; they just fade away"—and announced his intention to "fade away." However, he also told Congress that there was "no substitute for victory." It was a stern rebuke of the concept of "limited war," and its bitter sting has never faded away.

Without MacArthur, the Korean War was fought to a stalemate. The shooting was ended by an armistice on July 27, 1953, but the nation remained divided along the 38th parallel. South Korea today prospers as a capitalist democracy. North Korea languishes as an isolated Communist nation under an absolute dictatorship. For 53 years, an uneasy peace endured. In 2006 North Korea successfully tested its first nuclear weapon and in 2015 claimed to have developed a thermonuclear (hydrogen) bomb. The threat of a proxy war becoming a nuclear war is now the threat of North Korea itself launching Armageddon.

Battle of Dien Bien Phu: The Domino Theory Emerges (1954)

The two world wars of the twentieth century drew the attention of general historians as well as military historians to the so-called major powers. From World War II there emerged from among these major powers two "superpowers," the United States and the Soviet Union. The geopolitical vision of most of the post–World War II era was shaped by the perceived role of the two superpowers, around which much of the rest of the world seemed to orbit. Because both superpowers possessed nuclear and then thermonuclear weapons, a major war between the two was (to use a word popular during the era) "unthinkable." Thus, the wars fought by small nations were seen not as civil wars (in the case of former colonies and vassal states) or as wars for independence (in the case of then-current colonies) but as proxy wars, means by which the superpowers could confront each other without risking escalation into a world war. The truth that has been repeatedly missed or deliberately ignored is that these wars were not, in fact, fought on behalf of the superpowers but were civil wars and revolutions that were, in some degree, hijacked by the superpowers.

Following World War II, Vietnam fought for its independence from France. Although two American presidents, Harry S. Truman and Dwight D. Eisenhower, hated French colonial imperialism, both supported the French in their efforts to retain control over Vietnam because they believed that an independent Vietnam would fall into the orbit of Communist China or the Soviet Union. Under both presidents, a great deal of American money and military support was poured into what was called the French Indochina War, which began in 1946. Despite the aid, the French could not defeat the insurgency. At last, in May 1953, General Henri Navarre, a veteran of the two world wars, instituted the "Navarre Plan," which was an effort to compel the independence fighters, the Viet Minh, to abandon their insurgent, or guerrilla, tactics and fight a showdown European-style battle against French soldiers. If the French army could defeat the Viet Minh on its own terms, the insurgency might not stop, but it would be degraded. The French could leave, and the fighting could be turned over to Vietnamese forces that were still loyal to France. Thus France would retain some control in Vietnam and the country would stay out of Communist hands.

Navarre decided to force a battle at the strategically located plain of Dien Bien Phu, in northwest Tonkin near the border with Laos. He sent in French paratroops in the fall of 1953, and in November and December the U.S. Far East Air Forces flew transports carrying French soldiers to Cat Bai, from which American civilian contract pilots or French aviators flew them to Dien Bien Phu. President Eisenhower and his military advisors were becoming concerned that the Viet Minh's leading general, Võ Nguyên Giáp, was poised to attack Hanoi (Vietnam's major northern city) and Haiphong (a major harbor). Giáp was also massing more men to attack at Dien Bien Phu. Eisenhower committed additional military aid, including B-26 bombers and reconnaissance aircraft. On January 31, 1954, he authorized the dispatch of some 300 U.S. airmen as ground crew to service the aircraft. They were the first substantial commitment of American military personnel to Vietnam.

Despite American aid, Navarre's position at Dien Bien Phu steadily deteriorated. Over weeks and then months, the French defensive perimeter contracted. On April 7, 1954, President Eisenhower presented to American reporters a rationale for assisting France in holding on to Vietnam. It was, he explained, not a fight against independence but a fight against Communism. "You have a row of dominoes set up," the president explained, "you knock over the first one, and what will happen to the last one is the certainty it will go over very quickly." Casually tossed off to the press, the "Domino Theory" would become the cornerstone not just for extending aid to the doomed imperial ambitions of France but also for ultimately committing hundreds of thousands of American soldiers and many billions of dollars of American treasure to a war in Vietnam that would span the presidencies of Eisenhower, Kennedy, Johnson, Nixon, and Ford, ending in the unification of Vietnam under a Communist government as the American military withdrew in defeat.

Dien Bien Phu was the beginning. Navarre had supposed that the Viet Minh could only fight as insurgents. He deliberately forced them into open confrontation with the French military. What he did not count on was the patient deliberation of Giáp and his troops. They fought neither as insurgents nor in a single showdown battle. Instead they set up a long siege beginning on March 13, 1954. Fifty-six days later, on May 7, the final French stronghold on the plain of Dien Bien Phu fell to Giáp's forces, forces loyal to the forces of the charismatic Communist leader Ho Chi Minh. Out of some 20,000 French troops at Dien Bien Phu, an estimated 1,571 to 2,293 were killed in action, with 5,195 to 6,650 wounded. The Viet Minh captured 11,721. It was a humiliating defeat inflicted at the cost of 4,000 to 8,000 Viet Minh killed out of a force of 64,500.

Herman Kahn Publishes *On Thermonuclear War:* Challenging the MAD Doctrine (1960)

During August 6–9, 1945, with the dropping of "Little Boy" on Hiroshima and "Fat Man" on Nagasaki, the world and its militaries entered the Atomic Age. It was the first historical age to be named for the very force that threatened to destroy it. The American monopoly on nuclear weapons ended on August 29, 1949, when the Soviets successfully tested RDS-1, an imitation of America's "Fat Man," yielding 22 kilotons of explosive nuclear energy.

Now the world had two, mutually hostile, nuclear powers, each of which busied itself with creating more, and more destructive, weapons. In October 1952 a third member, Great Britain, joined what some began calling the "nuclear club." There was now talk of "nuclear weapons proliferation." France joined in February 1960 when it test-fired "Gerboise Bleue" (Blue Jerboa) in Algeria, at the time a French colony. From an American point of view, at least Britain and France were friendly Western nations—though France under Charles de Gaulle was notoriously independent of its allies. Far more ominously, the People's Republic of China tested a nuclear device on October 16, 1964.

By this time, the destructive ante had been upped by the development of a new type of nuclear device. It was called the thermonuclear bomb, the hydrogen bomb, or simply the H-bomb. Whereas the first generation of nuclear weapons—atomic bombs, or A-bombs—were fission devices that detonated when a mass of "fissile material" (enriched uranium or plutonium) was forced into supercriticality, creating a massive nuclear fission reaction, H-bombs were fusion weapons. In these, energy from "primary" fission reactions was used to trigger secondary fusion reactions between isotopes of hydrogen. The magnitude of energy released by fission—the splitting apart of atomic nuclei—is very great. That produced by fusion, the coming together of atomic nuclei to form more nuclei and subatomic particles, is much more energetic. "Little Man" exploded with the force of roughly 22 kilotons (22,000 tons) of TNT. "Ivy Mike," the first H-bomb tested—on November 1, 1952, by the United States—yielded 10.4 megatons, the equivalent of 10.4 *million* tons of TNT. On November 22, 1955, the Soviet Union successfully tested its first hydrogen bomb, RDS-37, which yielded 1.6 megatons.

By the early 1960s, the megatonnage multiplied with each H-bomb tested. On October 30, 1961, the Soviets detonated the most powerful weapon ever tested in the atmosphere, the so-called Tsar-Bomba, which yielded 58 megatons. More nations joined the club. Today, the United States, Russia, the United Kingdom, France, China, India, Pakistan, and North Korea are known to have nuclear weapons, and Israel is believed to possess them.

Even as weapons proliferated, it was generally calculated that the two superpowers in themselves possessed nuclear and thermonuclear arsenals sufficient to destroy civilization—indeed all life on Earth—several times over. In political and military circles, talk turned from ways to defend against nuclear and thermonuclear war to strategies to deter such a conflict. The prevailing doctrine held that only by engaging in a nuclear arms race, increasing one's own nuclear stockpile, would the enemy be discouraged from making a nuclear first strike. It was the classic scenario of dime novels, in which gunfighters in the Old West stared each other down in what was called a "Mexican standoff": *We're both armed. If you shoot, I will shoot, and we both will die.* Of course, in the new Atomic Age and Thermonuclear Age, such a death match would almost certainly engulf the world. The horror of these weapons was that, as powerful as the initial blast was, radiation and subsequent contamination (fallout) multiplied the death toll.

Full-scale war, it seemed to most people, was now off the table because it meant a universal Armageddon—doomsday. Military and geopolitical strategists spoke of "mutual assured destruction," which made for a very appropriate acronym: MAD.

Deterrence indeed proved powerful, but it hardly prevented war. Many "brushfire" wars, proxy wars, were fought and continue to be fought in the Atomic Age. Even without the deployment of nuclear weapons, many of these wars have been highly destructive. The Korean War (1950–1953) cost some 678,405 lives, perhaps even more. The Vietnam War (1955–1975) death toll has been estimated at between 1,362,494 and 4,249,494 killed. This being the case, in 1960 Herman Kahn, a military strategist at the government-subsidized RAND Corporation strategic policy "think tank," published *On Thermonuclear War.* He argued against the basic tenet of MAD—use of nuclear and thermonuclear weapons would mean mutual destruction—and presented scenarios in which a nation could win a nuclear, even a thermonuclear, war. He was not arguing for a nuclear first strike but was questioning the ultimate credibility of a purely thermonuclear deterrent. He held that it was the duty of a nuclear power to create war plans that contemplated "the unthinkable."

Kahn's book was less about tactics and strategy than about knowing when to commit to atomic war in order to achieve what he called the better of two "Tragic but Distinguishable Postwar States"—one in which everyone is killed and the other in which many are killed, but the side with the will to use the weapons in a timely and well-planned manner emerges from the war greatly depleted but still intact.

"Disasters," Kahn wrote, "come in very different sizes," and he amassed a voluminous amount of data to support his contention that nuclear and thermonuclear weapons were indeed terrible—but they were nevertheless weapons, not suicide devices. He specifically argued for ending the prevailing U.S. nuclear policy of planning to hit a so-called optimum mix of civilian and military targets and instead plan on ways to strike exclusively against Soviet missile sites and airfields in an effort to radically degrade the enemy's offensive capacity. While virtually everyone—politicians, the public, and the military—thought of nuclear and thermonuclear weapons as the ultimate means of "total war," war that made no distinction between combatants and noncombatants, Kahn argued for focusing these massively destructive weapons exclusively against offensive military targets. For better or worse, Kahn's book has remained a powerful challenge to deterrence. Whether this increases the probability of a nuclear exchange or increases the probability of surviving such an exchange remains a vexing question. But it dares political leaders and military strategists to *think* about how they could use the most destructive weapons ever devised.

The Cuban Missile Crisis: Strategy at the Thermonuclear Brink (1962)

MAD, "mutual assured destruction," was the cornerstone of the deterrence doctrine that dominated strategic war policy in the post–World War II Atomic Age. The idea was simple: If the superpowers each had apocalyptic stockpiles of nuclear weapons, neither side would dare be the first to use them—for the simple reason that mutual destruction was assured by the sheer amplitude of the stockpiles. No rational actor would act first.

A turning point in the credibility of MAD came on October 16, 1962, when President John F. Kennedy was shown photographs taken two days earlier by American U-2 "spy planes" revealing construction of a Soviet SS-4 medium-range ballistic missile (MRBM) launch site at San Cristóbal in western Cuba, some 90 miles off the coast of Florida. The range of the SS-4 could deliver nuclear warheads to any number of U.S. East Coast and Midwest cities.

Tension in Cuban-American relations was not new. Since the Spanish-American War (1898), American influence hung heavily over the island nation. Even after 1934, when the United States gave up all formal control over its sovereignty, Cuba remained closely bound to U.S. companies, especially fruit and sugar producers. In 1959 Fidel Castro led a revolution overthrowing the corrupt but pro–United States regime of Fulgencio Batista and establishing a Communist government in Cuba. Over the next two years, Castro brought Cuba into the Soviet orbit. During the administration of U.S. president Dwight Eisenhower, the Central Intelligence Agency devised a plan to overthrow Castro. Eisenhower's successor, Kennedy, inherited the plan and barely hesitated to authorize its implementation. Having assembled a force of anti-Castro Cuban exiles, the CIA led an invasion at the Bay of Pigs on April 17, 1961. CIA intelligence reported confidently that the people would rise up to join the invaders. They did no such thing, however, and the invasion was a fiasco—crushed in three days. Not only was the United States humiliated, but the Bay of Pigs fiasco drove Castro further into the Soviet camp. Castro was convinced that the Americans would again attempt an invasion, so he welcomed a Soviet offer to build missile bases in Cuba.

Soviet premier Nikita Khrushchev wanted maximum leverage over the United States. After meeting with the newly installed President Kennedy at the

Vienna Summit on June 4, 1961, the Soviet leader concluded that the young president was both naive and weak. In October 1961, East German police began disrupting the free passage of U.S. and British diplomats between the East and West sectors of divided Berlin in divided Germany. The U.S. military commander in West Berlin, General Lucius D. Clay, ordered American tanks and infantry to stand by at Tempelhof Airport. In response, on October 27, 1961, 33 Soviet tanks rolled up to the Brandenburg Gate, which marked the division between the West and East sectors. A tense standoff between U.S. and Soviet military forces developed, lasting from about five o'clock in the afternoon to eleven o'clock the next morning, when both sides finally stood down.

Berlin, the great postwar flashpoint, was very much on Kennedy's mind when he learned of the Soviet missiles in Cuba. No military plan existed to deal with this threat. To accept the missiles meant accepting the presence of mass destruction on America's doorstep. To respond aggressively against them was

This U-2 reconnaissance photo over Cuba shows Soviet missile emplacements.

NATIONAL ARCHIVES AND RECORDS ADMINISTRATION

likely to trigger World War III—if not immediately, then via Soviet retaliation in Berlin.

Avoiding any impulsive response, the president assembled under his brother, Attorney General Robert F. Kennedy, a 14-member Executive Committee (EXCOMM) of the National Security Council and charged it with formulating options for a response intended to remove the threat without igniting Armageddon. EXCOMM proposed five alternatives:

1. No response.
2. Rally and apply international diplomatic pressure to compel the Soviets to remove the missiles.
3. Bomb the missile installations and destroy them.
4. Invade Cuba.
5. Set up a naval blockade of Cuba to interdict, board, and inspect ships suspected of carrying missiles or personnel and turn them back. Since a blockade was technically an act of war, it could be more innocuously described as a "quarantine."

The military advisors, the Joint Chiefs of Staff, unanimously recommended combining options 3 and 4—a massive air assault followed by an invasion—arguing that the Soviet Union would never go to war to save Cuba. Kennedy objected, however. He believed that even if the air attack destroyed every single missile before any could be launched, and even if the invasion succeeded completely, the Soviets might still retaliate against Berlin or directly against the United States. In either case, the ultimate outcome would almost certainly be nuclear war. Moreover, what if the U.S. air strikes failed to destroy all the missiles? What if some were fired? Even a very limited nuclear attack against American cities would demand an all-out thermonuclear response against Soviet targets. World War III in that case was a certainty.

Kennedy also rejected launching an air attack without a follow-up invasion. He believed that this, too, would provoke the Soviets into at least overrunning Berlin. Moreover, if such a move was seen as a response to the U.S. air attack against Cuba, JFK feared that even NATO allies would condemn America for "throwing away Berlin" because the president was unwilling to peacefully resolve the Cuban crisis. If NATO dissolved as a result, the balance of power between the United States and the Soviet Union would change radically.

Of course, doing nothing was also a nonstarter. By process of elimination, therefore, the naval quarantine remained the only viable option. It was the proactive military action least likely to provoke a major war. At the same time, based on additional U-2 photography showing yet more missiles deployed in four separate sites, the president also prepared to launch an air attack and invasion. The entire 1st Armored Division and five infantry divisions were sent to Georgia for quick deployment, and the Strategic Air Command (SAC) positioned its nuclear-armed B-47 Stratojet bombers at civilian airports within striking range of Cuba. SAC's larger nuclear-armed B-52 Stratofortresses were sent aloft, flying patterns that positioned them to attack not only Cuba but the Soviet Union itself.

At seven o'clock on the evening of October 22, President Kennedy addressed the nation via a television broadcast on all three networks. He announced the discovery of the missiles, and he declared his intention to take all steps necessary for defense. No one who heard the speech could doubt that the world was on the brink of thermonuclear war.

Much of the global population breathlessly awaited the first contact between Soviet vessels and the ships of the quarantine. During the suspense, EXCOMM member George Ball cabled the U.S. ambassadors to Turkey and NATO, informing them that the president was contemplating an offer to withdraw U.S. Jupiter missiles from Turkey in exchange for the withdrawal of Soviet missiles from Cuba. Ball deliberately sent the message "in the clear"—uncoded—knowing the Soviets would intercept and read it. The idea was to set up a back-channel offer to remove the Jupiter missiles, which were, in fact, obsolete and already scheduled for retirement. Making them part of a deal would allow the Soviet premier to save face at home.

On October 24 the first Soviet cargo ships approached the quarantine line—and turned back. "We're eyeball to eyeball, and I think the other fellow just blinked," Secretary of State Dean Rusk remarked of the development.

The thermonuclear bullet had been dodged—but the missiles that had already been delivered to Cuba were still being erected there, and Kennedy continued to contemplate an invasion. This time, it was EXCOMM that persuaded him to await Khrushchev's response to the back-channel offer. In the end, the president quietly agreed to remove missiles from the Turkish-Soviet border in exchange for Khrushchev's removal of all missiles from Cuba, and the stalemate was broken on October 28. On the following day, the president suspended the quarantine, and by November 2 the missile bases were being dismantled.

This brush with Armageddon was a turning point that joined diplomacy with military tactics and strategy to reintroduce a rational basis for upholding the premise of MAD. The Cuban Missile Crisis demonstrated both the complex fragility of peace in the Cold War era as well as the possibility of averting World War III.

The Arab-Israeli War of June 5–10: Three Fronts, Six Days, Total Victory (1967)

Israel was born in war. The impetus for the creation of a "Jewish homeland" came from the Zionist movement begun in the late nineteenth century, but the Holocaust of World War II, in which at least 6 million Jews were murdered in a Nazi program of genocide, gave the founding of Israel a unique urgency. The country's independence was declared on May 14, 1948, and the next day the member states of the Arab League and other forces declared war. The United States recognized Israel 15 minutes after its creation, and as Egypt leaned toward alignment with the Soviet Union, American military support for Israel grew stronger.

The new nation won its war of independence and a second Arab-Israeli War shortly thereafter. It maintained itself on a continual war footing. The conflict fought from June 5 to June 10, 1967, the "Six-Day War," was the Third Arab-Israeli War. Shorter than many individual battles, it was more decisive than most battles and many wars. Israel's victory was not only total but also enormously consequential. Military historians and warfighters continue to study it as an object lesson in efficient combat.

Following the 1956 Suez Crisis, in which Israel, with the cooperation of the United Kingdom and France, invaded Egypt, the United Nations acted to stabilize the volatile region by sending a United Nations Emergency Force (UNEF) to occupy the Sinai, the desert peninsula from which Egypt often mounted military operations against Israel. As a result of the Suez engagement, Israeli forces had taken control of the Sinai but obeyed a UN order to hand over control to the UNEF. Eleven years later, in 1967, Egyptian president and prime minister Gamal Abdel Nasser demanded that the UNEF withdraw. It did—and in short order, Nasser imposed a blockade on shipping through the Straits of Tiran, the narrow seaway between the Sinai and Arabian Peninsulas, separating the Gulf of Aqaba from the Red Sea. His intention was to strangle Israel by closing off its major port, Eilat.

Having wrapped Egypt's fingers around Israel's neck, Nasser mobilized Egyptian forces, together with those of Egypt's ally Syria, along the border created by the UN-mediated armistice of 1949. Israel responded by mobilizing as well. The world was not surprised by this point and counterpoint. But it believed that Israel was now doomed. Egypt, Syria, Jordan, and Iraq menaced the country from three sides. A well-executed, well-coordinated operation would laterally dismember Israel, effectively driving it into the sea.

In the past, since the First Arab-Israeli War, Israel had hunkered down defensively while conducting typically brilliant guerrilla assaults and small-unit operations. The nation's political and military leadership—indeed, all the nation's principal leaders had extensive military experience—appreciated that, this time, the threat was too grave for a defensive response and small-scale action. Israel assumed the offensive directly after mobilization.

At the urging of Israeli chief of staff Yitzhak Rabin, the Israeli Air Force launched a massive preemptive aerial campaign on June 5. It targeted two dozen enemy airfields, destroying on the ground more than 400 Egyptian, Syrian, Jordanian, and Iraqi aircraft—virtually all of the Arab allies' airpower. The Arabs' warfighting capability was fatally degraded by this overwhelming strategic assault. The world took note. The most powerful Arab militaries in the region had united against a tiny country. That country had destroyed their combined air forces—in a single day.

Israel pressed its offensive. Under the overall command of Defense Minister Moshe Dayan, ground troops of the Israeli Defense Forces (IDF) surged over the Sinai Peninsula to seize Jerusalem's Old City, Jordan's West Bank, the Gaza Strip, and the Golan Heights. Israeli soldiers occupied these critical objectives—by

Israeli airborne troops prepare to board transports to the Sinai during the Six-Day War.
GOVERNMENT PRESS OFFICE (ISRAEL)

which the entire area around Israel could be dominated—before a UN-sponsored cease-fire was declared on June 10, 1967.

The combined deployed Arab strength in the Six-Day War was about 409,000 men. Against this, the IDF sent 264,000 regulars and first-line reservists. Although Israeli forces were very well equipped from modern Western sources—with modern armor and aircraft (of the 450 planes in the Israeli air force, 286 were first-line combat-operational warplanes)—IDF forces were outnumbered nearly 2 to 1. What made the difference, besides aggressiveness and brilliant tactics, was the unique 50/50 "tooth-to-tail ratio" of the ground forces. That is, combat ("tooth") personnel were evenly divided with support ("tail") personnel. Most armies at this time, including the U.S., British, and Arab forces, had a 20/80 tooth-to-tail ratio. In short, the relative *combat* strength of Israeli versus Arab forces was not nearly as unequal as the raw numbers suggested. No one was more surprised by this than the Arabs themselves.

The Israelis also recognized that the Egyptian, Syrian, and Iraqi air forces were equipped with numerous Soviet-supplied MiG-21 fighters. In the Israeli inventory, only the French-made Mirages and the Super Mystère fighters could come close to matching the Soviet aircraft in air-to-air combat. For this reason, Rabin was determined to go for broke with a preemptive strike that destroyed the MiGs on the ground, before they could get into action. From the beginning, then, the Israelis had air supremacy. This and the rapid possession of Jerusalem's Old City, Jordan's West Bank, and the Gaza Strip were crucial to victory. But the final decisive prize was the Golan Heights.

When June 9 dawned, only one of the Arab armies originally arrayed against Israel remained in the field: the 13 brigades of Major General Ahmed Souedani's Syrian army. This force was well dug in on the Golan Heights, at the point where the northeast border of Israel meets Lebanon to the west and Syria to the east. During the first four days of the war, Souedani pounded the Israeli kibbutzim in Galilee with artillery fire. Now the IDF turned its attention to the Heights.

Souedani's 40,000 troops were deployed behind strong fortifications. Israeli brigadier general David Elazar attacked with half that number and 250 tanks. These proved sufficient to destroy the Syrian defenses by June 10. When Al Quneitra, the principal town of the Golan Heights, surrendered to Elazar, Souedani asked for a cease-fire.

Military historians deem the Six-Day War to be among the swiftest and most complete victories ever recorded. Arab casualties (killed, wounded, captured, and missing) numbered 17,967. Materiel losses were heavy: 965 tanks and nearly 500 aircraft. Israeli casualties were 5,515, plus the loss of 394 tanks and 46 aircraft. Faced with threats on three sides, Israel had launched a three-sided offensive, which demonstrated to the region and the world the combat effectiveness of this diminutive nation.

The Tet Offensive: Pyrrhic Victory in the Vietnam War (1968)

For Americans, 1968 began as just another year. For those Vietnamese who had grown up with the traditional 12-year animistic calendar, it was the start of the Year of the Monkey. That meant the Vietnamese New Year, which began at the end of January, was *Tet Mau Than*, the "Feast of the First Morning of the Year of the Monkey." The North Vietnamese leadership had a special plan to celebrate it. This "First Morning" would be the first morning of a general uprising intended to tear South Vietnam apart. To ignite such a movement, a massive offensive was planned. Its aim was nothing less than to prompt the South at long last to look to the North, to unify under the Communist government of Hanoi.

It was an opportune time for a major push. Without the support of the United States, the government and military of South Vietnam could never prevail against the North, which drew support from the People's Republic of China as well as the Soviet Union—and which was also driven by a nationalist passion for true independence. In the meantime, support for the war was rapidly waning in the United States, where an antiwar movement gained increasing traction with each passing month. In this time of softening American resolve, Hanoi commenced its series of massive offensives. The first strikes came along the border until, suddenly, on Tet, January 30, 1968, the offensive exploded nationwide.

Communist forces hit major cities and military bases from Quang Tri and Khe Sanh near the Demilitarized Zone (DMZ) in the northern region of South Vietnam to Quang Long near the country's southern tip. Even the newly constructed U.S. embassy in Saigon was targeted. Airmen were forced to take up rifles to defend Tan Son Nhut Air Base, just outside Saigon.

Far to the north, near the DMZ, the U.S. Marine outpost at Khe Sanh was completely cut off by Viet Cong, the National Liberation Front (NLF) guerrilla army that operated in the South. The attack began on the first day of Tet, January 30, 1968, and Khe Sanh was held under heavy siege through mid-March. In defense of the besieged Marines, U.S. Air Force B-52s and fighter bombers flew over 24,400 sorties, dropping an estimated 100,000 tons of ordnance. In addition, food, ammunition, and other supplies were continuously air-dropped to the isolated Marines. Sometimes the goods were delivered by parachute; but when enemy fire was at its hottest, the crews of lumbering C-123 and C-130 cargo aircraft just pushed the supplies out the door during a low-altitude flyover.

The Tet Offensive was relentless, rolling out in three phases from January 30 to March 28, 1968, and then from May 5 to June 15, and finally from August 9 to September 23. It took a heavy toll on U.S. and Army of the Republic of Vietnam (ARVN) forces, but the offensive was actually far costlier to the North Vietnamese Army (NVA) and the Viet Cong (VC). Of an estimated 84,000 attackers, it is believed at least 45,000 were killed. Measured by any tactical yardstick, the U.S.-ARVN defense against the Tet Offensive was an unalloyed triumph. The offensive was clearly intended to destroy the fighting spirit of an already badly demoralized South Vietnam. Yet, by the numbers, it had precisely the opposite effect. Shortly after the outbreak of the Tet Offensive, ARVN deserters began voluntarily returning to service—some 15,000 by the end of the offensive. In addition, nearly a quarter-million South Vietnamese young men volunteered for military service during the period of the offensive.

The effect was very different in the United States. As perceived in America, the initial three-week campaign was a devastating victory for the Communists. It persuaded many Americans, not just the public but also politicians and policymakers, that the Vietnam War was indeed unwinnable. Reporting high enemy casualties meant little to Americans, who saw casualties among *their* young men having risen from 780 per month during 1967 to 2,000 a month in February 1968. Indeed, the American public had been lied to so much about the progress of the Vietnam War that few believed official military data demonstrating that the Tet Offensive was far from a U.S.-ARVN defeat. Nor did it help that the U.S. Air Force performed very poorly during this period. The "kill ratio"—North Vietnamese aircraft shot down versus U.S. aircraft lost—was now 1 to 1. It was the worst performance in the history of American aerial combat.

Since roughly 1966, U.S. lawmakers were becoming divided into "hawks" (war supporters) and "doves" (peace advocates). The Tet Offensive hardened the division and markedly increased the ratio of doves to hawks. In March, a distorted news story reported that General William Westmoreland, the chief U.S. commander in Vietnam, was asking for 200,000 more men to be committed to the war. This sent a shock wave of rage through a wide swath of the American public. Antiwar demonstrations became increasingly frequent, bigger, and far more boisterous. Public opinion polls taken in mid-March revealed that 70 percent of the American people favored a phased withdrawal of U.S. forces from Vietnam to commence immediately.

President Lyndon B. Johnson, who had vastly expanded war during his term, took steps to begin a gradual American withdrawal. Nevertheless, by the end of 1968, the number of American troops in Vietnam would reach a high of 536,000. Although the U.S.-ARVN counter to the Tet Offensive was an objective military victory, the events of Tet came across to most Americans as a massive psychological and moral defeat. On March 31, 1968, President Johnson made two stunning television announcements. He declared his intention to restrict bombing above the 20th parallel, a step intended to open the door to a negotiated settlement of the war. Next he announced that he would not seek another term as president. He forthrightly acknowledged that his record of advocacy of the war was tearing America apart and had become an obstacle to peace negotiations. The defense against the Tet Offensive thus stands in modern military history as a stark example of a Pyrrhic victory—a victory that takes such a devastating toll on the victor as to constitute a defeat.

My Lai Massacre and the Pentagon Papers: The Road to an All-Volunteer Force (1969–1971)

The first the American public heard of it was on September 6, 1969, when an Associated Press (AP) teletype clattered in newspaper offices across the United States: "Ft. Benning GA. An army officer has been charged with murder in the deaths of an unspecified number of civilians in Viet Nam in 1968, post authorities have revealed. Col. Douglas Tucker, information officer, said the charge was brought Friday against 1st Lt. William L. Calley Jr., 26, of Miami, Fla., a two-year veteran who was to have been discharged from the service Saturday."

It was not much information—and the brief story got Calley's rank wrong; he was a second lieutenant—but the story did not die. On October 22, 1969, nearly two months after the AP wire, a freelance journalist named Seymour Hersh got a phone call from one of his Washington sources. He told him he had "a fantastic story" about "a guy down in Benning who is being held on a charge of murdering 70 to 75 Vietnamese civilians" in a hamlet called My Lai 4 in the Son Tinh District of South Vietnam's south-central coast.

Hersh chased the lead. He interviewed Calley on November 9 and wrote a story the next day. He took it to *Life* and *Look*, the two most popular glossy magazines in the country at the time. They wanted no part of it. So Hersh contacted an obscure start-up news bureau called Dispatch News Service. DNS contacted about 50 newspapers and managed to sell the story to 35 of them for $100 each. They ran it on November 12 and 13, 1969.

The story failed to catch fire—a fact that drove Hersh all the harder. He turned up eyewitnesses, including Paul Meadlo, a 22-year-old farm boy from West Terre Haute, Indiana, who had served in the Charlie Company platoon led by Calley. He explained that they had been ordered to sweep through the My Lai hamlets, which were supposedly harboring Viet Cong. Meadlo told Hersh how he and the other soldiers "began gathering up" villagers. They stood about 40 "in one big circle in the middle of the village." Meadlo reported that Calley said, "You know what I want you to do with them." Calley then left for 10 minutes, returned, and said, "Get with it. I want them dead."

Hersh wrote this and more. Now the story burst into a flame that became a conflagration. Soon the *Cleveland Plain Dealer* published horrific photographs of what was now being called the "My Lai Massacre." They had been taken by Ron Haeberle, a combat photographer attached to Charlie Company. Haeberle risked criminal prosecution both for the unauthorized release of the photographs and for failing to report the atrocities he witnessed. Nevertheless, the images

These unidentified women and children are about to be killed by U.S. Army soldiers of Charlie Company in the My Lai Massacre on March 16, 1968. The photograph is by Ronald L. Haeberle, a combat photographer who leaked the images.
LIBRARY OF CONGRESS

were beyond shocking. One, showing the bodies of women and children lying in the ditch where they had been gunned down, was published internationally as an antiwar poster. It was overlaid with the text of an exchange between CBS newsman Mike Wallace and Paul Meadlo:

Q: And babies?

A: And babies.

William Calley Jr. was convicted by court-martial of murdering 22 South Vietnamese civilians but, after three years of house arrest, was released when a federal judge ruled that the verdict had been prejudiced by pretrial publicity. Nobody knows precisely how many Vietnamese civilians were killed in the My Lai Massacre. The official U.S. estimate is 347, while the Vietnamese government puts the toll at 504. Victims ranged from 1 year to 84 years old.

Thanks to the work of a determined journalist and the existence of a free press, Americans learned that the Vietnam War was a dirty war—or at least that some soldiers committed war crimes of the most heinous kind. Whether Charlie Company was the rule or the exception when it came to American troop conduct, Hersh neither determined nor said. But many Americans began to see the war as tainted by barbaric racism. Thanks to another set of journalists and a conscious-stricken military analyst named Daniel Ellsberg, America and the world also came to conclude that the Vietnam War was the product of lies.

In June 1971 the *New York Times* began publishing a series of articles on a voluminous secret government study of the origins of American involvement in the Vietnam War. It came to be known as "The Pentagon Papers," and it revealed that for three decades the U.S. government had not only bungled its handling of the Vietnam War but had intentionally deceived the American people about its foreign policy.

The document was officially titled *The History of the U.S. Decision Making Process in Vietnam* and had been commissioned by Secretary of Defense Robert McNamara, an appointee of John F. Kennedy, who also served in the administration of Lyndon Johnson until he resigned in 1968. Daniel Ellsberg, a professor at MIT, laboriously photocopied and then leaked the 2-million-word document to *Times* reporter Neil Sheehan. Ellsberg had worked for the RAND Corporation "think tank," collecting and analyzing the thousands of documents that made up the study. In the course of his work, he became—like McNamara himself—disillusioned about the Vietnam War. Also like McNamara, Ellsberg stopped working for the government; but unlike the former secretary of defense, he felt compelled to make public what he knew. At great personal risk, he leaked the document.

The Pentagon Papers told a twisted tale of conflict, muddled thinking, covert action, and deliberate lies in the crafting of Vietnam policy during every presidential administration from Harry S. Truman to Lyndon Johnson. Exposed was the role of the CIA and the complicity of President Kennedy in removing and assassinating South Vietnam's president, Ngo Dinh Diem. Revealed was the jaw-dropping and heartbreaking fact that the Gulf of Tonkin Resolution, supposedly a response to a North Vietnamese attack on the U.S. destroyer *Maddox* in international waters, had been written months in advance of that reported attack—an incident that had occurred in North Vietnamese territorial waters, been deliberately provoked, and greatly exaggerated. It was a phony pretext on the basis of which Congress gave President Johnson a "blank check" to wage war in Vietnam. Americans also discovered that Johnson had repeatedly lied when he denied having no long-term strategy for Vietnam. In short, the Pentagon Papers confirmed what the most radical antiwar activists had been claiming—for years.

President Richard Nixon was initially rather delighted with the Pentagon Papers revelations because they exposed the malfeasance of mostly Democratic administrations. But he quickly decided that he could not allow the leaking of classified government documents to go unchallenged. He ordered Attorney General John Mitchell to threaten the *Times* with charges of espionage. When the *Times* proved unimpressed, Mitchell secured a temporary injunction from the federal courts blocking further publication.

But it was too late. the *Washington Post* and *Boston Globe* had received portions of the Pentagon Papers and, because the injunction was lodged only against the *New York Times,* continued to publish—until they too were restrained. The papers united in an appeal to the Supreme Court, which ruled six to three on June 30, 1971, in favor of freedom of the press under the First Amendment. The newspaper-reading public continued to devour the Pentagon Papers, which savaged the government's credibility with the American public and allies alike. Doubtless, the revelations damaged various intelligence operations. Yet the revelations gave the anti-Vietnam War movement fresh credibility and respectability. Ellsberg's act of conscience, made public by a free press, accelerated the end of an unpopular and fundamentally unjust war. Even more enduringly, the revelations of My Lai and the Pentagon Papers were lessons in the limits of warfighting without public support. These two events put the nation on a course toward ending the peacetime military draft in the United States. On January 27, 1973, less than two years after publication of the Pentagon Papers, Secretary of Defense Melvin R. Laird announced the creation of the All-Volunteer Force (AVF). It transformed the U.S. military and the concept of military service in America.

Limits of Military Superpower: The Iranian Hostage Crisis (1979–1981)

The United States emerged from World War II as the greatest superpower on the planet. Backed by the combination of its robust economy and powerful military, the nation took a leadership role in the recovery of Europe and other parts of the world and in generally shaping the geopolitics of the second half of the twentieth century. The experience of World War II made America a military superpower. But as the world's old colonial hegemonies were dismantled during the postwar years and as former colonies and client nations—from nationalist or religious motives or a mixture of both—rose up, the limits of superpower military status became increasingly apparent. Smaller nations used insurgent tactics to wage asymmetric warfare, leveraging their limited resources in ways that challenged much larger and more powerful nations.

The United States confronted such a challenge beginning on November 4, 1979, when 500 Iranians stormed the American embassy in Tehran and took 52 American diplomats and citizens hostage. They were held for 444 days, until January 20, 1981. The crisis that was ignited ended President Jimmy Carter's political career and helped usher Ronald Reagan into the White House, yet it also set the stage for the major scandal of the Reagan administration.

The hostage-taking was carried out by Muslim Student Followers of the Imam's Line, an organization of Islamic fundamentalist students who supported the Iranian Revolution that overthrew the Shah of Iran. The abduction, endorsed by the Ayatolla Ruhollah Khomeini, founder of the Islamic Republic of Iran, was an act of vengeance against U.S. president Jimmy Carter, who had supported Shah Mohammad Reza Pahlavi, a longtime U.S. ally, and who had given the exiled and ailing shah permission to come to the United States for medical treatment. The hostage-taking was a humiliation for both Carter and the United States. A rescue attempt, Operation Eagle Claw, on April 24, 1980, failed miserably and had to be aborted. America seemed both to the world and to many Americans a helpless giant. Such was the power of asymmetric warfare tactics.

The Iran Hostage Crisis, as it was called, was a drag on the Carter presidency and contributed to the defeat of Carter's bid for a second term. To rub salt into the outgoing president's wound, Khomeini delayed the release of the hostages until January 20, 1981, the day Ronald Reagan was inaugurated. In an act of profound grace and patriotism, the new president commissioned Carter to fly to Wiesbaden, West Germany, as his special emissary to meet the hostages at a military hospital, their last stop before returning to the United States.

The timing of the release of the hostages redounded to Reagan's political benefit, but a short time later, a new round of kidnappings, inspired by the event in Iran, took place in war-torn Lebanon. Most of these hostages were destined to remain in captivity, their whereabouts unknown, their kidnappers unidentified, throughout the Reagan presidency. This situation gave rise to a complex covert plan to trade arms to Iran—of all places—in exchange for Iranian assistance in freeing the hostages.

Marine lieutenant colonel Oliver North, a close associate of CIA director William Casey, had the idea of using the cash proceeds from the sale of arms to Iran to fund the right-wing anti-Sandinista rebels, the "Contras" in Nicaragua—something President Reagan very much wanted to do, even though Congress, controlled by Democrats, had passed an amendment outlawing the use of U.S. funds to support the rebels. North's covert plan seemed to Reagan a foolproof way to defy Congress—despite warnings from White House staff that doing so might result in impeachment.

North's plan soon went awry, and an obscure Middle Eastern magazine broke the story that led to the revelation of the Iran-Contra affair. As in Nixon's Watergate scandal, the White House issued conflicting statements, and Reagan held press conferences that the day's news immediately contradicted. Reagan appointed a presidential commission headed by Senator John Tower to investigate. Tower produced a report that was nothing less than a scathing indictment of the president. Congress then formed a special committee to investigate, and a special prosecutor was appointed. President Reagan managed to weather the Iran-Contra affair without legal consequence, but the scandal hobbled the final days of his administration. The American public was left feeling that, once again, the United States, superpower though it was, could not effectively manage covert, small-scale warfare. Iran-Contra, a bizarre outgrowth of the Iran Hostage Crisis spurred the American military community to study asymmetric methods of warfare to compete in a world less and less defined by just two superpowers. American warriors had to learn to compete on new, unconventional battlefields.

The Gulf War: The Architecture of
Coalition Warfare (1990)

On August 2, 1990, the Iraqi army invaded its neighbor Kuwait after Iraqi president Saddam Hussein unilaterally declared that nation's annexation. Within a week, Kuwait was completely occupied. The U.S. administration of President George H. W. Bush feared that Iraq planned to use Kuwait as a platform from which to attack south into Saudi Arabia, which, like Kuwait, was a major oil producer. President Bush responded to the invasion by freezing Iraqi assets in American banks, imposing a trade embargo, and securing United Nations resolutions supporting military action against the invasion.

Saddam had a well-deserved reputation as a ruthless dictator, willing to kill and willing to take casualties to his own people and forces. Indeed, Iraq had the fifth-largest standing army in the world, and there was widespread anxiety in America that fighting a war against this man would be very costly. U.S. confidence in its military had long been undermined by what some called the "Vietnam syndrome"—the long, dark shadow cast by military failure in a war that was a nightmarish quagmire. There was widespread belief that the American military of 1990 was not up to the task of fighting a large army controlled by an absolute dictator who would stop at nothing.

President Bush was not a charismatic or inspiring leader by nature, but he set about building popular confidence in the armed forces, rallying popular support for the war that was about to begin. He embarked on a major effort to ensure that the United States would not stand alone against Iraq. Not only did he secure UN backing, Bush also reached out to the Arab League, which on August 3 condemned the invasion and demanded Iraqi withdrawal. It was clear to the president that most of the Arab world recognized Saddam Hussein as a regional threat, and much of the rest of the world saw Iraq as a threat to worldwide energy resources, including the great Hama oil fields of Saudi Arabia. President Bush went beyond the UN and commissioned his secretary of state, James Baker, to build an international military coalition against Iraq. In short order, Afghanistan, Argentina, Australia, Bahrain, Bangladesh, Canada, Czechoslovakia, Denmark, Egypt, France, Germany, Greece, Hungary, Honduras, Italy, Kuwait, Morocco, the Netherlands, New Zealand, Niger, Norway, Oman, Pakistan, Poland, Portugal, Qatar, Saudi Arabia, Senegal, South Korea, Spain, Syria, Turkey, the United Arab

Emirates, and the United Kingdom joined the United States to create a force of 660,000 military personnel in theater. U.S. forces constituted 74 percent of this body. Operation Desert Shield, the buildup phase of the response against Iraq, involved 48 nations, 30 of which provided military forces and 18 furnished economic, humanitarian, and other noncombat assistance. Desert Shield began on August 7, 1990, and was intended first and foremost to defend Saudi Arabia against invasion. It included a naval blockade of Iraq. U.S. Air Force fighters began to arrive at Saudi air bases immediately, and on August 9 advance elements of the U.S. Army contingent arrived. By the end of October, 210,000 U.S. Army and Marine troops had been deployed, in addition to 65,000 troops from other coalition nations.

While deliberately assembling the coalition and preparing for war, President Bush issued an ultimatum to Saddam: Withdraw immediately and completely from Kuwait. The dictator countered with an offer to withdraw only if there were simultaneous withdrawals of Syrian troops from Lebanon and Israeli troops from the West Bank, Gaza Strip, the Golan Heights, and southern Lebanon. Morocco and Jordan approved this proposal, but Syria, Israel, and the entire U.S.-led anti-Iraq coalition rejected it.

As the January 15, 1991, UN Security Council deadline for Iraqi withdrawal approached, the U.S. Congress on January 12 authorized the use of military force to drive Iraq out of Kuwait. Operation Desert Shield became Operation Desert Storm the day after the deadline passed. On the evening of January 16,

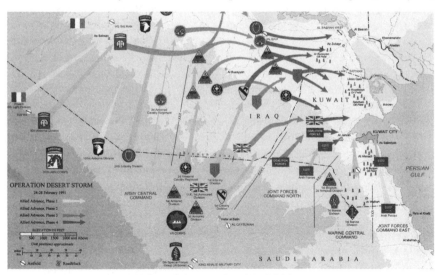

Operation Desert Storm, February 24–28, 1991.
UNITED STATES MILITARY ACADEMY

1991, President Bush delivered a globally broadcast address. "Tonight," he said, "28 nations, countries from five continents—Europe and Asia, Africa, and the Arab League—have forces in the gulf area standing shoulder to shoulder against Saddam Hussein. These countries had hoped the use of force could be avoided. Regrettably, we now believe that only force will make him leave."

With that, a massive air campaign was unleashed against Iraq and Iraqi positions in Kuwait. Over the next five weeks, coalition pilots flew more than 88,000 missions, with losses of 22 U.S. aircraft and 9 planes from other coalition countries. The Iraqi air force offered almost no resistance, but Iraqi ground forces did fire obsolescent Soviet-made "Scud" surface-to-surface missiles against targets in Israel and Saudi Arabia. Saddam hoped to goad Israel into joining the war, thereby alienating the Arab members of the coalition. Deft U.S. diplomacy persuaded Israel not to enter the conflict; the Scuds, in any case, did little damage.

The air campaign prepared the way for the ground campaign, led chiefly by U.S. general H. Norman Schwarzkopf. The overwhelming air supremacy of the coalition kept Iraqi reconnaissance aircraft from discovering anything about the deployment of coalition ground troops, and the ground offensive was launched at 4:00 a.m., February 24, 1991. The army's XVIII Airborne Corps was positioned on the coalition's left flank. This unit was to move into Iraq on the far west and, striking deep within the country, cut off the Iraqi army in Kuwait, isolating it from support and reinforcement from the north. The French 6th Light Armored Division would cover the XVIII Airborne Corp's left flank during this operation. The center of the ground force consisted of the U.S. VII Corps, the U.S. 2nd Armored Cavalry, and the British 1st Armored Division. These units were assigned to move north into Iraq after the left and right flanks had been secured, then make a sharp right turn to advance into Kuwait from the west to attack Iraqi units there, including the elite Republican Guard. The right flank of the attack—mainly U.S. Marines—was tasked with breaching Iraqi lines in Kuwait.

The attacks on the first day were intended, in part, to screen the main attack and to deceive the Iraqis into thinking the principal assault would come on the coast of Kuwait. Iraqi defenses were well developed, but only light resistance was offered, and many Iraqi prisoners were taken. By Day 2 of the ground war, French troops secured the left flank of the coalition advance, and U.S. forces cut off all avenues of Iraqi retreat and reinforcement. The U.S. 24th Division ended its advance in the southern city of Basra, Iraq, which sealed the remaining avenue of escape from Kuwait.

With the Iraqis in Kuwait occupied on the right, the XVIII Airborne Corps made a surprise attack on the left, in the west. By nightfall of February 25, the XVIII Airborne Corps was turning east into Kuwait. When the corps encountered units of the Republican Guard, this elite Iraqi unit simply broke and ran. By February 27, however, with the 24th Infantry having taken Basra, the Republican Guard was bottled up, and its Hammurabi Division attempted to engage the XVIII Airborne Corps in a delaying action to allow the remainder of the Republican Guard to escape. The Hammurabi Division was wiped out.

A cease-fire was declared at 8:00 a.m. on February 28, shortly after Iraq had capitulated on U.S. terms. The ground war had lasted just 100 hours. Kuwait was liberated at the cost to the coalition of 95 killed, 368 wounded, and 20 missing in action. Iraqi casualties were perhaps as many as 50,000 killed, 50,000 wounded, and 60,000 taken prisoner. Both Iraq and Kuwait suffered extensive destruction of infrastructure, and the environmental damage caused by Saddam's acts of destruction throughout the Kuwaiti oil fields, including raging oil fires and the dumping of crude oil into the Persian Gulf, would take many months to repair. Not only had the declared mission been accomplished, but confidence in the American military had been restored. As for military history, a new "best practices" model of coalition building had been created—one that, tragically, would not be followed when George H. W. Bush's son, George W. Bush, took the nation to war against Iraq for a second time, on March 20, 2003.

From the F-117A to the Predator: The Rise of Stealth and Drone Weapons Technology (1989–1994)

For centuries, even millennia, warfare had two domains, the land and the sea, which were developed as battlespaces in that order. The emergence of the air as a domain required considerable advancement in technology. The Montgolfier brothers successfully made manned flights in hot air balloons during 1782–1783, and in 1794, during the French Revolutionary Wars, members of a *compagnie d'aérostiers* (company of aeronauts) went aloft in tethered hydrogen-filled balloons to perform reconnaissance at the Battle of Fleurus (June 26). But it was not until 1903 that the United States' Wright Brothers achieved flight in a heavier-than-air craft. Very quickly, the military potential of such aircraft was envisioned, and by World War I (1914–1918), airplanes were used for reconnaissance, artillery observation, and bombing (mostly tactical, but also against civilian populations). Pursuit, or fighter, aircraft attempted to shoot one another out of the sky and also provided close-air support for ground operations.

Combat aircraft in World War I were often quite colorful—as were the pilots, who were pictured as latter-day knights engaged in one-on-one combat. Subsequent wars brought greater sophistication and introduced more sophisticated camouflage as well as night-flying technologies. But it was on November 10, 1988, that military aviation reached an unprecedented turning point. After several years of rumor and speculation in both the popular and aerospace press, the U.S. Air Force went public with an announcement that its inventory now included 52 Lockheed F-117A light-strike fighter aircraft. They were specifically designated as "Stealth" fighters. This meant they extensively employed stealth technologies designed to reduce their visibility and detectability—in short, to make them nearly invisible. Stealth technologies reduce the reflection and emission across the electromagnetic spectrum, including radar, infrared, visible light, and radio frequencies. Stealth also extends to the audio realm. The aircraft are designed to minimize the noise of their engines.

The F-117A was first used in combat during Operation Just Cause in Panama (December 20–24, 1989), which targeted for overthrow and capture Panamanian dictator Manuel Noriega. Judgment on the aircraft's performance was equivocal, but when the F-117A was used in January–February 1991 during

Operation Desert Storm in Iraq, results were superb. The stealth fighter created extensive disruption of Iraqi command-and-control operations during the air war, which prepared the way for the brief and decisive ground war that followed.

In the meantime, on July 17, 1989, a U.S. stealth bomber, the Northrop B-2, made its first flight. Like its fighter counterpart, the bomber used special materials and coatings to reduce electromagnetic emissions. Also like the F-117A, the B-2 was shaped to create a minimal radar cross section. While the F-117A was essentially an extreme delta-wing design, the B-2 was virtually a flying wing. The compromise between aerodynamic design and stealth design created stability problems in the F-117A, which required continual correction from a digital "fly-by-wire" system. By building on existing flying wing design models (dating from as far back as 1940), the B-2's shape more successfully reconciled stealth with aerodynamic stability.

Stealth aircraft are intended to penetrate deeply into enemy air defenses, and the B-2 was specifically designed to deliver nuclear and thermonuclear weapons against Soviet missile sites during a nuclear war. The fall of the Soviet Union during 1990–1991 reduced the demand for this extremely expensive strategic aircraft.

For all the advantages stealth offered, aircraft such as the F-117A and the B-2 were still burdened by a feature of flight the Wright brothers had introduced:

A B-2 Spirit stealth bomber soars over the Pacific after having been refueled in flight, May 30, 2006.

U.S. AIR FORCE PHOTOGRAPH BY STAFF SERGEANT BENNIE J. DAVIS III

the requirement for a pilot and, often, additional aircrew. As early as 1911, just eight years after the Wrights' first flight, Elmer A. Sperry, founder and president of the Sperry Gyroscope Company, became interested in applying remote radio control to aircraft. His idea was to create a flying bomb controllable from the ground (or from a ship) without the onboard presence of a pilot. Due to the limitations of radio technology, servo linkages between radio equipment and aircraft control surfaces, and feedback systems, so-called flying drones—unmanned aircraft—remained on the periphery of weapons development until World War II. Germany developed the V-1 flying bomb, a cruise missile that was not controlled remotely but was merely aimed and launched from the ground, with in-flight stability and course-holding maintained by an onboard gyroscopic inertial guidance system. The V-1 was an inaccurate weapon, descending to impact a target when its fuel ran out. But if the objective was to terrorize a large city, like London, the V-1 proved to be a successful demonstration of unmanned combat flight.

It was not until 1971, when the U.S. Navy developed MASTACS (Maneuverability Augmentation System for Tactical Air Combat Simulation) that existing practice target drones (BQM-34A aircraft) were modified with MASTACS technology and shown to be highly maneuverable when flown by remote control. These were the immediate precursors of combat UAVs (unmanned aerial vehicles), though the emergence of truly practical combat UAVs awaited the development of advanced digital technology beginning in the 1990s. On July 3, 1994, the first flight of the General Atomics Aeronautical MQ-1 Predator took place. It was initially conceived as an unarmed reconnaissance and forward observation platform but was soon modified to carry and fire two AGM-114 Hellfire missiles and other munitions. By 2001 the RQ-1 Predator was the primary U.S. Air Force and CIA UAV for offensive operations. Using satellite GPS and related technologies, these aircraft could fly their missions in such places as Iraq and Afghanistan while being controlled from bases within the United States. In recent years, more and more sophisticated stealth technology has been applied to the design of UAVs, and the aircraft have been made larger—large enough to carry virtually any type of munition, including nuclear and thermonuclear weapons. Fighter UAVs, intended for air-to-air combat, are in rapid development; because they carry no human pilot, their maneuverability is not limited by consideration of high G-forces that would be incompatible with the ability of a human pilot to maintain consciousness or even survive.

Stealth, drone technology, and the combination of the two are bringing aspects of warfare to a new moral crossroads. Today it is possible to conduct major combat remotely, as matters of life and death, target selection, and decisions to attack or not to attack increasingly assume the dimensions of a video game "played" far from the point of impact.

The Bosnian War: European Tribalism (1992–1995)

The military history of Europe is rich with extreme violence, culminating in the two great "world" wars of the twentieth century. Yet following World War II, Europeans had reason to believe that the worst was behind them, that Europe was becoming increasingly united, and that two of the historically most prolific causes of war, religious differences and racial or ethnic tribalism, were things of a less enlightened past. During 1992–1995, the continent found itself confronting a shocking turn in a military history that, it seemed to many, had lost its capacity to create any more shocks.

The Balkan nations have never been strangers to both nationalist and ethnic strife. The Treaty of Versailles that ended World War I (1914–1918) created the Kingdom of the Serbs, Croats, and Slovenes out of two independent states, Serbia and Montenegro, and what had been provinces of the now-dissolved Austro-Hungarian Empire. In 1929 the awkward name of this collection of states was changed to Yugoslavia. In the aftermath of World War II (1939–1945), the Yugoslav monarchy become a Communist republic under the leadership of Josip Broz Tito, a strongman prime minister and, later, president, who seemed to hold the ethnically disparate republic together through sheer charisma and force of will. Under Tito, Yugoslavia uneasily united six "republics": Serbia, Croatia, Bosnia and Herzegovina, Macedonia, Slovenia, and Montenegro. Two additional "provinces" were annexed to the country, Kosovo and Vojvodina.

After governing Yugoslavia since 1953, the 88-year-old Tito died in 1980. Very quickly, Yugoslavia began to fall apart. Slovenia and Croatia each declared independence, followed by Macedonia. This process unfolded against the backdrop of the decline of the Soviet Union and, with it, European Communism. During 1989–1990, the decline became outright collapse, and Bosnia and Herzegovina was swept up in a rising tide of nationalism. After Croatia and Slovenia left the Yugoslav federation in 1991, Bosnia's Catholic Croats and Muslim Slavs approved referenda on February 29, 1992, calling for the establishment of an independent, multinational republic as well. The Bosnian Orthodox Serbs, however, refused to secede from the diminished Yugoslavia, which was now dominated by Serbia. This refusal triggered a civil war later in 1992, which tore apart Bosnia and Herzegovina.

Three ethnic and religious groups had been living side by side under a Communist government in Bosnia. A savage civil war broke out among them now. The flames of this ethnic and religious conflict were vigorously fanned by Serbia's president, Slobodan Milosevic. Claiming a duty to protect the Serb ethnic minority living in Bosnia, Milosevic sent arms and other support to the Bosnian Serbs. The Bosnian federal army, which was dominated by ethnic Serbs, began shelling the Croat and Muslim neighborhoods in the Bosnian capital city of Sarajevo. This act of violent persecution prompted much of the international community to impose a variety of economic sanctions on Serbia in a bid to degrade its capacity to supply Bosnian Serbs with weapons and other materiel. The sanctions failed, however, to prevent Bosnian Serb guerrillas from carrying out brutal campaigns of "ethnic cleansing" against Muslims and Croats. Their objective was to "clear" certain areas for the exclusive occupation of Bosnian Serbs. When the international community sent relief workers to what was now a region on the verge of starvation, they were met by gunfire.

By July 1992, millions of Bosnians had become refugees. And although most of the human rights abuses were perpetrated by the Bosnian Serbs with the support of Milosevic's Serbia, the Croats and the Muslims responded with ruthless retaliatory raids, conducting campaigns of ethnic cleansing in the areas *they* controlled. The "former Yugoslavia," as the region was typically called, had descended into tribalism.

As the war ground on, destroying not only lives but also what had been a reasonably thriving economy, the Muslims and Croats of Bosnia agreed to a truce early in 1994 and united to oppose the Serbs. In August 1994 the confederation agreed to a plan formulated by the United States, Russia, Britain, France, and Germany, by which Bosnia would be divided 51 percent versus 49 percent, with the Serbs getting the smaller percentage. While the Muslims and Croats agreed on the plan, the Serbs kept fighting. In 1994 and 1995 Bosnian Serb forces conducted mass killings in Sarajevo, Srebrenica, and other, smaller towns, which the United Nations had designated as safe havens for Muslim civilians.

A far-reaching arms embargo imposed by the United States and the Western European powers did nothing to diminish, let alone stop, the war. Quite possibly, it may have had the unintended consequence of depriving Muslims and Croats of desperately needed arms, thereby putting them at an even greater disadvantage against the Serbs.

Concluding that the Bosnian situation was intolerable, in April 1994 NATO, with strong U.S. participation, launched air strikes against Serb positions in Bosnia. Despite suffering heavy losses, the Bosnian Serbs continued to fight, blocking all attempts at humanitarian aid and even holding under detention a 24,000-man U.N. peacekeeping mission. Nevertheless, the Muslim-Croat alliance had been making measurable military progress against the Bosnian Serbs. By September 1995 the alliance had reduced Serb-held territory in Bosnia to less than half the country, precisely the percentage specified in the peace plan endorsed by the Muslims and Croats.

With the reduction of their territory an accomplished fact, the Bosnian Serbs finally came to the peace table. On December 14, 1995, with Muslim and Croatian leaders, Bosnian Serb leaders signed the Dayton Peace Accords, brokered by the United States in a series of conferences held at Wright-Patterson Air Force Base, outside Dayton, Ohio. The major provision of the accords was the creation of a federalized Bosnia and Herzegovina, divided between a Bosnian-Muslim/Bosnian-Croat federation and a Bosnian-Serb republic. In addition, the accords guaranteed that refugees would be allowed to return to their homes, people would be permitted to move freely throughout Bosnia, and the human rights "of every Bosnian citizen" would be monitored by an independent commission and an internationally trained civilian police force. The accords also provided for the prosecution of individuals found guilty of war crimes.

The peace achieved essentially by dividing the small country of Bosnia into three ethnically homogenous, self-governed areas was an uneasy one. Less than a year later, violent civil unrest erupted in the southern Yugoslavian province of Kosovo as the Kosovo Liberation Army (KLA) launched guerrilla attacks on Serbian police forces. Early in 1998, Milosevic sent troops to Kosovo to crush its bid for independence, and full-scale civil war was under way. The war was ended by a U.S.-led military intervention under the auspices of NATO, which launched the largest allied military assault in Europe since World War II, forcing Milosevic to withdraw his forces.

"The First War of the Twenty-first Century": 9/11 and the Era of Endless American War (2001–)

At the end of World War II in 1945, the dawn of a military era of nuclear and thermonuclear "superweapons," the widely held assumption was that wars would increasingly become contests between major powers and superpowers. Instead, the military history of the post–World War II era was dominated by a variety of wars between asymmetric powers as relatively small insurgent nations or factions went up against the established major powers and even the superpowers, the United States and the Soviet Union. What few anticipated was the leveraging of extreme asymmetric warfare in acts of terror capable of creating mass destruction far beyond the small number of perpetrators involved. Moreover, perhaps no one could have imagined the long-term consequences of such asymmetric terrorism, namely a state of open-ended, perhaps endless war.

The act of terror in question is all too familiar. At 8:45 a.m. (EDT) on the morning of September 11, 2001, a Boeing 767 passenger jetliner, American Airlines Flight 11 out of Boston, struck the north tower of the World Trade Center in lower Manhattan, penetrating the building like a guided missile.

In bustling Manhattan, the collision drew instant and extensive live television news coverage. A real-time broadcast of thick black smoke pouring from the gaping tear in the silver skin of the 110-story skyscraper was accompanied by stunned newscaster narration. The nation's eyes were focused on the scene when another 767 (United Airlines Flight 175) impacted the south tower of the World Trade Center at 9:03. Because the cameras were present and rolling, much of world saw this impact as it happened. One thing was clear, the reason that both these impacts looked like guided missile attacks was that they were. The planes had been steered into the towers in the first attack directly against U.S. territory since the Japanese attacked Pearl Harbor, Hawaii, on December 7, 1941.

President George W. Bush was in a Sarasota, Florida, second-grade classroom reading aloud to schoolchildren when his chief of staff, Andrew Card, entered the room and whispered in the president's ear. Bush listened to the children read for a time before leaving the classroom and announcing on television at 9:30 that the United States had suffered "an apparent terrorist attack." Thirteen minutes after this announcement, a Boeing 757 (American Airlines

Flight 77) barreled into the Pentagon, U.S. military headquarters. At 10:05, back in Manhattan, the south tower of the World Trade Center collapsed. Five minutes after this, at 10:10, United Airlines Flight 93 plowed into the soil of rural Somerset County, Pennsylvania. Eighteen more minutes elapsed before the north tower of the World Trade Center fell.

Before the day was through, the news media reported that the airplane downed in Pennsylvania had been headed for the White House or the U.S. Capitol. Americans were also informed that all four aircraft had been hijacked by terrorists—"suicide hijackers" belonging to al-Qaeda (Arabic for "The Base"), an Islamist jihad organization led by a Saudi national named Osama bin Laden. He was committed to a holy war against Israel, the United States, and the West generally.

Perpetrated by an "army" of just 19 men, the four attacks killed 2,893 at the World Trade Center, 189 at the Pentagon (including the 64 passengers and crew of Flight 77), and 40 in the crash of Flight 93 in Pennsylvania. "We have just seen the first war of the twenty-first century," President Bush told the nation. Eight days later, on September 20, speaking before a joint session of Congress, he warned the ruling Taliban of Afghanistan—under whose protection bin Laden operated—that the United States would attack unless it turned over "all the leaders of al-Qaeda who hide in your land." President Bush began the war against the Taliban on October 7, 2001. As of February 2019, the War in Afghanistan had lasted 17 years and 4 months, the longest war in U.S. military history.

During the summer of 2002, the public, politicians, and media pundits debated where the so-called war on terrorism should be fought next. The Bush administration made a dubious case for invading Iraq, whose dictator, Saddam Hussein, had survived the Persian Gulf War of 1990–1991, which had been led by Bush's father, George H. W. Bush. The younger Bush argued that Saddam may or may not have had a direct connection with the events of 9/11 but identified him as an enemy of the West who would not rest until Islamist forces again attacked the United States—this time with "weapons of mass destruction" (WMDs), perhaps biological weapons, perhaps nuclear, perhaps both. The president took the United States to war against Iraq on March 20, 2003. Although principal American forces were withdrawn on December 18, 2011, after the war had lasted 8 years, 8 months, and 28 days, Iraq continues to be threatened by violence, and American president Donald J. Trump has proposed using it as a platform for American forces to monitor Iran, a nation against which the United States may yet go to war.

The Bronze Soldier of Tallinn: Cyber Becomes the New Battlefield (2007)

On April 27, 2007, the City Council of Tallinn, Estonia's capital, voted to move a Soviet World War II monument, "The Bronze Soldier of Tallinn," from a downtown city park to the Defense Forces Cemetery outside the city proper. Estonia had been occupied by the Soviet Red Army in World War II and was a Soviet state until the dissolution of the USSR in 1991. The nearly 70 percent of the Estonian population who are ethnic Estonians thought of the Bronze Soldier as a hateful artifact from the days of Soviet oppression. The country's ethnic Russians—about 25 percent of Estonia's population—regarded the monument as a sacred memorial to Red Army heroism. The decision to relocate it sparked protests and even riots.

By 2007 Estonia was widely nicknamed "e-Stonia" because it was so thoroughly wired, its 1.3 million citizens more completely networked and dependent on the internet than most other people in the world. Two years earlier the Estonian government had put most of its operations entirely online. All official documents were executed and signed electronically, cabinet meetings were conducted in cyberspace, and Estonians began voting online. By 2007, 61 percent of the Estonian population accessed their bank accounts online exclusively, and 95 percent of all banking transactions were electronic.

From a military point of view, no nation presented a richer cyber target than Estonia. The protests and riots that broke out at the end of April 2007 were immediately followed in cyberspace by a barrage of distributed denial of service (DDoS) attacks. Tens of thousands of linked computers swamped key Estonian websites with log-on requests, thereby effectively disabling them. Some of the attacks emanated from individuals, but most were carried out by international botnets, networked computers normally used by disreputable e-commerce providers to disseminate spam. Because large-scale botnet assaults in 2007 were costly and complex to mount, their use implied state support. Indeed, during the attacks, Russian online forums and chat rooms hummed with calls to action and even included explicit instructions on how to participate in the DDoS attacks. The servers of a government network designed to handle 2 million megabits of traffic per second were flooded with some 200 million megabits per second. The websites of the Ministries of Foreign Affairs and Justice were forced to shut down, and the majority Reform Party website was defaced with digital graffiti that included a Hitler-esque cookie-duster moustache scrawled across the face of Prime Minister Andrus Ansip. On May 3 the DDoS botnets were unleashed against Estonian private-sector websites and servers, quickly forcing most of the country's banks to shut down. Ripples of the attack reached well into the international banking community.

Throughout the cyber siege, Moscow denied involvement in the attacks, the volume of which peaked on May 9, the Russian anniversary of the end of World War II. By this time, the Estonian government had scrambled to respond by quadrupling the data capacity of its systems, and the attacks began to subside. On May 15, however, Russian hackers managed briefly to disable the national toll-free emergency phone number.

To this day, there is no definitive evidence conclusively connecting the Russian military or civilian government to the cyberattacks, but circumstantial evidence abounds. Konstantin Goloskokov, a leading member of a pro-Kremlin Russian youth organization called Nashi, admitted that Nashi had been involved. Goloskokov was not only a Nashi activist but also assistant to Sergei Markov, a Duma Deputy (the equivalent of a U.S. member of Congress). Indeed, Nashi (a Russian word meaning "ours," it is the short form of Youth Democratic Anti-Fascist Movement, "NASHI") is officially funded by *private* Russian business interests, but its creation on April 15, 2005, was enthusiastically endorsed by the Russian government. By 2007 it was receiving the vigorous endorsement of prominent government figures, including Vladislav Surkov, at the time first deputy chief of the presidential staff and, since December 2011, Russia's deputy prime minister.

The Estonian government had no doubt that Russia was waging cyber war. Estonia had joined the European Union and had also become a member of NATO in 2004. During the cyberattacks, NATO rushed to consider invoking Article 5 of the NATO treaty, by which each member pledges to consider an attack on any member as an attack on them all. In the end, NATO leadership backed down. As the Estonian minister of defense explained, "At present, NATO does not define cyber-attacks as a clear military action. This means that the provisions of Article V of the North Atlantic Treaty . . . will not automatically be extended to the attacked country."

When the NATO treaty was enacted in 1949, cyberspace existed neither as a concept nor, of course, as a battlespace—the equivalent of land, sea, and air. Article 5 could be triggered only by an "armed attack." As NATO leaders saw it, a cyberattack was not an "armed attack." Yet as Sarwar Kashmeri, national security expert and fellow at the Peace & War Center of Norwich University, put it, "Technology had transformed NATO's ring of steel around its members to a fence of tissue paper."

There is some truth in this. Nevertheless, after the 2007 cyberattack on Estonia, NATO began planning cyber defenses for itself and its members. A NATO policy on cyber defense was quickly approved in January 2008, and on May 14, Estonia, Germany, Italy, Latvia, Lithuania, the Slovak Republic, and Spain signed a memorandum of understanding formally establishing the Cooperative Cyber Defense Centre of Excellence (CCDCOE) in Tallinn. Both Turkey and the United States signed on before the end of 2008, and other members joined between 2010 and 2013.

The thinking of the defenders was nevertheless far behind that of the aggressors. In 1999 two Chinese air force colonels, Qiao Liang and Wang Xiangsui, published a book known in English as *Unrestricted Warfare*. The "age of technological integration and globalization," the authors argued, the age of the internet just then emerging, had "realigned the relationship of weapons to war, while the appearance of weapons of new concepts, and particularly new concepts of weapons, [had] gradually blurred the face of war." In all ages past, war was defined exclusively by the use of armed force. Now, the Chinese colonels asked, "Does a single 'hacker' attack count as a hostile act or not? Can using financial instruments to destroy a country's economy be seen as a battle?" Attempt to answer such questions using the traditional definitions of war, the authors warned, and they will remain unanswerable. "When we suddenly realize that all these non-war actions may be the new factors constituting future warfare, we have to come up with a new name for this new form of war: Warfare which transcends all boundaries and limits, in short: unrestricted warfare."

Qiao and Wang's book predicted that cyberspace would increasingly figure as a battlespace for what the authors called "war in which information technology is used to obtain or suppress information." In such a war, "there is nothing . . . that cannot become a weapon"; therefore, "our understanding of weapons must have an awareness that breaks through all boundaries." A "single man-made stock-market crash, a single computer virus invasion, or a single rumor or scandal that results in a fluctuation in the enemy country's exchange rates or exposes the leaders of an enemy country on the internet, all can be included in the ranks of new-concept weapons," weapons "that are closely linked to the lives of the common people." The "digital fighter is taking over the role formerly played by the 'blood and iron' warrior" so that "warfare is no longer . . . an exclusive imperial garden where professional soldiers alone can mingle."

On June 23, 2009, the United States recognized the emergence of cyberspace as the fourth domain of war—after land, sea, and air—by creating the U.S. Cyber Command (USCYBERCOM) with a mission to "conduct full spectrum military cyberspace operations in order to enable actions in all domains, ensure U.S./ Allied freedom of action in cyberspace and deny the same to our adversaries."

Index